RICHELIEU AND HIS AGE

Richelieu and his Age

Edited by

JOSEPH BERGIN

and

LAURENCE BROCKLISS

CLARENDON PRESS · OXFORD
1992

Oxford University Press, Walton Street, Oxford OX2 6DP
Oxford New York Toronto
Delhi Bombay Calcutta Madras Karachi
Petaling Jaya Singapore Hong Kong Tokyo
Nairobi Dar es Salaam Cape Town
Melbourne Auckland
and associated companies in
Berlin Ibadan

Oxford is a trade mark of Oxford University Press

Published in the United States
by Oxford University Press, New York

British Library Cataloguing in Publication Data
Data available
ISBN 0-19-820231-8

Library of Congress Cataloging in Publication Data
Data available
ISBN 0-19-820231-8

Set by Best-set Typesetter Ltd., Hong Kong
Printed and bound in Great Britain by Biddles Ltd.,
Guildford and King's Lynn

To two long-suffering academic wives:
Sylvia and Alison

Editorial Preface

The appearance of this book coincides with the 350th anniversary of the death of Cardinal Richelieu. In a year of notable anniversaries and new beginnings, this is one historical milestone that may understandably be overlooked, especially outside France. It is our hope that this volume will serve as a reminder that the modern world is as much the product of the vision of politicians as of the imagination of scientists and the courage of explorers. The chapters which follow were specially commissioned for this volume, and were all presented as papers to a conference held at Magdalen College, Oxford, in March 1991. The conference brought together virtually all the scholars in the British Isles currently working on the history of sixteenth- and seventeenth-century France. The papers provoked a lively and stimulating discussion from which all the authors benefited enormously.

The editors would like to thank all the participants at the conference who helped, each in his or her own way, to make this volume possible. Though it may be invidious to mention particular individuals by name, special thanks must go to Professor John Elliott whose unsurpassed knowledge of seventeenth-century Spanish history ensured that Richelieu and the problems of France were never discussed in isolation from contemporary events across the Pyrenees. The editors would also like to thank the British Academy for subsidizing the attendance of Professors Hermann Weber and A. Lloyd Moote at the conference, which made it possible to bring an international flavour to an otherwise Anglo-Irish event. Most of all, however, our sincerest thanks go to our fellow contributors for their exemplary response to editorial demands at every stage of this volume's gestation. On all occasions they co-operated positively and quickly with sometimes fierce and often detailed questions and suggestions from us concerning the early drafts of their contributions. We can only hope that they will be satisfied with the end result, and that they will regard the whole enterprise as worthwhile as we do ourselves.

In preparing this volume the editors are particularly indebted to Oxford University Press. Tony Morris and his colleagues responded enthusiastically to the idea of a volume of essays to commemorate the 350th anniversary of Richelieu's death and have worked hard to ensure that the volume appeared on time. Finally, a brief mention must be made of our two families. Co-editing a book at a distance is not without its difficulties and tends to be carried on by evening telephone calls. Numerous meal- and bath-times have been interrupted by lengthy conversations about the cardinal and his policies. We would like to take this opportunity to apologize to our children in particular. We sincerely hope that by spending so much of our time immersed in the unstable era of the Thirty Years War, we have not perpetrated lasting domestic disruption.

Paris and Oxford 1992

Acknowledgements

The editors would like to thank the following institutions for permission to reproduce photographs of works from their collections: the Bibliothèque Nationale, Paris, and the Barber Institute of Fine Arts, the University of Birmingham.

Contents

List of Plates

List of Maps

List of Abbreviations

AAE CP	Archives des Affaires Étrangères, Correspondance politique
AAE France	Archives des Affaires Étrangères, Mémoires et documents, France
AG	Archives de la Guerre
AN	Archives Nationales
APW	*Acta Pacis Westphalicae*, ed. M Braubach and K Repgen (Münster, 1962–).
ASV	Archivio Segreto Vaticano
AUP	Archives de l'Université de Paris (Bibliothèque de la Sorbonne)
Avenel	D. L. M. Avenel, *Lettres, instructions diplomatiques et papiers d'état du cardinal de Richelieu* (8 vols.; Paris 1853–76).
BI	Bibliothèque de l'Institut de France
BN	Bibliothèque Nationale
BS	Bibliothèque de l'Université de Paris/Sorbonne
Grillon	P. Grillon, *Les Papiers de Richelieu: Section politique intérieure. Correspondance et papiers d'état* (6 vols. to date; Paris, 1975–).
Isambert	Jourdan, Decrusy, and Isambert, *Recueil général des anciennes lois françaises* (28 vols.; Paris, 1821–33).
MS Fr.	Manuscrit français
MS Lat.	Manuscrit latin
Naf	Nouvelles acquisitions françaises
Richelieu, *Mémoires* SHF	Richelieu, *Mémoires*, ed. Société de l'Histoire de France (10 vols.; Paris, 1907–31).
Richelieu, *Mémoires* MP	Richelieu, *Mémoires*, 3 vols.; ed. J. Michaud and J. J. F. Poujoulat (Nouvelle collection des mémoires pour servir à l'histoire de France, 2nd ser., 7–9; Paris, 1850).
Richelieu, *Test. pol.*	Richelieu, *Testament politique*, ed. Louis André (Paris, 1947).

Note on Quotations

Quotations in French are cited in their original orthography except that an acute accent has been added to past participles where necessary to aid the reader's understanding. Quotations from other languages (e.g. Latin) have been translated into English and the original placed in the footnotes.

Note on Contributors

Joseph Bergin is Reader in History at the University of Manchester. He is author of several books on early seventeenth-century France, including *Cardinal Richelieu: Power and the Pursuit of Wealth* (New Haven, Conn., 1985), and *The Rise of Richelieu* (New Haven, Conn., 1991). He is currently working on the French Church in the first half of the seventeenth century and a general study of seventeenth-century France.

Richard Bonney is Professor in History at Leicester University and an expert on French administrative history of the ancien régime. His books include *Political Change in France under Richelieu and Mazarin 1624–1661* (Oxford, 1978), and *The King's Debts* (Oxford, 1981). He has recently been a visiting professor at the Sorbonne and at present is engaged in organizing a large collaborative study of the growth of the early-modern state.

Robin Briggs is Fellow of All Souls, Oxford, and a specialist on French social and cultural history. Among his publications is the recent *Communities of Belief: Cultural and Social Tensions in Early-Modern France* (Oxford, 1989). At present he is preparing a book on witchcraft in Lorraine.

Laurence Brockliss is a Tutor and Fellow in Modern History at Magdalen College, Oxford. He is particularly interested in the history of French education and science in the early-modern period and his publications include *French Higher Education in the Seventeenth and Eighteenth Centuries: A Cultural History* (Oxford, 1987). He is the editor of the journal *History of Universities* and is currently working on early-modern French medicine.

Edric Caldicott is Professor of French at University College, Dublin. He has published articles in both English and French on seventeenth-century historical and literary topics and in 1989 received the *Prix de l'Académie française* for his work on Molière. His publications on art patronage include a study of Gaston d'Orléans in R. Mousnier (ed.), *L'Âge d'Or du Mécénat* (Paris, 1985).

A. Lloyd Moote is Professor of History at the University of Southern California, Los Angeles. His many publications include *Revolt of the Judges* (Princeton, NJ, 1971), a study of the Fronde, and the recent *Louis XIII, the Just* (Berkeley, Calif., 1989). At present he is working on themes of regicide and the court-favourite in the seventeenth century.

David Parrott is Lecturer in History at the University of York and works on the French army. He wrote his doctoral dissertation on 'The Administration of the French Army during the Ministry of Cardinal Richelieu' (University of Oxford, 1985), and since then he has published a number of articles on French military history and foreign policy in the first half of the seventeenth century. He is currently expanding his thesis into a book.

Hermann Weber is emeritus Professor of Modern History at the University of Mainz and was the first director of the German Historical Institute in Paris. He is the author of many articles on French political and social history in the seventeenth century, and is an expert on Richelieu's foreign policy before France entered the Thirty Years War. None of his work has so far appeared in English.

INTRODUCTION

Joseph Bergin and Laurence Brockliss

With one or two exceptions, serious historical studies devoted to the ministry of Cardinal Richelieu only began in the Third Republic, thanks especially to the Herculean efforts of Avenel in gathering together and publishing many of the cardinal's more accessible papers.[1] Though far from complete—the archives of the Quai d'Orsay were originally closed to Avenel—his editorial labours made it possible for the first scholarly biographies to be written. The most notable of these was the six-volume monument to Richelieu that began issuing from the pen of Gabriel Hanotaux in 1893, the year before he became France's foreign minister.[2] The verdict of French historians like Hanotaux at the turn of the twentieth century on Richelieu's ministry was unequivocal. The cardinal was one of the truly great figures, not just in the history of France but in the history of Europe. At home, Richelieu laid the foundations for the French absolute monarchy by taming the great nobility, subduing the military might of the Huguenots, and centralizing the state bureaucracy under the all-seeing eye of the royal council and its intendants. Abroad, Richelieu prepared the ground for the glorious diplomatic and military achievements of Louis XIV. Through his successful intervention in the Thirty Years War, he destroyed once and for all the international power of the Habsburgs and restored the tarnished prestige of French arms. To historians who belonged to a nation still smarting from its humiliation by Bismarck, Richelieu came to appear as a saviour of France. Before he entered the council in 1624 the country seemed on the brink of collapse after sixty years of intermittent civil war. By the time he died in 1642, the state had been reconstituted, and France had become both a nation and a great power. France, too then, had once had a Bismarck. Moreover, Richelieu was the greater of the two men, for he had achieved the much greater feat of rising above the petty, religious obsessions of his age to place the needs of the state and nation first. Although a cardinal, Richelieu was the first great European secular statesman, an

---

[1] The last vol. of Avenel's work appeared in 1876 but it was primarily a publication of the Second Empire. See list of abbreviations, above.

[2] G. Hanotaux and duc de La Force, *Histoire du cardinal de Richelieu* (6 vols.; Paris, 1893–1947).

ardent promoter of the doctrine of *raison d'état* and the balance of power.[3]

For much of the twentieth century this picture of Richelieu the modern man, who was somehow ahead of his time, was largely accepted. It is still the impression conveyed by his most recent popular French biographer, Michel Carmona.[4] However, there are few academic historians in Western Europe or North America who would now support this traditional picture, for over the last twenty years one of the two panels in the diptych has been seriously defaced. Following the research of Anglo-American historians especially, most historians no longer subscribe to the notion that Richelieu was an innovative and effective administrator who single-handedly pointed the ship of state in the direction of absolutism.

In the first place, since the appearance in the early 1950s of Victor-Lucien Tapié's account of Louis XIII's reign, much greater attention has been placed on the role of the king as the ultimate arbiter of government policy.[5] Far from being a cipher as has been usually thought, Louis the Just has increasingly been seen as a pivotal figure, a man whose moods and interests were sufficiently strong and independent for Richelieu to have, at the very least, to take account of, and not infrequently to bow to them.[6] At the same time, numerous detailed studies of the administrative structures of ancien-régime France as a whole have made it clear how difficult it was for Richelieu, or indeed any minister, to exercise creative authority, however active or supportive the king might be. Richelieu's ministry, then, far from being a period of innovative state-building, has come to seem one of 'make-do and mend'. Indeed, it is clear that the most 'creative' administrative achievement of the cardinal's ministry, the permanent introduction of the intendants, was actually unintentional, the simple result of acute fiscal necessity in a time of war.[7] If Richelieu had plans for the internal reform of the French state, then administrative inertia and the primacy of foreign policy ensured that they were never put into effect. On his death much of

---

[3] The parallel between the two men finds a distant but distinct echo in the fact, recently noted by Robert Knecht, that Bismarck and Richelieu were long the only two European statesmen readily recognizable to the educated British public. See R. J. Knecht, *Richelieu* (Profiles in Power; London, 1991), p. vii.

[4] M. Carmona, *La France de Richelieu* (Paris, 1984); id., *Richelieu: L'Ambition et le pouvoir* (Paris, 1983).

[5] V.-L. Tapié, *France in the Age of Louis XIII and Richelieu*, Eng. trans. (Cambridge, 1974).

[6] The two most recent revaluations of Louis XIII are Pierre Chevallier, *Louis XIII, roi cornélien* (Paris, 1979), and A. Lloyd Moote, *Louis XIII, the Just* (Los Angeles, Calif., 1989).

[7] See esp. Richard Bonney, *Political Change in France under Richelieu and Mazarin 1624–1661* (Oxford, 1978).

the authority of the modern state continued to lie in noble and private hands. This was particularly true of the army, still in the 1630s a ragtag affair in the hands of petty Wallensteins.[8] As a result, Richelieu was never able to rely on the state apparatus as such in order to implement his or the royal will. Royal officials in the first half of the seventeenth century served themselves first, so that obedience and co-operation had to be bought in key institutions through the use of patronage and ties of kinship.[9] Richelieu, moreover, was no different in this respect from the judges, bureaucrats, churchmen, and governors whose services he negotiated or purchased. One of the most telling blows to the traditional Olympian picture of the chief minister was the revelation that, like his contemporaries, he too was serving the crown for the material good of himself and his family.[10]

In the last twenty years, then, the established interpretation of Richelieu has suffered considerable damage. His political skills have been increasingly seen as being directed as much towards political survival and personal enrichment as towards the challenges of creative state-building. Worse still, his reforming clothes would appear to have been stolen by his arch-rival Olivares who, if still regarded as a failure by historians, is at least credited with a reform programme which he attempted, albeit with disastrous consequences, to implement.[11] Yet although Richelieu's reputation may have been cut down to size, he is emphatically not about to disappear from the historical agenda. A statesman who has fascinated (and often appalled) *gens de lettres* since the time of his death can hardly have received a proper evaluation if he appears in the light of recent research to be reduced to the level of the common political herd. Richelieu was clearly more than just a highly successful political 'boss', the great political survivor in a notoriously unstable environment. However little he may have changed the character of the French state, there remains the fact that he and the circles associated with him during his long ministerial career were the authors of numerous, wide-ranging *projets* and *avis* which aimed to establish social stability, enhance royal authority, and promote the material

---

[8] David Parrott, 'The Administration of the French Army during the Ministry of Cardinal Richelieu' (D.Phil. thesis; Univ. of Oxford, 1985).

[9] The most detailed account of government through clientage is Sharon Kettering, *Patrons, Brokers and Clients in Seventeenth-Century France* (New York, 1986).

[10] Joseph Bergin, *Cardinal Richelieu: Power and the Pursuit of Wealth* (New Haven, Conn., 1985).

[11] J. H. Elliott, *Richelieu and Olivares* (Cambridge, 1984); id., *The Count-Duke of Olivares: The Statesman in an Age of Decline* (New Haven, Conn., 1985).

and spiritual well-being of the king's subjects.[12] This reforming impulse cannot be ignored by historians merely because concentration on administrative change has shown how unsystematic and unintended the growth of the French monarchy's power actually was. Indeed, recent research has made it all the more crucial to examine further the origin, scope, and achievements of Richelieu's reform proposals, especially in areas, such as church policy, where little has been hitherto said. Moreover, the diptych is not to be reduced to a single panel. By focusing attention on Richelieu's role in the creation of the absolute state, Anglo-American and French historians have largely neglected his diplomatic activities. In so far as those historians who take a positive view of the cardinal's reforming intentions see the pace and direction of change as being determined by the needs of war, this seems a curious oversight, one which is doubtless explicable in terms of current fashion.[13] Richelieu's diplomacy clearly was out of the ordinary, even if it bore a resemblance to the anti-Habsburg policies of the Valois and Henri IV. Richelieu, a cardinal, consistently championed alliances with Protestant powers, and in doing so appeared to ruin the chance of wiping out heresy at home and abroad. Any attempt to replace the traditional picture of Richelieu with one more carefully and sensitively drawn must confront this enigma. What, it can still be asked, was the purpose of Richelieu's diplomacy? Did the nationally minded historians at the turn of the twentieth century misunderstand his foreign policy, too?

The purpose of the essays in this collection is to take the long-running *procès de Richelieu* a step further. Together they constitute an attempt to deepen our understanding of the constraints under which Richelieu worked, but also to look at his multifarious activities in a more positive light than has been the case in recent years. One contemporary French historian might regard the whole endeavour as a waste of time. It is Christian Jouhaud's contention that Richelieu studies epitomize the subjectivity of all historical inquiry. Always hiding his true face behind a succession of masks, Richelieu invites the historian to construct an image according to individual fancy. Scholarly inquiry is thus reduced to an intellectual game.[14] The editors of this volume are more sanguine about the prospects of

---

[12] Many of these remain unpubl. The modern edn. of Richelieu's papers, which is far more complete than Avenel's, has so far only reached 1631: see Grillon in list of abbreviations above.

[13] There are few serious English-speaking historians of early modern foreign policy. Most are found in Jeremy Black (ed.), *The Origins of War in Early-Modern Europe* (Edinburgh, 1987).

[14] C. Jouhaud, *La Main de Richelieu, ou le pouvoir cardinal* (Paris, 1991).

historical understanding. While recognizing the inevitable subjective influences on historical writing, they remain convinced (naïvely perhaps) that an increase in data and information leads to a fuller understanding. Historians of our time will doubtless prove to be no less influenced by contemporary private and public concerns than were their predecessors a century ago, but it is surely legitimate to claim that their judgements will be better informed. Our changing picture of Richelieu the creative state-builder is largely the outcome of detailed work in the French archives: had it been an imaginative construct built on shallow documentary foundations, it would not have carried much conviction. The essays presented here, it is hoped, will convince for the same reason. They, too, are the result of detailed, often original, research in French libraries and archives. Significantly, most of their authors are historians who have already made major contributions to undermining the traditional image of the cardinal, which was, in any case, strongly dictated by Richelieu's own statements of his intentions and interpretations of the events of his time, especially as enshrined in his so-called *Mémoires* and *Testament politique*.[15] Contemporary historians, whether they are concerned with seventeenth-century France or not, would generally agree that a credible view of any major political figure or development should be based on a careful evaluation of political rhetoric and reality, of intentions and achievements. Richelieu studies must be an on-going event, a constant task of revaluation as continual research in the archives throws up new information to refine and sometimes even refute earlier views.

The volume opens with an essay by A. Lloyd Moote on the role of the favourite in the first half of the seventeenth century. According to Professor Moote, Richelieu's position in the French state is best understood by the term 'minister-favourite', in that he had a foot in both court and government. 'Minister-favourites' were common political animals in the period and before Richelieu came to power the position in France had already been occupied by Concini, Luynes, and La Vieuville. What marked Richelieu off as different (compared with his predecessors) was his longevity in the office. Moote relates this to Richelieu's skilful handling of the king on whose favour he ultimately depended. Richelieu had learnt from the mistakes of his predecessors. He was careful not to appear too greedy and to present policies as the king's not his own. In that way he

---

[15] The best edn. of Richelieu's memoirs was publ. by the Société de l'Histoire de France in the first 3 decades of this cent.: see Richelieu, *Mémoires* SHF. Unfortunately, the edn. is incomplete. For the period 1631–8 it is still necessary to use a 19-cent. edn. such as that by Michaud and Poujoulat: see Richelieu, *Mémoires* MP.

made it more difficult for those who coveted his position to mount a challenge. Also as a cardinal, he had certain advantages which meant that failure would end in rustication rather than violent death. Richelieu's primary aim was to stay in power for otherwise he could achieve nothing. Retention of power, however, was dependent on royal favour and Louis XIII could be easily approached by potential rivals. This reminds us of the fragility of Richelieu's position as chief minister, not least because one of his bitterest political enemies, Gaston d'Orléans, was heir apparent during most of his years in office. Professor Moote's essay is an obvious starting-point for any revaluation of the cardinal, and acts as the necessary bridge with the work on Richelieu of recent decades.

In the second essay, devoted to foreign policy, the volume turns its attention to one of the ways Richelieu used his hard-won authority. Its author, Hermann Weber, is a German scholar who represents a powerful indigenous tradition. While French and Anglo-American scholars have paid little attention to Richelieu's diplomacy in the past forty years, this has emphatically not been true of their German counterparts. In their case, Richelieu's foreign policy has been the subject of abiding interest through their concern to understand the genesis and course of the Thirty Years War. Their work, moreover, has been extremely innovative and undermined conclusively the traditional view of a proto-nationalist Richelieu striving to push back the frontiers of France to her natural boundaries. Unfortunately, this work has not been translated and remains virtually unknown to the English-speaking world. It is for this reason that an essay by one of the most productive members of this German historical school has a rightful place in this volume of revaluation.

Professor Weber's essay is an original contribution, the fruit of a lifetime's research into and reflection on Richelieu's foreign policy. It is his contention that Richelieu's policy should be viewed as inter-nationalist rather than nationalist, and Christian rather than secular. Richelieu, he believes, was anxious to establish a permanent peace in Christendom. This was to be done by frustrating the hegemonic ambitions of the House of Habsburg which had continually at-tempted to expand at the expense of independent princes. By build-ing alliances with other states France would create a system of collective security whereby the independent princes of Europe would guarantee each other's territory. Richelieu had limited territorial aims: all he sought were bridgeheads across the Rhine and the Alps so that France could come to the aid of princes in trouble without delay. Alliances could be made with princes irrespective of con-fessional allegiance. In the contemporary world of international power-play the Habsburgs were using religion as a cloak for secular ambition.

Some readers may well find Professor Weber's interpretation of Richelieu's foreign policy too clear-cut, dependent, as it is, on the cardinal's memoirs and the memoranda that he prepared for the king and ambassadors. It might therefore be argued that Weber is really only revealing how Richelieu wished to present his policy to his monarch and the outside world. However, Weber has clearly defined the terms of the discourse in which the cardinal's foreign policy was conducted, and this was manifestly not a secular rhetoric of national aggrandizement.

Discourse, in this case the discourse of internal reform, is also the subject of the following essay. Robin Briggs's attempts to penetrate the meaning of Richelieu's various memoranda on internal reform by placing them in the context of a much wider movement for reform in the early seventeenth century. Briggs concludes that there was nothing novel about Richelieu's reform proposals in the 1620s, which seem to have been drawn at random from conflicting reform programmes espoused by contemporaries. This leads the author to suspect that Richelieu's reform initiatives had an important political function. In a period of political instability where a variety of interest groups (the church, the nobles, the universities, and so on) vied to place their demands before king and council, there were other ways to consolidate support than by simple bribery. In his attempts to hold on to power in the first years of his ministry, Richelieu tried to please as many reforming constituencies as possible. Consequently, it is not too surprising that internal reform should tend to fall from his political agenda after 1630. Briggs's argument is provocative but extremely stimulating. If some readers may feel that he is as prone to over-simplification as Weber, there can be no doubt that he provides us with a completely new way of understanding the purpose of the famous 1625 *Règlement* and other projects with which Richelieu was associated. No longer will it be sufficient to see Richelieu as a reformer *manqué*, a radical frustrated by the outbreak of war.

There can be no doubt, on the other hand, that war played some part in undermining Richelieu's reform intentions. This is demonstrated clearly in the essay by Richard Bonney on Richelieu and the French finances. Much of this describes the history of government income and expenditure in the Richelieu era and beyond in a much more detailed way than hitherto. It will be of considerable assistance to historians wishing to understand the significance of the *tour de vis fiscal* usually attributed to the Richelieu ministry, and more generally the taxpaying capacity of seventeenth-century France. Of particular interest in the light of the largely aborted attempt to introduce *élus* into the *pays d'états* is Bonney's careful study of the tax differential between the centre and the periphery.[16] The concluding section of the essay, however, examines Richelieu's radical proposal towards the end of his life to replace the *taille* by a sales tax. Previous historians have treated this proposal as insignificant or evidence that the cardinal had no economic sense. Working from hitherto unknown documentation, Bonney is convinced that it was in fact a serious and realistic proposal, but one that exigencies of war necessarily confined to the drawing-table.

War also had a profound effect on Richelieu's ability to pack the army command with his political supporters, as is shown in the following essay by David Parrott. Richelieu's approach to army appointments, it would seem, was highly conservative, for he accepted that commanders should be drawn exclusively from members of the great aristocracy and he made no attempt to create a 'professional' officer corps. His aim was not to fill the chief army posts with ideological supporters but simply with scions of aristocratic families, such as the Condé, who shared the same political enemies and rivals as himself. Richelieu's policy was highly successful in the period of his ministry to 1636 for the number of armies in the field at any one time was small (and they were often commanded by the king or the cardinal anyway). But once France was committed to total war there were just too many armies and too few eligible candidates for command. The policy then broke down, thereby hampering the war effort to the extent that generals in the field were not necessarily the cardinal's relatives or allies. The legacy left over for the Mazarin regime to confront was an extremely dangerous one, as the events of the Fronde would all too clearly demonstrate.

However, Richelieu did not always use his powers of patronage in such a conservative and unfruitful fashion. Joseph Bergin in his essay on Richelieu and the episcopate shows that in some areas of government the cardinal used his influence over appointments extremely creatively. Strangely, given that Richelieu was an erstwhile bishop and cardinal, the history of episcopal appointments during his period in office has been completely neglected by historians. It is a subject which enables us, moreover, to approach the political relationship between Louis XIII and his chief minister from an unusual angle. By studying the character of episcopal appointments, Bergin is able to show conclusively that the cardinal put the 'abuse', as it appeared to

---

[16] Richard Bonney, *The King's Debts: Finance and Politics in France 1589–1661* (Oxford, 1981), did not look specifically at the history of government finance under the cardinal.

certain reformers and critics, of the royal right to nominate to most of the kingdom's sees to very good effect. At the beginning of the Richelieu era there was only a handful of bishops, like Richelieu himself, dedicated to the values of the Counter-Reformation. By the time that he died, in contrast, he had been able to fill the sees with clients who were also ideological allies in the broadest sense. Richelieu's work in the church suggests that the cardinal's institutional conservatism did not necessarily preclude reform.

It falls to Edric Caldicott to examine the role of the chief minister as patron of the arts. The subject is a vast one, and the author has chosen to deal with it with particular reference to the design of the galleries in the Palais-Cardinal and the château at Richelieu. In this case Richelieu used patronage for his own self-glorification. The portraits and scenes depicted in the paintings in the two galleries were intended to convey an image of Richelieu as the guardian of French prestige and the hammer of the over-mighty subject. At the same time, however, Caldicott is anxious to stress that Richelieu was well aware of the potential of art as a prop to the monarchy. He had gained his appreciation of art and its power from the example of Marie de' Medici and he encouraged a reluctant Louis XIII to emulate his own purposeful munificence. In the event it was Louis XIV, himself brought up in the Palais-Cardinal, who would follow Richelieu's lead and make art a full-blown instrument of state. Arguably, this was Richelieu's one enduring contribution to a specifically French form of state-building.

In the concluding essay on Richelieu and education Laurence Brockliss demonstrates the difficulty of effecting change when patronage possibilities were limited. Richelieu wanted to cut dramatically the number of arts colleges in France from a fear that they were detrimental to social stability. As most of the colleges were run by the regular orders, however, he had little way of realizing his ambition. Nor could he do much to ensure that the *noblesse d'épée* studied the humanities and philosophy, although this was something that he believed was essential for the lasting peace of the realm. A clientage system, where patron and client were bound together for mutual benefit, could scarcely be used as an instrument for changing patterns of behaviour: clients after all were not Pavlovian dogs. On the other hand, there was one educational institution over which Richelieu exercised a much more direct authority—the Paris faculty of theology. In consequence, the cardinal was able to begin to turn a quarrelsome and self-important intellectual debating-chamber into a useful tool of the crown and the Counter-Reformation.

It need hardly be said that this collection of eight essays examines only a cross-section of Richelieu's wide-ranging activities as chief minister. His attitude towards the Huguenots, the great nobility, and the parlements are only touched on tangentially here. His well-known interest in overseas trade and the navy are hardly mentioned at all.[17] Ideally, a volume like this should contain several more essays on these and other important aspects of Richelieu's ministry, so that a more comprehensive account of the cardinal's activities could be presented to the reader. But the constraints of time, space, and cost precluded such an ambitious undertaking. Nevertheless, despite its evident lacunae, we hope that a picture of Richelieu the chief minister does begin to emerge from this collection of essays, one which is in many respects both positive and novel. Richelieu in power seems to have been a man with four abiding concerns.

In the first place, he was always concerned with maintaining the confidence of the monarch and establishing the reputation of himself and his family: here the essays only confirm what historians have been repeating for several decades. Secondly, he was anxious to build up the reputation of France and the French king among the princes of Europe. He did not present his policy, however, as an expansionist one and always stressed that his aim was perpetual peace based on collective security. If we take his protestations at their face value, then Richelieu's diplomacy was conservative, almost medieval, whatever its consequences. The cardinal, appropriately, was an exponent of the just war.[18] Thirdly, Richelieu showed an enduring interest in reforming the state. Although his espousal of reform was probably in part a political tactic, he does seem to have genuinely sought means of enhancing the crown's authority, and ensuring social stability (the two of course were connected). As in his foreign policy, he seems in many ways a conservative: social stability was to be attained in particular by tieing the peasant to the soil and the artisan to his workshop. But again there seems to be a significant religious dimension. His dislike of duelling, venality, even the high taxation of the peasantry, all have a strong moral dimension. It is not surprising to find, then, that Richelieu was committed to church reform. By ensuring a properly motivated and well-educated higher clergy he aimed ultimately to establish the Counter-Reformation firmly in France and, presumably, to win the Huguenots back to the fold by force of example.

---

[17] The standard work on Richelieu's economic plans remains Henri Hauser, *La Pensée et l'action économiques du cardinal de Richelieu* (Paris, 1944).

[18] For the development of the theory of the just war, see F. H. Russell, *The Just War in the Middle Ages* (Cambridge, 1977).

Running through the volume as a whole is the suggestion that Richelieu's ecclesiastical status played a much greater part in his activities than has normally been thought. He was indeed *Cardinal* Richelieu, a churchman closely and unusually attuned to both Erasmian humanism and the Counter-Reformation, and with a taste for princely magnificence and self-projection reminiscent of the great prelates of the Renaissance church. He was a man of God who saw himself as striving to realize what he viewed as a juster social and moral order. His concomitant ability to satisfy a demanding monarch, to advance himself and his family socially and materially, to recruit a political clientele, and gradually but methodically to impose men of his own choosing in areas as diverse as the royal council, the army, the navy, and the provinces do not make him a Bismarck *avant la lettre* or a modern political boss, but rather a historical figure who had both the temperament and the intellectual gifts necessary to steer his course in the unpromising and intractable environment of seventeenth-century power politics.

RICHELIEU AS CHIEF MINISTER

A Comparative Study of the Favourite in Early
Seventeenth-Century Politics

A. LLOYD MOOTE

Of all the roles that Cardinal Richelieu played, that of chief minister
to Louis XIII astounded contemporaries and posterity the most by
its success.[1] Generation after generation of scholars have sought to
understand Richelieu's 'system' by categorizing it as a *ministériat*,
and his function as that of *premier ministre*.[2] *Ministériat* or 'ministerial
government' is a useful term in so far as it suggests that Louis XIII
ruled primarily with ministers, working individually and collabora-
tively in and out of the royal council; and the complementary term
'chief minister' surely captures the reality that from 1624 to 1642
Richelieu was *the* mediator between king and council, acting both as
intimate adviser to the king (in a *maître–serviteur* relationship, in the
language of the day) and powerful controller of his fellow ministers
(a protector–*créature* relationship).[3] However, the terms *ministériat*

I would like to express my gratitude to the British Academy for a subvention to participate at
the Richelieu conference; to fellow conferees for questions on my draft paper, and especially to
Laurence Brockliss and Joseph Bergin for their superb editorial suggestions; to J. Michael
Hayden and John B. Wolf for comments on variants of the paper; and to the Guggenheim and
Haynes Foundations, National Endowment for the Humanities, and Univ. of Southern Calif.
for financial support underwriting research. The essay is dedicated to Orest Ranum, in
appreciation of our discussions on Richelieu, favourites, and related themes over the past 28
years.

[1] See the classic panegyric by G. Hanotaux and duc de La Force, *Histoire du cardinal
de Richelieu* (6 vols.; Paris, 1893–1947); and the more nuanced trilogy by M. Carmona:
Marie de Médicis (Paris, 1981), *Richelieu: L'Ambition et le pouvoir* (Paris, 1983), and *La France
de Richelieu* (Paris, 1984). For contemporary assessments, see Scipion Dupleix, *Histoire de
Louis le Juste XIII du nom* (Paris, 1643), 2; Charles Vialart, *Histoire du ministère d'Armand Jean
du Plessis Cardinal duc de Richelieu* (2 vols.; n.pl., 1650), i. 4.

[2] See Étienne Thuau, *Raison d'état et pensée politique à l'époque de Richelieu* (Paris, 1966),
104–40, 226–41, 351–8. There is a useful summary in Françoise Hildesheimer, *Richelieu: Une
certaine idée de l'état* (Paris, 1985), 53–7.

[3] On patronage terminology, compare Yves Durand (ed.), *Hommage à Roland Mousnier:
Clientèles et fidélités en Europe à l'époque moderne* (Paris, 1981); and S. Kettering, *Patrons,
Brokers and Clients in Seventeenth-Century France* (New York, 1986), 18–22. On conciliar
government and master–*créature* relations within it, see Pierre Grillon, 'Lettre du secrétaire

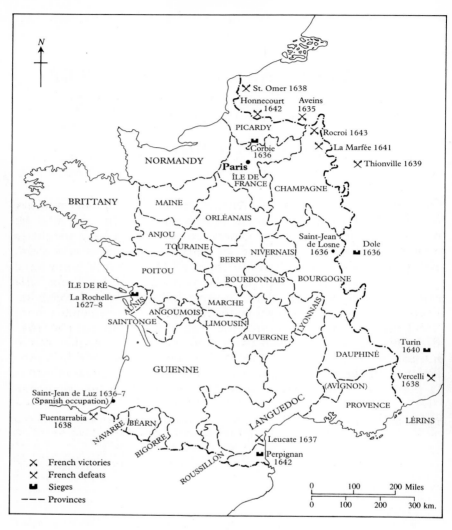

Map 1.1
The Provinces of France in the Early Seventeenth Century and the Sites of
Military Engagements

and 'chief minister' are too rigid and anachronistic to do full justice to the complex working of government in the age of Richelieu, shaped as it was by personal relationships and social habits that cut across formal institutional lines.[4]

As is well known, under Richelieu there was no formal *office* or *charge* of *premier ministre*. In fact he held no conciliar title other than minister of state, though his fellow ministers were quick to address him as 'le premier ministre de l'état'.[5] To add to the confusion, the contemporary term officially used was the more modest *principal ministre*, and it did not slip into any official documents for Richelieu until perhaps five years after his coming to power,[6] whereas it routinely designated his immediate predecessor, La Vieuville. Richelieu scholars have even referred grudgingly to a 'La Vieuville ministry', and called him 'un premier ministre absolu pendant six semaines'.[7] Paradoxically, those who presided formally over the council as *chef du conseil*—Cardinal de Retz, 1618–22, and Cardinal de La Rochefoucauld, 1622–4—were its weakest members.

Official terminology did not essentially change until the Peace of the Pyrenees in 1659, when Richelieu's successor, Cardinal Mazarin, and his Spanish counterpart, De Haro, were designated as 'prime and principal ministers'.[8] Thus the classic period of the chief minister and *ministériat* in France, which political history assigns to the regimes of Cardinals Richelieu and Mazarin from 1624 to 1661,[9] was barely recognized officially before it ended with Louis XIV's famous pronouncement on Mazarin's death that the government of his affairs, entrusted to the late cardinal, would henceforth be directed by himself.[10]

We will therefore have to go beyond formal titles and into the

d'état Claude Bouthillier au cardinal de Richelieu', in Durand (ed.), *Hommage*, 71–89; Roland Mousnier *et al.*, *Le Conseil du roi de Louis XII à la Révolution* (Paris, 1970); R. Mousnier, *Les Institutions de la France sous la monarchie absolue* (2 vols.; Paris, 1974–80), ii. 132–52.

[4] The classic critique is by Orest Ranum, *Richelieu and the Councillors of Louis XIII* (Oxford, 1963), 1–2.

[5] Grillon, i. 222–3. D'Aligre to Richelieu, 22 Oct. 1625. A *mémoire* for Mazarin in late 1643 refers to a pension for Richelieu as 'chef du conseil et premier ministre': AAE France 847, fo. 177.

[6] Grillon, iv, doc. 677, 21 Nov. 1629, royal *lettres patentes*; instructions to Marillac as *garde des sceaux* on Richelieu's status: AAE France 779, fo. 221.

[7] Carmona, *Richelieu: L'Ambition et le pouvoir*, 410; Hanotaux and La Force, *Richelieu*, ii. 549.

[8] J. H. Elliott, *Richelieu and Olivares* (Cambridge, 1984), 50.

[9] The outstanding work is R. J. Bonney, *Political Change in France under Richelieu and Mazarin* (London, 1978), which also recognizes their precursors, Concini and Luynes, as chief ministers, but ministers without their right to preside over the council which stemmed from their dignity as cardinals.

[10] See John B. Wolf, *Louis XIV* (New York, 1968), 134–5.

murky world of political practice in our quest for an understanding of Richelieu's ministerial *modus operandi*. The feature of court politics in early seventeenth-century Europe that interests us here is the common existence of what contemporaries called royal 'favourites'. These were individuals who had special favour with their monarch that transcended any formal office or function at court. This special relationship brought to the favourites and those close to them material and other benefits that were similar to those handed out to others at court, but far exceeded them in quantity and variety. For the purpose of understanding where Richelieu fits into this scheme of favour, I shall distinguish three types of favourite, although contemporaries did not employ any such precise typology: 'personal favourites', 'political favourites', and what I shall call the 'minister-favourite'.

The purely personal favourite was one who received wealth, honours, and royal household offices, but who did not use his special 'private' relationship with the monarch to influence public royal policy. By contrast, a political favourite was someone who amassed personal favours and also used them and favour with the royal benefactor to influence public affairs. At the risk of creating another formulaic term to replace the anachronistic 'chief' or 'prime' minister, I shall denote as 'minister-favourite' a third type of favourite who combined personal favour and public influence in such a way as to become the leading adviser to the ruler without holding any special office of chief minister, in some cases without holding any ministerial post whatsoever.[11] Contemporaries, while not settling on a generally agreed title for this pre-eminent royal adviser, could easily identify him, whatever his individual favours and offices might have been, and whatever the source of his hold was over the royal patron and master, whether it derived from a monarch's physical attraction to or emotional reliance on the adviser, sheer respect for proffered advice or mere reliance on experience in state service. The minister-favourite appeared almost routinely in early seventeenth-century France, and frequently elsewhere, to the envy of many, the admiration of some, and to the acknowledgement of all. This was, indeed, the 'age of the minister-favourite'.[12]

---

[11] Wolf, *Louis XIV*, perceptively notes this reality in titling his ch. on Louis XIV's breaking with the tradition, 'The New Government: There shall be No Minister-Favorite'. Contrast Ernest Lavisse (ed.), *Histoire de France depuis les origines jusqu'à la Révolution* (9 vols.; Paris, 1900–11), vii, pt. 2, who captioned his corresponding ch., 'Le Premier Ministre'.

[12] The best intro. is Antonio Feros, 'Kings, Councils and Favorites in the Spanish Monarchy, 1550–1620', paper given to the European History Seminar, Johns Hopkins University, 21 Feb. 1991. See also the comparative study by Elliott, *Richelieu and Olivares*, ch.

In France there were six such individuals or family teams in an almost unbroken fifty-year sequence, between 1610 and 1661. During Louis XIII's childhood and adolescence, the Italian couple, Concino Concini and Léonora Galigaï, were personal and political favourites of the ruling queen mother, Marie de' Medici (1610–17). The three fellow Italians fell in a *coup d'état* mounted by the restive young monarch's friends that left Concini assassinated, his wife executed for sorcery, and the queen mother banished to Blois.[13]

After seizing power, Louis ruled with his own succession of four favourites. For five years, Charles d'Albert, duke and constable of Luynes, shared royal favours with his two brothers. The arrangement was natural for the young king, for the middle-aged Luynes had not only won his heart, but helped him to topple his mother and her favourites, and displayed the political skills of making friends of potential royal enemies and containing those who were an unavoidable threat to king and favourite—especially the queen mother.[14]

Upon Luynes's premature death of purple fever in 1621, a chagrined monarch repented of having given so much to one subject. For the rest of his life, Louis XIII kept his vow never to let a personal favourite be his political adviser. This meant that his personal favourites fell when they tried to interfere with statecraft or supplant the king's minister-favourite, with Barradat being disgraced in 1626 and Cinq-Mars executed in 1642. During the same period, three experiments were made by royal councillors at being minister-favourites with the help of governmental experience that Concini and Luynes had lacked, but without their emotional hold on the ruler.

The first two of these experiments ended almost immediately in disgrace. Chancellor Nicolas Brûlart de Sillery and his son, the principal secretary of state, Puysieux, were banished early in 1624 after only a year of ascendancy in the royal council, having fallen victims to royal anger at perceived peculation and disregard for the king's will. Their successor, Marquis Charles de La Vieuville, son-in-law of the royal treasurer, Beaumarchais, and *surintendant des finances*, who had joined the now rehabilitated queen mother in turning the king's wrath against the Sillerys, was imprisoned in

2, 'Masters and Servants', 32–59; Elizabeth W. Marvick, 'Favorites in Early Modern Europe: A Recurring Psychopolitical Role', *Journal of Psychohistory*, 10 (1983), 463–89; Jean Bérenger, 'Pour une enquête européenne: Le Problème du ministériat au XVIIe siècle', *Annales: Économies, sociétés, civilisations*, 29 (1974), 166–92.

[13] Hélène Duccini's new study, *Concini* (Paris, 1991), appeared too late to be incorporated into this essay. It supersedes older biographies by Fernand Hayem, Alfred Franklin, and George Delamare.

[14] The most sympathetic portrait of the much maligned Luynes is Berthold Zeller, *Le Connétable de Luynes* (Paris, 1879).

August 1624 for similar state crimes that had been brought to Louis's attention by Marie and her long-time adviser-favourite, Richelieu.[15]

Louis XIII's initially reluctant experiment with the man whom La Vieuville had allowed into the council in April 1624 lasted for eighteen years until Richelieu's death in 1642. In Cardinal Richelieu we see a curious amalgam of past personal and political favouritism. The cardinal-minister had both the administrative experience capable of making him a political favourite to the king, and a keen appreciation of personal favouritism.[16]

Richelieu had begun as a hard-working bishop in his diocese at Luçon, then served as secretary of state during the last five months of Concini's regime. Finally, as adviser to Marie while she worked her way back into her son's favour, the former bishop and now cardinal by royal recommendation displayed a political shrewdness and wisdom that gradually gained the respect of the king. By appointing Marie's adviser to the royal council in 1624, Louis overlooked Richelieu's earlier association with the hated Concini and an overbearing administrative style that Louis had likened to 'tyranny' seven years before.[17]

If Richelieu was not also Louis XIII's personal favourite, he was a seasoned veteran of personal favouritism. As a protégé of Concini, the bishop of Luçon had written letters of 'creaturely' devotion, sought futilely to secure Marie's authorization to resign from the council in early 1617, yet failed to perceive the extent of the king's anger with the entire Concini ministry.[18] Marie de' Medici had looked kindly upon the bishop of Luçon during Concini's ascendancy, then as her personal *chef de conseil* during the transition to her exile at Blois. After being exiled at Avignon by the king and his favourite, who were both suspicious of his advisory role, Richelieu was recalled by them to Marie's side in 1619 to moderate her behaviour following her flight from Blois and raising of a rebel army. He remained her acknowledged *créature*, *surintendant*, and president of her council, with personal and political influence that some attri-

---

[15] On the Sillerys and La Vieuville, the most accurate contemporary account is Robert Arnauld d'Andilly, *Journal inédit* (2 vols.; Paris, 1888–1909), separately paginated annually for 1621–4. The relevant archival correspondence is voluminous.

[16] Two quite different studies of Richelieu's rise are drawn on here: Joseph Bergin, *The Rise of Richelieu* (New Haven, Conn., 1991); Elizabeth W. Marvick, *The Young Richelieu: A Psychoanalytical Study in Leadership* (Chicago, 1983). See also the controversial appraisal by C. Jouhaud, *La Main de Richelieu, ou le pouvoir cardinal* (Paris, 1991).

[17] [Duc de Chaulnes], *Relation exacte de . . . la mort du mareschal d'Ancre*, ed. J. F. Michaud and J. J. F. Poujoulat (Paris, 1837), 461.

[18] Examples of Richelieu's letters are in Avenel, i. 183–6, 194–5. His relations with Concini, Marie, and Louis XIII, as seen by Richelieu after his fall, are in AAE France 772, fos. 56–9.

būted to unnatural causes, until she abruptly dismissed him as the drama of the Day of Dupes began to unfold in November 1630. One should add that when Richelieu was serving as Marie's favourite and Luynes as Louis XIII's, each had played an intricate game of trying to insinuate himself into the other's favour, with a view to dominating his rival.[19]

Richelieu's protégé and successor, Jules Mazarin, resembled him as a cardinal and minister of state, governing for an equally long period of eighteen years. However, Cardinal Mazarin reverted to the example of Concini and Luynes in holding both personal and political favour with Louis XIII's widow, Anne, during her regency for Louis XIV. A seasoned Italian diplomat and then diplomatic agent of Richelieu, Mazarin entered Louis XIII's council on his patron's death, won the dying king's friendship, and went on to be the intimate partner of his widow. While no marriage contract has been found, there was no doubt that the new queen mother was emotionally as well as politically attached to this naturalized Frenchman.[20] Like Richelieu, Mazarin was hated by political rivals; unlike his patron, he was forced by élite and popular opposition into voluntary exile twice during the Fronde, in 1651 and 1652; but again like Richelieu, he survived until his death following his recall by Anne and Louis XIV after the Fronde in 1653.[21]

Beyond France's borders there were also many prominent minister-favourites during this time.[22] One thinks immediately of Sweden's Oxenstierna, Spain's Lerma and Olivares, England's Buckingham, Strafford, and Laud, and Austria's Khlesl and Eggenberg. Their careers and those of the French minister-favourites who preceded and followed Richelieu can tell us much about his own brand of royal favouritism. This group of minister-favourites comprised men of radically differing personalities: witness the cautious Luynes, Lerma, and Mazarin as opposed to the dramatic flourishes of Concini and Olivares. The domineering and ambitious Richelieu, who persevered in the long run as minister to Louis XIII—but not in the short term as *créature* of Concini—has to be set side by side with that equally driving autocrat, killed by companions of an outraged young Louis XIII. Socially, the favourites ranged from cadet branches of the

---

[19] Richelieu's correspondence with Luynes and the latter's fellow minister *créatures* is in AAE France, 771, 772, 775.

[20] See Ruth Kleinman, *Anne of Austria, Queen of France* (Columbus, Oh., 1985).

[21] The best study of Mazarin is Georges Dethan, *Mazarin: Un homme de paix à l'âge baroque 1602–1661* (Paris, 1981). The relevant government correspondence in the archives still awaits intensive exploration.

[22] See Bérenger, 'Le Problème du ministériat'.

greatest noble families (Olivares) to unremarkable civil-service *robe* nobility (the Sillerys), and on down to the son of a pastry-cook (Khlesl). One can only conclude that neither an individual's personality nor a particular social background guaranteed success. We will have to look very closely to discover Richelieu's special magic.

It does not lie necessarily in the titles and offices the cardinal held; all of the official vehicles of authority open to royal favourites had perils as well as advantages. This was true even of the office that historians have associated most closely with Richelieu's rise to and retention of power, the cardinalate. Like Emperor Matthias's favourite Khlesl, who had been bishop and then cardinal, Richelieu drew on the prestige, connections, and authority of both honours. In particular, being bishop of Luçon had helped propel him into the limelight of the concluding session of the Estates General of 1614–15 as orator for the first estate; and without the cardinal's biretta, he could not easily have taken precedence over all other ministers as he did at Louis XIII's council in 1624, by claiming that privilege as previously granted to Cardinals de Retz and de La Rochefoucauld.[23]

What else did the cardinal's robes give this ambitious man? Perhaps he used them as had Khlesl to place him socially above the grandees who had a much more distinguished pedigree.[24] The pointed comparisons made by Richelieu's pamphleteers with the distinguished cardinal-ministers of France's and Spain's past, Amboise and Ximenes, give further credence to the view that the minister-favourite was made more powerful in the public eye by donning his red hat, although the comparison with Ximenes turned most powerfully on their common fortune of being cardinal-warriors who helped save their country by military rather than religious acumen.[25]

There were two weaknesses in wrapping oneself in the cloak of religion, however. In the first place, taking holy orders prevented Richelieu from having an immediate family as his base of power through strategic marriages, office-holdings, and other benefits of Richelieu's royal favour. Secondly, being a cleric did not necessarily protect a favourite from royal disgrace, plots by the envious, or even death. In fact being a cleric could invite deadly attacks. The donning of the cardinal's hat in the service of his royal master during an age of Catholic revival and reform must surely have drawn attention

---

[23] On Richelieu's manipulation of his dignity as bishop and cardinal, see Bergin, *Rise of Richelieu*, 118, 243.

[24] On Khlesl, see R. J. W. Evans, *The Making of the Habsburg Monarchy, 1550–1700: An Interpretation* (Oxford, 1979), 43, 60–2, 64–7, 138.

[25] Elliott, *Richelieu and Olivares*, 98, 98 n. 42.

uncomfortably to the secular side of Richelieu's career, notably concerning his support of Louis XIII's military campaigns against fellow Catholic rulers. When grumbling against his power and policy recommendations led nobles to consider assassinating the cardinal-minister, Richelieu may well have been saved only by the scruples that the arch-conspirator, Louis XIII's brother, had about killing a priest; several of Gaston's fellow-conspirators, who were not so scrupulous but felt they needed princely validation of such a high crime, awaited in vain his signal to proceed.[26]

Past and contemporary European history were replete with examples of clergy in state service who met a fate that Richelieu escaped. The cardinal's generation could recall the rapid fall from grace and in one case murder of two famous servitors of past English monarchs, Archbishop Thomas à Becket of Canterbury and Cardinal Wolsey. Richelieu's own fall from early favour in 1617, despite being a bishop and almoner to the queen, was mirrored in the disgrace a year later of the Spanish royal favourite Lerma, almost immediately after he had been elevated by the pope to the purple.[27] That same year Cardinal Khlesl was unceremoniously consigned to a monastery by the future Emperor Ferdinand II.[28]

Richelieu was scarcely in his grave before his cardinal-minister successor Mazarin, and a counterpart in England, Archbishop Laud, fell into hard times. Laud's rank as archbishop of Canterbury may have delayed his trial and death for four years after his fall, until the English revolutionaries were joined by the more religiously radical Scots.[29] However, his office did not save him from the initial act of impeachment and imprisonment in the Tower of London at the end of 1640 for being 'an actor in the great design of the subversion of the laws . . . and of religion',[30] nor eventually from his attainder and execution in January 1645. Mazarin used his position as cardinal to prevent an entry in 1643 to the regent Anne's council of his rival and Gaston's favourite, the abbé de La Rivière.[31] However, the cardinalate did not prevent rivals from plotting Mazarin's overthrow or death in the so-called *cabale des importants* of 1643–4. Neither did

[26] Jean-Marie Constant, *Les Conjurateurs: Le Premier Libéralisme politique sous Richelieu* (Paris, 1987), 122–9, 147–65.

[27] J. H. Elliott, *The Count-Duke of Olivares: The Statesman in an Age of Decline* (New Haven, Conn., 1986), 35–6.

[28] Evans, *Habsburg Monarchy*, 65, 67. Evans adds, regarding Khlesl's disgrace by Matthias's successor Archduke Ferdinand, 'imagine Richelieu kidnapped by Gaston d'Orléans!' Yet one can, indeed, imagine something like that, had Gaston ascended to the throne. Richelieu feared it in 1626, 1627–8, and 1630.

[29] I owe this insight to Laurence Brockliss.

[30] Derek Hirst, *Authority and Conflict: England, 1603–1658* (Cambridge, Mass., 1986), 196.

[31] AAE France 850, fo. 16 (newsletter).

it shield him against an avalanche of *Mazarinade* pamphlets of 1648–52 that can only be described as scatalogically tinged character-assassination tracts, nor the indignity of two self-imposed exiles in 1650–2, and the placing of a price on his head by Frondeurs.

The difference between the long-term continuity of Richelieu's ministry and the serious, if temporary, troubles of Mazarin during the Fronde, can possibly be linked with the former's good fortune in being a priest and the latter's decision to become a cardinal without ever taking holy orders. But it was Richelieu's French birthright, the fact that his monarch was a man, and perhaps some character traits, not the mantle of sacred office, that spared him virtually all of the sexual slurs made against his naturalized French successor, tainted in Frondeur legend with being Italian, and supposed lover of Anne of Austria, the foreign-born queen mother, as well as of his own relations and of members of his own sex.[32]

If the honour of being a cardinal was a mixed blessing for a minister-favourite, the most prestigious council offices were even less propitious vehicles of favour. La Vieuville's post as finance minister was tainted by links to private financiers of the state. Alleged corruption triggered his imprisonment in 1624, just as it rationalized the incarceration of Mazarin's would-be successor, Fouquet, in 1661. Sully's success under Henri IV was not to be repeated.[33] Similarly, the chancery failed in the making of any minister-favourite. While Oxenstierna in Sweden served as chancellor to two monarchs, Gustavus Adolphus and Christina, from 1612 to 1644,[34] Brûlart, lifetime chancellor in France from 1607 to 1624, barely escaped legal investigation after his brief time of overriding power in 1623. Chancellor Séguier never headed the royal council, although he did become titular head of the temporary council that the rebel princes Gaston and Condé established near the end of the Fronde in Paris with the claim that this special body was acting on behalf of the monarch and opposed only to Mazarin.[35]

[32] In addition to the voluminous literature on the *Mazarinades*, see esp. C. Jouhaud, *Mazarinades: La Fronde des mots* (Paris, 1985); Hubert Carrier, *La Presse de la Fronde, 1648–1653: Les Mazarinades*, i. (Geneva, 1989); Marie-Noëlle Grand-Mesnil, *Mazarin, la Fronde, et la presse, 1647–49* (Paris, 1967); and Jeffrey Merrick, 'The Cardinal and the Queen: Sexual and Political Disorders in the Mazarinades', American Historical Assoc. paper, Dec. 1991.

[33] See R. J. Bonney, *The King's Debts: Finance and Politics in France 1589–1661* (Oxford, 1981); Julian Dent, *Crisis in Finance: Crown, Financiers and Society in Seventeenth-Century France* (Newton Abbot, 1973).

[34] See Michael Roberts, 'Queen Christina and the General Crisis of the Seventeenth Century', in Trevor Aston (ed.), *Crisis in Europe* (London, 1965), 206–34.

[35] A. Lloyd Moote, *The Revolt of the Judges: The Parlement of Paris and the Fronde, 1643–1652* (Princeton, NJ, 1971), 344.

The path to power from royal household and related military offices was the most treacherous of all.[36] The assassinated Concini and Buckingham, like the long-term survivors Lerma and Olivares, and Luynes whose favour was waning when he died, all founded their power in royal household offices—as first gentleman of the prince's bedchamber, master of the royal stable, or royal falconer. Similarly Concini, Luynes, and La Vieuville each held a pivotal military post, as marshal, constable, and captain of the king's bodyguards respectively.

Behind the varieties of personality, social background, and career trajectory lay some broader contemporary trends that helped shape the fortunes of favourites, and force us, once again, to look critically at the traditional historical interpretation that Richelieu's unique qualities constituted the major shaper of his destiny, or, as one scholar has contended, that his *ministériat*, 'en grande partie le fruit de circonstances, était modélé sur la personalité exceptionelle du cardinal'.[37] The broader external 'causes' are reflected in the popular cartoons of early seventeenth-century European political culture that featured the ship of state navigating stormy waters.

We remember best Richelieu's efforts to enlist this metaphor in his never-ending propaganda campaign to portray himself as especially effective in steering the early seventeenth-century royal vessel through the troubled sea of foreign threats and internal subversion. With Louis XIII at the helm, and his cardinal-minister as the anchor, French subjects were reassured that all was safe:

> Va navire, ne crains; ton pilote est un Dieu.
> Jamais ancre ne fut en plus Riche Lieu.[38]

What this depiction deliberately overlooked was the hidden subtext that the political sea upon which Richelieu was cast buffeted every contemporary royal vessel, brought on board and seasoned all the favourites in the ways of navigating the waters, and in addition charted much of the route that each of them took.

The most obvious general factor contributing to the age of the minister-favourite was the conjuncture of a generation of weak rulers—remarkably dull, unimaginative, and at times capricious, either too lazy or too hesitant to take charge of the ship of state in the way that Philip II, Elizabeth, and Henri IV had done a short generation before. The personalities of Philip III and IV, James I and Charles I,

---

[36] On the Spanish court, see J. H. Elliott, *Spain and its World 1500–1700* (New Haven, Conn., 1989), 145; on England, J. P. Cooper, *Land, Men and Beliefs* (London, 1983).

[37] Thuau, *Raison d'état*, 239.

[38] Carmona, *Richelieu: L'Ambition et le pouvoir*, illus. 20, 'Richelieu et la barque de l'État'.

Matthias and Louis XIII, gave would-be favourites an unusual
opportunity to capture the ear of their bewildered monarchs, but also
constituted obstacles to holding on to power.

Louis XIII presented special problems. Though always feeling
the need to rely on a confidant, he had strong general notions of
the directions he wanted his state to take, and had also developed a strong sense of the characteristics he wanted in his advisers.
Richelieu's success was to come in large part from his ability to fit
the political and psychological needs of a *maître* of some calibre.[39]
The task was beyond the capacities of his predecessors, even though
they managed part of the king's political agenda. Richelieu took note
of this for his own career in reflecting on Concini's pluses and
minuses. The cardinal had no quarrel with Concini's aims: 'Il avoit
pour principal but d'élever sa fortune aux plus hautes dignités où
puisse venir un gentilhomme, pour second désir la grandeur du
Roi et de l'État, et, en troisième lieu, l'abaissement des grands
du royaume [à cause de] leurs intrigues de cour.'[40]

Concini's mistake, however, as Richelieu noted elsewhere in his
memoirs, was to combine flaunting his family fortune with its com-
plement of aspiring to appear more powerful than the ruler: 'Il était
si vain que, ne se contentant pas de la faveur et du pouvoir de faire
ses affaires, il affectoit d'être maître de l'esprit de la reine et son
principal conseiller en toutes ses actions.'[41] In an even more biting
epitaph for a political rival whose peremptory relations with the
prickly Louis XIII he wished to avoid himself, the cardinal referred
to 'l'ambition que La Vieuville avoit de n'avoir ni maître ni com-
pagnon dans l'administration des affaires'. According to Richelieu,
this fatal flaw was accompanied by that finance minister's too narrow
focus on his own interests: 'il n'étoit pas moins attentif à ses intérêts
que les autres [favoris, i.e. Luynes and the Sillerys], beaucoup moins
capable de penser aux publics'.[42]

Recently historians have concentrated on the wars of the age as a
more pervasive cause of the phenomenon of the minister-favourite
than weak royal leadership alone.[43] Even the soldier-king, Gustavus
Adolphus, and the strong-minded Emperor Ferdinand II turned to
their trusted advisers Oxenstierna and Eggenberg, just as the less
self-confident Philip IV looked to Olivares, Charles I to Buckingham

---

[39] A. L. Moote, *Louis XIII, the Just* (Berkeley, Calif., 1989), 155–74. See also Elizabeth
W. Marvick, *Louis XIII: The Making of a King* (New Haven, Conn., 1986).
[40] Richelieu, *Mémoires* SHF ii. 228.
[41] Ibid. ii. 157.
[42] Ibid. iv. 21.
[43] The most persuasive presentation of this theme is Elliott, *Richelieu and Olivares*.

and Strafford, Louis XIII to La Vieuville and Richelieu, and Anne of Austria to Mazarin.

War clouds favoured Richelieu's ascension to the role of minister-favourite in 1624, because no one else in the French royal council could sort out conflicting religious and secular interests for Louis XIII as he faced the Thirty Years War, the Huguenot challenge, and the Valtelline quagmire. However, wartime success was hard to come by. At the outbreak of the Thirty Years War in 1618, Khlesl had been disgraced because his conciliatory treatment of the Protestant Bohemian rebels was anathema to the militant future Emperor Ferdinand II. Olivares was eventually dismissed for wartime failures; Strafford was executed following an act of attainder by his parliamentary opponents who feared that he might turn the royal army against them; and Mazarin was forced into exile in large part because of his association with the interminable and costly Franco-Spanish sequel to the Thirty Years War. Even Richelieu's record during his first two years, perhaps the most crucial in the wake of La Vieuville's quick political demise, was singularly unimpressive diplomatically and militarily.

Eventually, success allowed Louis XIII to be depicted as a warrior king, confidently employing his sword and a shield bearing Richelieu's image to crush his enemies at La Rochelle and the Susa Pass.[44] Richelieu's critics were so frustrated that they accused the cardinal of keeping the Habsburg war going to render himself indispensable to his master. But the ongoing uncertainties of war and diplomacy make it doubtful that the cardinal-minister saw it that way.

A complementary argument has been made that a 'revolution in government', involving the wartime expansion of civil and military personnel, government taxation, and bureaucratic paperwork, led monarchs trained primarily to head a court to turn over the burden of technical administration to a 'chief minister or favourite'.[45] However, governmental expansion was a long-term process that was in operation before 1610 and after 1661. We must therefore look for something within that particular phase of the state-building process. Recent scholarship has pointed to patron–client relations as the glue that bonded two rival centres of contemporary power: the expanding warfare state in search of order and obedience; and the 'overmighty subjects' whose time-honoured but eroding local seats of power,

---

[44] Frontispiece by Michel Lasne to a thesis by Laurent de Brisacier, 1632, reproduced in André Tuilier (ed.), *Richelieu et le monde de l'esprit* (Paris, 1985), 309, 312; illus. 42, notice no. 80.

[45] Geoffrey Parker, *Europe in Crisis 1598–1648* (Glasgow, 1979), 54–66; Conrad Russell, 'Masters or Servants', *London Review of Books* (5–19 July 1984), 13, as cited by Feros, 'Kings, Councils and Favorites', 27.

wealth, and prestige were increasingly dependent on reinforcement by court-brokered offices and honours.[46]

Richelieu's generation of fortune-seeking nobles of sword and *robe* extraction, as well as would-be-noble commoners, played a role in the evolution of the uses of royal patronage that differed from that of the immediately preceding and succeeding generations. They were far less destructive than military leaders and provincial governors during the late sixteenth-century wars of religion, who tore apart the fabric of the political–social order.[47] Yet they were more frantic in their quest for favour than the tamed nobility at Louis XIV's Versailles as imagined by sociologists and reconstructed by historians,[48] for the Sun King's subjects knew that their power derived largely from state patronage.[49] The court society of Louis XIII's day was thus rather Hobbesian in nature, driven by subjects' fears of losing power both at the centre and periphery of the state, envy of those who had it, and intense ambition to secure it for themselves. The tensions reflected in that scramble for power have even been depicted as producing a new modern culture centred on money, ambition, and individuality.[50] Whether the goal was land, marriage, credit, or the resources of the burgeoning state, ambitious individuals, families, and factions looked to the political centre in their quest of wealth, honours, and power.[51] Hence d'Avenel's reflection

---

[46] See J. Russell Major, 'The Revolt of 1620: A Study of Ties of Fidelity', *French Historical Studies*, 14 (1986), 391–408; Pierre Lefebvre, 'Aspects de la "fidélité" en France au XVIIᵉ siècle: Le Cas des agents des princes de Condé', *Revue historique*, 250 (1973), 59–106; and Kettering, *Patrons, Brokers, and Clients*.

[47] See *inter alia* Robert R. Harding, *Anatomy of a Power Élite: The Provincial Governors of Early-Modern France* (New Haven, Conn., 1978).

[48] Norbert Elias, *The Court Society* (New York, 1984); Emmanuel Le Roy Ladurie, 'Versailles Observed: The Court of Louis XIV in 1709', in his *The Mind and Method of the Historian* (Chicago, 1981), 149–73.

[49] See William Beik, *Absolutism and Society in Seventeenth-Century France: State Power and Provincial Aristocracy in Languedoc* (Cambridge, 1985).

[50] Jonathan Dewald, *Aristocratic Experience and the Origins of Modern Culture: France, 1570–1715* (Los Angeles, Calif., 1992). Dewald's examples are drawn from every generation within this time period, but one can detect an intensification of the process in the early 17th cent.

[51] See e.g. BI Godefroy 268, fo. 219, Luynes to Nérestang, 3 Nov. 1618, luring Concini's former creature with the bait of providing for his children; AAE France 775, fos. 217–21, Schomberg to Richelieu, 10 Aug. and 4, 16, 23 Sept. 1622, brokering the distribution of Cardinal Retz's benefices deemed 'very important' for his relatives. The related secondary literature is substantial, featuring Françoise Bayard, *Le Monde des financiers au XVIIᵉ siècle* (Paris, 1988); Daniel Dessert, *Argent, pouvoir et société au grand siècle* (Paris, 1984); Jean-Louis Flandrin, *Families in Former Times: Kinship, Household and Sexuality* (Cambridge, 1979); Kettering, *Patrons, Brokers, and Clients*; Mark Motley, *Becoming a French Aristocrat: The Education of the Court Nobility, 1580–1715* (Princeton, NJ, 1990); Marvick, *The Young Richelieu*; and her unpubl. paper 'Fidelity, Kinship and Affect: Notes on the Politics of Louis XIII's Court in 1638'.

on the nobility of Richelieu's time: 'Le gentilhomme peut encore devenir riche en jouant un rôle politique par la volonté du roi, il n'est plus assez riche par lui-même, pour exercer ce rôle grâce à sa fortune . . . La fortune privée de l'aristocracie est désormais trop mince pour constituer encore une puissance sociale.'[52]

Increased social scrambling for the favours of the state gave the fullest opportunity to royal favourites to act as brokers of wealth and power. As is suggested by the subtitle of Joseph Bergin's recent study of Richelieu's fortune, 'Power and the Pursuit of Wealth',[53] several overlapping practices were involved here. As royal advisers, the favourites seemed to concentrate on the exercising of power on behalf of the state. Yet in the manipulation of royal patronage, they operated much like other ambitious subjects from the court, military, or *robe* nobility, or even non-noble social climbers, all of whom were eager to win either honourable titles or ignoble but profitable tax leases. Indeed, the favourites gave out royal favours to others in their social circles as well as to themselves.

In effect, as they put on these several hats, royal favourites tended to blend together and monopolize favour and power in one gigantic windfall of the age of war, state-building, and the court society. It is doubtful that Richelieu and his fellow favourites separated state interest and self-interest in their own minds any more clearly than they and their royal masters separated religious and secular reasons of state.[54] For favouritism led to statecraft, if only to protect one's investment; and statecraft necessitated dispensing the favours that bound subjects in loyalty to both the favourite and his royal master. Inevitably, a considerable portion of correspondence between royal favourites, their ministerial *créatures*, and other clients, concerned the giving and obtaining of royal favours.[55]

If we place Richelieu's particular blending of favour and power within the wide range of contemporary courtly behaviour, we find him somewhere in the middle between the two extremes of avarice and self-denial.[56] On the one hand, he was no Cardinal de La Rochefoucauld, who could hardly be brought around either to exercise power and enjoy lucrative benefices, or let Richelieu and his precursor-favourites freely dispense those favours to their own

---

[52] Georges d'Avenel, *La Noblesse française sous Richelieu* (Paris, 1901), 176.

[53] *Cardinal Richelieu: Power and the Pursuit of Wealth* (New Haven, Conn., 1985).

[54] On reason of state and religion, see William F. Church *Richelieu and Reason of State* (Princeton, NJ, 1972).

[55] BI Godefroy 52 has correspondence between Ambassador Cesy and Luynes in 1621, with allusions to the necessary mixing of a minister-favourite's 'interests particuliers' and 'vertu'.

[56] On the tensions between public power and private interests, see esp. Dewald, *Aristocratic Experience*, ch. 6: 'Money and the Problem of Power'.

clients.[57] On the other hand, in pursuing power and favour without any qualms, Richelieu concentrated less on obtaining and dispensing favours and devoted more time and energy to what we would call public service than had his one-time rival Luynes. The contrast between Richelieu and Concini was even greater. Precisely where Cardinal Richelieu stood can be understood by a close comparative examination of the techniques of favouritism during his age. All of the minister-favourites of early seventeenth-century France, but especially Richelieu, Luynes, and Concini, had in common three personal strategies in their exercise of royal favour. Firstly, through royal generosity they acquired a quasi-private patrimony of lucrative pensions, offices, tax-farm leases, and land. Secondly, they all advanced their extended families through patronage, prestigious marriages, and other alliances with the greatest noble dynasties of the realm. This family strategy greatly elevated the status of the favourites who, as a rule, were either of lesser court-based nobility or state-service lineage; and it was fully in keeping with the contemporary belief that success had to be shared with one's relations. Thirdly, the favourites placed their own supporters in the royal household, councils, and other civil, military, and ecclesiastical offices. This conformed to the contemporary custom of patrons creating the fortune of their client-*créatures*. And it gave the patron extra eyes, ears, and voice within the entourage of members of the royal family as well as the council.[58]

Concini and his wife undoubtedly thought initially of using their friendship with Marie de' Medici as *premier gentilhomme de la chambre du roi* and *dame autour de la reine mère* primarily to make a fortune. They were especially interested in controlling the leasing of tax farms and appointments to venal office.[59] Thanks to Léonora, they acquired the lands and the marquisate of Ancre in Picardy; Concini became the marshal of Ancre; and the couple began to round out their domain with his military governorships.

On the advice of the baron de Lux, the marshal of Ancre came to see his governments as a power base, and a haven in case of court hostility.[60] His growing control over the wealthy, strategic north-

---

[57] J. Bergin, *Cardinal de La Rochefoucauld: Leadership and Reform in the French Church* (New Haven, Conn., 1987), 133–4.

[58] There is a fine summary of Richelieu's application of the 2nd and 3rd strategies in Flandrin, *Families*, 20–1.

[59] Fernand Hayem, *Le Maréchal d'Ancre et Léonora Galigaï* (Paris, 1910), 67–70, 108, 261–5.

[60] François Duval de Fontenay-Mareuil, *Mémoires*, ed. J. F. Michaud and J. J. F. Poujoulat (Paris, 1837), 63.

eastern province of Picardy was one of the points of contention after 1614 between rebel grandees, who were jealous of his favour, and the queen mother and her favourite who insisted on seizing the governorship of Picardy from the noble rebel, Longueville. Having almost prevented the peace treaty of Loudun in 1616 by his intransigence, Concini settled for shifting his power base to Normandy as its lieutenant-general, and as governor of Pont de l'Arche, Caen, and Quillebeuf.[61] Yet for all his self-serving patrimonial interests, he used his provinical strongholds and troops under him for the royal cause.[62]

Luynes's patrimony-building began where Concini's ended. Louis XIII gave all of the fallen favourite's governorships to him. Luynes then shrewdly traded his Norman base for the top provincial spot in Picardy (using the intermediate trading-chip of the government of Île de France). His governorship of Picardy, along with that of Amiens, coupled with his brother Chaulnes's provincial lieutenancy, gave Luynes a spectacular patrimony that had eluded all of Concini's guile and blustering.[63] Siri claims that he would have preferred Provence, and more so Britanny, both of which fell later to Richelieu's clan, but the price demanded by the governors, Guise and Vendôme, was too high.[64]

Luynes also had an eye for the political use of patrimony. As lieutenant in Normandy, he hosted Louis XIII's first Assembly of Notables at Rouen; the notables were suitably impressed, currying favour with the new favourite as well as giving a vote of confidence to the policies and actions of king and favourite.[65] Luynes's later acquisitions in Picardy had an obvious strategic importance when he became constable of France. Favourite and monarch could risk striking out against southern rebel Huguenot towns, knowing that an attack on Paris from the Spanish Netherlands would be less likely than if Picardy were in the hands of a restive grandee.

In Richelieu's case the largess bestowed, first by Marie de' Medici and then by Louis XIII, was staggering. He was as opportunistic as Luynes—witness his wresting of the La Rochelle area bloc

---

[61] Hayem, *Maréchal d'Ancre*, 67–70, 108, 261–5.

[62] BN MS Fr. 3804, fos. 25–6, Concini to Montigny (in his hand, n.d.); Paul Phélypeaux de Pontchartrain, *Mémoires*, ed. J. F. Michaud and J. J. F. Poujoulat (Paris, 1837), 347, 352, 367, 370; Hayem, *Maréchal d'Ancre*, 175–80.

[63] *Relation exacte de la mort du Mareschal d'Ancre*, 465; Fontenay-Mareuil, *Mémoires*, 131 and 141.

[64] Vittorio Siri, *Mémoires secrètes . . . contenant le règne de Louis XIII* (36 vols.; Amsterdam, 1774–84), xix. 193–4.

[65] Fontenay-Mareuil, *Mémoires*, 126–7; V.-L. Tapié, *France in the Age of Louis XIII and Richelieu* (Cambridge, 1974), 95.

of governorships from a would-be rival for Louis XIII's favour, Marshal Jean de Toiras, victor over the English amphibious attacks on the area in the mid-1620s. He was not above obtaining from fallen rivals private estates or regional posts coveted by previous favourites for their maritime commercial and strategic importance. Le Havre, Honfleur, and several other places became suddenly available in 1626 from Marshal Ornano and other fallen rivals, thanks to the smashing of the Chalais conspiracy against Richelieu and Louis.[66]

Yet heeding the lessons he had learned as *créature* of Concini and Marie de' Medici, the cardinal-minister was exceedingly careful to make these acquisitions from disgraced, imprisoned, or dead adversaries appear to be forced on him by the king, or paid for from his own wealth. How different from Concini's insisting that he be paid for services rendered as governor and marshal.[67] Nevertheless, Richelieu was also reimbursed, albeit very indirectly.[68] And during the crisis of the Day of Dupes the cardinal behaved like his former patron in contemplating fleeing to Le Havre.[69]

The favourites were almost as interested in the second strategy of advancing their relations as they were in caring for their own patrimonies. Concini made his sister abbess at Caen; Léonora secured for her brother the abbey of Noirmoutiers and the archbishopric of Tours. On one occasion Concini's sister repaid him handsomely, raising a band of troops to join his forces against noble rebels.[70] Luynes carried on the tradition. His family had administrative control over Picardy, the Bastille, and Vincennes, leading to friendship with the imprisoned Condé and ultimately to allying the liberated prince with the king against the rebel queen mother and Huguenots.[71] The governorship of Blaye, gateway to Guienne and key to keeping local grandees in check, was awarded to Luynes's brother, Luxembourg.[72] On the other hand the coming to court of Luynes's distant relations 'in boatloads'—the sarcastic term was Louis XIII's—resulted in favours that no one has ever associated with state-building.[73]

[66] See Grillon, i. 545–55. AAE France 783, fos. 27–9, for a list of the governments of Ornano, who died in prison while awaiting trial for treason.

[67] BI Godefroy 268, fo. 35, Concini to Villeroy, 20 Sept. 1615, and the Dollé-Nérestang correspondence.

[68] Bergin, *Cardinal Richelieu*, esp. 82–3.

[69] Henri-Auguste de Loménie de Brienne, *Mémoires*, ed. J. F. Michaud and J. J. F. Poujoulat (Paris, 1838), 52.

[70] Pontchartrain, *Mémoires*, 302; *Relation exacte*, 465; Fontenay-Mareuil, *Mémoires*, 90.

[71] See Siri, *Mémoires secrètes*, xx. 161–2; Richelieu, *Mémoires* SHF ii. 253.

[72] Fontenay-Mareuil, *Mémoires*, 154.

[73] See L. Moreri, *Grand Dictionnaire historique* (18th edn., 18 vols.; Amsterdam, 1740), i. 225–7; Henri de Rohan, *Mémoires* (Paris, 1837), 516.

Richelieu's relations also came in boatloads;[74] and more than one proved a personal embarrassment for the cardinal and a handicap for the state, notably his nephew François de Pont Courlay, general of the Provençal galleys and governor of Le Havre, whom he eventually had to disgrace in 1639 after virtually renouncing him as his client three years before.[75] We only need to recall that the visibility of Richelieu's family was reduced by the atypicality of its history, his own clerical status depriving him of children to favour. His sibling Alphonse acted throughout his life more like a self-effacing surrogate Cardinal de La Rochefoucauld than an *alter ego* to Cardinal Richelieu. His oldest brother, Henri, was killed in a duel in 1619, thereby halting a very promising career at court, and forcing Richelieu, in Fontenay-Mareuil's words, to rely thereafter on strangers, 'often of little reliability'.[76]

The favourites' complementary tactic of forging family alliances with the great noble families in France reveals remarkably few differences between Richelieu and his two prime predecessors. Indeed, one could just as easily say that they were like him in using alliance strategies in the service of the state, as to say that Richelieu was like them in using alignments for personal and family enhancement.[77] Like Concini and Luynes, he allied himself with the king's powerful cousin, Condé. The Condé connection served the state, as well as the interests of all three of these favourites, by bolstering royal authority against restive or rebel grandees. Eventually the policy failed under Concini and Marie, who arrested the prince in 1616. Luynes and Richelieu subsequently faced a more pliable Condé. The prince was grateful to Luynes for restoring his freedom and placing him in the royal council in 1619, and to Richelieu for persuading Louis XIII to bring him back to court in 1626 despite Condé's second falling out with state policy that had triggered his angry withdrawal from the council in 1622. Richelieu stayed in power long enough to strengthen the family alliance with a marriage between his niece Claire Clémence de Brézé and Condé's son in 1641; his precursors were forestalled in anticipating this achievement by the tender ages of Concini's children and by Luynes's death.[78]

---

[74] See Lavisse, *Histoire de France*, vi, pt. 2, 436–9, for a short list, and Bergin, *Cardinal Richelieu*, for a thorough and measured evaluation.

[75] Avenel, v. 569, Richelieu to Pont Courlay, 26 Aug. 1636. A good summary of Pont Courlay's chequered career is in Kettering, *Patrons, Brokers, and Clients*, 24–5. See also Ch. 5 by David Parrott, below.

[76] Fontenay-Mareuil, *Mémoires*, 139–40.

[77] On Richelieu, see Orest Ranum, 'Richelieu and the Great Nobility: Some Aspects of Early Modern Political Motives', *French Historical Studies*, 3 (1963), 184–204.

[78] On Condé, see Ch. 5 below.

Private interest looms greater in other marital alignments. Concini sought to join the rich and famous grandee families; but the youth of his children, changing court politics, and perhaps a foreigner's fear of antagonizing the French nobility thwarted proposed marriages with the Soissons, Vendômes, and Guises. He never pushed his four nieces forward the way that Luynes, Richelieu, or the naturalized Mazarin advanced the cause of their family dynasties. Indeed, he felt compelled to defend what his family had acquired in the patriotically sounding pamphlet, *L'Italien français*. By contrast, the marriage of Luynes's brothers to wealthy heiresses and the elevation of his lands and theirs to duchies looks much like a blueprint for the string of family weddings and titles arranged by Richelieu. The cardinal was opportunistic during his years in the wilderness, entering into a marriage alliance with Luynes as part of a peace treaty ending the second war between Marie de' Medici and Louis XIII. He was thwarted in reaching into royal and quasi-royal blood when prospective Soissons and Lorraine in-laws spurned his family. But he still managed marriages with the powerful Épernon clan of Guienne, and with the Harcourts, Brézés, Pont Courlays, and Guiches.

How comparable were the favourites in the third strategy of controlling royal household, council, and other offices? There was certainly progression from early favourites to Richelieu in terms of expanded control over the royal family. On the other hand, the placing of *créatures* and allies in military, civil, and ecclesiastical offices was every bit as marked under Concini as under Richelieu. Nor does the brilliance of Richelieu's almost total control over Louis XIII's council after 1635[79] detract from the considerable success that Concini and Luynes had in moulding the conciliar membership to their liking. The only sharp contrast was with the very incomplete conciliar control exercised by the Sillerys and La Vieuville; Richelieu had a decade to work out his system, while his immediate predecessors had only a few months.

In his handling of the royal family, Richelieu built on the foundations laid by his predecessors. Concini and Marie had trusted the middle-aged Luynes to be merely the young Louis XIII's falconer and personal favourite, and paid for their mistake when favourite and monarch overthrew them. Luynes kept watch on the young monarch by having himself or one of his brothers regularly in Louis's presence; and by securing the appointment of the supposedly

---

[79] See the classic study by Ranum, *Councillors of Louis XIII*; and the set of documents in R. J. Bonney, *Society and Government in France under Richelieu and Mazarin, 1624–1661* (London, 1988).

docile Jesuit priest, Arnoux, as confessor-*créature*, and replacing him when he turned against the favourite. Luynes also tried to control Marie, first by making Richelieu his own client and her adviser, and later by ending the second war between Marie and Louis XIII with a peace treaty that included a marriage between Luynes's nephew, Combalet, and Richelieu's favourite niece, the future Duchess of Aiguillon. The plan worked initially, for Richelieu supplanted Marie's hard-line confidant Ruccelaï.[80] However, Richelieu proved more dangerous as a client than Ruccelaï had as an enemy, by making Luynes's *créature* and fellow minister, Déageant, his own client, and currying favour with others in the royal circle. During Richelieu's own time as minister-favourite, he adopted Luynes's marriage strategy with equally unsuccessful results. A cousin of the cardinal was married to Puylaurens, favourite to the king's brother and heir, Gaston; but the new in-law promptly betrayed king and cardinal by encouraging Gaston to rebel.

Richelieu appears more innovative in his determination to avoid as much as possible a rift between Louis XIII and his mother, brother, and wife. Perhaps the cardinal was shrewder than Luynes, whom Louis remembered with bitterness long after his death as intensifying the feud between king and queen mother following her exile in 1617. The cardinal also saw as a mistake La Vieuville's dismissal of Gaston's governor, Ornano, who had originally been beholden to Luynes's circle, but also had a reputation for making the heir happy; one of Richelieu's first recommendations when he replaced La Vieuville was that Louis bring back the heir's favourite.

Yet surely the cardinal's paramount concerns in mediating royal family relations were less innovative than they were a blend of traditional state interest and his obvious self-interest. He was seeking to cover himself in case the sickly Louis should die and Gaston succeed him, just as he was attempting to keep the ever unpredictable Gaston and Marie from giving any noble revolt against king and cardinal the legitimation of their support as members of the royal family. Acting as the 'honest broker' did not always work, to be sure, as Ornano's arrest for encouraging Gaston's independence, Gaston's own frequent revolts, and Marie's spectacular flight from France after the Day of Dupes show. However, Richelieu enormously strengthened his relations with Louis XIII by trying to keep Marie content, Gaston satisfied, and Anne docile.

Richelieu's other means of keeping Louis close to him—choosing

---

[80] See Siri, *Mémoires secrètes*, xix. 197; and the more modern accounts by Hanotaux and La Force, *Richelieu*, ii, and Carmona, *Marie de Médicis*.

a personal favourite and confessor for the king who were the cardinal's *créatures*—were unoriginal and almost fatally flawed. Just as Marie and Concini had thought they controlled Luynes, Richelieu assumed that he had control over Barradat and Cinq-Mars, who entered deadly conspiracies against him. He was more fortunate with Saint-Simon *père*, a constant messenger and bridge between king and cardinal. Like Luynes, Richelieu was undercut by royal confessors, notably Fathers Suffren and Caussin.[81]

In other appointments, from the army to the judiciary, Concini and Galigaï's hand can be seen time and again. The protection and expansion of their private financial interests eventually led them to oust council members who blocked their financial designs and to influence royal policies that affected their fortune. They played a role in the dismissal of Sully and then Jeannin from the finance ministry; and they ousted Chancellor Brûlart and du Vair, keeper of the seals, for failing to authorize lucrative contracts. Their personal agents of long standing, Mangot and Barbin, ultimately settled in as keeper of the seals and finance minister, and Concini's *créature*, Richelieu, became secretary of state.[82]

Government correspondence during the Concini era suggests that the council was unstable but that there was sufficient co-operation to ensure that it functioned relatively efficiently in respect of both public and private matters,[83] despite the Italian favourite's oppressive demands of his minsterial *créatures*.[84] Concini may have stayed away from the council by calculation, knowing that he had the ear of the queen mother and need not risk any visibility that would increase popular envy. His habit of remaining at his provincial base away from court during some crucial personnel changes seems equally calculated, like Luynes's propitious delay in becoming a council member immediately after Concini's murder, and Richelieu's habit of placing himself at a distance from the king during major crises like the Chalais affair.

Luynes's decision to enter the council, and actively engage in

---

[81] See BI Godefroy 15, fos. 376, 404–5, 408.

[82] On council changes, see esp. Fontenay-Mareuil, *Mémoires*, 43, 70, 89, 101–9, 113.

[83] BN MS Fr. 3657, fos. 106, 124, 139, 145, 149, Mangot to Béthune, Sept.–Nov. 1616; BN MS Fr. 3804, fos. 19, 22, 25–6, 29, Marie (Richelieu) to Montigny, 1 and 12 Mar. 1617; Concini to Montigny, 2 June 1616. See also BN MS Fr. 3799, fo. 72, Concini to Jeannin, 28 Feb. 1611; BI Godefroy 268, fos. 39–41, 46, 76–7, 126–7, Louis de Marillac to Nérestang, 11 Sept., 11 and 22 Oct. 1615, 18 Jan. 1616; Marie (Richelieu) to the pope, nominating Léonora's brother to the cardinalate, 4 Dec. 1616.

[84] Richelieu, *Mémoires* SHF i. 168–9; Robert Arnauld d'Andilly, *Journal, 1614–1620* (Paris, 1857), 292.

its debates as constable and eventually acting keeper of the seals, marked an advance on Concini's council strategy. The new favourite never controlled the council completely, yet persuaded Louis to add to the council 'greybeards', purged by Concini and now restored by the king, a number of persons involved in the *coup d'état* of 1617. Luynes's brother, Chaulnes, and cousin, Modène, *créatures* like Tronçon and Cardinal de Retz, and eventually allies like Condé, gave the king's favourite a solid base of support in the council. Like Concini, Luynes had difficulty finding a reliable finance minister. He turned first to Barbin's assistant, Déageant; after that *créature* turned to Richelieu, Luynes replaced him with the talented military and civil servant Schomberg. Luynes also had to contend with uncertain career civil servants like the Sillerys and the independent du Vair. To obviate the problem, Luynes also worked closely with Louis XIII in private to review all policy-making before and after council sessions.[85]

Richelieu must have learnt much about council control during the Luynes era and the following two years when Marie re-entered the royal court and council. He was in constant correspondence with Luynes and other council members from 1617 to 1621,[86] then acted as Marie's confidant to tell her what to say in the council meetings of 1622–3. He especially relied on Marie's *créature* and in-law, Louis de Marillac, who acted at court as his informant, advocate, and virtual client. Thus, during the scramble for royal favour immediately following Luynes's death, Marillac informed Richelieu of the good offices he had undertaken on his behalf: 'Je vous adverteroy particulierement que jay recogneu que les ministres vous redoutent et vous veullent faire craindre par Argos [Louis XIII] comme favori et ambitieux. Jay trouvé moyen de remedier à cella aupres du Roy et de luy en changer l'impression . . .'.[87]

Richelieu's early years in the council after 1624 are shrouded in mystery, for he had to contend with a mixed group of holdovers from the ministries of the three previous royal favourites. Nevertheless, he moved with astonishing speed to build on past connections. We can trace the development of affection and devotion in two of his long-time *créatures*, Schomberg as minister without portfolio (1624–32) and d'Effiat as finance minister (1626–32).

---

[85] See AAE France 774, esp. fos. 53–4, Brûlart to Puysieux, 22 June 1621 (involving the Sillerys, Schomberg, and other council members attending the king); fos. 56–7, Puysieux to Brûlart, 22 June 1622 (showing Luynes's interaction with the council).

[86] See e.g. AAE France 771, fos. 112, 114, 118–19, 123, 384–6, correspondence of Richelieu with Luynes, Déageant, and Jeannin, late 1617; AAE France 775, Luynes's letters to Richelieu in 1621.

[87] AAE 775, fos. 88–90, Louis de Marillac to Richelieu, 29 Dec. 1621.

As early as 1622, d'Effiat had expressed his 'creaturely' support for Richelieu through Louis de Marillac. Soon after Richelieu's entry to the royal council in 1624, d'Effiat wrote directly to the cardinal of his complete confidence that the new minister was uniquely qualified to give France 'nostre guérison totalle' despite his hesitation to enter state affairs.[88] It is not surprising that d'Effiat became Richelieu's fellow minister in charge of finance two years later.

Schomberg's relationship with Richelieu can be traced back all the way to the periods of Concini's and Luynes's favour. They were in close touch in 1617 when the then bishop of Luçon was foreign secretary and Schomberg a military-diplomatic 'troubleshooter' on the Franco-German border. Immediately after Luynes's death in 1621 we find Schomberg capitalizing on the opportunity to inform Richelieu, through Marie, of the favourite's demise, and adding, 'pour moi, je ne recevré pas un petit contentement quand l'occasion me sera offert de vous tesmoigner combien je suis vostre serviteur'. A year later, Schomberg dutifully and warmly congratulated Richelieu on securing the cardinal's biretta. At the beginning of 1623, just after Louis dismissed him as finance minister, Schomberg took care to acknowledge Richelieu's letter of condolence, combining this with a gracious as well as self-interested reference to the latter's own 'prosperity'. Richelieu and Louis XIII brought Schomberg back immediately after La Vieuville's fall;[89] and that patient *créature* of the cardinal soon expressed on paper his eagerness to serve his fellow minister and patron.[90]

Michel de Marillac, co-superintendant of finances from 1624 to 1626, and then keeper of the seals until his disgrace on the Day of Dupes in November 1630, exemplified a second type of early councillor. He and Richelieu were collaborators and fellow *créatures* of Marie de' Medici rather than having their own patron–client arrangement. Despite Marillac's past refusal to 'faire la cour aux favoris de son temps . . . au mareschal d'Ancre et au connestable de Luines',[91] he worked closely with the new minister-favourite until royal policy shifted from suppressing Huguenot rebellion to engaging in the Mantuan campaign against Louis XIII's fellow Catholic

---

[88] AAE France 775, fo. 215, Marillac to Richelieu, 21 Oct. 1622; Grillon, i. 88–90, d'Effiat to Richelieu, May 1624.

[89] On the respective roles of king and adviser in 1624, see Moote, *Louis XIII*, 167.

[90] Schomberg to Richelieu: AAE France 774, fo. 212, 15 Dec. 1621; AAE France 775, fo. 220, 16 Sept. 1622; AAE 778, fo. 11, 12 Jan. 1623; AAE France 778, fo. 219, 6 Nov. 1624, publ. with minor omissions by Grillon, i. 126. On Richelieu's relations with Schomberg in 1616–17, see Antoine Aubery, *Mémoires pour l'histoire du Cardinal Duc de Richelieu* (2 vols.; Cologne, 1666), i. 17–35; BN MS Dupuy, fo. 145, Mangot to Béthune, 23 Nov. 1616.

[91] Nicolas Lefevre de Lezeau, 'Histoire de la vie de Messire Michel de Marillac', BN MS Fr. 14027, fo. 80[r].

Habsburg rulers. Richelieu's ability to tolerate and control Marillac until the Day of Dupes resembles Luynes's accommodating style, and is in sharp contrast to the Sillerys and La Vieuville who allowed rivals, La Vieuville and Richelieu, into the council and were quickly overthrown by them.

Like his predecessors, Richelieu had to contend immediately with another difficult type of councillor, one who was independent-minded but without ambitions. The best example is Chancellor d'Aligre, who had been the king's own choice as keeper of the seals and chancellor, and who wrote letters of fulsome praise to Richelieu,[92] only to be relieved of the seals in 1626 for failing to back the council's decision to arrest Gaston's favourite, Ornano.[93]

It took Richelieu twelve long years out of a total of eighteen to assemble a team which was independent of his precursors' stamp, bore no loyalty to Marie de' Medici, and showed no trace of uncertain political leanings. Even then he resembled Luynes in leaving some unattached figures in the council. Was this by design, by chance, or out of necessity? Beneath the tightly knit team-work of the 1630s lay rivalries among his own *créatures*, which caused the war secretary, Servien, to be dismissed over disputes with the finance minister, Bullion, and secretary of state, Chavigny, in 1636.[94] There was also Bullion's unique status among Richelieu's *créatures* of having direct access to the king.[95] Finally there was the quite different autonomy of the Loménie–Brienne and Phélypeaux–Pontchartrain lineages. They had made the two least important secretaryships of state virtual family fiefs, and they disdained playing any significant role as clients of Richelieu. Historians assume that their functions were too minor for Richelieu to control, or even that he kept everything except routine paperwork from their portfolios. However, they were very close to the king, and their distance from Richelieu served the state well. At the Day of Dupes, Louis XIII on his own initiative entrusted Henri-Auguste Loménie de Brienne with taking the seals from the disgraced Michel de Marillac, and informing Marie that he had considered that long-term *créature* of hers a traitor for over a year. It was to Louis Phélypeaux de La Vrillière

[92] Grillon, i. 222–3, D'Aligre to Richelieu, 22 Oct. 1625.
[93] See David J. Sturdy, *The D'Aligres de la Rivière: Servants of the Bourbon State in the Seventeenth Century* (Woodbridge, 1986), 20–45.
[94] See esp. BI Godefroy 310, fos. 189–90. On Servien's relations with Richelieu and Bullion concerning personal financial entanglements involved in his fall, see AAE France 847, fos. 136–8. For similar conflicts among Richelieu's clients within the broader governing structure, involving the Condé and Épernon-La Vallette clans, see Marvick, 'Fidelity, Kinship and Affect'.
[95] Ranum, *Councillors of Louis XIII*, 37–9. Richelieu's close relations with Bullion from 1624 on appear in the latter's papers, BN MS Fr. 6556, esp. fos. 42–6, 120, 122–3, 126.

that the monarch turned to draft and present his last will and testament.[96]

What do these comparisons of Richelieu and his fellow favourites tells us about his performance as 'chief minister' to Louis XIII? My first conclusion is that their political techniques had more in common than even the most revisionist studies of the cardinal-minister have shown. Favouritism worked consistently to the benefit of the monarchy, the favourite, and the enormous network of the favourite's *créatures*, friends, and relations. This is not in itself surprising, since the techniques of favouritism reflected the political culture and social drives of the age more than they did the peculiarities of an individual favourite's social status, career path, or personality.

Even some of the state-building accomplishments of Louis XIII that Cardinal Richelieu has been credited with were intimately connected with self-serving techniques which he shared with his fellow favourites. Richelieu himself acknowledged the statecraft of Concini's personal alignments with individual members of the great nobility and of his conflicts with other grandees (imprisoning Condé, leading an army against the rebel forces in the north-east). Luynes operated by personal diplomacy that sought to subdue the Huguenots through a personal alliance with their leader Rohan, and used his influence with Condé to check the ambitions of the rebel queen mother. Richelieu's own relationships with the great nobility had the same complex agenda of serving state, grandees, and self.

The inevitable reaction to the techniques of the favourites by disgruntled subjects leads us to a second conclusion. It was very difficult to avoid falling from power either through conspiracy, assassination, or revolt by subjects; or through dismissal by a monarch intent on protecting his own reputation and state resources in the face of charges that his adviser was tyrannizing over ruler and subjects, and monopolizing royal favours that a previous generation of subjects had shared.[97]

Each favourite was charged with being at least as bad as the past ones. Richelieu's own propaganda weapons against his predecessors were duly turned against him. As Olivares's star began to rise in Spain and Richelieu's in France, the story of the fifteenth-century Constable Alvaro de Luna's fall from favour and execution was popularized in both Spanish plays and a history in French, in order to attack the current Spanish and French favourites, Lerma's son and Constable Luynes. Ironically, the history, probably commis-

---

[96] See Brienne, *Mémoires*, 64, 66–8; Ranum, *Councillors of Louis XIII*, 29, 68–71; Moreri, *Dictionnaire*, vii. 164.
[97] See Bérenger, 'Le Problème du ministériat', 177, 191.

sioned by Richelieu, was later reprinted as an indictment of his own 'tyranny'.[98] How then, we must ask, did Richelieu survive the avalanche of criticism that brought down Buckingham through assassination, Strafford and Laud by revolution, Mazarin temporarily by massive rebellion, and others like Lerma, Olivares, Concini, Puysieux, and La Vieuville by court manœuvring and royal acts?

Richelieu's finesse in handling Louis XIII's sensitivity has been much studied. However, there is still something new to be said about it from the perspective of the history of contemporary favourites. First, the prior evolution of government by favourites served the cardinal well. By 1624 the focus of the favourite had evolved from favour itself to a complex intertwining of state and personal interests, along with a shifting of the primary talents of the minister-favourite from courtly skills to administrative expertise. The courtiers Concini and Luynes had thus been succeeded by experts on judicial and diplomatic affairs in the Sillery family, and the financier La Vieuville. Richelieu was admirably suited to play the role of minister-favourite at that precise time, for he did not lack in the courtly ways necessary to control patronage, yet he had considerable experience in administrative matters, to which the king was paying increasing attention, despite spells of ennui. The cardinal-minister was a courtier on his father's and eldest brother's side and by his own training at Pluvinel's academy; he was of the *robe* and its traditions through his mother, his earlier office of secretary of state, and, one could argue, by having been a conscientious administrator of his diocese.

Richelieu was also well situated to deal with the evolution of the other key functionary in the contemporary history of the minister-favourite, the monarch. Louis XIII had changed from an uncertain adolescent, who gave up more power and influence to a favourite than he felt comfortable with, into a stubborn adult with set limits to what he would relinquish. Richelieu protected his position with the king in three ways: by not engrossing office, making the best of his ecclesiastical dignity, and above all pretending he did not actively seek wealth for himself. The first two strategies were employed as much out of chance as by choice. The third he learnt from the unfortunate experiences of his predecessors and of his own early career.

We may never know why Richelieu assumed no ministerial portfolio, and remained content with the simple administrative title of minister of state. Whatever the reason, the absence of a high-

---

[98] See Elliott, *Richelieu and Olivares*, 34–5; Thuau, *Raison d'état*, 223.

sounding civil or military office must have allayed Louis XIII's fears of seeing yet another ambitious subject taking advantage of him. So, too, did his wearing of the purple, since the previous councillor-cardinals, Retz and La Rochefoucald, had prestige but were non-threatening. More calculating was Richelieu's habit during his entire tenure as minister-favourite of not flaunting his favour the way his predecessors had. His first, and arguably his most terrifying, experience of trying to act disinterested came after the assassination of his patron, Concini. Fearful of being prosecuted for too close an association with Concini's patronage-mongering, he wrote down the secret defence known to us as the *Caput Apologeticum* (1618). In it Richelieu stressed his integrity and complained that his behaviour was misunderstood: 'Il [Richelieu] n'estoit point intéressé; maintenant c'est vanité . . . en un mot les vertus d'un homme en faveur luy sont vices en disgrace'. In its conclusion, he emphasized his unequivocal loyalty to the crown, describing himself as 'fils de père qui a tousjours servy les Roys, et en sy peu qu'il a peu l'a tousjours fait luymesme'.[99] In 1626 Richelieu brooded again, this time over the first challenge to his ministerial career, and the charge by Chalais's friends 'qu'on disoit que ledit escurier [Barradat] n'estoit pas favori, mais bien Calori [Richelieu], qui estoit et ministre et favori tout ensemble'.[100]

Richelieu was stunningly successful in winning the parsimonious Louis XIII over to his side against such accusations. In 1624 he wrote a memorandum to the king suggesting that Constable Lesdiguières, Puysieux, and La Vieuville had made Louis XIII look stingy while taking credit for favours that the king gave to other subjects. In a brilliant inversion, Richelieu pledged to have the monarch take credit for the dispensing of all favours, while shouldering the responsibility himself for any favour denied by royal grace.[101] He made a case of referring to himself and his own 'creaturely' beneficiaries as *gens de bien*,[102] of looking as if even his council appointments of 1624 had been thrust upon a reluctant subject, and claiming that his disinterested service cost the king far less than any other royal servitor.[103] The most famous articulation of his strategy with Louis XIII is his *Testament politique*: 'Jamais l'homme de bien ne pense à s'enrichir aux dépens du public en le servant. Comme ce

---

[99] He also pointedly associated the ministers of 1610–16 with Concini's 'enrichment' from gifts and secret funds (*comptants*). See Avenel, vii. 416–422; and AAE France 772, fo. 58 (Apr. 1618).

[100] Grillon, i. 546. See Grillon, i. 548–51, cataloguing Richelieu's alleged favours for himself, family, and friends, with a vigorous self-defence.

[101] See AAE France 779, fos. 9–14, 18, and Grillon, i. 104–5, 116–22.

[102] BI Godefroy 15, fo. 401, Richelieu to Père Coton, 1 Dec. 1622.

[103] D'Avenel, *Noblesse*, 174. See also Bergin, *Cardinal Richelieu*.

seroit un crime d'avoir telle pensée, rien n'est plus honteux à un prince que de voir ceux qui ont veilli en le servant, chargés d'années, de mérite et de pauvreté tout ensemble.'[104]

Richelieu, however, was not just able to keep the king's confidence. What has equally puzzled historians was the cardinal's good fortune in preventing the direct envy and hatred of his ministry by disgruntled subjects from turning into a successful conspiracy against his power or life.[105] Part of the explanation must lie in the evolution of the position of minister-favourite in early seventeenth-century France. In the first place, Richelieu survived because he had the king's backing, including the protection of the unprecedented extension of royal treason laws to include defamatory attacks on the monarch's policies and policy advisers.[106] This protective shield was featured in the writings of Richelieu's apologists, who noted that 'les voies de fait contre ceux qui sont en faveur auprès des Princes, sont qualifiées du crime de lèse-majesté d'autant que, sous l'ombre du serviteur, on en veut communément au Maître'.[107] In the second place, his survival can be attributed to the way he handled relations with his enemies, friends, rivals, and *créatures*. Like his long-term counterpart across the Pyrenees, Olivares, who abhorred the appellation, *privado*, Richelieu fended off some criticism by eschewing the epithet of *favori*.[108] He was castigated more for his tyranny than his 'interests', and his tyranny was difficult to attack on moral grounds since it was in the service of the king and state. Those who persisted in opposing him knew that he was direct and forthright in telling them whether they could expect favours, political support from the king, or any hope of royal mercy if they crossed the line to treasonous words and deeds.[109] As for Richelieu's collaborators, their

---

[104] *Test. pol.* 311.

[105] Concini's ideological defence that the crown should monopolize the granting of favours had singularly failed him. Jeffrey K. Sawyer, *Printed Poison: Pamphlet Propaganda, Faction Politics, and the Public Sphere in Early Seventeenth-Century France* (Los Angeles, Calif., 1991), 118. Precisely the same weak line of defence was adopted by an apologist for the beleaguered La Vieuville, who sought to justify the king's appointing and favouring of all the earlier royal favourites since 1614 from Concini to the Sillerys. *Response à la voix publique envoyée de la cour* (1624), 10–14, 19–21, 28–9.

[106] Ralph Giesey, Lanny Haldy, and James Milhorn, 'Cardin Le Bret and Lèse Majesty', *Law and History Review*, 4 (1986), 23–55; Church, *Richelieu*, 184–6, 206, 221, 375, 406.

[107] Paul Hay du Chastelet, *Recueil de diverses pièces pour servir à l'histoire* (Paris, 1635), as quoted in Thuau, *Raison d'état*, 241. This protective posture is given divine-right sanction in L'Estoile's *Sacrifice des muses*: 'Etre votre ennemi, c'est l'être de mon Roi. Et l'être de mon Roi, c'est l'être de Dieu même'. Ibid. 245.

[108] Elliott, *Count-Duke of Olivares*, 169–70.

[109] The scruples of men like duc d'Épernon, former royal favourite under the Valois and Marie de' Medici, and now independent of Richelieu although governor of Guienne and father of one of Richelieu's *créatures*, Cardinal La Vallette, are shown in rich detail in Constant, *Les Conjurateurs*, 125–45.

correspondence reveals a special tone of devotion that went beyond normal 'creaturely' language.[110]

Richelieu's survival stands out in sharp relief when compared with the record of his successor. Admittedly, Mazarin had a more difficult task in so far as he was a foreigner, inheritor of a long and costly war, minister to a Spanish-born queen mother, and labouring during a royal minority. On the other hand, his self-effacing manners and ingratiating charm mirrored the best in Luynes. One would have thought that here was someone who could surpass his fellow cardinal in operating unostentatiously from the platform of minister without portfolio and cardinal of the church. Yet Mazarin seems to have been weak precisely where Richelieu was strong.

Cardinal Mazarin's wealth at the end of his career was immense, 37 million *livres* by comparison with Richelieu's 22 million—perhaps the greatest fortune ever amassed by an early modern French royal servitor.[111] More damaging was that for all his proclaiming of his selfless state service, he did not cover his tracks well. The *Mazarinade* pamphlets of the Fronde had little difficulty concentrating on both his perceived corruption and tyranny. Mazarin was caricatured as swimming with Concini beside the ship of state, stirring up the troubled waters with hated *monopoleurs* who shared his profit-taking from the state coffers.[112]

In his handling of relations with friends, collaborators, *créatures*, rivals, and enemies, Mazarin appears to have been equally unfortunate.[113] He tried to win over everyone with pleasantries, gifts, and vague promises, in contrast to Richelieu's more selective and direct style. Very shortly, few trusted Mazarin, or so it seemed.[114]

---

[110] e.g. Grillon, i. 126, Schomberg to Richelieu, 6 Nov. 1624, closing with the wish 'de vous honorer tousjours plus que personne du monde et de vous dire avec le plus passion . . .'; AAE France 780, fos. 33–4, d'Effiat to Richelieu, 25, 27 and 28 Jan., 9 and 24 Feb., 15 and 30 Mar. 1625, concerning his being out of favour with the king, but being restored to the king's good graces by Richelieu's 'protection', which he had pleaded for 'pour le mémoire de Mr de Beaulieu'; AAE France 780, fos. 351–3, Bullion to Richelieu, 1 and 30 Mar. 6 Apr., 9 Oct. 1625, expressing similar thanks for protection against 'calumnies' about his accounts of receipts and expenditures on mission.

[111] Daniel Dessert, 'Pouvoir et finance au XVIIᵉ siècle: La Fortune du cardinal Mazarin', *Revue d'histoire moderne et contemporaine*, 32 (1976), 161–81; J. Bergin, 'Cardinal Mazarin and his Benefices', *French History*, 1 (1987), 3–26. Twenty-one abbeys held by Mazarin are listed in BN MS Fr. 15715, fo. 9. Richelieu's benefices at death are listed in AAE France 846, fos. 155–6.

[112] George Dethan, *The Young Mazarin* (London, 1977), illus. 41.

[113] See Sharon Kettering, 'Patronage and Politics during the Fronde', *French Historical Studies*, 14 (1986), 409–41. Julian Dent, 'The Role of Clientèles in the Financial Élite of France under Cardinal Mazarin', in J. F. Bosher (ed.), *French Government and Society 1500–1850* (London, 1973), 48, suggests that Mazarin 'had no time to attract a clientèle' in 1643. But Richelieu did so long before 1624.

[114] Moote, *Revolt of the Judges*, 67; Dethan, *Mazarin: Un homme de paix*, stresses the positive side of Mazarin's exceptional reliance on personal relations.

Despite employing all the techniques of building fortune, favour, and power, he seems to have been late to develop a strong clientele of noble governors,[115] late to build up a party in the parlement of Paris,[116] even late in developing a clientage among his fellow clerics.[117] Those whom he thought were his friends or *créatures* deserted him in astounding numbers during the Fronde, including the obsequious Séguier.[118]

Mazarin survived, of course, with the support of a faithful few led by the queen, to whom he was bonded by personal and political favour as well as by being godfather to Louis XIV. During the Fronde Mazarin developed his own remarkable team of Le Tellier, Lionne, and Richelieu's banished colleague, Servien.[119] He finally found in Nicolas Fouquet someone to run the state's finances effectively and loyally, and in Colbert someone to manage his own finances without scruple. After the Fronde those who had vilified or betrayed him came over to his side. But Mazarin, pleasant, bright, and diplomatically skilled as he was, was no Richelieu. After Richelieu the phenomenon of the minister-favourite continued; after Mazarin it ended. Changing political structures and social agendas undoubtedly played a large part in the demise of the minister-favourite as a constant fixture at the French court. Louis XIV's personality also played its role, as did Mazarin's frequent advice that as an adult he should rule without a minister-favourite (after the current favourite had departed from this life, to be sure).[120] Yet one cannot help wondering what would have happened to the political practices of late seventeenth-century France had Louis XIV been served as political favourite by Cardinal-Duke Richelieu.

[115] Kettering, *Patrons, Brokers, and Clients*, 161. Cf. Bonney, *Political Change*, 292–4; J. Russell Major, *Representative Government in Early Modern France* (New Haven, Conn., 1980), 623, quoting Mazarin to Lionne, Mar. 1651.

[116] Moote, *Revolt of the Judges*, 287–8, 302.

[117] See Pierre Blet, *Le Clergé de France et la monarchie 1615–1666: Étude sur les assemblées générales de 1615 à 1666* (2 vols.; Rome, 1959), ii. 4–9, 118–19.

[118] Dethan, *Mazarin*, 253, 255. On his difficulties, see Madeleine Foisil, 'Parentèles et fidélités autour du duc de Longueville gouverneur de Normandie pendant la Fronde', in Durand, *Hommage*, 153–68. For one of his rare successes in winning over a *créature* of the deceased Richelieu, see Jean-Pierre Labatut, 'La Fidélité du duc de Navailles', ibid. 183–97.

[119] On Mazarin's early assembling of *créatures* in and near the council, see AAE France 847, fo. 2, Brézé to Servien, 3 Aug. 1643; AAE France 850, fo. 26, Mazarin to Servien, 29 Aug. 1644; BI Godefroy 218, fos. 122–5, Lionne to Anne of Austria (1646); BI Godefroy 310, fo. 190, on Le Tellier as his *créature* after Richelieu's death (1643). For the end of the Fronde, see BN MS Fr. 6891, correspondence of Mazarin with Le Tellier and the Fouquet brothers, Oct. 1652. For conciliar changes during his ministry, see BI Godefroy 310.

[120] See Wolf, *Louis XIV*, 68–77, 133–9.

2

'UNE BONNE PAIX'

Richelieu's Foreign Policy and the Peace
of Christendom

HERMANN WEBER

In a survey of French foreign policy for the years 1624–42, the years
when it was shaped principally by Richelieu, an attempt to identify
its general characteristic features must begin with his efforts to
secure peace. The attainment of peace was the main objective of
French policy throughout this era, and the programme was conceived and diplomatically articulated in countless *avis*, memoranda,
and directives. The French persisted in their will for peace, and it
was proclaimed insistently as propaganda to both a French and a
European public. And if in the process the formula 'une bonne paix'
appears with considerable frequency, it was used not merely as a
decorative tag but in order to underline their deliberate intention to
give this peace a very particular quality. 'Une bonne paix' was
throughout these years a realistic political programme.

This first observation, however, must immediately be linked to a
second, namely the fact that during all this time peace was never
achieved. True, there were peace treaties,[1] but their scope was
restricted and they had little effect on the general course towards
peace. On the contrary, in fact, it is more characteristic of these
eighteen years that localized conflicts escalated in significance until
the whole of Europe ended up as the terrain for a global dispute.
And since this course was chiefly the work of France (and thus of
Richelieu), the fact that peace policies failed forces us to consider a
third point, the question of their proponents' sincerity. According to
Fritz Dickmann, no statesman contributed as much as Richelieu to
'prolonging the struggle in Europe, until finally he was outlived by
the war itself'. 'Whether tragic or guilty', Dickmann continues, 'the

---

Trans. from the German by Robert Vilain of Christ Church, Oxford. The editors would like to
thank Manchester Univ. for helping to defray the cost of the trans.

[1] The treaties of Monçon with Spain (1626), Susa with Savoy (1629), Cherasco with the
emperor (1631), and the treaty with England (1629).

effect of Richelieu's policies was destructive, and even though they
were concerned with the problems of peace, they were fatal to peace
itself'.[2] An investigation of Richelieu's peace politics must therefore
be concerned not only with their conception and practice, but also
with the questions of their manifest failure and of whether or not
they were sincerely propounded.

The following survey is structured along the lines of the main
aspects of Richelieu's peace politics as he himself formulated them.
Of overriding importance for the whole is his aim to attain a *paix de
la chrétienté*; and for this to be *une bonne paix* three further goals had
also to be presupposed: *une paix générale, une paix sûre*, and *une paix
prompte*. Accordingly, these form the four sections of this survey.

I

Looking through Richelieu's memoranda, directives, and letters, it
very soon becomes noticeable that whenever the question of 'peace'
is raised, it is most commonly 'the peace of Christendom' that is at
issue. Neither the 1643 general directive for peace negotiations in
Westphalia, nor Richelieu's preceding drafts, were a first attempt by
the French king to achieve 'une bonne Paix en toute la Chréstienté'.[3]
And this is true not only of the period when the ravages of the Thirty
Years War had affected large areas of Europe and when securing peace was important to a correspondingly large number of
parties. Solutions to the conflicts in Upper Italy, the Valtelline, or
Mantua, had already been extended in significance beyond their local
boundaries and connected with the establishment of the peace of
Christendom,[4] and the settlement of bilateral disputes was also seen
from this perspective.

---

[2] '... dazu beigetragen, das europäische Ringen zu verlängern, bis schliesslich der Krieg
selbst ihn überlebte' and 'Ob Tragik, ob Schuld, Richelieus Politik war von zerstörerischer
Wirkung und, obwohl mit den Problemen des Friedens beschäftigt, für diesen selbst
verderblich', Fritz Dickmann, *Der Westfälische Frieden*, 4th edn. (Münster, 1977), 52–3. The
early death of Dickmann was a great loss, for his work was of seminal importance for a new
assessment of Richelieu's peace policies in German historiography.

[3] *APW*, I, *Instruktionen*, i (*Frankreich, Schweden, Kaiser*), revised by Fritz Dickmann *et al.*,
58–123. Here p. 62. The general directive of 30 Sept. 1643 belongs to the ministry of Mazarin,
but it is based on drafts prepared by Richelieu at the end of Dec. 1636, Feb./Mar. 1637, and
Aug./Sept. 1641. For the background to the general directive and the dating of the early
drafts, see the intro. in *APW* I. i. 1–16. The same vol. also includes an edn. of the different
versions.

[4] For the *avis* of 1624 on the question of the Valtelline, see Richelieu, *Mémoires* SHF iv.
203–12. For Mantua, see e.g. the directives for Bautru's mission to Spain at the end of 1628 in
ibid. viii. 235–46.

The peace of Christendom was a fundamental component of Richelieu's foreign policy. This objective provided a framework and set up a yardstick for all practical peace policies, in other words for every effort designed to lead to contractual agreement on the establishment of peace. What are we to understand by 'the peace of Christendom'?

When Richelieu speaks of establishing the peace of Christendom,[5] he does not intend it primarily in the sense of bringing to an end a state of war affecting the whole or parts of Christendom. He is envisaging rather an end to a much more general threat to this peace. For Richelieu the situation of Christendom was characterized by Spain's aspirations to a universal monarchy, which she sought to establish with the help of the Holy Roman Empire, and which he thus saw as involving the whole house of Habsburg.[6] It is from this perspective that even the dispute over the Valtelline derived its broader significance.[7] Richelieu interpreted Spain's ambitions as aiming to subject the smaller states of Christendom, notably in Italy and the Holy Roman Empire, to Spanish Habsburg interests. But the pope was also to be linked into the Spanish Habsburg system. And in so far as it was a platform for repelling more powerful opponents to such a usurpation of control—France, chiefly—the whole of Christendom would ultimately have to submit to this pretention to universal power and authority on the part of the Spanish-

---

[5] Richelieu does not, to my knowledge, explain or more precisely delimit his concept of Christendom. He uses the traditional formulation that refers in a general sense to all Christian states. It is nevertheless noteworthy e.g. that the formulation used in Richelieu's draft B1 for the general directive, 'de tous les Princes de la Chréstienté', is replaced in the final version B2 by 'de toute la Chréstienté', which stresses its unified nature more strongly: see *APW* I. i. 62, ll. 11–12 and 40–1. For the fundamental significance of the B1 and B2 versions, see *APW* I. i. 30–1. The rival concept of 'Europe' is met less often. For a general account of the changing use of this terminology since the 16th cent., see Helmut Gollwitzer, *Europabild und Europagedanke: Beiträge zur deutschen Geistesgeschichte des 18. und 19. Jahrhunderts* (Munich, 1964); and for the period of the Westphalian peace negotiations see Alphonse Dupront, 'De la chrétienté à l'Europe: La Passion westphalienne du nonce Fabio Chigi', in *Forschungen und Studien zur Geschichte des Westfälischen Friedens* (Schriftenreihe der Vereinigung zur Erforschung der Neueren Geschichte, 1; Münster, 1965), 49–84.

[6] Richelieu's opinion respecting Spanish ambitions was already evident in his short first ministry. In the instructions given to Schomberg in 1617, the latter was expressly ordered to reassure his German contacts that the Spanish marriage would not entail a revision of France's existing alliances with the German princes to the advantage of Spain. On the contrary, 'il fauldra prendre occasion de leur tesmoigner, à nostre proffict, que nous ne désirons point l'advancement d'Espagne; nous offrans, qoyque discrettement, à les assister contre les pratiques que le roy d'Espagne faict pour faire tomber avec le temps les couronnes de Hongrie et de Bohème, celle du roy des Romains et l'impérialle, sur la teste de l'un de ses enfans'. If not in so many words, the text conjures up the nightmare of a Spanish universal monarchy, by which the Habsburg system of the age of Charles V might be renewed. For these instructions, see Avenel, i. 208–35 (the quotation is from p. 223); also Richelieu, *Mémoires* SHF i. 135 n. 1.

[7] See the *avis* of 1624 (above n. 4).

dominated house of Habsburg. This is the basic line of argument behind Richelieu's last drafts for the directives at the peace negotiations.[8]

The phrase 'peace of Christendom' thereby acquires a very specific quality. It is not a question simply of putting an end to a condition where peace does not reign. The threat to peace posed by Spain and the Habsburgs is a threat made to the liberty of Christendom by the tyranny of a Spanish universal monarchy,[9] and this was the context in which Richelieu understood the 'peace of Christendom'. It also implied, of course, an end to military conflicts that had arisen from this Spanish claim or the moves to resist it. But far more than that, it signified the establishment of a condition in which Christendom was no longer exposed to such a threat, a condition in which—to put it in positive terms—the liberty of Christendom was re-established and guaranteed for evermore. The 'peace of Christendom' was understood primarily as a durable framework for peace that preserved all the powers of Christendom in untroubled coexistence and liberty.

There are good grounds to suppose that behind Richelieu's conception of peace in these terms there lay already the idea of a balance of power. Admittedly, he had not programmatically expressed a notion for the achievement of the balance of power in Europe. But the idea that a group of forces with France at its centre would serve as a counterweight to Habsburg preponderance was itself an integral component of Richelieu's state of ordered peace and within this idea the concept of a balance was already implicitly expressed.[10] For

[8] *APW* I. i. 63. For the question of the universal monarchy of the house of Habsburg in the Thirty Years War, see Franz Bosbach, *Monarchia Universalis: Ein politischer Leitbegriff der frühen Neuzeit* (Schriftenreihe der Historischen Kommission bei der Bayerischen Akademie der Wissenschaften, 32; Göttingen, 1988), 87–106.

[9] 'Liberté de la Chrétienté' or 'Liberté publique' is only ever used in this sense. See e.g. Richelieu, *Mémoires* SHF viii. 210, where it is said of the fall of La Rochelle that the allies saw in it, amongst other things, a hope for 'l'affranchissement général de toute l'Europe de dessous le joug de la tyrannie de la maison d'Autriche'. This may be taken to apply in a narrower sense to the relationship between the emperor and the imperial estates, as in the passage from ibid. x. 159: 'Enfin, l'Empereur, sous divers prétextes d'apparence spécieuse, mais de nulle solidité, prenoit le train de se rendre maître de l'Allemagne et la réduire en une monarchie absolue, anéantissant les lois anciennes de la république germanique, sur lesquelles est fondée l'autorité impériale'.

[10] I believe that the idea of balance played a more important part in Richelieu's thought than is supposed by Konrad Repgen in his essay 'Der Westfälische Friede und die Ursprünge des europäischen Gleichgewichts', in Repgen, *Beiträge zu Grundfragen der neuzeitlichen Geschichte*, ed. K. Gotto and H. G. Hockerts (Paderborn, 1988), 53–66. See also Wolfgang-Uwe Friedrich, 'Gleichgewichtsdenken und Gleichgewichtspolitik zur Zeit des Teutschen Krieges', in Wolf D. Gruner (ed.), *Gleichgewicht in Geschichte und Gegenwart* (Hamburg, 1989), 18–59, and Hermann Weber, 'Chrétienté et équilibre européen dans la politique du cardinal de Richelieu', *XVIIe siècle*, 166 (1990), 7–16, which has further examples. See also Georges Livet, *L'Équilibre européen de la fin du XVe à la fin du XVIIIe siècle* (Paris, 1976).

one thing, this idea corresponded to a conception of the unity of Christendom as a body whose limbs performed different functions while remaining organically integrated into the whole.[11] And for another, Richelieu saw this balance as already implicit in the geographical division of Europe and as such corresponding to a divinely ordained order.[12]

This leads us on to a further aspect of Richelieu's conception. The French peace policies that served the interests of Christendom in this manner were also highly favourable in many respects to fundamental interests of the French monarchy.

Most important of these was the transformation of the French monarchy's self-image into political reality. In one of Richelieu's most famous statements about international affairs, the *avis* to the king of early 1629, the cardinal categorically declared it the aim and desire of his king 'de se rendre le plus puissant monarque du monde et le prince le plus estimé'.[13] This pre-eminence in power and reputation were united, realized, and justified precisely by his ful-filling the role that took the whole of Christendom as its field of operation. The Most Christian King of France was to be not only the supreme arbiter in Christendom, but above all its protector,[14] and for Richelieu this function as protector was sufficient to justify all possible kinds of political and military intervention on the part of France.[15] Being guarantor for the peace of Christendom was the culmination of this function, and the respect that the French king thereby gained thus also justified his right to be the greatest power in

[11] See 1 Cor. 12: 12–30. In ch. 5, s. 1, of Richelieu, *Test. pol.*, the image of the body is frequently applied to the unity of the state. Richelieu makes the generalizing remark that 'un tout ne subsiste que par l'union de ses parties en leur ordre et en leur lieu naturel' (p. 256).

[12] 'Il me semble que la providence de Dieu, qui veut tenir les choses en balance, a voulu que la situation de la France separât les Etats d'Espagne pour les affaiblir en les divisant' (*Test. pol.* 408).

[13] 'Advis donné au Roy après la prise de la Rochelle pour le bien de ses affaires' (13 Jan. 1629): Grillon, iv. 24–47. Here p. 24.

[14] See Hermann Weber, 'Dieu, le Roi et la chrétienté: Aspects de la politique du cardinal de Richelieu', *Francia*, 13 (1986), 233–45. Richelieu claimed the role of arbiter for the French king as early as 1616: cf. Avenel, i. 213. On the role of arbitrator, see also Rudolf von Albertini, *Das politische Denken in Frankreich zur Zeit Richelieus* (Beihefte zum Archiv für Kulturgeschichte, 1; Marburg, 1951), 145–6. The full range of the role of protector is made clear e.g. in Richelieu's *Mémoires* where he looks back over the year 1630 in connection with the Mantua affair. See *Mémoires* MP ii. 307: 'toute la chrétienté, ravie d'une action si magnanime, reconnoît le Roi pour restaurateur de la liberté commune, et le puissant protecteur des princes foibles contre la violence des plus puissans'. Note the integration of the Mantua affair into the framework of the whole of Christendom!

[15] Regarding the fundamental significance of protection in Richelieu's political thought, see the conclusion to Hermann Weber's *Frankreich, Kurtrier, der Rhein und das Reich 1623–1635* (Pariser Historische Studien, 9; Bonn, 1969), 391–5.

Christendom.[16] Power and stature were no longer the instrument
and product of tyrannical abuse, but fulfilled instead an ordering
function that was the basic duty of every force within its own sphere
of influence.[17] In the case of the Most Christian King, however,
whose position amongst the princes of Christendom was like that of
the sun amongst heavenly bodies,[18] this ordering function had to be
exercised beyond the boundaries of the kingdom of France and
extended to the whole of Christendom. French policies with the
peace and freedom of Christendom as their goal thus constituted
a legitimate means of realizing the French king's pretensions to
becoming the most powerful monarch and most highly respected
prince in the world. Furthermore, being in accordance with the will
and design of God, they could be certain of a blessing from above.

France's fundamental interest in a peace policy for the benefit of
the whole of Christendom was linked to much more pragmatic considerations, too. Richelieu on several occasions clearly stated his
conviction that France was not in a position to survive prolonged
wars in which she had to rely on her strength alone.[19] This was
because of the country's economic situation, because of its internal
tensions, and not least because Richelieu believed that France was,
basically speaking, not a warlike nation: the French preferred
spontaneous action and swift success but were in no position to
sustain military commitment over a long period. France therefore
needed peace, and the peace of Christendom, eliminating as it did all
possibilities of conflict, represented maximum security better than
any other course.

A French foreign policy that aimed at 'peace in Christendom' was
thus a realistic political programme commanding serious attention.
This is by no means to stress purely altruistic motives that take
no account of French interests. On the contrary, efforts towards
the peace of Christendom brought the interests of Christendom
into perfect alignment with the interests of France and the French
monarchy. They guaranteed freedom for Christendom and were
simultaneously the best means of promoting the Most Christian

---

[16] For the relationship of power and reputation, see *Test. pol.* 372–5.

[17] On this point see also Hermann Weber, 'Richelieu théoricien politique', in R. Mousnier
(ed.), *Richelieu et la culture* (Paris, 1987), 55–66.

[18] This comparison appears in the propaganda literature on the 'mystère de la monarchie'
that was disseminated after the assassination of Henri IV and at the beginning of Louis XIII's
reign, summarized in R. Mousnier, *L'Assassinat d'Henri IV* (Paris, 1964), 226–36. See
Richelieu, *Mémoires* SHF vii. 239, 'le Roi comme un vrai soleil, s'éleva au plus haut du ciel sur
l'horizon de la chrétienté'.

[19] See e.g. Richelieu, *Mémoires* SHF v. 187–8, viii. 107–22; *Mémoires* MP iii. 103; and
above all *Test. pol.* 383–400.

King's mission to take a leading role in the affairs of Christendom. And ultimately they promised the land and its people the relaxation of tension that they sorely needed in order to flourish properly. On top of all this, the policy fitted perfectly into a theocentric world-view and was in accord with the will of God for order. This, at least, was Richelieu's conception.

It is far from certain, however, that every member of the council of state and other important court circles, including even the king himself, supported Richelieu in his plans for the long term. Opposition came from the *dévots*, for example, who were increasingly influential until the Day of Dupes at the end of 1630. The very question of respect for the interests of Christendom raised problems: the group around Cardinal Bérulle, the queen mother, and Marillac, the keeper of the seals, for example, took exception to the inherent contradictions of this policy when, for instance, it called for the co-operation of Protestant powers. Was it proper, they asked, for Catholic France under the Most Christian King to ally herself with heretics against the Catholic king of Spain and thus at the same time neglect the fight against heresy at home? Was it not desirable on the contrary to strive at overcoming the confessional split by means of an alliance of Catholic powers, and was a Catholic peace not therefore to be given priority?[20] It was obvious that Richelieu's priorities were different—though his position was not taken up lightly or without a view in the long term to the ultimate re-establishment of the confessional unity of Christendom.[21] As far as the immediate conflict with the Habsburgs was concerned, he thought he had no other choice.

This was not the only challenge to Richelieu's intentions. On the Day of Dupes the king had decided in favour of his chief minister, but did this also constitute approval of his peace policy? In the summer of 1634 the voice of a war faction made itself heard at court, a faction that took only French interests into account when considering a decision for or against open war, and at the beginning of August the king joined them by declaring himself in favour of open war. The arguments were raised again in the summer of 1635 in connection with the declaration of war. Richelieu, however, believed that the question could only be settled from the perspective of the

---

[20] On this point see W. F. Church, *Richelieu and Reason of State* (Princeton, NJ, 1972), 126–72; Georges Mongrédien, *La Journée des Dupes* (Paris, 1961); and the summary in P. Chevallier, *Louis XIII roi cornélien* (Paris, 1979), 319–407. See also Richelieu, *Mémoires* SHF v. 206 ff.; *Mémoires* MP ii. 204 ff., 222–6, 239, and 271.

[21] Pierre Blet, 'Le Plan de Richelieu pour la réunion des protestants', *Gregorianum*, 48 (1967), 100–29.

peace of Christendom, and attempted to delay as long as possible the execution of the king's decision. It was only with the imprisonment of the archbishop-elector of Trier by Spain that a declaration of war was justified from this perspective. At this point, in Richelieu's eyes, a declaration of war was not only legitimate but imperative, for both sides were appearing on the stage of Christendom in their traditional roles: the Spanish king as oppressor, and the French king as protector of the freedom of Christendom.[22]

This, then, is an outline of the framework and aims of the policies Richelieu adopted to secure peace. What were the main features of their practical execution? What were the means for attaining the 'bonne Paix de la Chréstienté'? First and foremost it was essential to establish a general peace.

II

The passage already quoted from the general directive for negotiations at the Peace of Westphalia is from the third paragraph of section 1, which reads in full:

Qu'elle [= Sa Majesté] désire seulement une bonne Paix en toute la Chréstienté et que les affaires soient en tel estat que, si les Espagnolz ne veulent vivre en repos par la considération de la raison, on puisse les y obliger par celle d'une bonne et puissante union, en laquelle le Roy ne veut entrer que pour contribuer à une si bonne fin sans aucun intérest.[23]

The basis for the peace of Christendom was thus a coalition, here no more precisely defined than that, but including France. Considering its function as a force to maintain peace in opposition to a force endangering peace, this coalition was clearly designed to act as a counterweight and establish a balance of power with Spain. There were two preconditions if it was to operate thus, namely that a system of alliances should be set up and that it should be incorporated as such into the peace negotiations and peace treaty. A peace

---

[22] On the disputes of summer 1634 about open war, see Hermann Weber, 'Vom verdeckten zum offenen Krieg: Richelieus Kriegsgründe und Kriegsziele 1634–35', in Konrad Repgen (ed.), *Krieg und Politik 1618–1648: Europäische Probleme und Perspektiven* (Munich, 1988), 203–18. On the situation after war was declared in 1635, see H. Weber, 'Zur Legitimation der französischen Kriegserklärung 1635', *Historisches Jahrbuch*, 108 (1988), 90–113. In the same context see id., 'Der König, die Melancholie und der Krieg: Ein Avis Richelieus aus dem Jahre 1635', in Ralph Melville *et al.* (eds.), *Deutschland und Europa in der Neuzeit: Festschrift für Karl Otmar Freiherr von Aretin zum 65. Geburtstag* (Veröffentlichungen des Instituts für Europäische Geschichte Mainz Abt. Universalgeschichte, 134; Stuttgart, 1988), i. 241–58. Among the war faction was notably Servien, secretary of state for war.

[23] *APW* I. i. 62.

policy had to fulfil these preconditions, and the principle of a general peace had to be strictly adhered to, in particular when the French king and his representatives entered into negotiations.

These conceptions were not developed immediately prior to the negotiations for the Peace of Westphalia, but had been a major component of Richelieu's foreign policy since 1624. As early as the dispute over the Valtelline it is obvious that he was trying to link the various areas of conflict north and south of the Alps so as to form a united front against Spain: Savoy and Venice, the Netherlands and England, Denmark and Sweden, and the Catholic and Protestant estates of the Empire were all involved in these attempts. The fact that by 1625–6 the question of the Valtelline had almost been solved was no reason to desist from them. On the contrary, in February 1626 Richelieu once again formulated a wide-ranging plan for preventing Spain from realizing its aims 'à la monarchie universelle', by means of a general campaign in the Holy Roman Empire that included England, Denmark, Sweden, Brandenburg, the Netherlands, Venice, Savoy, and other states not named specifically, and which was to be supported by military and financial involvement on the part of France.[24]

The same is true of the crisis over the succession in Mantua. The agreement, drafted on 11 March 1629, signed initially by Savoy, Mantua, and Venice, was to be open to other states in order to 'procurer le repos de l'Italie et de toute la Chrétienté'. It was not sufficient, so ran the agreement, for these states to limit themselves to providing military assistance for the duke of Mantua, 'mais qu'il étoit du tout nécessaire d'empêcher qu'à l'avenir il ne pût plus arriver de semblables inconvéniens, au préjudice de la sûreté de tous les princes et de la paix de la chrétienté'.[25] It was stated quite explicitly that the aim of the alliances extended beyond the immediate, restricted military purpose, towards establishing a general peace of Christendom.

But apparently in flagrant contradiction to his stated goal of a general peace in Christendom, Richelieu rejected the treaty between the emperor and France that had been signed in Regensburg on 13 October 1630 by the French representatives, Brûlart de Léon and Père Joseph. Richelieu's particular reason for doing this—that

[24] 'Advis sur les affaires présentes qu'a le Roy en février 1626': Grillon, ii. 294–300, here esp. pp. 296–9.
[25] Richelieu, *Mémoires* SHF x. 166. On the agreements, see Hermann Weber, 'L'Italie du Nord dans la politique de Richelieu', in *Genova e Francia al crocevia dell'Europa (1624–1642): Atti del Seminario Internazionale di Studi, Genova 25–27 Maggio 1989*, in *I tempi della storia: Bollettino del Centro di studi sull'età moderna*, 2 (1989), 29–58.

a general peace was at issue here—seemed to give the lie to his declared intent to establish a general peace of Christendom.[26] So too did his refusal to renounce alliances and their resulting obligations, which were seen by others as a threat to peace, and his resultant demand that the treaty be limited exclusively to the disputes in Italy. Even close confidants of the cardinal had shown no misgivings about signing the treaty and had greeted the news of its completion with enthusiasm.[27] It would surely not be too much to see in this event an indication of how far Richelieu's politics were a very personal affair. Unlike his closest colleagues at court and in Regensburg the cardinal recognized immediately that the articles of the Regensburg treaty were irreconcilable with his own conception of the general peace of Christendom and the steps he had already taken towards its realization.

Indeed, Richelieu's opinion that Spain was seeking to fulfil its ambitions towards a universal monarchy by allying itself with the emperor had won alarming confirmation from the very conflict over Mantua whose settlement was intended by this agreement, and in particular from the new dimensions that this conflict had taken on after the emperor's political and military intervention. But since the fall of La Rochelle in October 1628, France had been free from the possibility of attack from behind and this security had been the prerequisite for a new political offensive whose aims had been expressed in the memorandum of 13 January 1629 quoted above. Attempts to find partners outside Italy were stepped up: these partners included on the one hand the Netherlands[28] and a series of imperial estates,[29] but on the other—and this was a completely new departure—the king of Sweden.[30] The negotiations with Gustavus Adolphus that had begun in 1629 reached their culmination in the Treaty of Bärwalde of January 1631. It was not the Regensburg

---

[26] *Mémoires* MP ii. 288–91.

[27] See Bouthillier to Richelieu, 20 Oct. 1630, AAE France 250, fo. 67, and the notes reproduced in this context in Grillon, v. 613–20, nos. 583–97, especially the 'Notes et documents sur le conseil tenu à Roanne le 27 octobre 1630'. See also Jörg Wollenberg, *Richelieu, Staatskunst und Kircheninteresse: Zur Legitimation der Politik des Kardinalpremier* (Bielefeld, 1977), 55–9.

[28] See Albert Waddington, *La République des Provinces-Unies, la France et les Pays-Bas espagnoles de 1630 à 1650*, i. *1630–1642* (Paris, 1895), *passim*.

[29] This was the aim of the mission undertaken by Marcheville in the autumn of 1629 and spring of 1630; his instructions of 8 July 1629 and 15 Jan. 1630 are in AAE CP Allemagne 6, fos. 292–9 and 7, fos. 2–3. See also Weber, *Frankreich, Kurtrier, der Rhein und das Reich*, 69–84. For the negotiations with Bavaria, see Dieter Albrecht, *Die auswärtige Politik Maximilians von Bayern 1618–1635*, (Schriftenreihe der Historischen Kommission bei der Bayerischen Akademie der Wissenschaften, 6; Göttingen, 1962), 211–62; Andreas Kraus, *Maximilian I.: Bayerns Grosser Kurfürst* (Graz, 1990), 166–71 and 185–7.

[30] Michael Roberts, *Gustavus Adolphus: A History of Sweden 1611–1632* (2 vols.; London, 1953 and 1958), i. 395–8 and 407–9. See also the account in *Mémoires* MP ii. 298–307.

treaty with the emperor but a new coalition—with Sweden henceforth as the new and decisive partner, and in conjunction with the Netherlands and German Catholic and Protestant imperial estates—that was to thwart Habsburg ambitions for a universal monarchy and to restore peace and security to Christendom.

Thus the course was set for the development that led from the entry of France into open war in 1635 to the start of peace negotiations of 1643. This is not the place to give a detailed account of the vicissitudes of these alliances, but instead a second aspect will be considered.

This system, as has already been observed, was geared to attaining peace in the whole of Christendom and as such was the logical preparation for the 'bonne et puissante union' to be referred to in the directive of 1643 as the basis of the peace of Christendom. It was thus not simply a question of bringing this 'union' into existence and keeping it together until peace negotiations could be started, using the weight of this union to make such negotiations possible. Rather, this union had to be incorporated into the negotiations and into the settlement itself.

The meaning of the formula 'paix générale' had in consequence been altered and refined somewhat. Richelieu's demand for 'paix générale' did not mean abstract universal peace *per se*, nor did it mean the universal validity of the terms of peace. Richelieu's formula quite concretely meant the inclusion of *his* system of alliances, or more precisely of the allies of France, into the negotiations and the peace treaty. The distribution of forces that he considered necessary for the maintenance of peace and freedom in Christendom was to establish itself in the negotiations and be enshrined lastingly in the treaty. The 'paix générale' referred principally to France's wishes regarding her partners in the negotiations and subsequent treaty, but this was supposed to be the means for attaining a universal peace settlement. The debate over how a general peace thus understood was to be made possible and effectively introduced was one of the fundamental problems of Richelieu's peace policy until his death. It became especially pressing when the expansion of the war that had been going on since 1635 reached the point where an all-inclusive peace was essential.

The scope of this essay makes possible only a brief summary of the mountain of difficulties with which Richelieu was then faced. Even if the individual partners of the coalition agreed in principle in their desire for universal peace (and this desire had been widespread since the beginning of the 1630s), what each understood by it was very different. What was expected of peace by Sweden, Denmark, the

Netherlands, Saxony, Brandenburg, Hesse, the League of Heilbronn, or possible supporters in the Catholic camp, was by no means the same thing in each case.[31] France's association with Sweden, of which Richelieu had such high hopes for a decisive effect in the military conflict with the Habsburgs, was at the same time an extremely heavy burden to him. The balance of interests shifted: Spain now played a less central role in the Thirty Years War, and the intervention of Sweden gave instead new importance to the Holy Roman Empire, northern Europe generally, and the question of religion—which had some effect on the commencement of peace negotiations. At home as well as in the enemy camp, willingness and opportunity for a general peace became dependent upon the most varied of allegiances.

After 1631 Richelieu was therefore obliged to work for the general peace in two directions at once: he had to ensure that all France's allies and dependants were able to take part in the negotiations, but he had as well to prevent separate negotiations and settlements amongst individual partners. This presented problems that were frankly insoluble.[32] The impossibility of their resolution was evident in the pope's protracted attempts at mediation, where the proposal for a peace congress in Cologne was finally abandoned because of the question of whether or not to admit Protestants. It was evident also in the effects of the Peace of Prague (May 1635), which bound above all the Catholic imperial estates, but also the electorate of Saxony, to the emperor and strengthened his position *vis-à-vis* the estates such that individual estates could be prevented from taking part in general peace negotiations. And it was evident not least in Sweden's repeated temptation to enter into separate negotiations with the emperor.

Finally it should not be overlooked that this, the first practical attempt at a peaceful solution for the whole of Europe, was confronted with a host of formal difficulties which could not be resolved due to the lack of previous experience, as Fritz Dickmann has rightly pointed out: 'The struggle to find an acceptable form for the negotiations and to fix the circle of participants, to establish the composition, place and time of the congress, took longer than did the peace negotiations themselves.'[33] Such formal questions were, how-

---

[31] For Sweden see Sven Lundkvist, 'Die schwedischen Kriegs- und Friedensziele 1632–1648'; for the estates of the Empire see D. Albrecht, 'Die Kriegs- und Friedensziele der deutschen Reichsstände'; both in Repgen, *Krieg und Politik*, 219–40 and 241–73 respectively.

[32] On this point see esp. Dickmann, *Westfälischer Frieden*, 59–117.

[33] 'Das Ringen um die Form der Verhandlungen und den Kreis der Teilnehmer, um Zusammensetzung, Ort und Zeit des Kongresses hat länger gedauert als die Friedensverhandlungen selbst.' Dickmann, *Westfälischer Frieden*, 79.

ever, ideal for concealing the strategic wranglings over principle and conception that made up the true network of contradictory interests of those taking part in the peace discussions, and with which Richelieu's system found itself confronted.

The favourable turn that the war had taken for France and her allies since the end of the 1630s was one of the reasons why Richelieu's stubborn insistence on general peace negotiations finally led to the creation of the necessary conditions: Sweden had been brought into line by a treaty signed in 1638 and renewed in 1641;[34] in December 1641 preliminary discussions between France, Sweden, and the emperor led to an agreement on the opening of peace negotiations admitting the participation of French and Swedish allies; finally, at the imperial Diet of 1640–1 in Regensburg, it was evident that there was an increase in the number of the estates who wanted a general peace with their participation as separate partners and which they wanted to achieve against the emperor's will.[35] The way that Richelieu had wished towards a 'paix générale' was cleared even before his death.

Important though these successes were, the ultimate goal of a 'bonne paix' had still not yet been reached. It would be attained only with a 'paix sûre'. And with this we reach the core of Richelieu's conception of peace.

III

What did 'secure peace' imply? On the one hand, of course, it meant that the terms of the peace should be implemented and respected. But it was of decisive importance that the *state* of peace should last. This had been a fundamental source of anxiety for Richelieu during the whole of his tenure of office, and which he voiced unambiguously in the general directive: 'l'expérience nous fait cognoistre que les Espagnolz ne gardent leurs Traittéz qu'en tant qu'il leur est utile et qu'ilz n'ont pas d'occasions de les rompre avantageusement . . . '.[36] It was so important to Richelieu for peace to be made lasting that he was even prepared to go as far as giving up other possible gains from the peace: 'la seureté du Traitté que l'on voudra faire estant bien establie, toutes les parties intéressées pourront se contenter

---

[34] On the question of the Swedish position see Michael Roberts, 'The Swedish Dilemma', in Geoffrey Parker, *The Thirty Years' War* (London, 1984), 156–61.
[35] See Kathrin Bierther, *Der Regensburger Reichstag von 1640–41* (Kallmünz, 1971), 227–31.
[36] *APW* I. i. 71.

de moindres conditions, la raison voulant qu'on estime plus un médiocre avantage, iors qu'il est certain, que de beaucoup plus grandz qui ne le sont pas'.[37]

The establishment of a 'paix générale' was the most important precondition for this security, but it was far from being the ultimate goal. The point was not merely to put an end to a state of war, and it was not to use the 'paix générale' to set up a balance between the various partners' interests and to force the opponent to acquiesce in the common will by presenting a united front. All this was naturally relevant to Richelieu's dogged insistence on universal peace. However, the requirement that all the allies of France and Sweden should be participants in the peace negotiations had a much more ambitious purpose, namely the realization of a conception of a peace that extended far beyond putting an end to the war. The factor that had governed Richelieu's policies from the very beginning, the existence within the power network of Christendom of a system of French alliances acting as a counterweight to the Spanish-dominated house of Habsburg and intended to keep its ambitions in check, was now to be amplified by the peace treaty into a factor regulating the future peace of Europe. How was the treaty to make this system of alliances efficacious in the future, too?

The security of peace was to be ensured by a guarantee enshrined in the treaty itself. The system of alliances was to be made effective by reason of this guarantee, because the guarantee came into operation when peace was threatened or broke down altogether. The system of alliances and the security of peace were thus intimately linked by this guarantee. A general peace—that is, the negotiations and the treaty made with the participation of all the allies—was the indispensable precondition for such a guarantee, but only by virtue of this explicit guarantee did the 'paix générale', or universal peace, become a 'paix sûre', a secure—that is, lasting—peace. 'Paix générale' and 'paix sûre' were not identical: their relationship was one of interaction.

This needs to be explained more precisely. Richelieu had managed to gain approval for a universal peace, but clearly he did not think that the system of alliances in force on the eve of the negotiations was an adequate basis for a secure future peace. This basis needed to be considerably broader. Section 4 of the general directive for the Westphalia negotiations (which derived from Richelieu's draft of 1637) speaks expressly of the creation of two leagues in Germany and Italy in which all 'Princes, Potentatz et Communautéz' were to be

---

[37] Ibid.

included. This was to be the initial object of the peace *negotiations*, but the result was to be adopted into the treaty itself. It was in this further development of the 'paix générale' that the decisive step towards 'paix sûre' was taken, which in this respect too was much more than a 'paix générale'. The guarantors of peace were to be not only the narrower group of participants that constituted the congress at the beginning of its deliberations, but all the members of those two leagues that the negotiations were to construct, 'estant spéciffié particulièrement par serment sur les Saintz Evangiles que touts lesdits Princes, Potentatz, et Communautéz s'opposent par négociations et par armes à tous ceux qui y voudront contrevenir'.[38] Thus the security of peace was ensured on the broadest possible basis. According to the formulations of the directive this guarantee of security was to be extremely general, aiming not at one particular power but at all possible enemies of peace. It could thus be accepted by all the signatories to the treaty. Only in this manner did peace become in its full sense *une bonne paix de la chrétienté*.

This was the pinnacle of Richelieu's conception of a balanced system of alliances as the means to peace. It was Fritz Dickmann who first analysed the extent and originality of the cardinal's 'system of collective security', not only as the goal of a political vision but as a realistic political operation. Richelieu had not invented the notion of a treaty guarantee based on a form of international law, and the promotion of the peace negotiations was not the first time he made use of it. The notion of security was already present in all the endeavours towards alliances of more restricted scope that had been made since the conflicts in Upper Italy. What was new was that, in conjunction with preparations for a peace congress, Richelieu had extended the principle of a guarantee of security fixed by treaty to the whole of Christendom.[39]

Finally, the concept of a guarantee for the security of peace had specific consequences for France. The preservation of peace by means of a universal guarantee certainly could not and did not mean that France would give up the leading role in any future order based on peace. This was especially true in regard of her capabilities for intervention should peace be threatened. The maintenance of peace had a political and a military component: the guarantors were to

[38] Ibid.
[39] See on this point Dickmann, *Westfälischer Frieden*, esp. 157–63, including more details on the origin and development of the notion of a guarantee. I am not able to prove that Richelieu had absorbed the ideas of Erasmus, Sully, Campanella, Grotius, or Rohan. But I am in complete agreement with Dickmann that the pragmatic Richelieu was the first to make a system of collective security the objective of a continuous, practical policy.

proceed against violations 'par négotiations et par armes'. The way France had previously conducted wars was by pursuing the double policy of direct and indirect war, and the guarantee system of collective security enabled her to continue the strategy of an indirect war. But even the possibility of direct military intervention on the part of France became an article of peace policy, seen in the higher perspective of the preservation of lasting peace. What was important was to stick to the principle that had dictated military aims since the campaigns in Upper Italy: even then military activity had been undertaken not to make extensive territorial conquest but to open up points of access and secure military bases.[40] What had referred in the early years to Susa, Pinerolo, Saluzzo, and Casale had been applied in the programmatic *avis* of 13 January 1629 to the whole area on the eastern borders of France and even to the sea.[41] In the following years this programme was systematically put into practice for these areas, partly by means of protection treaties and the like, partly by military action—where the safeguard of right was always loudly emphasized.[42] This military strategy was part also of the policies designed to secure peace. It found its logical continuation in the territorial demands that preceded all peace initiatives up to and including the negotiations for Westphalia, where it is stated in the first section of the general directive 'qu'ainsy que Pignerol est nécessaire au Roy comme une porte pour le secours de l'Italie, ainsy il est important que Sa Majesté ne soit pas séparée de l'Allemagne, affin qu'elle soit en estat de ne souffrir pas les oppressions qu'on pourroit faire à divers Princes qui y possèdent des Estatz'.[43] These territorial concessions ensured that possible military action would back up the guarantee commitments. The search for concessions was not motivated by any desire for conquest but as part of the terms by which peace was ensured.

The 'paix sûre' thus had a triple basis: it required the participation

---

[40] See Richelieu's *avis* of May 1625 (Grillon, i. 181–6) and of Apr. 1628 (ibid. iii. 202–10). See also Richelieu, *Mémoires* SHF ix. 611–12; *Mémoires* MP ii. 150, 155, and 188–9.

[41] *Avis* of 13 Jan. 1629: Grillon, iv. 25–6.

[42] On this point see H. Weber, 'Richelieu et le Rhin', *Revue historique*, 239 (1968), 265–80, and his *Frankreich, Kurtrier, der Rhein*; Wolfgang Stein, *Protection Royale: Eine Untersuchung zu den Protektionsverhältnissen im Elsass zur Zeit Richelieus 1622–1643* (Schriftenreihe der Vereinigung zur Erforschung der Neueren Geschichte, 9; Münster, 1978); Rainer Babel, *Zwischen Habsburg und Bourbon: Aussenpolitik und europäische Stellung Herzog Karls IV. von Lothringen und Bar vom Regierungsantritt bis zum Exil (1624–1634)* (Supplement to *Francia*, Deutsches Historisches Institut Paris, 18; Sigmaringen, 1989). Seminal on the question of legitimation is Fritz Dickmann, 'Rechtsgedanke und Machtpolitik bei Richelieu: Studien an neuentdeckten Quellen', *Historische Zeitschrift*, 196 (1963), 265–319.

[43] Cf. the general directive, *APW* I. i. 63, and its execution, 75–6 and the following sections.

of all the states of Christendom in setting up the treaty; it could rely on a guarantee based on international law and given by all the contracting parties; it preserved the option of military intervention for France. In this manner lasting peace was to be established: peace *for* the whole of Christendom and ensured *by* the whole of Christendom. Because the option of military intervention was preserved, the French king maintained his dominant role as the chief protector of Christendom—as it was unambiguously formulated in the preamble to the general directive.[44]

Thus Richelieu's achievements at his death were not only to have ensured that the way was open for a 'paix générale'. His conception for a 'paix sûre' was also adopted into the general directive that his successor, Mazarin, drew up on the basis of his drafts for the commencement of peace negotiations. The next and last section of this essay is devoted to a final assessment of how successful Richelieu's peace politics ultimately were.

IV

The agreement that was made in 1648 after laborious negotiations was not the realization of the *bonne paix de la chrétienté* that Richelieu had fought for. Two of its principal goals had not been achieved, or had been attained only imperfectly. (1) Neither Spain nor the Netherlands were amongst the signatories (they had already signed a special treaty in 1646), and fighting between France and Spain continued until 1659. (2) The terms of the guarantee that had been so fundamental to Richelieu's conception of a 'paix sûre' were so formulated that they were 'far removed from what Richelieu had originally intended'[45]—in particular, the two alliances of all the 'Princes, Potentatz et Communautéz' of Germany and Italy did not come about. There were other differences, too, but it was the abandonment of the two main pillars of Richelieu's system, universal peace and collective security, that ultimately condemned his political efforts at peace to failure.

This failure becomes all the more evident if the cardinal's own

---

[44] Ibid. 59: 'que jamais Prince n'a tant eu de guerre et que jamais Prince ne l'a tant aborée, aussy si l'on considère celle où il s'est engagé, comme celles qu'il n'a peu éviter, esgalement èz unes et èz autres l'on verra que la seule obligation de donner à ses sujectz catholiques le libre exercice de leur Religion, les contenir en leur devoir, chastier leur rébellion, et conserver la Paix dans la Chrestienté, luy a fait prendre les armes, sachant qu'il estoit obligé comme Roy à qui Dieu avoit donné son auctorité, de le faire révérer et employer sa puissance pour la deffense des Princes qu'on vouloit opprimer. . .'.

[45] Dickmann, *Westfälischer Frieden*, 341–2, quoted from p. 342.

ideal time-scale is adduced as a means of judging the progress and
result of his policies. 'Une paix prompte' was his frequently expressed wish, but during the long eighteen years in which he guided
French policy no *paix de la chrétienté* came about, and another six
years elapsed after his death before the Treaty of Westphalia was
completed. But in this respect was not Richelieu himself chiefly
responsible for the failure of his ultimate goal? Was it not he who
had used his peace politics to prevent a swift denouement? To repeat
Fritz Dickmann's verdict cited at the beginning of this essay, no
statesman had contributed as much as Richelieu 'to prolonging the
struggle in Europe until finally he was outlived by the war itself'.[46]
Does not, then, the cardinal's failure to pursue a swift peace bring
into question the sincerity of his commitment to a Christian peace?

A considered answer to this question requires further reflection on
the principles which determined Richelieu's political thinking and
action. A key element of Richelieu's art as a statesman was without
doubt his ability to apply the factor of *time* judiciously.[47]

Il y a certaines occasions auxquelles il n'est pas permis de délibérer longtemps, parce que la nature des affaires ne le permet pas. Mais, en celles
qui ne sont pas de ce genre, le plus sûr est de dormir sur les affaires,
récompenser par la promptitude de l'exécution le délai que l'on prend pour
les mieux résoudre.

This was the recipe he gave to his king in his *Testament politique*,[48]
and in the chapter on the effectiveness of 'négotiation continuelle' he
explains, 'Il faut poursuivre ce qu'on entreprend avec une perpétuelle
suite de dessein en sorte qu'on ne cesse jamais d'agir que par raison
et non par relâche d'Esprit, par indifférence des choses, par vascilla-
tion de pensées et par résolutions contraires.'[49] Consideration of the
time factor was a matter for reason; reason was to decide which were
fit goals for action; and in the pursuit of these goals action had to
allow itself to be guided by reason.[50] Ranke admired in Richelieu's
avis his 'clear-sightedness, taking into account the remotest consequences'.[51] Richelieu's political actions were determined by the
long-term perspective of his aims, as reason demanded they should
be. Any other mode of action could lead to dangerous short-circuits.
'L'expérience fait voir que si on ne prévoit de loin les desseins où on

---

[46] See above, n. 2.   [47] Elliott, *Richelieu and Olivares*, 155.
[48] *Test. pol.* 335.   [49] Ibid. 352.   [50] See Ibid. 325–9.
[51] '...[der] Scharfblick, der die zu erwartenden Folgen bis in die weiteste Ferne
wahrnimmt...', Leopold von Ranke, *Französische Geschichte vornehmlich im XVI. und XVII.
Jahrhundert*, intro. Otto Vossler (2 vols.; Stuttgart, 1954), i. 147.

veut se porter, quand on est sur le point de leur exécution on se trouve court', he told the king in 1627.[52]

Given Richelieu's political style, then, progress towards the peace table was guaranteed to be slow. Urgent though the immediate need for a 'paix prompte' might be, the ultimate goal of a 'paix sûre' must not be jeopardized because of it. Reason demanded that security, not speed, should determine the appropriate time-scale: 'Paix sûre' had priority over 'paix prompte'. What were the effects of this principle on Richelieu's peace policy?

It must first be observed that during the whole of Richelieu's tenure of office this problem of time-scale never affected peace negotiations proper. Richelieu's policy was geared to creating the *conditions* for peace negotiations, and he did not experience the start of the negotiations themselves. Nevertheless, the creation of these conditions was itself governed by the long-term perspective of his ultimate conception of the peace. It was principally a matter of getting agreement on a 'paix générale'. The difficulties here, not only with France's opponents but with her own allies, were extraordinarily complex, as may be seen from the summary in the previous paragraphs. But this practical problem was exacerbated by another, whose influence is felt most strongly in the matter of time-scale: Richelieu's fundamental mistrust of Spanish politics.

Richelieu was not only convinced that Spain was dictating the policy of the emperor,[53] but also that she was responsible for preventing the settlement of the material differences between France and the Empire. In the tactics for negotiation adopted by the Spanish he saw above all a catalogue of cunning, dishonesty, and slyness. That had been true in Upper Italy and continued to be true now in the 1630s.[54] It was chiefly a matter of presenting hindrances to the institution of peace negotiations. Both directly and indirectly

---

[52] 'Mémoire pour faire voir au roi', 15 Aug. 1627: Grillon, ii. 392.

[53] 'Nous savons, il y a longtemps, que l'aigle impérial sert à S. M. Catholique de ce que le faucon sert au fauconnier; il le fait voler pour prendre la proie, et puis la lui ôte.' Thus Richelieu, *Mémoires* SHF viii. 265, quotes the French ambassador Bautru in his negotiations with Olivares in 1628. On the relations between Spain and the Empire, see Hildegard Ernst, *Madrid und Wien 1632–1637: Politik und Finanzen in den Beziehungen zwischen Philipp IV. und Ferdinand II*. (Schriftenreihe der Vereinigung zur Erforschung der Neueren Geschichte, 18; Münster, 1991).

[54] e.g. regarding the negotiations over the Valtelline in 1625, Richelieu, *Mémoires* SHF v. 110; regarding Mantua and the mediation of the papal legates, memorandum of 20 Apr. 1628, Grillon, iii. 202–10, esp. p. 203; for a reproduction of Bautru's discussions in 1628–9, Richelieu, *Mémoires* SHF viii. 251–72; for Mazarin's negotiations in the spring and summer of 1630, *Mémoires* MP ii. 188–9, 203, 209, 220–2, and 228; for Mazarin's attempts to secure peace after 1635, see his efforts at mediation in autumn 1635 and in 1636–7, ibid. ii. 661–72 and iii. 4, 188, and 194–9, respectively.

Richelieu repeatedly sought to ascertain clearly whether or not Spain seriously desired peace and under what conditions.[55] He wished to be certain how reliable the statements of Spanish representatives were, in direct conversations or through intermediaries. He wanted the extent of their authority to be unambiguously stated, and he expected the results of negotiations to be irrevocable.[56] As long as he was dissatisfied on these points, or experienced the opposite of what he expected, he was plagued by the suspicion that Spain was stalling, trying to steal a march on him, deceive, or simply show him up. He sincerely feared that France might be forced publicly into the role of the petitioner seeking peace to cover her own weakness. This would have been an intolerable insult to the king's reputation, which above all had to remain untainted in negotiations of this kind.[57] Conversely, mistrust and suspicion dictated France's own negotiating technique. This consisted in highly cautious, tentative, and secretive manœuvring, in which the opponent (Spain) was expected to make preliminary offers of surrender on points which France herself was not prepared to concede.[58] This profound mistrust stayed with Richelieu until the last,[59] and it was ultimately this mistrust that determined his conception of the order of peace.[60]

Richelieu was convinced that only a determined demonstration of strength could force Spain to accept conditions opening the way for the swift re-establishment of peace and freedom in Christendom.[61] How could such pressure be brought to bear? Richelieu certainly did not settle for direct military pressure from the outset. An extensive

---

[55] Bautru's embassies to Spain in 1628–9 and 1632 (where his mission was to drive Olivares to such a pitch of anger that he would come out with what he really thought: 'échauffant souvent le comte d'Olivarés pour apercevoir la vérité dans ses colères', *Mémoires* MP ii. 420); the embassies of Saint-Étienne and Charbonnières to the emperor in 1633–4; Barault's embassy to Spain in 1634. What most clearly emerges from this is the importance of the mediation by the papal legates. See Auguste Leman, *Urban VIII et la rivalité de la France et de la Maison d'Autriche de 1631 à 1635* (Mémoires et travaux publiés par des professeurs des Facultés catholiques de Lille, 16; Lille, 1920), *passim*; K. Repgen, *Die römische Kurie und der Westfälische Friede*, I. *Papst, Kaiser und Reich 1521–1644*, i (Bibliothek des Deutschen Historischen Instituts in Rom, 34; Tübingen, 1971), *passim*. See also Richelieu, *Mémoires* MP iii. 188.

[56] See the directives for Saint-Étienne and Charbonnières in 1633 (*Mémoires* MP ii. 447–50); for Charnacé and Brezé in 1635 (ibid. iii. 10–20, and the instructions, pp. 20 and 23); and for Charbonnières in 1634 (ibid. ii. 548–51).

[57] The same mistrust also occupied the other side. On Olivares in particular, see Elliott, *Richelieu and Olivares*.

[58] *Mémoires* MP iii. 201–3.

[59] See the memorandum of Nov. 1642 in Avenel, vii. 176.

[60] See the passage from s. 4 of the general directive cited above: 'l'expérience nous fait cognoistre que les Espagnolz ne gardent leurs Traittéz qu'en tant qu'il leur est utile et qu'ilz n'ont pas d'occasions de les rompre avantageusement', *APW* I. i. 71.

[61] e.g. Richelieu's *avis* of 15 Sept. 1629, Richelieu, *Mémoires* SHF x. 340–3.

system of alliances could have the desired effect, but did not exclude the possibility of war. Richelieu's position was unambiguous: if reason could not prevail, war was a perfectly legitimate means of forcing one's opponent to accept peace.[62] But he wanted to make sure that any measures that provided for or initiated a war with the Habsburgs, and especially that any passive or active participation in such a war on the part of France, would be understood in this light. War was the *ultima ratio* of his peace policies. This had been his position in summer 1634 when faced with the king and the war party at court, who were prepared to embark immediately upon open war. In Richelieu's eyes recourse to war would only be justified 'si après avoir tenté toutes sortes de moyens raisonnables pour porter les Espagnols a une juste Paix, je ne tenois pour tres asseuré, que la guerre est, non seulement le plus court, mais le seul moyen qui les y peut contraindre'.[63] And even during the winter of 1634–5 he had wanted to give peace negotiations a last chance as 'moyens raisonnables'. But then, after this long prevarication, open war also proved not to be the quickest way to achieve peace, or at least not the peace that Richelieu intended. Now, moreover, for the sake of a quick solution, a situation arose that put Richelieu's conception at risk within his own camp. In a memorandum from 1637 this crisis is described with perfect clarity. The extended duration of the war was incurring high costs that the country could no longer raise and which were giving rise to general dissatisfaction. But more than that, there was a general feeling against the war:

Un autre mal est en cette guerre que le sentiment d'icelle est en peu d'esprits. Je ne dis pas que peu d'esprits l'éprouvent, car la demonstration en est claire, et n'y a personne raisonnable qui ne confesse qu'elle est juste, mais je dis que peu d'esprits en sentent l'interest. Car la disposition des peuples ne regarde que son repos, et ne se soucie pas des interests de l'estat, tant que de soi meme . . . et quand je dis les peuples, je ne dis non seulement la populace de la campagne et des villes, mais aussi tous les parlements les officiers, les ecclesiastiques et la plus part de la noblesse de la campagne . . .[64]

---

[62] *Mémoires* MP ii. 204–5 and 206. See also Roland Mousnier, 'Richelieu, cardinal et principal ministre, chrétienté et guerres dynastiques', in *Genova e Francia al crocevia dell'Europa*, 7–27.

[63] 'Avis donné au Roy au commencement de Juin 1634.' AAE CP Hollande 16, fos. 464ᵛ–88, here fo. 480ᵛ–81.

[64] 'Sur l'estat des affaires du Royaume.' AAE France 256, fos. 108–10ᵛ, here 108ᵛ. In the same memorandum there is an interesting explanation of why the war was just: 'Ceste guerre est juste dans le droit des gens, elle est juste devant Dieu, qui veut et aprouve que nous conservions notre liberté, nos droits et notre dignité, et n'oblige ni les Rois ni les Estats a souffrir que l'on les en prive, et par consequent il est juste de faire la guerre pour s'y

That this was the prevailing mood at court, and that it threatened to endanger Richelieu's plans became clear in 1637 during the crisis initiated by the king's confessor, Père Caussin, and in the Cinq-Mars conspiracy of 1641–2. In both cases a quick and direct peace was to be concluded with Spain by circumventing or even eliminating Richelieu.[65] The king, who had not been unsympathetic to these plans, only came fully back into line with Richelieu's conception two weeks before the cardinal's death.[66]

Richelieu himself had periodically considered another way out of the dilemma of a swift peace that was not attainable even by war, which reveals another understanding of 'paix prompte'. In spring 1637, when attempts to bring together a peace congress in Cologne were looking increasingly like coming to a dead end, Richelieu declared himself prepared to accept a cease-fire. At first sight this seems paradoxical, since a cease-fire would have had to last ten or fifteen years if there was to be a reasonable hope of its leading eventually to a 'paix prompte'![67] But in this case it is clear that a swift peace did not necessarily have to mean a peace that put an immediate end to the state of war by a peace treaty. 'Swift' in this context meant swiftly proceeding negotiations, once the necessary preconditions had been agreed to, and because they had been agreed in advance. A long gap before the negotiations proper began was not in contradiction to Richelieu's demand for a 'paix prompte', but perfectly in harmony with it.

In this light, therefore, it is difficult to speak of culpability, in the sense of culpable omissions or delays, when assessing Richelieu's peace politics. For Richelieu it was quite legitimate, indeed essential, to decide upon the duration of negotiations, and the appropriate time for making resolutions, from the perspective of their ultimate goal. This goal was the *paix de la chrétienté*, to be attained by way of a 'paix sûre'. Richelieu's policies were oriented around this goal, and the appropriate and necessary time-scale of a 'paix prompte' was also subject to it.

maintenir. Les moyens de cette guerre sont a la vérité facheux, mais si la guerre est juste, ce n'est pas contre la justice de la faire par des moyens qui en soy ne sont pas justes: si l'on n'en a point d'autres, car les moyens ne sont pas considérés par l'injustice qu'ils sont en soy, mais comme instrumens d'une juste querelle. Mais l'injustice qui est dans les moyens necessaires nous oblige a tenir bride en main proceder avec grande circonspection pour ne pas pecher en nous mesme et envers Dieu du côté de leur injustice.'

[65] See Chevallier, *Louis XIII*, 539–46 and 583–600 respectively, and Elliott, *Richelieu and Olivares*, 146 ff.

[66] M. Carmona, *Richelieu: L'Ambition et le pouvoir* (Paris, 1983), 691–2.

[67] *Mémoires* MP iii. 201–2. Cf. also the 'Sixiesme party de Trêfue qui se peut convertir en Paix' in the supplementary directive of 1642 (*APW* I. i. 156–8), which assumes a 20-year cease-fire in the case of a peace treaty's not being possible.

The last and seemingly decisive question that arises from all this is not one of the execution of Richelieu's peace policies, but of their practicability. There is no doubt that France needed peace and that Richelieu wanted peace. The country needed time to recover from the internal crises that had shaken it almost continually since the wars of religion. She needed peace in order to make herself internally stable again. Ultimately, France had also to look to the future and the promise of new vigour and new riches offered by overseas expansion, and to be able to imitate and compete with the Netherlands and England, she needed peace. There were clear initial signs of such a policy in the 1620s.[68] But this presupposed that there were no longer grounds to fear a threat to exterior and internal security from Spain. In Richelieu's analysis this threat was to more than France: it culminated in the Spanish ambition to establish a universal monarchy and as such affected the whole of Christendom. Spain's threat to France therefore had to be removed by putting an end to the threat to the whole of Christendom.

The peace of Christendom was in France's interests, but it was not pursued exclusively in the light of French interests, for Richelieu was also considering the advantage of the whole of Christendom. And it is surely not going too far to suggest that the cardinal saw this not only as a matter of political pragmatism but also one of moral duty. Research in recent years has repeatedly acknowledged that in him *homo politicus* never excluded *homo religiosus* and that he tried to bring the one facet into harmony with the other.[69] In his theologically oriented view of the temporal world's duty to create order, the dimensions of peace extended well beyond the merely political. It is also worth noting that out of Richelieu's precise notions about the cause of unrest in Christendom, and about the measures necessary for regaining and securing peace, there arose obligations for political action whose dimensions also far exceeded the logical necessities of political rationality. The interests of France were not combined with the interests of Christendom because of any Machiavellian *raison d'état*. They were united in the conviction that the kingdom of France had a divinely ordained function in respect of both France and Christendom. Thus they found not only their legitimation but also their binding nature. The search for peace therefore had in principle to be the search for a swift peace. Richelieu did not only

---

[68] See H. Hauser, *La Pensée et l'action économiques du cardinal de Richelieu* (Paris, 1944), esp. 48–73 and 121–42.

[69] Besides the earlier studies by Hassinger, Church, Dickmann, Thuau, Wollenberg and Elliott, see also Jean de Viguerie, 'Richelieu théologien', in R. Mousnier (ed.), *Richelieu et la culture*, 29–42, and Mousnier, 'Chrétienté et guerres'.

treat the numerous inquiries, interventions, and negotiations with which he was confronted throughout his tenure of office seriously and responsibly as the material for his policies. There is no doubt that he also hoped for swift success. But—and this is the corollary—this was never allowed to degenerate into a search for peace at any price.[70] The *bonne paix de la chrétienté* could only derive from the combination of a 'paix générale' with a 'paix sûre', and in his efforts to achieve this long-term goal Richelieu fully accepted that even his contemporaries would see in him the greatest obstacle to a 'paix prompte'.[71]

The modern historian would agree with this judgement in the sense of a bare statement of fact. But would he agree with it also as an accusation of guilt? It seems to me that this first attempt to transform a noble vision of peace in Europe into political reality ought rather to command our admiration, and that its failure ought to provoke us to more reflection.

In the introduction to his *Idee der Staatsräson*, Friedrich Meinecke asked

. . . why is it not possible then for the properly understood interest of the states themselves, co-operating by reason of ethical motives, to induce them [the states] to unite and freely restrict the methods of their power politics, to abide by Law and Morality, and to develop Institutions of International Law and the League of Nations to a full and satisfactory efficiency?

Meinecke's answer is this:

Because no one of them will trust another round the corner. Because no one of them believes for certain about any of the others, that it would abide by the agreed limitations in absolutely every instance and without exception;

---

[70] See e.g. *Mémoires* MP ii. 206.

[71] The Peace of Westphalia not only meant the failure of Richelieu's peace policy, but also heralded a period of European politics where the self-interest of states was dominant and completely suppressed a diplomacy built on the needs of Christendom. This was esp. true of the hegemonic policies of Louis XIV. Clearly the problem then became one of whether a lasting peaceful European order could best be built on the balance of power or a hegemonic system. See L. Dehio, *Gleichgewicht oder Hegemonie: Betrachtungen über ein Grundproblem der neueren Staatengeschichte* (Krefeld, 1948). This had already exercised Richelieu and would dominate the 18th cent. See also H. Duchhardt, *Gleichgewicht der Kräfte, Convenance, Europäisches Konzert: Friedenskongresse und Friedensschlüsse vom Zeitalter Ludwigs XIV. bis zum Wiener Kongress* (Darmstadt, 1976). It was in this context, and as a reaction to the destructive consequences of the armed conflicts of the second half of the 17th cent., that there begins with the abbé de Saint-Pierre a whole series of peace plans, aiming to solve the crisis of the European order brought about by Louis XIV. For these, see M. G. Bottaro Palumbo, *Ch.-I. Castel de Saint-Pierre e la crisi della Monarchia di Luigi XIV*, i. *1658–1710* (Genoa, 1983). However, the plans also belonged to a line of utopian schemes which been repeatedly floated since the Renaissance. The best overview of this literature is still K. von Raumer, *Ewiger Friede: Friedensrufe und Friedenspläne seit der Renaissance* (Freiburg, 1953).

but on the contrary suspects that in certain instances that other would once again lapse into following his own natural egoism.[72]

The analysis of Richelieu's peace politics and their failure seems to me substantially to confirm this judgement. One might ask whether man's nature makes his dream of universal peace impossible to realize. The description of this or that policy, or the examination of this or that success or failure, should not prevent us from reflecting occasionally on this fundamental question.

[72] F. Meinecke, *Machiavellism: The Doctrine of Raison d'État and its Place in Modern History*, Eng. trans. with intro. by W. Stark (London, 1957), 15.

3

RICHELIEU AND REFORM
Rhetoric and Political Reality

ROBIN BRIGGS

Je croys qu'une des raisons qui vous a aultant empesché d'entrer aux affaires, estoit le peu d'apparence de rencontrer de l'honneur, n'y ayant personne qui ne veit la France en plus misérable estat qu'il se puisse estre. La malice du temps avoit fait perdre l'opinion vénérable qu'on doibt avoir du souverain, qui n'est plus en l'estime qu'elle doibt estre, comme les continuelles révoltes qui ont esté jusques à aujourd'huy le monstre[nt], . . .

Qui pourra espérer et trouver remeddes à tant de maulx, s'asseurant de conduire le navire à bon port au milieu de tant de tempestes? Où est le médecin politique qui respondra de restablir la santé, quand la maladye a surmonté les puissances naturelles?

Among the letters of congratulation which greeted Richelieu on his appointment to the council, that by the future *surintendant* d'Effiat stands out for its harsh realism about the state of France. In a remarkably succinct analysis he pointed out the decline in royal authority, the divisions of the church, the Protestant problem, the behaviour of the grandees, and the results of the sale of office. Justice was venal, merchants were leaving trade to invest in office, and France was unable to trade on equal terms with her neighbours; in consequence the people were poor, revenues did not match expenditure, and the problems were made worse by the need to pay pensions to the grandees. Against this dismal picture d'Effiat did set an ideal vision in which all groups performed their proper functions, so that for example 'la Noblesse s'employe aux choses glorieuses', while a peaceful people are optimistically seen blessing the king and 'payant avec amour' his taxes. He declared his faith that God would show Richelieu the path to follow among all these precipices, 'estant par là que nostre guérison totale doibt arriver, ou nostre mort est asseurée sans remedde'.[1]

Although d'Effiat expressed his views with unusual clarity, there was nothing original about them. The nautical and medical meta-

---

[1] Grillon, i. 88–90, d'Effiat to Richelieu, May 1624.

phors for the state were virtually as old as political thought itself, while the analysis of France's specific problems belonged to an established tradition, with which Richelieu was equally familiar. A clear line runs from the *cahiers* of the Estates General of 1614–15, through the discussions of the Assemblies of Notables of 1617 and 1626–7, Richelieu's own reform proposals of 1625, the Code Michaud of 1629, and the *Testament politique* compiled in the late 1630s. Despite some differences of detail and emphasis, these documents clearly drew heavily on one another; they also looked back even further, to earlier meetings of the Estates and to the great royal ordinances of the sixteenth century. Their central idea is a simple one, with a strongly traditional, even scholastic, basis. What should be a harmonious and ordered polity has been corrupted, by malice or error, and can only be restored to full functionality by the removal of the intrusive elements. Earnest seekers after that fabled beast, the society of orders, may perhaps think, like the pursuers of the yeti, that they see large footprints here.

More examples of thinking of this type can be found in another short document from 1624, 'Pour remédier aux désordres plus pressans', which appears to be a working paper from Richelieu's *cabinet*. The two points which indicate the decadence of the state are said to be the decline of royal authority and excessive luxury, in clothes, food, and furnishing. The remedy for the latter is that familiar recourse of baffled traditionalists, sumptuary legislation. The main thrust of the document, however, is in another direction. What is essential, while awaiting 'un plus ample réglement, et surtout pour contenir les Grands soubzs l'autorité royale, qui est le seul pivot sur lequel tourne l'Estat', is to find ways of supporting a powerful armed force 'par le moyen duquel chacun soit retenu dans le devoir par l'apréhension d'un prompt chastiment'. This will create a situation in which the king 'se puisse faire redouter à ses voisins', and 'la facilité sera beaucoup plus grande pour prévenir le mal et remédier à loisir aux désordres dont il convient purger l'Estat.' What we may scent here already is a whiff of realism and *raison d'état*, with an ominous suggestion that the patient is to be force-fed some very nasty medicine indeed.[2] Despite these hints, however, the document is typical of many in its reliance on metaphor at crucial moments. Problems may be identified in specific terms, but solutions tend to be disappointingly vague. This is hardly surprising, for the immediate

---

[2] Grillon, i. 141–2. As the editor points out, some of the document found its way into the *Testament politique*.

domestic problems facing any ministry raised difficult, often embarrassing, issues, and regularly demanded responses which diverged sharply from conventional assumptions. Whether it was in dealing with the Huguenots, venality of office, the grandees, or the royal finances, ministers were forced to take many decisions for which their only defence had to be one of expediency. The result was a permanent tension between rhetoric and political action, and this will be the central subject of this chapter.

Richelieu himself encountered the long-running discussion which circled uncertainly around these issues as a member of the Estate of the Clergy in 1614–15, in the debates and *cahiers* of the Estates themselves, and almost certainly in some of the numerous political pamphlets they evoked. During his brief first ministry he had to deal with noble rebels who borrowed various elements from the grievances of the Estates to justify their resistance, a technique he himself was party to during the major revolt of 1620. By the time he rejoined the Council in 1624 he had surrounded himself with a group of political thinkers and writers who manipulated these themes with considerable skill. We do have to recognize that most of the documents on which we rely to establish his personal attitudes, like the 1624 paper already cited, are of uncertain provenance, yet this is in some ways positively helpful. Richelieu never made the foolish attempt to function as an autonomous political entity, conjuring up brilliant policies unaided and in isolation. This is precisely the anachronistic image which the legend of the great cardinal is liable to generate, and from which we need to escape. In a very fundamental sense he appears to have been a team man, who operated through multiple circles of friends, allies, and dependants. This tendency is already evident in his early ecclesiastical career, so that it appears to be as much temperamental as a function of the political world in which he moved; in 1624 he already stood out from all possible rivals in this respect.[3] The point needs emphasis, since it is rather too easy to generalize from Richelieu's own example, and think that other ministers naturally operated in the same way. In fact it is hard to think of any other French statesman of the whole century who even begins to compete in terms of the range of his advisers and contacts; the nearest is probably the minister's great admirer Jean-Baptiste Colbert. Richelieu certainly took care to retain his own liberty of action, partly by encouraging some diversity of view among his entourage, yet he could hardly avoid being influenced by the general

---

[3] J. Bergin, *The Rise of Richelieu* (New Haven, Conn., 1991), esp. 107–15, 230–1, 262–5.

tone of their opinions. This did mean that in a sense he was the minister of the previous regime's critics, much as Olivares was the minister of the *arbitristas* whom those critics so much resembled.[4]

In the short term at least this was a tactically astute position, since men of virtually every persuasion seemed to agree that France was in a very bad state. There was abundant political support waiting to be mobilized by a government which held out hopes of competence and stability. La Vieuville had tried to exploit the possibilities, but lacked both the necessary abilities and a sufficiently wide political base. In his attempts to gather all real power into his own hands he had only emphasized these defects, repeating the error of Luynes when he combined the great offices of constable and *garde des sceaux* in his own person. It was not just that no one man could perform all the duties, nor that the favourite's lack of qualifications for either risked making him a laughing-stock. A successful *ministériat* positively required a team, something which the lack of recent examples may have obscured; to cumulate positions was at once to reveal one's lack of capable allies, and to accept direct responsibility for any failure. Like many other aspects of French political life, these problems could not be discussed openly at the time, since there was a prevalent myth that only the king himself could legitimately head the government. Louis XIII was sufficiently aware of the difficulty to try and take control himself after the death of Luynes, putting on his father's mantle, but the immediate effect was to destabilize the situation further.

It could be argued Richelieu gained enormously by being excluded from any share of power before 1624; the king had time to discover (however subconsciously) that he needed a capable first minister, while the numerous blunders of 1617–24 provided a large stock of excuses for the first period of the ministry.[5] The efforts of Richelieu himself and his numerous propagandists have permanently affected our vision of this period, so that the summer of 1624 is liable to appear instinctively as a watershed between confusion and order, failure and success. In many ways, as will be seen later, this is thoroughly misleading, yet the new ministry did manage some deft tricks to seize the political initiative. This often involved exploiting the kind of political rhetoric already mentioned, invoking images of sickness and decadence to imply that France was now on the way to recovery. The essential message was that the fault lay with men more

---

[4] Bergin's ch. on the episcopate (ch. 6 below) provides an excellent example of the way Richelieu used advice from his entourage, while maintaining his own freedom of action.

[5] The best account of this period is now that by Bergin, *Rise of Richelieu*, esp. 239–59.

than with structures, so that a change of personnel at the top could bring drastic improvements. Richelieu's own thinking is presumably reflected in his *Mémoires*, but also in the account given by Scipion Dupleix, whose *Histoire de Louis le Juste* seems to have been rather similar in emerging from what was virtually a collaborative effort. The historian, often criticized by his contemporaries for undue servility, left a description of how the cardinal had the work read out to him, provided vital information, and corrected the drafts.[6]

Dupleix suggested three main causes for France being 'languissant, enervé et foible' in 1624: the behaviour of the Huguenots and the grandees, and the ambition of Spain, which led her to foment internal divisions in France.[7] Earlier, when describing how Richelieu was recalled 'à la direction des affaires d'Estat, qui estoient en très-grand desordre', he had attributed previous failures to a whole series of faults. Ministers had displayed a lack of application, generals and troops had proved inadequate, showing a severe lack of military discipline, the finances were exhausted, state secrets were known to France's enemies, yet those of other powers remained unknown to the ministers. He then finished with 'et (qui pis est) que l'on donnoit impunité aux rebellions et autres crimes des Grands, et que l'on achettoit leur fidelité au poids d'or'. Dupleix claimed that all these defects had been reversed under Richelieu, before going on to list twenty marvels of the ministry; these were mostly military and diplomatic, and number eighteen went so far as to allege

... que depuis huit cent ans la Monarchie Françoise allant tousjours en decadence, et nos Rois estans plus empeschés à conserver leur Etat, que disposés à conquester, nous en voyons aujord'huy estendre heureusement les limites avec la gloire du nom François, le contentement de nos alliés, la confusion de nos ennemis, et l'estonnement de tout l'Europe.[8]

The attempt to portray Louis and Richelieu as reversing an unfavourable trend which went back to the immediate successors of Charlemagne is something of an extreme case. It may perhaps reflect the pessimistic view many French observers took of their national history since the largely unsuccessful wars of François Ier and Henri II, which had ended with the unfavourable peace of Câteau-Cambrésis and the long agony of the religious wars. The pamphlet literature surrounding the Estates General of 1614 bears witness to such feelings, with many writers sounding a note of puzzled dismay.

---

[6] É. Thuau, *Raison d'état et pensée politique à l'époque de Richelieu* (Paris, 1966), 224–5.

[7] S. Dupleix, *Histoire de Louis le Juste, XIII du nom, roy de France et de Navarre* (Paris, 1635), 255.

[8] Ibid. 4–6.

It is striking how for virtually all the authors the answer lay in the firm assertion of authority; it was the style rather than the mode of government which was contested. To judge from these writings, and the debates in the Estates General, absolutism had already won the public debate by default.[9] The experience of the later sixteenth century must have weighed heavily here, not least through the association of several anti-absolutist theses with either the 'monarchomach' Huguenot writers or the Catholic League. The shift in opinion within the political nation can be well seen in Bodin's movement from a 'constitutionalist' to an 'absolutist' position, and had been largely confirmed by Henri IV's success in restoring peace to France.

Fervent public displays of support for the young Louis XIII emphasized how a king still too young to rule could be a major political asset, a symbolic figure effectively immune from attack. The enormous investment in the king as the unifying force in French society reflected both the widespread fears of renewed instability, and the discredit which had fallen on any suggestion that civil society should have a share in power. Apparent ideological agreement did not, however, offer any reliable solution to the everyday political problems of the years after 1610. The reappearance of aristocratic rebellion, then of religious war, seems to have engendered a renewed wave of pessimism, although Louis XIII's obvious good intentions preserved the monarchy from direct criticism. The idea that France was suffering from deep-seated maladies, which called for suitably vigorous remedies, was taken up by Richelieu and his writers, notably Fancan, in pamphlets aptly entitled *Discours salutaire et avis de la France mourante*, or more simply just *La France mourante*.

Ideas about the need for reform were not confined to any one group, and there was a very significant tradition within governmental circles themselves. The policies pursued under Henri IV and Sully were far from being forgotten, for although ministers might change rapidly, there was substantial continuity at the level of *conseillers d'état* and *maîtres des requêtes*. Recent historians have rightly laid great stress on the crucial role of this group from the 1630s onward, but this should not obscure the important part they already played as the practical agents of royal power. This was, of course, the back-

---

[9] J. M. Hayden, *France and the Estates General of 1614* (Cambridge, 1974); R. Chartier and D. Richet (eds.), *Représentation et vouloir politiques: Autour des États-Généraux de 1614* (Paris, 1982); J. Cornette, 'Fiction et réalité de l'état baroque (1610–52)', H. Duccini, 'La Vision de l'état dans la littérature pamphlétaire au moment des États-Généraux de 1614', and id., 'Discours et réalité sociale: Le Révélateur des pamphlets', all in H. Méchoulan (ed.), *L'État baroque, 1610–52* (Paris, 1985).

ground from which Marillac and some other ministers emerged. Although such men might be generally sympathetic to many of the proposals emanating from the Estates General, there were some important differences. Where what we may characterize as the Estates tradition stressed the need to restore social harmony as the means to renewed political stability, the conciliar tradition placed the primary emphasis on bolstering royal authority. No doubt the years of weak government after 1610 had been particularly frustrating for these men, who might naturally link low-level disobedience and obstruction with the growing sense of political drift and the threat of renewed internal conflict. Close supervision of the financial and judicial officials in the style of Sully was part of their preferred approach, while the final suppression of the local estates in Guienne in 1622 suggests that the establishment of a standardized fiscal system remained a desirable objective in their minds. This does not mean, as Russell Major would have it, that there was a serious commitment to a long-term reform plan on these lines. The evidence points towards a much more pragmatic attitude, which sought to advance royal authority on a local and piecemeal basis. In the case of Guienne there were much better reasons for changing the tax system than existed elsewhere. Taxes were not levied by true provincial estates, but by some ten separate local assemblies, which constituted an administrative nightmare yet could only put up relatively weak resistance to the crown in a direct confrontation. As this example may suggest, the conciliar tradition was primarily directed towards pragmatic issues of everyday political management, usually related to the multifarious tensions between centre and periphery.[10]

It would be an absurd simplification to suggest that there were clearly distinct 'Estates' and 'conciliar' traditions, which stood in opposition to one another. Contemporaries would have been baffled by any such dichotomy, not least because of their intense dislike of anything which suggested deep-seated conflict. Yet provided we remember that it is an artificial construct, the distinction may alert us to the very real divergences beneath the surface. The superficial similarities between all proposals for reform were strong, so that various eclectic combinations were possible, yet beneath them there lurked profound differences which the political language of the day was not really able to articulate. Most crucially, was the crown a benign, relatively distant protector of local power structures, or a

---

[10] J. R. Major, *Representative Government in Early Modern France* (New Haven, Conn., 1980), 266–94, 484–5. The attack on the estates of Guienne was launched by Sully in 1603; the *élections* were withdrawn in 1611, but reintroduced definitively in 1621–2.

powerfully interventionist force acting in the name of some greater national good? The answer was bound to be some mixture of the two, yet individuals could occupy widely separated points on this spectrum. The same terms and concepts were being appropriated by men whose unstated assumptions were frequently incompatible. This question could be extended more widely, to ask if there was any agreement on the so-called 'fundamental laws', or on the point at which royal absolutism became tyranny and might possibly be resisted. Once a ministry embarked on any serious effort at reform these hidden rocks would represent a constant danger, even supposing the ministers could agree on which course they were steering (to borrow the ship-of-state metaphor). A further complication arose from the need to attract and retain the support of a king whose political education had been negligible, but whose personal opinions were both strong and somewhat incoherent.[11]

Grandiose schemes of whatever kind would in any case have been quite inappropriate to the political situation in which Richelieu found himself in the early years of his ministry. The cardinal's long and tortuous rise to power had taught him some hard lessons, shaped him into a skilful political operator, and left him with a complex set of obligations and liabilities towards others. Above all, he had to justify himself to a hostile and suspicious king without alienating his established patron, Marie de' Medici. It hardly needed Richelieu's acute political intelligence to see that major reform proposals were highly dangerous; all recent precedent suggested they would fail, gravely damaging the credit of any minister who was too closely associated with them. One may wonder how much he would have welcomed the publication in the *Mercure français* for 1624 of Olivares's plans for a reform of the Spanish monarchy, which seemed to imply the need for a French response—in many ways this was much more the position associated with his rival La Vieuville, who had sought to present himself as the much-needed general reformer.[12] As seen from Paris in the years between 1624 and 1627, both the international and the domestic horizons looked very threatening, so that it needed all Richelieu's skills to avoid being dragged down by the same difficulties which had defeated his predecessors and made way for his own ascent. Sheer survival had to be his first priority, with

---

[11] For an interesting discussion of the king's upbringing, see E. W. Marvick, *Louis XIII: The Making of a King* (New Haven, Conn., 1986).

[12] *Mercure Français*, 9 (1623–4); this is a separate 80-pp. section at the start of the vol., whose *privilège* was issued in Mar. 1624. For La Vieuville's ambitions, Bergin, *Rise of Richelieu*, 246–50.

the corollary that he should preserve as much liberty of action as possible by not setting himself specific goals.

Had Richelieu fallen at this stage, historians would probably describe his foreign policies as just another chapter in a long story of French débâcles. In this sphere he still displayed much of his old impetuousness, which comes out vividly in the *mémoire* he wrote for the king in May 1625. At the outset of Olivares's *annus mirabilis* his rival confidently announced 'il semble que toutes choses conspirent maintenant à rabattre l'orgueil de l'Espagne', going on to claim: 'maintenant tout tremble sous la terreur des armes de la France. Jusques icy tout a succédé à souhait.' Soon there was to be a rude awakening, as the cardinal's first anti-Spanish coalition collapsed, while the ambiguous treaty of Monzón only partially disguised the failure to win control of the Valtelline. This was far from being the 'sure and honourable' peace he had anticipated as the way to avoid simultaneous conflicts at home and abroad. The same *mémoire* does also reveal much greater realism on just this point, pointing out the dangers that the Huguenots will again exploit a foreign war for their own ends, possibly with Spanish help. Richelieu clearly sensed the dilemma this posed, although he could not articulate it with total clarity; because the Huguenots lay low when the king was strong, it was almost impossible to take advantage of their relative military weakness. Perhaps it was his experience of the feebleness and division of the rebels of 1620 which led him to write contemptuously of the 'impuissance' of the grandees, whom he regarded as the only other source of internal danger.[13]

The one clear gain made by the government in 1625 came from using the alliances with the English and the Dutch to compensate for its own lack of naval power; ships provided by the allies defeated Soubise off La Rochelle, allowing the royal forces to regain control of the islands of Ré and Oléron.[14] Richelieu's anxiety, as well as his adroitness, is demonstrated by the decision to summon an informal Assembly of Notables at the end of September, to consider whether French intervention in the Valtelline should continue. Autocratic rulers only resort to consultations of this kind when they want to cover themselves against possible failure, and this occasion was no exception. The same year saw the preparation of the *Règlement pour*

---

[13] Grillon i. 181–6. For the foreign policy difficulties, R. Pithon, 'Les Débuts difficiles du ministère de Richelieu et la crise du Valtelline, 1621–1626', *Revue d'histoire diplomatique*, 74 (1960), 298–322.

[14] C. de la Roncière, *Histoire de la marine française* (6 vols.; Paris, 1899–1932), iv. 466–76; G. Lacour-Gayet, *La Marine militaire de la France sous les règnes de Louis XIII et Louis XIV* (3 vols.; Paris, 1911), i. 66–70.

toutes les affaires du royaume, a lengthy plan for internal reforms found among Richelieu's papers. This has often been treated as a kind of blueprint for the whole ministry, testimony to the vision and determination of its presumed author. Such a view is hard to square with the actual contents of this curious document, whose main author may in fact have been Bishop Miron of Angers.[15]

The *Règlement* begins with a somewhat jejune proposal for reform of the royal council, which was never implemented. After its most substantial section, on reform in the church, it suggests severe action against duels, reform of the royal household, and the end of venal office-holding. The use of *comptants* to prevent proper accounting is to cease, pensions and salaries are to be reduced, the demesne to be resumed, and a *chambre de justice* held to check peculation by the financiers.[16] Hospitals are to be reformed, the able-bodied and idle poor punished, the number of colleges reduced and regulated, and sumptuary laws renewed. This collection of ill-assorted measures certainly includes practical steps to which Richelieu was already committed, such as the *chambre de justice* and the attack on duelling. As a programme for reforming the kingdom, however, it cannot be taken very seriously. The inadequacy of the section on venality of office, mostly lifted from the *cahiers* of the Estates General, is symptomatic of the general lack of conviction. The only genuinely impressive element is the discussion of ecclesiastical matters, which of course represents the one area in which the cardinal and many of his entourage had extensive personal experience. The emphasis on reform of the clergy was in fact shrewdly calculated to appeal both to a pious king and to those clerical circles from which Richelieu drew so much of his support and political strength. At a time when his foreign policy risked alienating the *dévots* there was much to be said for reminding them of his commitment to the central policies of the Tridentine reform. Had the document been published as a propaganda manifesto it would have been very well judged by many contemporaries, but its banal commonplaces are very far removed from what the ministry was actually to bring about.

One should in fairness add some other documents from the same period, in which there is mention of further topics, such as maritime policy and governorships, which figure prominently on the govern-

---

[15] Grillon, i. 248–69; for Miron's involvement J. Petit, *L'Assemblée des Notables de 1626–1627* (Paris, 1936), 37.

[16] *Comptants* were secret payments, increasingly used to pay interest far higher than the legal limits on royal borrowing. The *chambre de justice* was an *ad hoc* court set up at intervals to fine the financiers for the benefit of the treasury.

ment's future agenda.[17] Many of the individual items from this group of papers are undoubtedly shrewd and worthwhile. In particular, there is still a great deal to be said for Hauser's favourable evaluation of Richelieu's economic vision, despite its multiple failures to deliver the rewards for which he hoped.[18] In this area, one can see the merits of assembling groups of specialist advisers, like the Razilly clan for maritime and trading questions. Nevertheless, looking at the material as a whole, it does seem evident that the cardinal and his ministers tended to flounder when it came to formulating strategic plans. There is little sense of an order of priority, nor of practical means of implementation, while tradition and innovation jostle one another uncomfortably. Richelieu may have wanted to emulate the commercial success of the United Provinces; he was certainly not prepared to envisage the social changes which would have been the necessary corollary. In his desire to render the nobility flexible and useful, yet leave it possessed of its major privileges, he was already entangled in one of the basic contradictions of the ancien régime. The inconsistency and uncertainty of his ideas on venality of office would soon become plain, while it was surely misguided to try simultaneously to curb spending through sumptuary laws (however ineffective) and to encourage trade. Whether ministers in the seventeenth century—or indeed much later periods—can be expected to produce convincing schemes for national regeneration is of course a moot point. It is tempting to give Richelieu credit for the attempt alone, although John Elliott's comparison between his efforts and those of Olivares makes the latter look the more determined reformer of the two.[19]

There is, however, another way to look at the whole problem, which may make better sense of what was going on. As a supreme political operator, Richelieu can never have forgotten that his first objective was simply to stay in power. The best way of all to achieve this would have been brilliant successes from his first policy initiatives; he may well have expected these, and was certainly claiming them in some of the early papers he wrote for the king. By the summer of 1626 the hollowness of such claims was becoming uncomfortably evident; his foreign policy initiatives were being blocked, with an unsatisfactory settlement in the Valtelline, the defeat of the Danes, and the collapse of relations with England. His

---

[17] Grillon, i. 242–7, 303–13, 321–38, 508–15, 524–7, 531, 569–70, 576–80. For maritime policy see also Lacour-Gayet, *Marine militaire*, i. 13–61.

[18] H. Hauser, *La Pensée et l'action économiques du cardinal de Richelieu* (Paris, 1944).

[19] J. H. Elliott, *Richelieu and Olivares* (Cambridge, 1984), 60–85.

handling of Protestant rebels had brought a further burst of criticism from many *dévots*, so that at this point the name 'cardinal de La Rochelle' had a very different sense from the one it would soon acquire. Richelieu's admirers have rightly stressed his sense of timing and capacity for patience, which can be illustrated by various quotations from the state papers of this period. He may well have sensed that soon enough there would be better opportunities; meanwhile he made energetic efforts to displace any blame on to others. Nevertheless, his position was becoming uncomfortably exposed, and he needed to watch his flank from three crucial directions. First and foremost there was Louis XIII himself; secondly, the wider royal family and the court; thirdly, public opinion, primarily among the crucial political élite represented by the high *robe* families of Paris.

Much recent scholarship, including the important biographies by Pierre Chevallier and Lloyd Moote, has shown that Louis XIII was far from being the feeble dependent creature of myth.[20] Yet it is still difficult to break away properly from the easy assumption that Richelieu was the real maker of policy, manipulating the king into compliance even against his better judgement. There were times when the minister was determined to secure certain outcomes, setting up memoranda and discussions to this end. Any reasonably astute practitioner of the political arts, however, knows that such techniques should be reserved for crucial occasions, not turned into a dangerously overbearing routine. How did Richelieu transform the king's attitude to him so rapidly, before the triumphs of 1628–31 had shown that he could deliver much of what he promised? The answer is surely that he involved Louis deeply in the business of government, laying a great range of possible policies before him, explaining the difficulties and contradictions, and making the king feel that he was in control. In many respects Richelieu needed to repeat the highly successful operation he had carried out to secure Marie de' Medici's trust, and no doubt he had once again learnt much from earlier experience.

In some ways we might see the 'duumvirate' as a highly developed tutorial relationship, but there were additional benefits for the cardinal. If the king took decisions after having the pros and cons laid out for him, then he shared the responsibility for failure; furthermore, opposition to policies established in this way was direct opposition to the monarch himself. The preparation of elaborate plans and discussions for action on many fronts created an im-

---

[20] P. Chevallier, *Louis XIII roi cornélien* (Paris, 1979); A. L. Moote, *Louis XIII, the Just* (Berkeley, Calif., 1989).

pression of ministerial energy and competence, which was probably better not disturbed by too many hasty attempts to put them into practice. Richelieu had every reason to feel deeply satisfied with the king's famous response to his offer of resignation in June 1626: 'Tout, grâce à Dieu, y a bien succédé depuis que vous y êtes: j'ai toute confiance en vous, et il est vrai que je n'ai jamais trouvé personne qui me servît à mon gré comme vous. C'est ce qui me fait désirer et vous prier de ne point vous retirer, car mes affaires iraient mal.'[21] Louis plainly did not think the first stage of the ministry a failure, despite the various set-backs it had witnessed. All such judgements are relative, and one must pay tribute to the skill with which Richelieu had made the best of several awkward situations; even more, perhaps, to the climate he had created around the king, which had as much to do with stage-management as with solid achievements.

There is a very perceptible difference between the sporadic and uncertain papers relating to domestic reform, and the massive series of documents covering the 'Chalais conspiracy' of 1626.[22] Once Richelieu was faced with a direct threat to his position he responded with a quite different level of intensity. How far the frenetic court politics of that year relate to serious conspiracies, rather than to some foolish talk among the intimates of Gaston and the queen, coupled with predictable hostility to the minister, remains almost impossible to judge. What can be said is that Richelieu exploited the situation brilliantly to place himself and Louis side by side, as the designated victims of treachery and as its investigators. Both men did sometimes show a tendency to paranoid fears on this count, which were liable to dovetail together; there may have been a shared need for enemies who would act as a focus for political action. On the broader front, it is striking that the notorious three great aims of the ministry, as expressed in the *Testament politique*, all involved gaining supremacy over enemies who were to be put down. The Chalais affair also gave the opportunity to restructure the ministry, with the disgrace of the chancellor d'Aligre allowing Marillac to be moved from the *surintendance des finances*, where he had performed unimpressively, notably over the virtually abortive *chambre de justice* of 1624, to the more suitable post of *garde des sceaux*.[23] A much greater gain was the

---

[21] Grillon, i. 353–4, Louis XIII to Richelieu, 9 June 1626.

[22] For the most important, Grillon, i. 382–402, 414–23, 449–50, 462–4, 477–9, 533–40.

[23] R. J. Bonney, *The King's Debts: Finance and Politics in France 1589–1661* (Oxford, 1981), 115–21, discusses Marillac's inadequacies as *surintendant*. As *garde des sceaux* (effectively chancellor) he was running those areas of the conciliar and judicial system in which he was most experienced and capable.

promotion of the clear-sighted d'Effiat as the new *surintendant*; his
performance was to be one of the great hidden factors behind the
successes of the next few years.[24] Although many of these men may
have declared themselves to be *créatures* of Richelieu, he never
committed the unpardonable crime of treating them as if they were
his ministers rather than those of the king; in addition he left them
extensive freedom of action in their own domains. This was at once
effective and politically adroit, for in the last resort blame for failure
could be attached to an individual, not to the ministry as a whole.[25]

One important advantage of keeping a multiplicity of reforming ideas in play was the appeal this held for the larger group of
politically aware individuals who staffed the central institutions of
the monarchy. *Conseillers d'état, maîtres des requêtes, parlementaires,*
and others could all find something with which to sympathize, as
many of them had with the Estates General. Talk of rationalizing
office-holding was not necessarily unwelcome to these men, who
might well gain from the limited reforms which were all that could
realistically be expected. It was for the eyes and ears of this group,
above all, that the major propaganda campaigns of the ministry
were intended. Richelieu's grasp of the importance of the press, the
pulpit, the theatre, and the salons as agencies of power may not
precisely count as a reform, but it was one of the most original
and successful features of his government.[26] Leading figures of the
Parisian *robe* were also involved through their participation in the
Assemblies of Notables, and through many less formal consultations
with ministers. The formation of what Pierre Goubert has called 'la
vision des grands commis', with its trenchant espousal of royal and
conciliar authority as the way to eliminate disorder in the state,
surely has its roots here.[27]

It would be harsh to suggest that the whole business was nothing
but window-dressing, and indeed if we see politics as process then it
all had plenty of meaning. This is very clear with the Assembly of
Notables summoned for the end of 1626. This was simultaneously a
piece of political theatre, a device to gain time and to outwit possible
opposition, and the springboard for some quite serious proposals. At
the first level it purported to celebrate the unity of the royal family,
notably with the integration of the newly married Gaston d'Orléans

---

[24] Ibid. 140–6, for the increase in revenue under d'Effiat.
[25] O. A. Ranum, *Richelieu and the Councillors of Louis XIII* (Oxford, 1963); unfortunately
this excellent study concentrates on the period after 1635.
[26] Several aspects of these policies are explored in Ch. 7 below, by Caldicott.
[27] P. Goubert, *L'Ancien Régime*, ii. *Les Pouvoirs* (Paris, 1973), 12–14, 49–55; R. J. Bonney,
Political Change in France under Richelieu and Mazarin, 1624–1661 (Oxford, 1978), 112–34.

(now 18) into the political world. At the second, Richelieu was again giving the impression of purposeful activity, yet in a form which minimized risk. A relatively modest slate of reforms was put before the hand-picked assembly, whose debates largely followed an agenda pre-set by the government. Acceptance of the proposals would be a notable confirmation of the cardinal's ascendancy; rejection, or the kind of emasculation which was actually employed, was more evidence of the unwillingness of his opponents to come to the aid of the crown. Such a manœuvre was essentially possible because there was no immediate crisis to give the assembly real leverage, and because its selected membership represented several different interest groups. When we look at the actual reforms proposed we find two which might offer significant assistance to the royal finances: the redemption of the demesne, and the creation of a standing army of some 20,000 men directly supported by the provinces. Even in combination they do not look like a satisfactory answer to the problems explained by d'Effiat in his speech on the financial situation, but the latter in particular might have been capable of further development. Any hope of a French equivalent of Olivares's Union of Arms was however killed by the way the Assembly watered down this proposal, as it did that for the demesne. The deputies were more amenable on some other points, notably the demolition of fortresses and the plans for commerce and the fleet.[28]

How far all this concerned Richelieu it is hard to judge; his numerous letters and papers from the first months of 1627 pay virtually no attention to the Assembly, leaving one to suspect that he had quickly written it off as an empty parade. On this evidence his own mind was full of the threat from England and the Huguenots, which the behaviour of the royal agents in the vicinity of La Rochelle was doing a great deal to exacerbate. It is difficult to judge the extent to which this was a deliberate policy; it would soon provide a great challenge which simultaneously offered a way out of the long-standing impasse represented by the Huguenots, lucidly identified by the cardinal in 1625.[29] Dealing with an emergency of this kind would in many ways pose easier problems, at the intellectual level, than the search for ways to reform the kingdom. By April 1628 he had certainly made up his mind, for after summarizing the various difficulties he advised the king:

[28] Petit, *L'Assemblée des Notables, passim.*

[29] Grillon, i. 226–33, 'Discours tendant à voir si, ayant la guerre avec l'Espagne en Italie, il faut la faire aussy au-dedans du royaulme', 25 Nov. 1625. For the broader context, D. Parker, *La Rochelle and the French Monarchy* (London, 1980).

Que toutes ces choses faisoient voir clairement que la France n'avoit peu
d'affaires, que sa maladie estoit de celles que les médecins appellent
compliquées, dont la guérison est d'autant plus difficile que ce qui est bon à
un genre de mal est préjudiciable à l'autre.

Que ce qui estoit le plus fascheux estoit la gangrène qui paroissoit
extérieurement venoit d'une cause interne, assez cogneue, mais à laquelle on
ne pouvoit toucher.

Que le vray remède à tous ces maux estoit la prise de la Rochelle. Si
on venoit à bout de ceste place promptement, les ennemis découverts
déposeroient, non leur mauvaise volonté, mais leur hostilité; les secrets
applaudiroient aux victoires du Roy, qu'ils eussent bien désiré troubler, et
nous aurions la paix partout si nous voulions.[30]

It may well have been with war against the Huguenots in mind
that Richelieu had pushed ahead so hard with the maritime programme, even when it meant offending such a powerful figure as
Montmorency. He knew that naval capacity would be crucial in the
forthcoming conflict, and was probably right to think that only his
own direct involvement would secure results. Needless to say,
the prospect of enhancing his own direct power must also have
been attractive, accompanied as it was by the governorships of Le
Havre and Brouage. His nomination in 1626 as 'grand-maître et
surintendant-général du commerce et de la navigation', with the
buying out of the rival admiralty jurisdictions, represented a serious
attempt to rationalize and revitalize royal administration in this field.
Naval expenditure rose sharply, from some 830,000 *livres* in 1624 to
around 1.5 million in the following years, then 4.6 million in 1628,
before settling down at over 2 million a year. France may not have
become a major naval power overnight, but her capacities were
greatly increased.[31] If the projects for new companies and trading
ventures—which appear to have been partly stimulated by the
example of the Spanish *almirantazgo*—were largely stillborn, this did
not indicate any loss of interest by Richelieu. It is doubtful whether
any state policies could have changed the face of French trade
quickly, while the later fate of Colbert's companies (and of the
almirantazgo) suggests that there were basic faults in the model being
applied.[32]

Alongside that of the Huguenots, another problem which no

[30] Grillon, iii. 203–4, 'Advis que le Cardinal donna au Roy à son retour de Paris, à La
Rochelle', *c*.20 Apr. 1628.

[31] L. A. Boiteux, *Richelieu 'grand maître de la navigation et de la commerce de France'* (Paris,
1955); Petit, *L'Assemblée des Notables*, 192.

[32] For the *almirantazgo* and its influence on Richelieu, Elliott, *Richelieu and Olivares*, 81,
and id., *The Count-Duke of Olivares: The Statesman in an Age of Decline* (New Haven, Conn.,
1986), 161–2.

ministry could avoid, however little it cared for wider reforms, was that posed by venal office-holding. Although there were a few pamphleteers in 1614–15 (whose motives it might be kinder not to question) who defended the sale of office on practical grounds, even they criticized its abuses, while more generally it was the subject of widespread execration. At the Estates General a third estate dominated by office-holders had defended the status quo adroitly, by tacking unacceptable conditions on to every proposal for change.[33] Their particular concern was to defend the *paulette* or *droit annuel*, the great innovation of 1604 which much enhanced their effective property rights in their positions. In the knowledge that a public defence of the system was impossible, the officials themselves advocated the abolition of the *paulette*, while rendering this impossible by tacking on demands for reductions in pensions and the *taille*. One set of semi-mythical arguments was thus employed to counter another, frustrating any attempt to discuss the real issues. In practice the *paulette* had proved a distinct political and fiscal success for the crown, yet the ministers themselves showed little enthusiasm for it after 1610. Debates about venal office tended to become confused by the double issue of the *paulette* in particular and venality more generally; only the most perspicacious saw that there was virtually no advantage in abolishing the first unless the latter was greatly reduced. At the Rouen Assembly of Notables in 1617–18 it seems to have been Louis XIII himself who decided that the *paulette* should not be renewed, despite the lack of any realistic plan to follow this up by widespread resumption or repurchase of offices.[34] During the revolt of 1620 Richelieu sought to exploit the resulting discontent by communicating with the parlements; Luynes reacted by hastily promising to restore the *paulette*, even if this was on harsh fiscal terms which were resisted until a much more favourable deal for the officials was reached in 1621.[35]

If one leaves questions of morality aside, it is hard to see that Louis XIII had any more to gain from trying to get rid of venal office-holding than he did from that other early policy decision to support the emperor against the Bohemian rebels. The whole issue of office-holding does in truth need revaluation in its wider context, for Mousnier's classic study is far from exhaustive. Did the sale of office really have the disastrous effects its opponents claimed, distorting French society and the national economy? It is easy to see why

[33] See n. 7 above; Duccini, 'Discours et réalité sociale', 388–405, is particularly concerned with these questions. Also Roland Mousnier, *La Vénalité des offices sous Henri IV et Louis XIII* (2nd edn.; Paris 1971), 599–600, 609–19.
[34] Mousnier, *Vénalité*, 633–6.   [35] Ibid. 636–7.

contemporaries reasoned in this way, much harder to know whether historians should accept their impressionistic judgements. Richelieu's own views on the subject are hard to read accurately; the early schemes to abolish venality plainly gave way at some point to the disabused realism of the *Testament politique*, but this change is impossible to date. In the 1625 reform plan what seems to be envisaged is that the officials will be allowed one sale or inheritance of their posts, free of any further payments to the crown, but that they will revert to the crown at the second vacancy. It is also suggested that the number of offices should be reduced to that of 1574; both projects closely echo the *cahiers* of the Estates General. No formal proposals to abolish either venality or the *paulette* were brought before the Notables in 1626–7, nor do they appear in the Code Michaud. A short unattributed note among Richelieu's papers relating to the Notables might suggest that second thoughts were already gaining ground. 'Il faudrait en outre modérer par le temps et par la mort des officiers le grand nombre d'offices où tout le monde emploie son bien et son argent, mais cette condition comme la suivante sont à considérer en temps et lieu et ne semblent maintenant de saison.'[36]

This was not the only view, however, for the *Avis à l'Assemblée de Messieurs les Notables*, a pamphlet which clearly had government backing (it was reprinted in the *Mercure*), included much more radical suggestions. After suggesting of the people that 'Cinq choses l'oppriment grandement, les Tailles, les Logements des gens de guerre, le Sel, les Aydes, et la mangerie des Officiers', the author went on to propose that the financial officials should be suppressed, being compensated by the payment of *rentes* on those sums they could demonstrate they had paid to the king. As for the judicial officials,

Il y a la dispense de quarante jours qui rend les Officiers comme hereditaires, la venalité qui les met en commerce, et le gain ordinaire est toleré qui les encherit. Il seroit à desirer qu'on peust guerir ces trois maladies tout d'un coup, mais il est bien mal aisé: tant de gens et si puissans dans l'Estat y sont interessez, que je craindrois que le remede ne fust pire que le mal. Il faut donc y aller pied à pied, et insensiblement. . . . La valeur excessive des Offices est le fondement de ce desordre. Il y en a pour cent millions d'or et plus en France: le seul moyen qu'on a de les frapper, c'est d'en oster les epices et les emoluments: d'une pierre vous frapperez deux coups: vous ferez ramender les Offices, et soulagerez grandement le peuple, qui n'a pas tant d'interest à la venalité ou à la paulette, comme à l'oppression qu'il sent, à cause des exactions de plusieurs Ministres de Iustice.

[36] Petit, *L'Assemblée des Notables*, 90 n. 75.

By this means there would be no more lawsuits within ten years, because the judges would have no motive to prolong them. Two important caveats were added, however, which rather undercut much of what had gone before. These reservations were so serious that they raise questions about the author's real intentions, perhaps suggesting that yet again the rhetorical attack on sale of office concealed an intention to preserve the status quo in reality. Firstly, it was crucial not to make all the officials discontented, unless at the same time great relief was given to the people. Secondly, there was no point in attacking hereditary rights in office without abolishing venality itself.[37]

These warnings were not sufficient to prevent a subsequent threat to remove the *paulette* in 1629–30, which was rather strangely combined with the simultaneous attempt to impose *élections* in several *pays d'états*; at this point the government's policy looks simply incoherent.[38] It was certainly very ill-advised, uniting a motley group of vested interests and factious nobles in a set of revolts which prefigured some very dangerous aspects of the Fronde. While one can suppose that the ultimate aim was quite cynical, to extract the maximum amount in what was effectively ransom money, this falls well short of accounting adequately for the course of events. The timing was dictated by the routine expiry of the *droit annuel*, granted for nine years at a time, which was always liable to be the occasion for dispute. It is quite conceivable that the ministers were so influenced by the general current of opinion that they felt unable simply to renew what they thought of as an abuse; only when they had reminded themselves of the dangers of not doing so would they yield to force of circumstance. This was to be the last occasion during the ministry when the office-holders were seriously threatened in this way, however, after a period during which they had experienced virtually constant uncertainty. It is not easy to square the brief reference in Richelieu's advice to the king, showing that he personally wished at the beginning of 1629 for the non-renewal of the *paulette* a year later (and 'abaisser et modérer les compagnies, qui, par une prétendue souveraineté, s'opposent tous les jours au bien du royaume'), with the lack of evidence from his correspondence for any specific interest in the topic during the year.[39]

In comparison with venality of office, some of the other elements

[37] *Mercure français*, 12 (1626–7), 775, 781–2, 787–9.

[38] Mousnier, *Vénalité*, 656–61.

[39] Grillon, iv. 25, 'Advis donné au Roy après la prise de La Rochelle pour le bien de ses affaires', 13 Jan. 1629. It would have been hard for any minister to disregard the contribution which the *parties casuelles* made to the royal revenues, as shown in Ch. 4 by Bonney, below.

in the various reform programmes were straightforward. The imposition of Tridentine discipline on the Catholic Church, massive task though it was, could begin with attacks on recognized abuses. Administrative and judicial problems might in theory be resolved by better definition of the remit of various bodies, and revision of the rules they applied. Hospitals, universities, communications, and trade also raised practical problems, so that it was at least plausible to hope that closer enforcement of regulations would improve the situation. The most difficult of the other areas were the nobles and the finances. Defining the membership of the nobility, and giving its members a suitable role in the state, exercised many minds without producing much in the way of answers. Reserved positions in the courts and military commands were two standard responses whose inadequacy was fairly obvious. Richelieu himself would show a consistent interest in encouraging them to participate in trade, with little positive result. The dejected conclusion to the relevant chapter in the *Testament politique* sums up a long and frustrating experience: 'On pourroit mettre en avant beaucoup d'autres choses pour le soulagement de la noblesse. Mais j'en supprime tous les pensées, après avoir considéré qu'ainsi qu'il seroit fort aisé de les écrire, il seroit fort difficile et peut-être impossible de les pratiquer.'[40] This seems a fair comment on the enormous literature concerning the supposed decadence of the French nobility produced since the 1560s. As with venality, commentators found it virtually impossible to get beyond the myths—in this case the Frankish conquest, genetic superiority, and military prowess—to a realistic analysis of the situation. Richelieu himself subscribed to much of this ideology, as emerges from the lengthy attempts by his propagandists to demonstrate the ancient lineages of his forbears. He also devoted much effort to ensuring that his family should join those of the grandees, yet there are suggestions in his policies and in the proposals put to the Notables of a wish to use the lesser nobility as a kind of counter-balance. By giving them positions in the council and in the bureaucracy, above all by using his military patronage to enlist them in his armies, the king could encourage their personal loyalty to the crown at the expense of the *grands* and their networks of *fidélités*.[41]

---

[40] *Test. pol.* 223.

[41] For this debate, see A. Devyver, *Le Sang épuré: Les Préjugés de race chez les gentilshommes français de l'Ancien Régime* (Brussels, 1973), esp. 56–154, 184–216; D. Bitton, *The French Nobility in Crisis, 1560–1640* (Stanford, Calif., 1970); A. Jouanna, *L'Idée de race en France au 16ᵉ siècle et au début du 17ᵉ siècle* (2 vols.; Montpellier 1981); id., *Ordre social: Mythes et hiérarchies dans la France du 16ᵉ siècle* (Paris, 1977); id., *Le Devoir de révolte: La Noblesse française et la gestation de l'état moderne, 1559–1661* (Paris, 1989), esp. 281–362. The chs. by

Ideas about the finances were hardly more promising than those about the nobles, mostly seeming to inhabit an ideal world, where the wildest optimism reigned. One is led to wonder how many of those involved could think quantitatively, in any meaningful sense. It was hardly to be expected, of course, that the potential contributors would volunteer new ideas to their own disadvantage, but government representatives often seemed to do little better. The Estates General had wanted the *taille* reduced to the level of 1576, while Richelieu and his advisers made quite implausible claims to the Notables about the beneficial results of redeeming alienated royal demesne, in which they cannot have had much faith themselves. These proposals are characteristic of many other reforms sponsored by the cardinal, in that they owed more to political expediency than to any long-term commitment. It is hard to resist the conclusion that everyone preferred not to look too hard at some unpalatable truths, although most of the figures prepared for the Notables, presumably by the exceptionally able *surintendant* d'Effiat, were all too gloomily accurate.[42] As will be discussed later, at some time Richelieu did formulate a much more ambitious (and probably impractical) plan to raise 42 million a year from an extended *gabelle* and a 5 per cent sales tax, but it seems almost certain that this scheme dates from the very end of the ministry.[43]

Over the four years immediately following the Assembly of Notables, with the siege of La Rochelle, the destruction of Huguenot military power, and the Mantuan war, Richelieu would enjoy the greatest sequence of triumphs of his whole ministry. He was also threatened with disaster, because the central support of his original political system was lost with his alienation from Marie de' Medici. This brought out the tensions within the ministry, and ever since Pagès's famous article the conflict which culminated in the Day of Dupes has been interpreted in rather over-simplified terms as a struggle between a peace party and a war party, between reform at home and glory abroad.[44] More recently Russell Major has intensified these claims, going so far as to describe the cardinal as an 'evil genius' who took the wrong turning. This argument rests on dubious claims that Marillac was personally responsible for an authoritarian

---

Brockliss and Parrott (below, Chs. 8 and 5) lay emphasis, respectively, on Richelieu's sustained interest in the political health of the lesser nobility, and the continued links between lesser nobles and grandees.

[42] *Mercure Français*, 12 (1626–7), 790–813.
[43] See Ch. 4 below, by Bonney.
[44] G. Pagès, 'Autour du "grand orage": Richelieu et Marillac, deux politiques', *Revue historique*, 179 (1937), 63–97.

style of domestic reform, which Richelieu rejected in order to pursue his foreign ambitions.[45] The merits of an outright assault on local rights and privileges seem less than obvious in any case, even if one believes the government was embarking on such policies before 1630 with a definite programme in mind. The rather piecemeal assault on the privileges of both officials and estates in 1629–30 is very hard to unravel, partly because Richelieu himself gave so little evidence of interest in it, but contemporaries must have been right to see the hand of the model *créature* d'Effiat as pre-eminent in these policies. It was not until two years after the Day of Dupes that Languedoc would finally be allowed to retain its traditional forms of government, at a substantial price. It is certainly hard to believe that the effective destruction of the local estates would have led to some kind of national renewal; they only operated to any effect in a small proportion of the country, and the cost to the crown in lost revenue was relatively modest.[46]

The area in which Marillac clearly took direct responsibility was the massive reforming ordinance irreverently nicknamed the Code Michaud, which was quite explicitly stated in its preamble to be the government's response to the various consultations dating back to 1614. Contemporary accounts make it clear, however, that he was the co-ordinator rather than the sole author, with for example Richelieu himself supervising the drafting of the articles dealing with maritime affairs.[47] The Code was criticized by the parlement of Paris on numerous grounds of detail, but above all because of the way in which it sought to reinforce conciliar authority (the real reasons for opposition may have had more to do with the prospect of tighter enforcement of the rules governing office-holding). The later record of the government does not suggest any reluctance to use conciliar power, any more than in deploying the *maîtres des requêtes* in the provinces. There is in fact a real problem over Richelieu's attitude to the Code Michaud, which most historians have passed over in silence, busy describing the campaigns of 1629 and the disputes they

---

[45] Major, *Representative Government*, 452, 571–82, 619–21. I can see nothing in any of the material associated with Marillac to suggest that he had viable and coherent plans for internal reform, which could somehow have altered the course of French history. Apart from his hostility to the *pays d'états*, his views are those of a conventional *dévot*, looking to reinforce a static social and political order. D. A. Bailey, 'The Family and Early Career of Michel de Marillac (1560–1632)', in M. P. Holt (ed.), *Society and Institutions in Early Modern France* (Athens, Ga., 1991), 170–89, reiterates Major's claims without providing any relevant evidence.

[46] For a more extended discussion, R. Briggs, *Communities of Belief: Cultural and Social Tensions in Early Modern France* (Oxford, 1989), 117–31.

[47] E. Everat, *Michel de Marillac* (Riom, 1894), 56–8, and L. Desjonquères, *Le Garde des sceaux Michel de Marillac et son œuvre législative* (Paris, 1908), 95.

fostered within the government. Why did the cardinal apparently lose interest so fast after the *lit de justice* of 15 January, so that his lack of support effectively encouraged the opposition to measures he clearly supported in principle?

Despite the assertions in his *Mémoires*, it seems highly probable that it was Richelieu rather than Marillac who insisted on trying to force the reforms through the parlement of Paris by the direct use of royal power, a high-risk tactic which was always likely to misfire.[48] At the extreme one could even suppose that this was a trap designed to discredit the *garde des sceaux*, who carried the blame for the ensuing tussle with the *parlementaires*. A more plausible interpretation is that the *lit de justice* was indeed Richelieu's own blunder, but one forced on him by the need to start the Italian campaign without delay. Whereas he quickly recognized that it would be best not to force the issue further, and was prepared to let the opposition have its head for the moment, Marillac obstinately kept pressing for a conclusion at a time when the government's main attention had to be directed elsewhere. The acting *premier président* of the parlement, Le Jay, told Richelieu the obvious truth: 'telles ordonnances hors de saison font des révolutions dans les esprits et donnent des fascheries et des mescontentemens grands; et cela joint à n^re appréhension de la rupture du droit annuel, qui est proche, mettant les conditions de toute personne dans l'incertain: tout meslé ensemble rend les esprits chagrins et faschés'.[49] Marillac's own letters on the question in 1629, in contrast, suggest real political obtuseness, which must have infuriated the cardinal.[50] The latter was always very skilful in making others carry the blame for failure, and the growing divisions over major policy options gave him particular incentives in this case.

There is clearly a basic truth in the picture given by Pagès, in the sense that the dispute between Richelieu and Marillac centred on the potential domestic consequences of an aggressive foreign policy. Yet his article does tend to over-simplification, even anachronism. Marillac's recorded statements suggest that he was less concerned with lost prospects of reform than he was terrified by the threat of massive internal disorder in the event of outright war with Spain.[51] Again it is easy to see how this exasperated Richelieu, for the logic of

---

[48] Everat, *Marillac*, 156–67, for an intelligent account of this complex affair, and pp. 68–89 for a summary of the Code; a shorter English summary in Major, *Representative Government*, 512–15. The text is in Isambert xv. 223–342.

[49] Grillon, iv. 318, Le Jay to Richelieu, 20 May 1629.

[50] Ibid. iv. 91–2, 215, Marillac to Richelieu, 8 Feb. and 17 Apr. 1629.

[51] Ibid. v. 76–7, 232–4, 391–3, 397–8, 405–7, 418–9, 427–34.

this position would oblige France to throw in her hand whenever a
serious confrontation loomed. Given that Louis XIII plainly had no
such intention, Marillac's querulous objections sound more like
simple fright than a viable political position. Nor should we read
Richelieu's famous memorandum inviting the king to choose between peace and war without close regard to its context. When he
laid out the consequences of keeping Pinerolo for the king he certainly set the choice up to ensure the outcome he wanted. His
comments on the domestic consequences were part of a 'worst case'
scenario, which might arise if Olivares reacted by declaring a general
war. It was an astute move to anticipate the criticisms which were to
be expected from Marillac and his supporters, for if the king had
already decided against them when reading the memorandum, they
would have little effect on him at the council.[52]

Some of the gloomy predictions may have come true after 1635; in
the intervening years, however, France had succeeded in retaining
her gains without a war, and it took a long sequence of further acts
of aggression to drive Spain to the point where Olivares reluctantly
decided to force one. The piecemeal nature of these events does
not suggest any grand plan, merely a remorseless logic of events
which might have carried any ministry along. Throughout this
period Richelieu plainly aimed to achieve his foreign policy objectives without a major war, and he came within a hair's breadth
of success. The crucial event was the defeat of his German and
Swedish allies at Nördlingen, surely the most disastrous battle of
the century for the peoples of continental Europe. The events of 5
and 6 September 1634 prolonged the conflicts in Germany, the
Netherlands, and northern Italy by more than a decade, and insti-
gated a twenty-four-year war between France and Spain. Ironically it
was the victors at Nördlingen who ultimately came off worst; it was a
battle which Spain in particular would have done well to lose, in
view of the way Olivares reacted by taking most of the wrong
options.[53]

During the years before 1635 the government can hardly be said to
have neglected domestic affairs entirely. D'Effiat's pragmatic management of the finances seems to have been more effective than most
of the loudly trumpeted plans of previous years, while in the early
1630s there was a major attempt to carry through the plans to
demolish redundant fortresses. When opportunities presented them-

---

[52] Ibid. v. 208–13, Richelieu to Louis XIII, 13 Apr. 1630.
[53] For a major revaluation of foreign policy in this period, see D. A. Parrott, 'The Causes of
the Franco-Spanish War of 1635–59', in J. Black (ed.), *The Origins of War in Early Modern
Europe* (Edinburgh, 1987), 72–112.

selves, the ministers reshaped the relationships between the crown and the *pays d'états* in common-sense ways which took account of widely differing local circumstances.[54] A mixture of coercion and compromise saw a significant increase in tax revenues from these provinces without provoking any serious political trouble after 1632; all the major popular revolts were in the *pays d'élections*. The year 1634 would see a striking range of initiatives, some happier than others. They included a major session of the *Grands Jours* at Poitiers, a widespread investigation of false nobles, an important edict on the *taille*, and Bullion's maladroit attempt to free the taxes from many of the payments previously made to the officials.[55] Many of the individual reforms envisaged in the Code Michaud were pursued, although outright successes were predictably rare.[56] As subsequent chapters in this book demonstrate, Richelieu sponsored a wide range of initiatives in domestic affairs down to his death.

Historians need to make a conscious effort to situate Richelieu in his own times, and not to envisage him in anachronistic ways. A reading of his papers leaves no doubt about his own sense of priorities, which reflected the experience of a man who had grown up during the last turmoil of the civil wars and was acutely aware of the fragility of the French state. To him, the dangers came from enemies who sought to prolong that fragility and weakness for their own ends. Spain and other foreign powers, the Huguenots, factious grandees—these were indeed his priorities, as tradition rather boringly tells us. Until they were overcome he saw little realistic prospect of finding suitable medicines for more complex and controversial maladies, and was well aware of the danger that violent prescriptions might kill the patient.[57] Yet he certainly did not repudiate the reforming traditions of his age; it was typical of a master politician of his type to use them for his own purposes, without ever allowing them to stand in the way of a ruthless quest for power, for both himself and his royal master. Historians are

---

[54] For some examples, see W. H. Beik, *Absolutism and Society in Seventeenth-Century France* (Cambridge, 1985), 130–3, 198–202; D. Hickey, *The Coming of French Absolutism: The Struggle for Tax Reform in the Province of Dauphiné* (Toronto, 1986), 161–78; and S. Kettering, *Judicial Politics and Urban Revolt in Seventeenth-Century France* (Princeton, NJ, 1978), 51–80.

[55] H. Imbert, *Les Grands Jours de Poitou: Registres criminels (1531, 1567, 1579, 1634)* (Niort, 1878), and *Mercure Français*, 20 (1634–5), 812–48; P. Deyon, 'A propos des rapports entre la noblesse française et la monarchie absolue pendant la première moitié du XVIIᵉ siècle', *Revue historique*, 221 (1964), 341–56; Bonney, *King's Debts*, 165–8; J. B. Collins, *Fiscal Limits of Absolutism: Direct Taxation in Early Seventeenth-Century France* (Berkeley, Calif., 1988), 98–107.

[56] For the attempts to continue with the Code, Everat, *Marillac*, 187–8.

[57] This last conceit was something of a commonplace; for examples see F. E. Sutcliffe, *Guez de Balzac et son temps: Littérature et politique* (Paris, 1959), 211.

curiously prone to regard the desire for power, one of the most basic of human appetites, as if it were a grave failing in a statesman. Such covert moralism can only diminish real understanding; as the exponents of *raison d'état* would stress, one has to deal with the world as it is, and recognize that power is the driving force of politics. The flexible realism which emerged as the leitmotif of Richelieu's domestic policies declared itself equally strongly in foreign policy, almost always the primary focus of his personal attention. It would be hard to improve on the reply to Marillac in May 1630, in which Richelieu describes war as 'un des fléaux dont il plaist à Dieu affliger les hommes', but points out that 'qui feroit la paix à des conditions honteuses ne la conserveroit pas longtemps'.[58] France could not operate by different rules to the other major states, and on this point at least Richelieu was a true Machiavellian. This is not to claim any direct influence of ideology on policy; Richelieu would almost certainly have behaved in exactly the same way if Machiavelli had never written, perhaps with less scruples, although he might have defended himself rather differently. Nor should we assume that he was as cynical as analysis of his policies often makes him seem. Historical judgement on such issues is bound to be highly subjective, but the evidence suggests that he was driven on as much by a sense of mission as by personal ambition, and that his interest in reform was perfectly genuine.

While there is a natural tendency to follow the cardinal's own view that foreign war and domestic reform were incompatible, this masks the ultimate paradox of the ministry. The conscious plans for reform were well-intentioned but jejune, undermined by a mixture of analytical weakness and archaism. Their reliance on argument by analogy is revealing, for it was precisely in this area that the new style of *raison d'état* broke most sharply with conventional wisdom, in an attempt to justify policies which seemed immoral to many contemporaries.[59] The really decisive changes, which gave the ancien régime monarchy its distinctive shape, were the creations of war. It was the desperate pressures of the conflict with Spain which forced a series of improvisations, justified only by necessity, which brought the crown into confrontation with many of the vested interests it would normally have respected. Nothing could exemplify this better than the domestic innovation for which Richelieu is now best remembered, the transformation of the intendants to form the basis

---

[58] Grillon, v. 260–1, 'Advis du cardinal de Richelieu en suite de celuy de la Reyne mère et du garde des sceaux de Marillac', mid-May 1630.
[59] Thuau, *Raison d'état*, 148–9.

of a new technique of government. Little as he may have had to do with this virtually unplanned development, it followed naturally from his extreme pragmatism, with its instinct for turning all available materials to advantage. The historical development of the French monarchy had already closed off many other possible routes to modernization, and in its own terms this expedient provided a brilliantly creative answer to the linked problems of venal office, royal finance, and local disorder. Although war may have involved great suffering and terrible risks, the morally inconvenient truth is that the state would emerge from it enormously strengthened, if also deeply flawed in its underlying fiscal and social structures. Whereas the conceptions of reform with which Richelieu began his ministry were inadequate and conventional, the effects of his political practices were more radical than he can ever have envisaged. This emphasizes a certain lack of realism in the political thinking of his day, which was precisely what made the complex of ideas associated with *raison d'état* so crucial to his regime.

4

LOUIS XIII, RICHELIEU, AND THE ROYAL FINANCES

RICHARD BONNEY

We need to start, perhaps, with an assertion that the subject to be studied is not simply Richelieu and the king's finances, but Louis XIII, his various ministers (including finance ministers), and the royal finances. The distinction may seem either self-evident or tautological, but it has taken the appearance of Lloyd Moote's biography of *Louis XIII, the Just* to reaffirm what should always have been evident: that from 1617, if not before, we are dealing with a king of age to rule personally, who at times sought to do so. A recognition that the king could, and did, dispose of ministers and ratify appointments, albeit under the guidance of his chief minister, is fundamental for an understanding of the development of his financial policy.[1] In 1624, 1636, and 1643, the king rid himself of the services respectively of La Vieuville, Servien, and Sublet des Noyers for reasons which had something to do with financial policy,[2] although other issues were involved; in 1636 and 1637 Bullion appealed directly to the king, when it seemed that Richelieu might

The author wishes to thank Dr Graham Smith for his computing advice and Dr Margaret Bonney for the statistical work and preparation of the graphs for this article. Research assistance from the British Academy and from the Economic and Social Research Council (award no. R000231968) for the E[uropean] S[tate] F[inance] D[ata]b[ase], an international collaborative project in data collection, is gratefully acknowledged by the author. A personal research award from the Leverhulme Trust has permitted the checking of figures and the consultation of additional MSS relevant both to this subject and to a projected study of the intendants of Louis XIV. The ESFDB datasets cited in this chapter may be consulted after 1993 via JANET/ERN at the ESRC Data Archive in the Univ. of Essex. A list of abbreviations used is given at the end of this chapter.

[1] A. L. Moote, *Louis XIII, the Just* (Berkeley, Calif., 1989), 105, 107–8, 167, 169, 171. One searches in vain e.g. for any real discussion of the king's control of financial policy in P. Chevallier, *Louis XIII, roi cornélien* (Paris, 1979). The title itself suggests that it is difficult to find Louis XIII at all in M. Carmona, *La France de Richelieu* (Paris, 1984), although at pp. 129–37 there is a discussion of 'le budget de la nation'.
[2] R. J. Bonney, *The King's Debts: Finance and Politics in France* (Oxford, 1981), 112, 160. Id., *Political Change in France under Richelieu and Mazarin* (Oxford, 1978), 15 n. 3.

dismiss him after the apparent failure of the war effort.[3] After Bullion's death, Louis XIII noted that he missed his firmness (did he also miss his corruption?), so that it is clear that the support was indeed forthcoming:[4] and after Bullion's death in 1640 the king also questioned Richelieu's judgement that Bouthillier was capable of managing financial affairs as sole *surintendant*.[5]

Louis XIII also discharged some royal expenditure himself and accounted to no one for it. Even if there is no evidence that he used the *comptants ès mains du roi* on anything like the scale of Louis XIV,[6] as far as the royal finances were concerned, so-called 'absolutism' nevertheless had a direct financial implication. However, Louis XIII displayed no great understanding of financial issues. Had the king possessed any real acumen in this area, could he seriously have thought in 1634 that open intervention in the Thirty Years War would cost just a million a year more than the annual subsidy to the Swedish and Dutch allies?[7]

It is difficult to analyse a thirty-three-year reign as one long financial period. Similarly, Henri IV's reign was too short, and the reign of Louis XIV too long, for a financial comparison of the reigns, in the manner of Saint-Simon's *Parallèle des trois premiers rois Bourbons*, to make any sense. We have, perforce, to see the seventeenth century in terms of ministries, not just because they form more coherent periods for discussion but also because of the political role of the chief minister or other important political figures. Richelieu exercised rights of nomination over the position of finance minister, the significance of which was commented upon by contemporaries. Shortly before he won the battle of Castelnaudary against the forces of the rebellious duc de Montmorency in Languedoc, Schomberg (himself a former *surintendant*) remarked to Richelieu on the appointment of Bullion and Bouthillier: 'c'est un choix digne de v[ot]re prudence, et duquel il n'y aura jamais sujet de se repentir. Ils estoient desja dans les affaires[;] la confiance, la suffisance et la probité y sont, et l'[o]n sy maintiendra par la

[3] Bonney, *Political Change*, 43. AAE France 820, fo. 258, 9 May 1636. AAE France 826, fo. 227, 25 Mar. 1637.

[4] O. A. Ranum, *Richelieu and the Councillors of Louis XIII* (Oxford, 1963), 165.

[5] Moote, *Louis XIII*, 171, and, ultimately, Ranum, *Councillors of Louis XIII*, 165.

[6] Thus the expenditure accounts for 1636, which do not include *comptants par certification*, contain payments by the king (*comptants ès mains du roi*) totalling 240,000 *livres*: BN Naf 164. The figures provided by Malet (see n. 12 below) indicate much higher levels of expenditure of this type by Louis XIV, and indeed this category is not specifically identified before 1661 in his tables. For the explanation of secret expenditure, see Richard Bonney, 'The Secret Expenses of Richelieu and Mazarin', *English Historical Review*, 91 (1976), 825–36.

[7] Bonney, *King's Debts*, 169. On the amount of the subsidy to Sweden: ibid. 163–4.

douceur de leurs humeurs et le pouvoir que vous avez sur l'un et sur l'autre . . .'.[8]

A brief introduction to the fiscal system inherited by Louis XIII, Richelieu, and the finance ministers in 1624 is necessary to set the context. Since the system was both complex and the product of a long period of evolution it defies simple analysis. The French kingdom had developed three main types of revenue: direct taxes, indirect taxes, and *affaires extraordinaires*. Under the category of direct taxes we place the *taille* and the *taillon* (although there were variants of these taxes within the provinces which retained provincial estates, the *pays d'états*). Prior to Richelieu's ministry, and during his early years in power, some of these direct taxes had been alienated, that is to say the right to collect them had been sold off to private individuals who collected what were known as the *droits aliénés*: these private rights were revoked in 1634. Subsequently, a number of new direct taxes were established under Louis XIII and Richelieu, most notably a new military tax called the *subsistances*. By the end of Richelieu's ministry, the revenue from these taxes was anticipated in the form of loans from financiers, on whose agents were conferred the right of collection. This is sometimes, incorrectly, referred to as the farming of direct taxes.[9] True revenue farming was exclusively reserved to the area of indirect taxes. The revenue farm was a fixed lease conferring exclusive rights of collection on the revenue farmer and his agents for a number of years. This system, which was largely created during Sully's ministry (1598–1611), virtually excluded royal officials from the administration of indirect taxes such as those on the consumption of salt (the various farms of the *gabelles*); drink (the *aides*); and on the circulation of goods in various parts of the kingdom allocated to particular farms (the *cinq grosses fermes* and the regional variants such as the farm of the *convoy et comptablie* of Bordeaux). The third main type of revenue, the *affaires extra-ordinaires*, comprised virtually everything else that did not fall under the other two categories. Strictly speaking, the 'extraordinary taxes' were those raised by the method of *traités*, or one-off tax contracts with financiers: the financier undertook to raise a fixed sum of money in return for a standard rate of interest. Such contracts might concern the establishment of new offices, or new annuities (*rentes*), or any of a plethora of fiscal expedients that had already been used

---

[8] AAE France 802, fo. 328, 5 Aug. 1632.
[9] There is much information on direct taxes in Bonney, *Political Change*, chs. 8 and 9 (pp. 163–213), and J. B. Collins, *Fiscal Limits of Absolutism Direct Taxation in Early Seventeenth-Century France* (Berkeley, Calif., 1988).

before 1624, and which were further developed by Louis XIII's and Richelieu's finance ministers.[10]

I

However influential the king and Richelieu might have been in the appointment or dismissal of finance ministers, once installed, the *surintendants des finances* were left to manage affairs without much in the way of direct royal supervision and only sporadic interventions by the chief minister. Louis XIII and Richelieu appointed only five *surintendants* in all: Bochart de Champigny, Marillac, d'Effiat, and Bullion and Bouthillier, of whom the last two served for the longest period, just over eight years (1632–40; Bouthillier remained sole *surintendant* until June 1643).[11] Stability rather than change was the order of the day, in marked contrast to periods of political upheaval such as the Fronde (when there were eight *surintendants* in five years). Yet though Richelieu's *surintendants* were in post longer than their successors at the time of the Fronde, the five separate changes of financial regime do not lend themselves to statistical analysis. It is therefore more appropriate to take Richelieu's ministry as a continuum and to compare it with five other ministerial periods in the seventeenth century. The ministries selected are those of Sully (here represented by the period 1600–10 only: he had been appointed *surintendant* in 1598 and was forced out of office in January 1611); the predecessors of Richelieu (the period 1611–23); Mazarin (for the years 1643–60 only: he died in March 1661); Colbert; and the successors of Colbert.

Before proceeding further, it is necessary to make some comment about the source material which permits this comparison to be made. In the absence of other manuscript sources covering a comparable period, Jean-Roland Malet (d. 1736, a chief clerk in the finance ministry whose tables of statistics were posthumously published in 1789) still remains the fundamental source for the financial history of the seventeenth century (that is, with the exception of the years 1657–61 and 1696–9 for which he provides no data). Whatever

---

[10] The system is explained in more detail in Bonney, *King's Debts*, 293–6, and in id., 'The State and its Revenues in *Ancien-Régime* France', *Historical Research*, 65 (1992), 150–76. There are also detailed articles by Françoise Bayard in *Dictionnaire du grand siècle*, ed. F. Bluche (Paris, 1990), 53 (*aides*), 585–6 (*fermes*), 593–6 (*financiers, fiscalité directe*, and *fiscalité indirecte*), 631–2 (*gabelle*), 1499–1500 (*tailles*), 1529–30 (*traités*).

[11] The list in Bonney, *King's Debts*, 285–6, has been confirmed by M. Antoine, *Le Dur Métier de roi* (Paris, 1986), 41 n. 37, and most recently by Bernard Barbiche in his contribution on the *surintendants* in *Dictionnaire du grand siècle*, ed. Bluche, 1494.

TABLE 1. Comparison of Malet's figures and the contemporary accounts for the year 1633

	Guénégaud's accounts	Malet
TOTAL REVENUE	57,450,336	57,464,923
Receptes générales (fo. 274^v)	8,376,504	8,374,393[a]
Bois (fo. 276)	580,751	580,474
Taillon (fo. 277)	1,115,794	1,115,794
Aydes (fo. 277^v)	2,179,884	2,179,893
Cinq grosses fermes (fo. 278^v)	1,618,401	1,618,401
Convoy de Bordeaux (fo. 279)	1,529,246	not itemized separately
Gabelles de France (fo. 281^v)	138,111	138,661
Other gabelles (fos. 282–3)[b]	1,385,392	1,464,392
Parties casuelles (fo. 293^v)[c]	28,236,934	28,231,028
Deniers extraordinaires (fo. 300^v)	11,019,968	10,418,987
TOTAL EXPENDITURE (fo. 310)	57,510,336	57,069,390
Comptants per certification (fo. 309^v)	19,127,444	29,752,935[d]

[a] Income from the *taille*, including both *pays d'élections* and *pays d'états*.
[b] Addition of separate items.
[c] Income from offices.
[d] The figure in Malet is also at variance with that compiled by the Chambre des Comptes (19,349,157 *livres*).

criticisms one may level at his figures, they form the only continuous set of financial statistics for the seventeenth century.[12] One of the few authenticated accounts from the period of Richelieu's ministry is that of Gabriel de Guénégaud for 1632.[13] This was presented to the council of finance on 30 May 1633 and was passed with the signatures of Chancellor Séguier, Bullion, Bouthillier, Mallier, and Particelli on 13 June 1633.[14] It is a relatively simple task to compare the figures in this manuscript with those presented by Malet (see table). The main problem is the breakdown of expenditure between

[12] J. R. Malet, *Comptes rendus de l'administration des finances du royaume de France . . .* (London, 1789). For his life and work, see R. J. Bonney, 'Jean-Roland Malet: Historian of the Finances of the French Monarchy', *French History*, 5 (1991), 180–233. The critical edn. of Malet's figures in the ESFDB is forthcoming in Margaret and Richard Bonney, *Jean-Roland Malet: Premier Historien des finances de la monarchie française* (Comité pour l'histoire économique et financière de la France; Paris, due out in 1993).
[13] The chief treasurer was in correspondence with Richelieu in the summer of 1632, 'afin que l'on ne me puisse imputer aucune faulte': AAE France 804, fo. 270, 19 July 1632.
[14] BI Godefroy 144, fos. 259–310. Cf. Bonney, *King's Debts*, 164 n. 4.

ordinary and extraordinary, where Malet's figures differ from those of the other sources for the period (although the figures for total expenditure are very close). In other respects, the similarity between the figures is striking.

The relative importance of different types of expenditure can be appreciated rapidly from Chart 1, which may perhaps help to overturn some preconceptions about the merits and demerits of certain ministers.[15] 'Extraordinary' expenses were higher during Richelieu's ministry, at 51 per cent of the total, than at any other time in the seventeenth century, with the exception of Mazarin's period as chief minister, when the figure reached nearly 66 per cent of the total. The much criticized predecessors of Richelieu, who used this type of expenditure for only 28 per cent of the total, were almost as prudent as the reforming Colbert, for whose period in office they comprised a mere 22 per cent of the total. The great reformer, Sully, whose reputation was secure in the eighteenth century as the last honest finance minister of the ancien régime—a reputation which, on the whole, has been reinforced by Aristide's recent study of his fortune[16]—used this type of expenditure almost as much as Richelieu and his *surintendants* did, for sums which amounted to 46 per cent of total expenditure, although in Sully's case the purpose was different.[17] In contrast, the much criticized successors of Colbert— Le Peletier and Pontchartrain (Malet's figures are complete only until 1695 and therefore do not include the whole of Pontchartrain's ministry)—used extraordinary expenditure much more sparingly, for a mere 14 per cent of the total.

The significance of this type of expenditure, chiefly *comptants par certification*, has been emphasized elsewhere[18] so that it is only necessary here to discuss its main aspects. The Chambre des Comptes audited expenditure in great detail, except for those expenses which were covered by the rules of government secrecy (*comptants*); under this category merely the total amount was presented for audit. Before Colbert's ministry, the secret expenses were abused by the government as a means of conferring excessive interest rates on financiers and of making other dubious financial transactions which it would

---

[15] ESFDB dataset \rjb\malet\malb009. Cf. chart 1 in Bonney, 'Jean-Roland Malet', 227, where the figures are calculated by decades for the entire 17th cent. A list of abbreviations used in charts and graphs is given at the end of this chapter.

[16] Isabelle Aristide, *La Fortune de Sully* (Comité pour l'histoire économique et financière de la France; Paris, 1990), who estimates (p. 92) his fortune in 1610, shortly before leaving office, at only 2.2 million *livres*.

[17] Malet characterizes such expenses under Henri IV and Sully as 'remboursements, intérêts d'avance &c' but after 1611 as 'Dépenses & gratifications par comptant'.

[18] Bonney, 'Secret Expenses'.

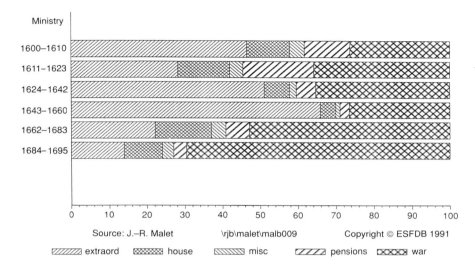

Chart 1: Categories of French royal expenditure by ministries, 1600–95

have been difficult to pass through the relatively open auditing process. In the years before 1661, much extraordinary expenditure took the form of paper transactions, including the deferring of actual payment from one accounting year to the next by the procedure known as the 'ordonnance de remise en d'autre Épargne'.[19] The greatly reduced reliance on extraordinary expenditure under Colbert reflects a conscious ministerial decision to avoid the public criticism which Foucquet's policy in the 1650s, and that of his predecessors, including Richelieu's *surintendants* (above all, Bullion),[20] had provoked. Thus the extent of reliance on extraordinary expenditure is both an index of the potential for corruption and a measurement of the autocratic nature of the ministry, of its unwillingness to submit detailed expenditure accounts to the auditing process of the Chambre des Comptes.[21]

The innovative nature of Richelieu's ministry is clearly demonstrated when extraordinary expenditure is removed from the cal-

---

[19] Bonney, *King's Debts*, 174.
[20] Ibid. 181–2.
[21] For growing unease of the Chambre des Comptes by 1631, and its later view that 1630 was the turning-point after which the abuses in financial administration reached disastrous proportions: ibid. 157–8.

culations (Chart 2).[22] Never again in the seventeenth century did expenditure on war fall back to the low levels of Richelieu's predecessors, to the relatively modest 49 per cent of ordinary expenditure under Sully, and almost 50 per cent under Jeannin, Schomberg, and La Vieuville. Military expenditure during Richelieu's ministry amounted to 72 per cent of ordinary expenditure. This was exceeded only under Mazarin and Colbert's successors; under Colbert himself the decade of peace in the 1660s reduced the proportion of military expenses to 68 per cent of ordinary expenditure. Here, then, was a significant change under Louis XIII and Richelieu: in proportionate terms, expenditure on pensions and the various royal households declined in significance, and with the exception of household expenses under Colbert (which rose to 19 per cent of the total, the same figure as under Richelieu's predecessors), this became the new balance of expenditure in the seventeenth century.

Since Malet provides no figures for extraordinary revenues after 1661 it is impossible to pursue this method of analysis for total revenues after this date, except by using other sources, but ordinary revenues may be analysed under the same ministries (Chart 3).[23] Here, the striking feature of Richelieu's administration, which has been commented on elsewhere in the context of Bullion's *surintendance*,[24] was the extent of its reliance on income from the *parties casuelles*. It reached the record figure for the seventeenth century of 46 per cent of ordinary income. Under Mazarin, income from this source rapidly declined in importance (to a mere 17 per cent), and the proportion fell further still under Colbert and his successors. It is clear that the fall was not quite so dramatic as Malet's figures seem to suggest because part of the income drawn from the world of office-holding was redefined under Colbert and his successors as 'extraordinary revenue'.[25] Even so, a fundamental change in revenue-raising occurred under Richelieu which was not repeated later; and the difficulties faced by the regency government in dealing with the office-holders at the outbreak of the Fronde were at least partly a consequence of the excesses of the previous administration. The corollary of reliance on the *officiers* as a mainstay of ordinary revenue was that those two sturdy revenues of the ancien régime, the *taille* and the revenue farms of indirect revenues, reached

[22] ESFDB dataset \rjb\malet\malbo10. Cf. chart 2 in Bonney, 'Jean-Roland Malet', 228, where the figures are calculated by decades for the entire 17th cent.

[23] ESFDB dataset \rjb\malet\malbo11. Cf. chart 3 in Bonney, 'Jean-Roland Malet', 229, where the figures are calculated by decades for the entire 17th cent.

[24] Bonney, *King's Debts*, 177, 198.

[25] This seems clear from AN KK 355, which enumerates additional taxes on *officiers* sometimes under extraordinary and sometimes under ordinary revenues.

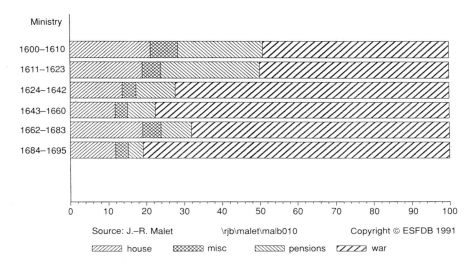

Chart 2: Categories of French royal expenditure by ministries, 1600–95
(excluding extraordinary expenditure)

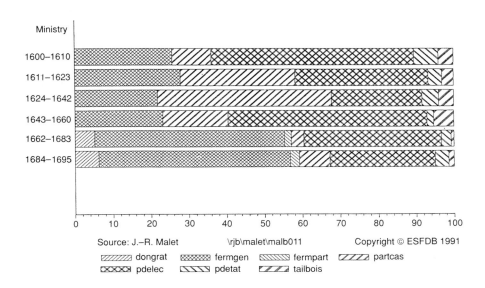

Chart 3: Categories of ordinary revenues of the French monarchy by
ministries, 1600–95

an all-time low for the seventeenth century, respectively just under 24 per cent and just under 22 of the total under Richelieu. In contrast to the picture for expenditure, the balance of ordinary revenues under Richelieu is at variance with the rest of the period. Not until the war of the Spanish Succession, it seems, would the relative fiscal burden fall so heavily on the *officiers* compared to the rest of the population.

This picture is further clarified if the various categories of ordinary and extraordinary revenue are viewed in quinquennial periods before and during Richelieu's ministry (Chart 4: the base period is taken to be Louis XIII's reign, to which is added the year 1644 to maintain even divisions by quinquennia).[26] Extraordinary revenues ('denextra' on the chart, *deniers extraordinaires* in Malet's terminology) do not predominate in the first quinquennium of Louis XIII's reign (1610–14); at 31 per cent of total revenue they were on a par with the income from the *taille* from the *pays d'élections* received by the treasury (as distinct from the levy in the provinces, an important difference which will be discussed later). Nor do they predominate in the second quinquennium, the period after the Estates General (1615–19), because the *pays d'élections* and the revenue farms remained more important, even if only marginally so, at respectively 29 per cent and 26 per cent of total revenues compared to 22 per cent for extraordinary revenues. Three quinquennia followed (1620–4, 1625–9, 1630–4) in which the *parties casuelles* predominated even in comparison with extraordinary revenues and gradually squeezed out the contribution from the *pays d'élections*.[27] Only in the quinquennium after France's entry into the Thirty Years War in 1635 did the extraordinary revenues achieve the predominance which they were to retain during the remainder of Richelieu's ministry.[28]

Once extraordinary revenues are excluded from the analysis, the predominance of the *parties casuelles* between 1620 and 1639 remains clear (Chart 5).[29] Income from this source at its high point in the years 1630–4 reached 55 per cent of ordinary revenue. Before 1620 and after 1640 income from the *pays d'élections* assumed its greatest

[26] ESFDB dataset \rjb\malet\malbo12.

[27] R. Mousnier, *La Vénalité des offices sous Henri IV et Louis XIII* (2nd edn.; Paris, 1971), 421, where the proportions are calculated as annual figures as a % of total income (i.e. including extraordinary revenues) for the years 1600–43. Mousnier noted (p. 422), 'c'est donc de 1620 à 1633 que cette importance relative est la plus grande'.

[28] These calculations appeared in Bonney, *King's Debts*, 313, but the definition of the categories has been modified subsequently in line with those used in Bonney, 'Jean-Roland Malet', 229, which included income from the *pays d'états* in the calculations as a separate item (and thus reduced the proportion of miscellaneous revenues).

[29] ESFDB dataset \rjb\malet\malbo13.

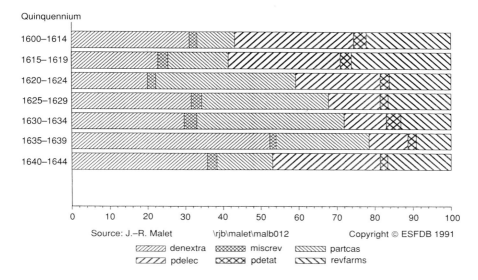

Chart 4: Categories of ordinary and extraordinary revenues of the French monarchy, 1610–44

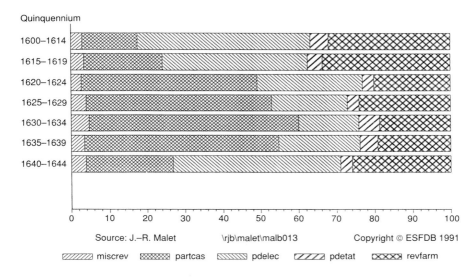

Chart 5: Categories of ordinary revenues of the French monarchy, 1610–44

proportionate significance: income from the areas without representative institutions accounted for 45 per cent of ordinary revenue in the years 1610–14, 38 per cent in the years 1615–19, and 44 per cent in the years 1640–4. Income from the revenue farms amounted to about a third of ordinary revenue in the first decade of Louis XIII's reign, but under a quarter in the second decade; it fell in the 1630s to under 20 per cent, but rose once more to just over a quarter of ordinary revenue after 1640. Consumption of salt and other commodities fell with the subsistence crisis of 1628–31 and the economic dislocation resulting from France's entry into the Thirty Years War; substantial remissions had to be accorded to the revenue farmers to prevent bankruptcy and the abandonment of their leases, and this proved to be the pattern in the 1640s.[30] Income from the *pays d'états* always averaged below 6 per cent in Louis XIII's reign.

II

There is a danger that in presenting proportions of revenue and expenditure for the seventeenth century a static impression of the overall 'budget' is given.[31] The figures were, of course, on the increase. Looking back on the reign of Louis XIII, and reflecting on the origins of the Fronde, Omer Talon concluded that more taxes had been raised by that king than all his predecessors put together. A better informed contemporary, writing in 1644, estimated that 700 million in *affaires extraordinaires* had been brought to the treasury since 1620, while the gains of the financiers on this type of transaction had amounted to 172 million.[32] The rise in secret expenditure, or expenditure by means of *comptants par certification*, in the reign of Louis XIII is clear from Graph 1, where other sources can be brought to bear on Malet's figures to establish a pattern.[33] A similar trend may be established from Malet's figures from the *pays d'élections*, the revenue farms, and the *parties casuelles* (Graph 2).[34] Wherever we look, the figures are on the increase. The treasury yield of revenues increased close to the declaration of war on Spain in

---

[30] Richard Bonney, 'The Failure of the French Revenue Farms, 1600–60', *Economic History Review*, 2nd. ser. 32 (1979), 18–19. The precise reason for the fall in income from the revenue farms in 1620–4 is less clear, except in terms of dislocation resulting from the revolts of the queen mother and the Huguenot revolt of 1621–2.

[31] On the question of the 'budget' see the sources cited in Bonney, 'Jean-Roland Malet', 208 n. 139.

[32] Both contemporaries cited by Bonney, *King's Debts*, 188–9.

[33] ESFDB dataset \rjb\malet\malgo31.   [34] ESFDB dataset \rjb\malet\malgo32.

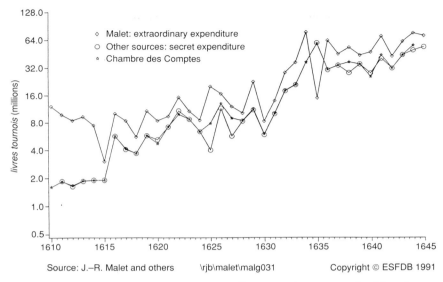

Graph 1: Malet's extraordinary expenditure totals compared with other sources, 1610–45 (semi-logarithmic scale)

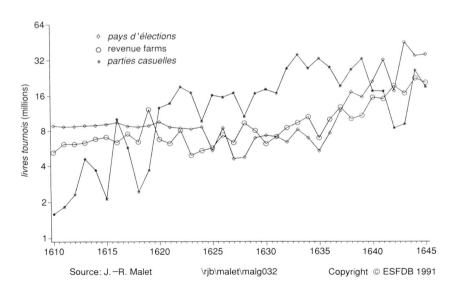

Graph 2: Semi-logarithmic graph of total receipts from the *pays d'élections*, revenue farms, and *parties casuelles*, 1610–45

1635; but as will be seen, the first real increase in taxation in the provinces had occurred earlier, before Richelieu's ministry.

Was the French intervention in the Thirty Years War financed by monetary expansion (which Bullion had hoped for in 1632)[35] or by borrowing and tax contracts—in short, by paper transactions?[36] This question can be partially resolved by setting the figures for mint output against the contracts for loans and *traités* (Graph 3).[37] There was a significant increase in mint output in the 1630s and 1640s, but on the whole this followed, rather than preceded, the revenue generated by loans and tax contracts (or more precisely, the agreement of contractors to loans and *traités*, since the actual income was often produced many months later). By 1636, Bullion was once more concerned at the lack of investment in loans and tax contracts, and the devaluation of that year was aimed at encouraging participation, since inactive cash deposits lost their value.[38]

When Malet's evidence concerning the treasury yield from the *pays d'élections* is presented according to ministries, the figures demonstrate a broad uniformity in the yield from direct taxes paid by the different regions throughout the seventeenth century (Chart 6).[39] This reflects a fiscal conservatism on the part of ministers: it was considered dangerous to meddle with the traditional allocation between one province and another. However, it also in some measure relates to the capacity to pay. Thus, the northern region (here defined as the *généralités* of Paris, Soissons, Amiens—including the Boulonnais—and Châlons) provided 15 per cent of the total income from the *pays d'élections* from the period of Sully's ministry until the end of Richelieu's ministry; from Mazarin's ministry onwards, this region provided about 20 per cent of the total. Under Richelieu, the central region (here defined as the *généralités* of Orléans, Tours, Bourges, and Moulins) provided under 18 per cent of the total income from the *pays d'élections*, its lowest proportion in the seventeenth century (under Sully the figure had reached 25 per cent of the total). In contrast, the south-east region within the *pays d'élections* (here defined as the *généralités* of Lyons, Riom, and Grenoble) provided a higher amount of revenue to the treasury than formerly

---

[35] Bonney, *King's Debts*, 171. For mint issues in France in this period: F. C. Spooner, *The International Economy and Monetary Movements in France, 1493–1725* (Cambridge, Mass., 1972).

[36] Bonney, *King's Debts*, 174–5.

[37] ESFDB dataset \rjb\kingdebt\kdg002.

[38] Bonney, *King's Debts*, 171. The devaluation of 1636 is discussed most fully in Spooner, *International Economy*, 181–2.

[39] ESFDB dataset \rjb\malet\malbo15. Cf. chart 5 in Bonney, 'Jean-Roland Malet', 231, where the figures are calculated by decades for the entire 17th cent.

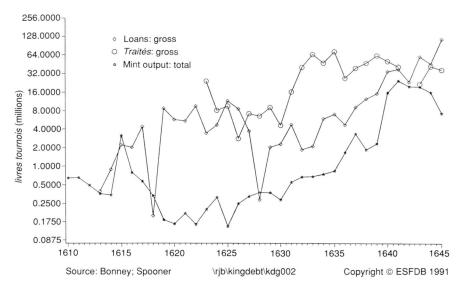

Source: Bonney; Spooner   \rjb\kingdebt\kdg002   Copyright © ESFDB 1991

Graph 3: Royal borrowing and *affaires extraordinaires*, 1610–45, set against mint output

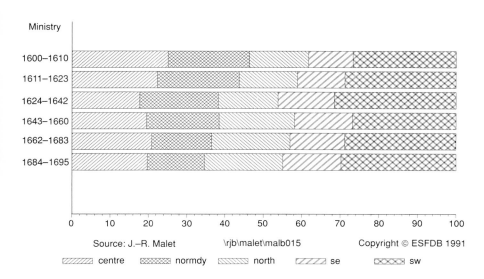

Source: J.–R. Malet   \rjb\malet\malb015   Copyright © ESFDB 1991

centre   normdy   north   se   sw

Chart 6: Receipts of direct taxes from the *pays d'élections* by region and by ministries, 1600–95 (some 14.7 per cent of the total), which remained about the level for the rest of the century. The south-west (here defined as the *généralités* of Poitiers, Limoges, Bordeaux, and Montauban—the latter established under Richelieu in 1635)[40] reached its highest point (some 31.5 per cent of the total) under Richelieu, declined markedly under Mazarin, and never rose again to the level of the first cardinal's ministry. Finally, Normandy (the *généralités* of Alençon—established under Richelieu in 1636—Caen, and Rouen) provided just over 20 per cent of the total under Richelieu, a somewhat smaller proportion than in Sully's ministry and under Richelieu's predecessors; this proportion fell consistently during the rest of the seventeenth century. When the figures are viewed in greater detail, and presented in quinquennial totals for Louis XIII's reign, the northern region within the *pays d'élections* (here defined as before) shows the greatest fluctuation, from as low as 12 per cent of the total at the beginning of Richelieu's ministry to as high as 20 per cent (Chart 7).[41] The south-eastern region within the *pays d'élections* was consistently the lowest contributor to the treasury (at between 12 and 15 per cent of the total); while the south-western region was consistently the highest (at between 27 and 32 per cent of the total).

What of the areas where provincial estates survived during Richelieu's ministry? Chart 8 takes Malet's evidence concerning the treasury yield from both the *pays d'élections* and the *pays d'états* and presents this for the whole of the seventeenth century, according to ministries.[42] The interest of this chart lies in the inclusion of the relatively small yield from the *pays d'états* ('pdetotal': the figures for the levy in the provinces themselves were much higher than was the yield to the treasury; a higher proportion of revenues was assigned to local expenses in the *pays d'états* than in the *pays d'élections*). In fact, the contribution of provinces with estates during Richelieu's ministry was the third highest for the seventeenth century: at over 15 per cent of the total, it exceeded the contribution of these areas under Sully, Richelieu's predecessors, and Mazarin (when the figure fell to a derisory 3 per cent of the total). Only under Colbert, and especially under his successors, was the contribution from the *pays d'états* significantly higher.

When these figures are viewed in greater detail for the relevant period, the rise in the contribution of the provinces with estates

---

[40] La Rochelle is added for the period after 1661.

[41] The year 1644 is added to maintain even divisions by quinquennia: ESFDB dataset \rjb\malet\malbo16.

[42] ESFDB dataset \rjb\malet\malbo17. Cf. chart 7 in Bonney, 'Jean-Roland Malet', 233, where the figures are calculated by decades for the entire 17th cent.

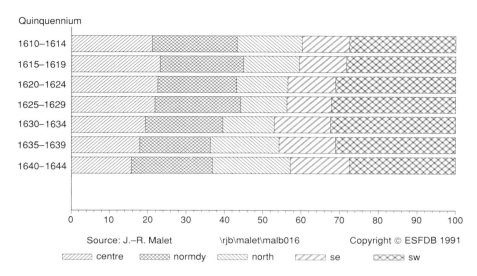

Chart 7: Receipts of direct taxes from the *pays d'élections* by region, 1610–44

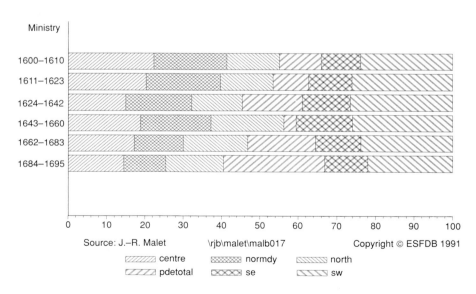

Chart 8: Receipts from the *pays d'élections* and the *pays d'états* by ministries, 1600–95 (chiefly direct taxes)

under Richelieu's ministry is confirmed (Chart 9).[43] The figures do not, however, substantiate Professor Major's view that it was Marillac who put the pressure on the *pays d'états* with the creation of *élections* in 1628.[44] Rather, the sudden increase in revenues from the *pays d'états* in the period 1630–4 can be accounted for by d'Effiat's insistence on high rates of payment by the provinces to compensate for the revocation in 1631–2 of *élections*, and the imposition on Languedoc of the regime of the edict of Béziers of 1632 (a measure which at least guaranteed a minimum amount of revenue to the crown). Revenue from this source increased from 13 per cent of the total in the years 1625–9 to 25.8 per cent in the years 1630–4. The contribution of the *pays d'états* relative to the *pays d'élections* fell back thereafter, with a dramatic fall in the last year of Richelieu's ministry. This does not necessarily imply that the fiscal burden in the *pays d'états* was reduced. It may be the case that in wartime Richelieu preferred political stability (and hence low taxes) in the frontier regions; but these areas also suffered from the billeting of troops who took what they wanted in addition to their legitimate entitlement under the levy known as winter quarter.[45]

These figures may be compared with those for the levy on the provinces (Chart 10).[46] Professor Collins provides the figures for the levy in fifteen *généralités* of the *pays d'élections* for 1597, 1599, 1600, 1607, 1609, 1620, 1634, 1640, and 1643; the years 1594, 1639, and 1647 have been added to those drawn from his table. The figures are not entirely comparable to those provided by Malet, for two reasons. One is that Malet always included a number of *généralités* omitted from Collins's list: thus the figures from eighteen *généralités* are incorporated in Charts 6–9 for the later part of Richelieu's ministry. Secondly, as Malet himself made clear, contemporary accounting practice before 1660 did not permit a detailed breakdown between the levy, the charges, and the net revenue.[47] Malet's figures therefore inform us about what, for want of a better term, we might call 'disposable treasury revenue', not the total levy on the provinces.

[43] ESFDB dataset \rjb\malet\malbo18.

[44] The provinces affected were Dauphiné, Burgundy, Languedoc, and Provence: J. R. Major, *Representative Government in Early Modern France* (New Haven, Conn., 1980). This thesis is discussed in Bonney, *Political Change*, 349–50, and id., 'Absolutism: What's in a Name?', *French History*, 1 (1987), 112 n. 92.

[45] For the edict of Béziers as a restriction on the levy in Languedoc: Bonney, *Political Change*, 380. The effect of military levies is discussed in W. H. Beik, *Absolutism and Society in Seventeenth-Century France* (Cambridge, 1985), 141. Since the *quartier d'hiver* was discharged locally, it affected the amount of tax revenue received by the central government.

[46] ESFDB dataset \rjb\colbo01. Collins, *Fiscal Limits of Absolutism*, 162.

[47] Malet, *Comptes rendus*, 182, quoted in Bonney, 'Jean-Roland Malet', 204.

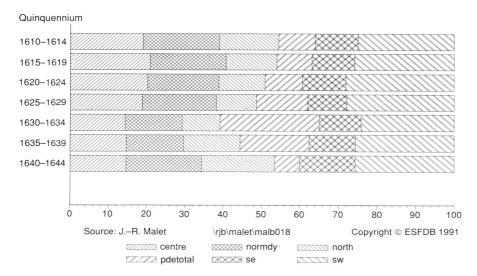

Chart 9: Receipts from the *pays d'élections* and the *pays d'états*, 1610–44
(chiefly direct taxes)

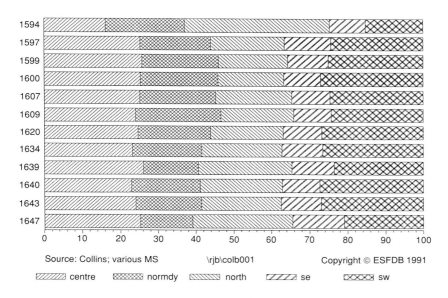

Chart 10: Direct taxes levied on the *pays d'élections* by region, 1594–1647

The figures in Chart 10, in contrast, are those for the levy. With the exception of 1594, when the Catholic League still controlled part of the kingdom, and when war taxation loomed large, the balance between the regions held reasonably steady for the levy, although less so than for payments to the treasury.[48]

The rate of tax increase in the provinces can only be ascertained from an analysis of local sources, since Malet's figures before 1660 do not enlighten us on this question. Professor Collins has provided us with two provincial series (Champagne and Normandy), respectively for the years 1602–34 and 1597–1643.[49] The series for the *élection* of Paris has been added for the years 1615–43 and the resulting graph presents the figures deflated in terms of silver value for this shorter period (Graph 4).[50] In a separate graph (Graph 5), the figures for the *élection* of Paris are presented over the longer timespan of 1615–1787, converted into index numbers to show the rate of growth from the base index of 1600–30, and recalculated on an eleven-year centred moving average so that the main trend can be seen without short-term fluctuations. The index numbers for the *taille* are also deflated by the value of grain in the same period so that the 'real' value may be perceived. The 'real' rate of increase in the period of the Thirty Years War remains impressive.[51] The figures for the *élection* of Paris show a doubling of the levy of direct taxes (including elements other than the *taille*) in the period of Richelieu's predecessors: by alienating direct taxes in the form of the *droits aliénés*, Luynes and Schomberg doubled the levy in the *élection* of Paris by 1621, to help pay for the war against the Huguenots. Shortly before the French declaration of war against Spain in 1635, the *droits aliénés* were revoked, which increased the treasury's share of the total fiscal burden to nearly a million *livres*, whereas the figure in 1625 had been under 0.4 million.[52] By the end of Louis XIII's reign, the *élection* of Paris would provide 1.4 million in direct taxes. This figure was slightly higher in nominal terms than the levy at the end of the seventeenth century. In 'real' terms, the levy actually declined in

[48] The figures for 1594 also include elements other than the *taille* ('a cause du domaine, aydes, impositions, tailles et crues y joinctes . . .'): BN MS Fr. 4680, fo. 15.

[49] Collins, *Fiscal Limits of Absolutism*, 150, 152–3.

[50] ESFDB dataset /rjb/ eleg002.

[51] ESFDB dataset /rjb/ eleg006. It is possible to calculate the total levy of the *taille* (i.e. *taille* plus *droits*) for only a few years in the period. For purposes of calculating the mean index numbers of the *taille*, the total levy has been used where available, with the principal of the *taille* (alone) filling in the gaps. The mean index numbers for the *taille* have also been deflated by dividing them by the index numbers for grain prices during the period, using the common base index of 1600–30 = 100. The grain figures were those of M. Baulant, 'Le Prix des grains à Paris de 1431 à 1788', *Annales: Économies, sociétés, civilisations*, 23 (1968), 539.

[52] Collins, *Fiscal Limits of Absolutism*, 136, 141.

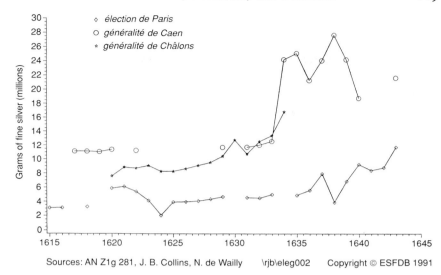

Graph 4: The value of the levy of the *taille* in the *élection* of Paris and in the *généralités* of Châlons and Caen, 1615–43, in metric tons (millions of grams of fine silver)

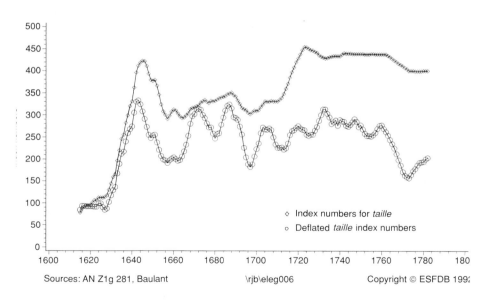

Graph 5: Eleven-year centred moving averages of index numbers for the *taille* in the *élection* of Paris, 1615–1787, set against 'real' *taille* index numbers (index 100 = 1600–30)

Louis XIV's reign from 1647 until the war of the Spanish Succession. The evidence from the *élection* of Paris is also of interest because it serves to test Professor Collins's argument that under Richelieu the maximum fiscal capacity of the state was reached in terms of the *taille*, at 30–35 million *livres*.[53] This argument is borne out by the accounts from Colbert's ministry onwards, where the limit of 40 million was breached only four times (in 1662, 1676, 1677, and 1678) in the seventeenth century.[54] We may estimate the fiscal burden on the *élection* of Paris at about 27.5 per cent of the *généralité* of Paris under Richelieu (it was somewhat higher at the end of the century, and may be calculated as 36 per cent of the burden on the *généralité* in the period 1688–1712)[55] and about 3.5 per cent of the total fiscal burden on the *pays d'élections*. A levy of 1.4 million on the *élection* of Paris at the end of Louis XIII's reign would thus represent a total levy in the *pays d'élections* in the region of 40 million. This was Bullion's estimate of the levy before the deduction of charges.[56]

III

By 1639–40, shortly before Bullion's death, the financial problems of the French monarchy had already become acute. In Bullion's words:[57] 'V[otre E[minence] a raison de desirer la paix extra-ordinairement. Jamais les finances ne furent en si mauvais estat. Tous les gens de finance ne veulent entrer en aucune traitté et les peuples ne veulent rien payer . . .'. According to Malet's estimate, *rentes* and *gages* absorbed a total of 45.8 million by this date, and Bullion had no choice but to cut back on payments: initially he suspended a quarter of the *gages*.[58] At the same time, cash expenditure had risen because of the war effort: in peacetime, it had been usual to pay 30 million at most in cash; the limit of such expenses in practice was 40 million unless new revenues could be found. There is

[53] Ibid. 219. Collins states the argument as a limit on 'direct taxation'; but since this term would include the new taxes of Louis XIV's reign, the *capitation* and the *dixième*, this formulation of the argument is incorrect.

[54] ESFDB dataset \rjb\kk355\kkd004.ssd, from AN KK 355.

[55] ESFDB dataset \rjb\genb001.

[56] In 1650, the *brevet* fixed the levy at 40.2 million, of which the *élection* was to carry 1.43 million. Similarily, in 1654, the *brevet* fixed the levy of the *taille* at 40 million; the burden on the *élection* of Paris (before reductions) was fixed at 1.43 million. For Bullion's estimate of the *taille* at '40 et tant de millions dont les charges deduictes il en revient 20 et tant de millions au Roy . . .': AAE France 819, fo. 97ᵛ, 'Memoire du Sr de Bullion sur les quartiers d'hiver' (1635).

[57] AAE France 834, fo. 116ᵛ, 25 Oct. (1639).

[58] Bonney, *King's Debts*, 179, and Malet, *Comptes rendus*, 94.

clear evidence that Richelieu was personally involved in establishing the priorities for expenditure.[59] The cardinal also intervened in the search for new revenues to meet such expenditure. On 2 January 1636, he met the great financier Pierre Puget de Montauron and discussed the first version of a scheme which was to become the *sol pour livre*, the 5 per cent sales tax introduced in November 1640.[60] He met Tubeuf to discuss the levy of the *subsistances* in the provinces in 1639.[61] It is also clear from Bullion's letters of the autumn of 1639 that the chief minister exercised a determining role in the main decisions (the *taxe des aisés*, the billeting of troops in Normandy after the extension of the *gabelle* into the small privileged region known as the *pays de quart bouillon*,[62] and the *affaires extraordinaires* necessary for 1640).[63]

This preoccupation of Richelieu and Bullion with the short term did not, however, preclude the hope that the war could be ended quickly and financial reforms brought about. In the last months before his death in December 1640, Bullion expressed the wish to Richelieu for 'une bonne reform[at]ion dans le royaume'.[64] Richelieu seems to have been influenced by Bullion's plans,[65] but devised his own set of proposals for restoring stability to the king's finances by creating a budgetary surplus for the first time since the ministry of Sully.[66] Royal expenditure was to be reduced drastically to 25 million 'after the peace'. All areas of royal expenditure were to be

---

[59] Bonney, *King's Debts*, 174. Bullion's last statements concerning the 40 million limit on cash expenses were shortly before his death. AAE France 835, fo. 257, 6 July (1640): 'les depenses presentes ne peuvent aller sans moyens extraordinaires et [il] faut touts les ans trouver pres de 40 millions à cause des advances pour le content'. AAE France 836, fo. 19, 9 Aug. (1640): 'l'estat que VE a ar[r]esté qui monte pour le content à 39 millions et tant de livres chose non imaginable dans le manquement des moyens extraordinaires'. AAE France 836, fo. 61, 29 Aug. (1640): 'l'ordre que VE avoit resolu pour l'année 1640 a esté excedé de plusieurs millions'.

[60] Bonney, *King's Debts*, 183–4, and AAE France 819, fos. 178, 217–18. Also AAE France 820, fos. 1, 27, and 28, 1 Jan. and 15 Jan. 1636.

[61] AAE France 833, fo. 31, 31 Jan. (1639).

[62] So-called because it enjoyed the right to free salt production, subject to paying the crown the equivalent of a quarter of the value of its production: M. Foisil, *La Révolte des Nu-Pieds et les révoltes normandes de 1639* (Paris, 1970), 152.

[63] AAE France 834, fos. 43 and 93, 1 Sept. and 11 Oct. (1639).

[64] AAE France 835, fo. 101, 7 May 1640. See Ranum, *Councillors of Louis XIII*, 146. A reform plan written in his hand was known to contemporaries and survives in the form of a copy entitled 'Ordre a préparer lors qu'il plairra à Dieu donner la paix au Royaume': BN MS 500 Colbert 194, fos. 273–4.

[65] With regard to the *rentes*, Bullion's plan was more detailed than Richelieu's although comparable figures were cited (5 million).

[66] Richelieu's own reform plan of 1639–40 is known to us under the title 'Du Card[in]al de Richelieu en 1640. Projet pour augmenter le revenu de Sa Ma[jes]té & descharger son peuple' with an accompanying 'Projet de despense après la paix': Bonney, *King's Debts*, 131 n. 1, 183. This document is transcribed for the first time in the appendix to this ch.

pruned and the need to reduce royal expenditure by abolishing the
comptants was recognized. This was explicitly stated in Bullion's
plan; Richelieu made no mention of the *comptants* except in the
context of *comptants ès mains du roi*, which were envisaged at the level
of a mere 300,000 *livres* per annum. The reduction in the military
establishment was to be so drastic that the king's ability to fight
another foreign war would have been seriously affected had the plan
been implemented. On the other hand, Richelieu envisaged a total
royal income of over 58 million and thus presumably a very useful
war reserve of 33 million a year. This royal income would be provided from a redistribution of taxes. The chief direct tax, the *taille*,
would be abolished. It would be replaced by the salt tax, which
would be extended uniformly throughout the kingdom (and would
raise 30 million) and the new 5 per cent sales tax (which would raise
12 million). The revenue raised from the salt tax would rise from 13
per cent to 51 per cent of the total; while the sales tax would provide
20 per cent of revenue at inception (Pie Chart 1).[67] The collapse of
extraordinary expenditure in Richelieu's proposals is evident from a
comparison of the figures for actual and projected expenditure
under the reform plan. From 56 per cent of the total, extraordinary
expenditure would fall to a mere 1.2 per cent (Pie Chart 2).[68]
The budget on military expenditure rose as a proportion, but had
declined in absolute terms. Household expenditure rose substantially
as a proportion of the total, as did pensions, under Richelieu's
reform plan.

The memoranda later edited by the *intendant des finances* Moreau
de Beaumont (1713–85), which amounted, among other things, to
the official history of the *gabelles* and the *aides*, explained Richelieu's
intentions:[69]

Il avoit formé le projet d'une imposition uniforme dans toutes les provinces
du royaume, avec une seule régie dans les marais salans dont le Roi se
rendroit propriétaire. Le prix du minot, pour subvenir à toutes les dépenses,
devoit être réglé, eu égard au nombre des habitans, à leur consommation
dans une année. Il se proposoit par ce moyen de supprimer une grande
partie des frais de régie & de ménager même des ressources qui missent en
état de diminuer les autres genres d'imposition. Ce projet diffère de celui de
François Ier, qui, à la vérité, avoit d'abord mis les marais salans sous sa
main, mais uniquement pour en constater l'état & jusqu'à ce qu'il eût

---

[67] ESFDB dataset \rjb\malet\mali006.
[68] ESFDB dataset \rjb\malet\mali005.
[69] J.-L. Moreau de Beaumont, *Mémoires concernant les impositions et droits. Seconde partie.
Impositions et droits en France* (vols. ii–iv; Paris, 1769), iii. 48.

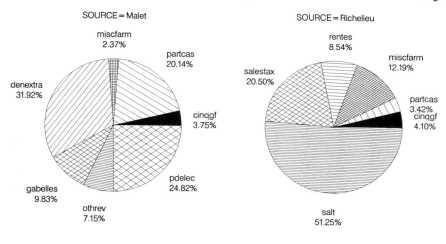

SOURCE = Malet

miscfarm
2.37%

partcas
20.14%

denextra
31.92%

cinqgf
3.75%

pdelec
24.82%

gabelles
9.83%

othrev
7.15%

SOURCE = Richelieu

rentes
8.54%

miscfarm
12.19%

salestax
20.50%

partcas
3.42%
cinqgf
4.10%

salt
51.25%

Sources: J.–R. Malet; AN K 891, no.2   \rjb\malet\mali006   Copyright © ESFDB 1991

Pie chart 1: Categories of French royal revenues in 1640 according to Malet and Richelieu's reform plan

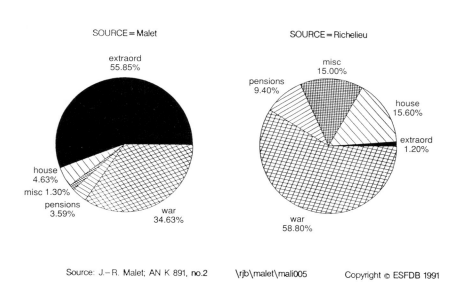

SOURCE = Malet

extraord
55.85%

house
4.63%

misc 1.30%

pensions
3.59%

war
34.63%

SOURCE = Richelieu

misc
15.00%

pensions
9.40%

house
15.60%

extraord
1.20%

war
58.80%

Source: J.–R. Malet; AN K 891, no.2   \rjb\malet\mali005   Copyright © ESFDB 1991

Pie chart 2: Categories of French royal expenditure in 1640 according to Malet and Richelieu's reform plan prescrit une forme d'administration & de régie relatives à sa nouvelle opération . . .

The memorandum on the *aides* suggested that the *sol pour livre* was less radical in its purpose:[70]

Il fut crée sur la fin du règne de Louis XIII, par l'édit de novembre 1640, pour subvenir aux dépenses de la guerre, une nouvelle imposition à l'instar de l'ancien sol pour livre sur toutes les marchandises vendues, revendues & échangées, sous le nom de *subvention générale du vingtième*. La déclaration du 8 janvier suivant changea cette perception & ordonna que le nouveau droit seroit payé à l'entrée suivant des tarifs d'évaluation.

Whether or not they were feasible,[71] Richelieu's revenue proposals in his reform plan must rate with the *capitation* of 1695 and Vauban's *Projet d'une dîme royale* (written *c*.1697 but only published in 1707) as one of the most revolutionary fiscal ideas of the seventeenth century. They were, of course, different in nature from subsequent experiments and proposals relating to direct taxation. France and England did not rely heavily on indirect taxes (unlike Spain) in the sixteenth and seventeenth centuries. Richelieu's proposals anticipated the eighteenth-century changes in these two countries, where the greater proportionate reliance on indirect taxes tended to reinforce the social position of the upper classes.[72] To the extent that one of the revenue proposals, the sales tax or *sol pour livre*, was actually implemented, the view that Richelieu and Bullion failed to introduce any 'really new tax schemes' is perhaps not quite fair[73]

[70] Ibid. iii. 346.

[71] The usual judgement on the plan is that they were not, and that they showed Richelieu's ignorance of financial questions: H. Hauser, *La Pensée et l'action économiques du cardinal de Richelieu* (Paris, 1944), 178. However, this verdict in turn rests on the inaccurate (and thus incomprehensible) figures in *Test. pol.* 437–8, 441–3. André's readings for the new salt levy and the sales tax were respectively 25,000 *livres* and 12,000 *livres*! Selections from the André edn. have now been re-ed. by Daniel Dessert: see Richelieu, *Testament Politique* (Brussels, 1990). André's figures are set beside those from the document cited in n. 66 above in the appendix. Moreau de Beaumont emphasized the fact that Richelieu's plans interfered with the right of the proprietors of the *salines* to sell their salt abroad. If salt was a proper subject for taxation, 'le commerce extérieur qu'il procure est un objet digne de la plus grande attention, & qui paroit difficile à concilier avec le projet que le Cardinal de Richelieu avoit formé': *Mémoires concernant les impositions et droits*, iii. 48.

[72] 'A Tax laid upon Land seems hard to the Landholder, because it is so much Money going visibly out of his Pocket. And therefore as an Ease to himself, the Landholder is always forwarded to lay it upon Commodities . . .'. Quoted by J. V. Beckett, 'Land Tax or Excise: The Levying of Taxation in Seventeenth- and Eighteenth-Century England', *English Historical Review*, 100 (1985), 304. See also P. K. O'Brien, 'The Political Economy of British Taxation, 1660–1815', *Economic History Review*, 2nd. ser. 41 (1988), 26–7, and J. Brewer, *The Sinews of Power: War, Money and the English State, 1688–1783* (London, 1989), 95–101.

[73] Ranum, *Councillors of Louis XIII*, 137.

(although the *sol pour livre* was Henri IV's *pancarte* under another name).[74] While Sully had not opposed the establishment of the tax proposed by the Assembly of Notables of 1596, he claimed that its levy was impracticable, while its projected yield was grossly inflated; and so it had proved to be under Henri IV.[75] But whereas at the time of Sully the proponents of the *sol pour livre* had asserted that it could raise 4–5 million, by 1640 the estimated yield had risen to a minimum of 12 million.[76] There can be little doubt that, in terms of the circulation of goods, the wealth was in the kingdom waiting to be taxed, at least in peacetime. The problem was a political and an administrative one: how to organize the levy in the face of resistance. Within two months of Richelieu's death, Louis XIII succumbed to political pressure and abandoned the tax altogether.[77] In the case of Richelieu's *grand dessein du sel*, we cannot be certain that the cardinal himself would not have abandoned it in the face of opposition, given his comments and his fiscal concessions after the revolt of the Va-Nu-Pieds.[78] So we are left with a scheme on paper for the wholesale transfer of revenues—71 per cent of income was to come from the two schemes taken together, the levy on salt and the sales tax—without any political certainty that either could be levied in the kingdom at large, dominated as it was by regional privilege. Nothing came of the plan, and perhaps nothing could have come of it without a recourse to force. In this respect, perhaps, if in no other, the implications of Richelieu's plan of 1640 were akin to those in Olivares's Grand Memorandum of 1624 to reform the constitutional and fiscal structure of the Spanish Habsburg monarchy.[79]

[74] *Les Œconomies royales de Sully*, ed. D. J. Buisseret and B. Barbiche (vol. ii, 1595–9; Paris, 1988), 138. Sully's judgement of the scheme is worth quoting: 'l'imposition du sol pour livre qui se leveroit sur toutes sortes de vivres, denrées et marchandises, tant menues peussent-elles estre, qui seroyent vendues en detail, du revenu de laquelle les autheurs d'icelle, comme s'ilz eussent trouvé la pierre philosophale ou les mines du Perou, faisoyent une grande parade, publiant que tel revenu monteroit à plus de quatre milions de livres, faisant un certain calcul sur la despence des particuliers, lequel à l'execution se trouva ridicule et impertinent'.

[75] Ibid. 142. Sully added that the tax would be so difficult to collect that it would attract 'toutes les haines et crieries des peuples et les plainctes, reproches et importunitez des demandeurs'. See Bonney, *King's Debts*, 50.

[76] Bonney, *King's Debts*, 184.

[77] Bonney, *Political Change*, 48 n. 3 and 328–30. Moreau de Beaumont pointed out that an additional levy on drink remained within the provinces subject to the *aides*, the levy of which remained 'difficiles et dispendieuse': *Mémoires concernant les impositions et droits*, iii. 346–7.

[78] His comments are cited in Foisil, *La Révolte des Nu-Pieds*, 157, 286. The main fiscal concession was the continuing special regime of the *pays de quart bouillon*.

[79] J. H. Elliott, *The Count-Duke of Olivares* (New Haven, Conn., 1986), 197–8. Id., *Richelieu and Olivares* (Cambridge, 1984), 73–4, 77, 84.

IV

In the end, it was not Richelieu the reformer, or crypto-reformer, of the royal finances who would be remembered, but the Richelieu of the alleged *tour de vis fiscal* and the corrupt financial regime of his clients, above all Bullion. The *Mazarinades*, which may be taken as a fair reflection of popular opposition to ministerial policies at mid-century, belaboured the disastrous consequences of Richelieu's administration of the royal finances. *La Vérité toute nue . . .* (1652) asserted that 'On ne sçauroit penser sans horreur à la maniere dont elles ont esté administrée depuis le temps du Cardinal de Richelieu. Au lieu de choisir des homes dignes de remplir la charge de Sur-Intendant, qui est la plus importante du Royaume, principalement durant vne aussi grande guerre que celle que nous soustenous depuis tant d'années', he had appointed d'Effiat and Bullion, with Cornuel, Bordier, Galland, Lambert, Le Camus, Bretonvilliers, Bordeaux, and Tubeuf in subordinate roles: 'Ie serois trop long', the author asserted, 'si ie voulois nommer tous ceux qui ont fait comme en vn moment tant de fortunes prodigieuses . . .'.[80] For subsequent generations, notably Boisguilbert and Malet at the beginning of the eighteenth century, the emphasis was solely on Richelieu's *tour de vis fiscal*. Boisguilbert considered that Richelieu doubled in ten years 'tous les revenus de la Couronne; on cria extrêmement contre lui; mais c'était avec la dernière injustice que l'on faisait ces plaintes, car cette augmentation était l'effet de celle de tous les biens du Royaume, qui avait plus que doublé pareillement . . .'.[81] Malet, too, judged that the reign of Louis XIII saw a substantial increase in taxation, for which Richelieu's foreign policy was largely responsible ('il donna peu au soulagement des Peuples, parce qu'il donnoit tout à l'agrandissement de la Monarchie qu'il gouvernoit').[82] The Richelieu of the reform plan had largely been forgotten, despite Véron de Forbonnais's recognition that there had indeed been a plan.[83] The judgement of Voltaire, who castigated the plan as 'gibberish', has

---

[80] H. Carrier, *La Fronde: Contestation démocratique et misère paysanne* (2 vols.; Paris, 1982), i (pp. 4–5 of the *Mazarinade*, which is reproduced in its original form). For the financiers under Louis XIII, see Françoise Bayard, *Le Monde des financiers au XVIIe siècle* (Paris, 1988).

[81] *Le Détail de la France* (1695), quoted in *Pierre de Boisguilbert ou la naissance de l'économie politique*, (INED, 2 vols.; Paris, 1966), ii. 649. See also ibid. ii. 914 (*Factum de la France*, 1707): 'tous les revenus du royaume doublèrent de son temps, ainsi que ceux du Roi, auquel n'ayant trouvé que 35 millions de rente, il en laissa 70 à sa mort'.

[82] Malet, *Comptes rendus*, p. xi, and BN MS Fr. 7752, pp. 7–8, quoted by Bonney, 'Jean-Roland Malet', 191.

[83] F. Véron de Forbonnais, *Recherches et considérations sur les finances de France depuis 1595 jusqu'à l'année 1721* (2 vols.; Basle, 1758), i. 238–44.

tended to be accepted.[84] Thus the link between the reforming endeavours of the first half of the seventeenth century, chiefly the *sol pour livre* (however misguided the fiscal base of the tax), and the projects of the second half, above all the *dîme royal* of Vauban, and the new taxes of the last wars of Louis XIV's reign (the *capitation* of 1695 and the *dixième* of 1710) has been lost. The historical verdict on Richelieu has thus been narrowed;[85] and Richelieu the oppressive minister, as well as Richelieu the *affairiste*, has become the new orthodoxy.

It may seem a logical extension of the argument that Richelieu had a 'conscious and perfectly realistic ordering of priorities', in both his public and private business affairs,[86] to argue that the chief minister was properly in charge of the actions of his subordinates, the *surintendants* and *intendants des finances*. If 'the decisions which shaped the history of his wealth were his alone',[87] why should this not have been true of financial policy in general? Such an extension of the argument is not necessarily warranted, for it would assume a greater capacity to control the detailed workings of government than was possible for a chief minister in the seventeenth century. As far as is known, Richelieu never attended the *conseil d'état des finances*; Mazarin only did so in the first week of November 1643,[88] though for a few days in 1659 he contemplated becoming a joint *surintendant* with Foucquet.[89] There had been talk of Richelieu heading a group of four finance ministers in 1624;[90] but with the appointment of Bochart de Champigny and Marillac at the end of August 1624 the talk had come to nothing. It is clear that experience in managing the crown's finances was of value to a retired minister in the task of managing his private wealth, as the example of Sully demonstrates.[91] But there is not a great deal of evidence that the lessons of managing a private fortune, by means of agents, helped in the task of controlling the king's finances. Bullion called Richelieu 'le meilleur mesnager en toutes fassons et pour les affaires publiques et pour les

---

[84] Voltaire commented on 'le galimatias sur les finances qu'on trouve au chapitre 9 du *Testament politique*' and concluded that the author was guilty of 'des fautes qu'un écolier ne commetrait pas'; either Richelieu was extraordinarily ignorant of financial questions or he was not the author of the *Testament politique*: quoted by André in *Test. pol.* 56, 495, 502.

[85] Though Carmona, it is true, has devoted a few lines to the proposed reforms: M. Carmona, *Richelieu: L'Ambition et le pouvoir* (Paris, 1983), 634–6.

[86] J. Bergin, *Cardinal Richelieu: Power and the Pursuit of Wealth* (New Haven, Conn., 1985), 67.

[87] Ibid. 68.

[88] Bonney, *Political Change*, 8 n. 2.

[89] Bonney, *King's Debts*, 1.

[90] Ibid. 114–15, and AAE France 778, fo. 196.

[91] Aristide, *La Fortune de Sully*.

finances du Royaume',[92] but the cardinal always disclaimed true expertise in such matters.[93] Whether or not we accept this disclaimer must depend not merely on the evidence of the creation of Richelieu's private fortune, fundamental though this is, but on the feasibility of the reform plan of 1640. If the chief minister's scheme was more than 'gibberish', and contained (as has been argued here) not merely an internal coherence but a certain realism predicated on the idea of a return to a *status quo ante*, then we arrive not merely at a better-informed verdict on Richelieu's knowledge of the royal finances but a quite different judgement of Richelieu the 'state-builder'. The permanence of the *tour de vis fiscal* was a consequence of the continuation of the war beyond Richelieu's death. It was not something consciously willed by the cardinal, contrary to the later views of Boisguilbert and Malet. It therefore follows that as late as 1642 the state might have been 'rolled back',[94] had those famous secret peace negotiations with Philip IV (perhaps even the secret negotiations involving Cinq-Mars) led to a peace settlement in Richelieu's lifetime. This was what the public at large had hoped for on the death of Louis XIII, and it was these aspirations which the regency government so conclusively failed to meet.

Abbreviations used in charts and graphs

centre	central region within *pays d'élections*
cinqgf	*cinq grosses fermes*
denextra	*deniers extraordinaires*
dongrat	*dons gratuits* ('voluntary grants' from estates)
extraord	extraordinary income or revenue
fermgen	*fermes générales*
fermpart	*fermes particulières*
gabelles	*gabelles* (various revenue farms concerning levy of the salt tax)
house	household expenditure of the royal family
misc	miscellaneous expenditure
miscfarm	miscellaneous revenue farms
miscrev	miscellaneous revenues
normdy	Normandy
north	northern region within *pays d'élections*
othrev	other revenues

[92] AAE France 836, fo. 141, 11 Nov. 1640.

[93] Ranum, *Councillors of Louis XIII*, 136.

[94] Although the precise administrative significance of Richelieu's proposals remains elusive, the reduction in expenditure could not have failed to make its impact by restricting bureaucratic development in France.

partcas	*parties casuelles*
pdelec	direct taxes from *pays d'élections*
pdetat	*pays d'états* (chiefly direct taxes)
pensions	expenditure on gifts and pensions
pdetotal	total revenue from *pays d'états*
rentes	savings from redemption or repurchase of *rentes*
revfarms	revenue farms
salestax	sales tax (*sol pour livre*)
salt	income from salt tax after Richelieu's proposed reforms
se	south-eastern region within *pays d'élections*
sw	south-western region within *pays d'élections*
tailbois	income from *taillon* and *bois*
war	military expenditure

APPENDIX

Two Versions of Richelieu's Proposed Reform of French Finances

I. PROJECTED ROYAL REVENUE AFTER THE EXPECTED PEACE TREATY

Testament Politique,
ed. André (pp. 437–8)

'Du Card^{al} de Richelieu en 1640
Projet pour augmenter le revenu de
Sa Ma^{te} & descharger son peuple'
(AN K 891, no. 2)

. . . en déchargeant entièrement le peuple de 17 millions de livres, qui reviennent maintenant aux Coffres du Roi des levées de la taille, la recette peut monter jusques à 50 millions, ainsi que l'état suivant le justifie clairement:

De l'imposition à mettre sur le sel sur les marais ou autrement en toutes les provinces du Royaume. Il en peut revenir au Roi, tous frais faits . . .

25,000

De l'imposition à mettre sur le scel soit sur les marais ou autrement en toutes les provinces du Royaume, il en peult revenir à Sa Ma^{te} . . .

30,000,000 de lt

Du sol pour livre de toutes les marchandises et denrées du Royaume . . .

12,000

Du sol pour livre sur toutes les marchandises et denrées . . .

12,000,000 de lt

Des aides . . .

400,000

De la ferme des Aydes par estimaon

2,000,000 de lt

De la réduction du rachat des rentes Constituées sur l'hôtel de ville . . .

De la réduction ou rachapt des rentes constituées en l'hostel de ville de Paris il en reviendra à Sa Ma^{te} à déduire sur les charges la somme de . . .

5,000,000

5,000,000 de lt

Des parties casuelles . . .

2,000,000

De l'ord^{re} des parties casuelles par estimaon

2,000,000 de lt

De la ferme de Bordeaux . . .

1,800,000

De la ferme du Convoy de Bordeaux & du nouveau subside imposé à Blaye & depuis transferé aud. Bordeaux . . .

1,800,000 lt

Des 3 livres pour muid de vin
entrant à Paris, nouvelle
imposition . . .

750,000

Des 30 sols anciens et nouveaux, dix
sols pour chacun muid de vin
entrant à Paris . . .

580,000

De la ferme des 45 sols au lieu des
péages et octrois, ci . . .

530,000

De la ferme de Brouage . . .

254,000

De la traité foraine de Languedoc,
épiceries et drogueries de Marseille
et 2 pour cent d'Arles . . .

380,000

Des Surtaux de Lyon . . .

60,000

Des Cinq grosses fermes . . .

2,400,000

Des nouvelles impositions de
Normandie . . .

150,000

De la Ferme du fer . . .

80,000

Des ventes des bois ordinaires des
Domaines . . .

550,000

TOTAL 50,483,000[a]

Des trois livres pour muid de vin
entrant à Paris de nouvelle
imposion . . .

750,000 lt

Des XXXs antiens & nouveaux, X
s. d'entrée sur chascun muid de vin
entrant à Paris . . .

580,000 lt

De la ferme des XLVs au lieu des
péages & octroys de la rivière de
Seine . . .

530,000 lt

De la ferme de Brouage . . .

254,000 lt

De la traitte foraine de Languedoc,
espiceries drogueries de Marseille &
pour cent [sic] d'Arles . . .

380,000 lt

De la ferme du tiers surtault de la
douanne de Lion . . .

60,000 lt

Des Cinq grosses fermes . . .

2,400,000 lt

Des nouvelles imposions de
Normandie dont bail a esté
nouvellem. ft . . .

150,000 lt

De la ferme du fer . . .

80,000 lt

Des ventes des bois ordinaires . . .

550,000 lt

59,483,000[b]

Sans y comprendre ce qui revient
des imposions des Tailles

[a] In fact, the total was 14,971,000 livres.

[b] In fact, the total was 58,534,000 livres, including 9 lt 13 s 'pour tonneau de Picardie'
(174,000 lt) and the farm of revenues from the river Loire (225,000).

2. PROJECTED ROYAL EXPENDITURE AFTER THE EXPECTED PEACE TREATY

Testament Politique, ed. André (pp. 441–3)	'Projet de despense après la paix' (AN K 891, no. 2)
	La paye de 10,000 chevaux soubz le tiltre de cent compagnies de gens d'armes qui n'estans enrollez que pour servir en cas de besoing ne recevront par an qu'un quar^{er} . . .
	1,300,000 lt
	La paye de 50,000 hommes du p^{er} ordre des legionnaires qui estoient enrollez dans les provinces & XXV regimens pour servir seullemt pour lors q. la nécessité le requerra ne recevront qu'une monstre pour les soldatz & quatre pour les officiers revenant à . . .
	1,200,000 lt
	La paye de 40,000 hommes de second ordre de gens de guerre actuellement servans qui recevront tous les jours leur pain & IIIIs de prest revenant à . . .
	6,000,000 de lt
	La paye de 4,000 chevaux legers payez de neuf mois au lieu qu'à présent ilz ne recoivent que 4 monstres de deux mois chascune revenans . . .
	1,600,000 lt
	La paye des garnisons extraord^{res} . . .
	1,000,000 de lt
La dépense de la [marine] de Ponant et de Levant ne sauroit être moindre que de 2 millions, ainsi qu'il paraît par les États particuliers qui en sont dressés . . .	La despense de la marine du ponant & Levant . . .
2,600,000 livres	2,000,000 de lt
Celle de l'artillerie reviendra à . . .	Celle de l'artillerie à . . .
600,000	. 600,000 lt
Celle des Maisons du Roi, de la Reine et de Monsieur à ci . . .	La despense des maisons du Roy, de la Royne, de Monsieur le Dauphin & de M^r frère unique . . .
3,600,000	3,500,000 lt

Les pensions des Suisses, dont on ne peut honorable s'exempter, sont de . . .

400,000

Les bâtiments coûteront . . .

300,000

Les ambassadeurs . . .

250,000

Les fortifications . . .

600,000

. . . les pensions et les appointements ne seront employés à l'avenir que pour . . .

2,000,000

Les [ordinaires] du Roy . . .

50,000

Les acquits patents . . .

400,000

Les parties inopinées & voyages . . .

2,000,000

Les nonvaleurs . . .

150,000

Les Comptants du Roy . . .

300,000

Toutes ces dépenses ne reviendront qu'à 25 millions[c]

Les pensions des Suisses . . .

400,000 lt

Les bastimens . . .

400,000 lt

Les ambassadeurs . . .

250,000 lt

Les fortificaons . . .

600,000 lt

Les pensions & apointemens . . .

2,000,000 de lt

Les ordinaires du Roy . . .

50,000 lt

Les acquits patents . . .

300,000 lt

Les parties inopinées & voyages . . .

2,000,000 de lt

Nonvalleurs par estimaon . . .

1,500,000 lt

Les Comptans du Roy . . .

300,000 lt

Somme de ce que dessus

22,650,000 lt[d]

[c] In fact, the total was 13,250,000 livres.
[d] In fact, the total was 25 million livres.

5

RICHELIEU, THE *GRANDS*, AND THE FRENCH ARMY

DAVID PARROTT

I

The great aristocracy has traditionally been accorded a secondary, and essentially negative, role in studies of Richelieu's ministry. As one historian pointed out in a recent article, the nobles in seventeenth-century France have been the victims of a crude historicism which sees the rise of royal absolutism as inevitable, and even praiseworthy, so that resistance by the nobility appears as mere short-sighted and futile obstructionism.[1] The great aristocratic families have largely been depicted as a group acted upon by 'new' historical forces, rather than political actors in their own right. Allocated an over-simplified social structure and an apparently shared and undisputed set of political objectives, the *grands* can be wrapped up in convenient assumptions about feudal anachronism and group selfishness. Thus packaged, they are pushed to one side of the historical stage, in good time to be unveiled a few decades later, safely locked up in the 'gilded prison' of Versailles.

A part of this traditional interpretation of the role of the aristocracy during Richelieu's ministry was grounded on an assumption which is no longer widely held: few historians now believe that Richelieu was intent on a political revolution aimed at destroying the privileges and power of the *grands*. However, it remains easy to slip into another historical simplification, which creates a single entity, the 'great nobility', which is treated as a homogenous, politically distinct, group within French society.[2]

I should like to record my thanks as ever to Dr Robert Oresko, who read this paper through for me, and whose comments and suggestions have proved unfailingly helpful.

[1] R. Briggs, 'Noble Conspiracy and Revolt in France, 1610–60, *Seventeenth-Century French Studies*, 12 (1990), 158–76, 159.

[2] e.g. O. A. Ranum, 'Richelieu and the Great Nobility: Some Aspects of Early Modern Political Motives', *French Historical Studies*, 3 (1963), 184–204; R. Mousnier, 'Monarchie contre aristocratie dans la France du XVIIe siècle', *XVIIe Siècle*, 31 (1956), 377–81.

While the *grands* represent an extremely small number of individuals in seventeenth-century France, it is misleading to suggest that this distinction gave them a single social rank. As all contemporaries recognized, the most important characteristic of the *grands* was their conscious internal stratification.[3] At the top of this ranking came those actually of the royal blood with undisputed places within an eventual succession to the crown: the king's immediate family—the children and grandchildren of France—and kinsmen of unbroken legitimate male descent, such as the prince de Condé and comte de Soissons. Distinct from these were the *grands* related to the king by illegitimate descent, the Longueville, the Angoulême and the Vendôme, whose status was a matter for debate and competition; the Longueville, for example, were engaged in a running struggle to obtain recognition as princes of the blood, with rights to the succession, through much of the seventeenth century. Henri II de Longueville's second marriage to the sister of the Grand Condé was certainly seen by contemporaries as a move to associate himself more closely with the direct line of royal succession.[4] A later agreement, made between the duke and Louis XIV, whereby the Longueville were to be recognized as of the royal blood in return for a greater degree of crown authority in the family's traditional governorship of Normandy, was a source of contention until the extinction of the family line in 1694.[5]

The next tier in the structure comprised those claiming princely, as distinct from royal, status, either through rights of succession

---

[3] J. P. Labatut, *Les Ducs et pairs de France au XVIIe siècle* (Paris, 1972), is one of the most useful studies of the aristocratic hierarchy, though by definition it is substantially concerned with a particular group within the structure. R. Mousnier, *Les Institutions de la France sous la monarchie absolue* (2 vols.; Paris, 1974–80), i. 125–8, 163–5; *Dictionnaire du grand siècle*, ed. F. Bluche (Paris, 1990), provides some useful analytical sections, but in the matter of individual and family biographies it should be consulted in conjunction with le Père Anselme de Sainte Marie [P. de Guibourgs], *Histoire généalogique et chronologique de la maison royale de France, des pairs, grands officiers de la couronne, de la maison du roi et des anciens barons du royaume* (3rd edn., 9 vols.; Paris, 1726–33), and F. A. de La Chesnaye-Desbois, *Dictionnaire de la noblesse . . .* (3rd edn., 19 vols.; Paris, 1866–76). An indication of the ranking of individuals amongst the *grands* can be found in the details of precedence connected with membership of the order of the Saint Esprit: F. de Flavigny, *Abrégé historique des chevaliers . . . de l'Ordre du Saint-Esprit* (Geneva, 1873).

[4] Duc de Saint-Simon, *Mémoires*, ed. A. de Boislisle (45 vols.; Paris, 1879–1930), xix, 66. The family's relationship to the royal line is reviewed in Anselme, *Histoire généalogique*, i. 219–23.

[5] R. Mettam, *Power and Faction in Louis XIV's France* (Oxford, 1988), 85–6. The interests and aims of the Longueville family were diversified still further by their possession of the sovereign principality of Neuchâtel; this offered not merely the possibility of claiming sovereign status, but the possession of a territory whose links as a co-alliée within the Helvetic Confederation provided crucial access to Swiss mercenaries, and whose geographical position, to the east of Spanish Franche-Comté, gave the territory great strategic importance.

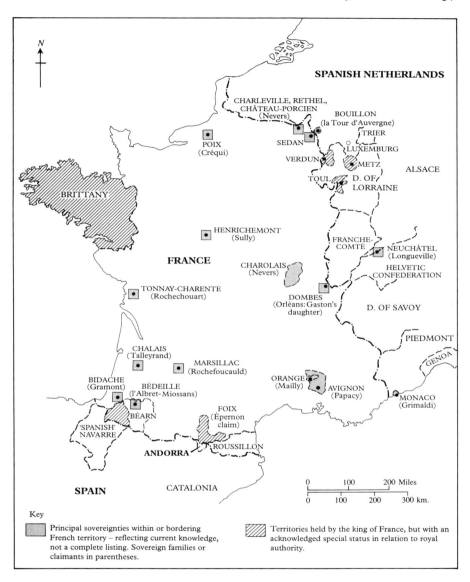

Map 5.1. Sovereign States or Semi-Independent Territories within or on the Borders of France in the First Half of the Seventeenth Century.

to foreign sovereignties, or through the possession of a sovereign territory enclosed within, or existing on, the borders of France. The scope for competition over ranking at this level was formidable, especially after the increase in the number of *princes légitimés* during the reign of Henri IV; this tier included such extended families as the Guise, which by the seventeenth century comprised half a dozen different lines, all of which could lay claim to the status of *princes étrangers* by reason of their uncontested rights as cadets of the house of Lorraine. While far from a consistently unified clan in pursuit of shared strategies and objectives, branches of the family retained a key role in aristocratic politics throughout the seventeenth century.[6]

Below this princely tier came the *ducs et pairs*. In most cases *seigneuries* were raised directly to the status of *duché-pairies*, with rapid registration of the *pairie* by the Paris parlement. This typical procedure was followed for the *seigneurie* of Richelieu in 1631.[7] However, there were also a number of nobles with ducal titles who had not received or who had not registered a *pairie*, yet who held a sufficient mass of power and influence to be counted amongst the *grands*. In a number of cases the crown specifically created *duchés à brevet* to rule out the possibility that a *pairie* would subsequently be registered and to emphasize the distinct rank of this group.[8] In other cases the reasons for the failure to register a *pairie* seem obscure: Mazarin had obtained the re-creation of the duché de Nevers for his nephew, Philippe-Jules Mancini, in 1661, but for unknown reasons it was never registered as a *pairie*; the Crevant d'Humières gained ducal rank in 1690 for the military services of the Maréchal, but in contrast to most comparable families who received promotion for military services, no *pairie* was subsequently registered.[9]

Amongst all these French dukes were notable families, the Épernon and the La Rochefoucauld, for example, who pressed claims to recognition by the crown as *princes étrangers* on the basis of possession of sovereign territories or of blood ties to sovereign dynasties. The Épernon had a number of strategies to achieve *prince étranger* status, based upon their close relations to the Foix family, with its

---

[6] Anselme, *Histoire généalogique*, iii. 485–503, provides biographical information about the ramifications of the Guise/Lorraine family, but no recent studies exist of the family in the 17th cent. See Labatut, *Ducs et pairs*, 351–69; A. Jouanna, *Le Devoir de révolte. La Noblesse française et la gestation de l'état moderne, 1559–1661* (Paris, 1989).

[7] J. Bergin, *Cardinal Richelieu: Power and the Pursuit of Wealth* (New Haven, Conn., 1985), 125–7.

[8] Labatut, *Ducs et pairs*, 357–8.

[9] Ibid. 113–4.

title to sovereign Navarre, upon their title to the princedom of Buch and on their designs concerning Metz, where they held the governorship.[10] In the same period, the La Rochefoucauld sought to achieve recognition as *princes étrangers* on the basis of possession of the princedom of Marcillac-Lanville.[11] The large numbers of principalities in the south and east of France, and the special cases of the provinces of Brittany and Navarre, with their separate and specific relationship to the French crown, presented considerable possibilities for advancement through family possession or close association.

There was nothing homogeneous therefore about the *grands*, and never had been. At every dividing line of the hierarchy individual families strove for promotion and competed with one another for precedence. Relative ranking was a constant source of dispute; and these disputes cannot be dismissed as being empty rivalries, carried on outside the arena of real politics by status-obsessed aristocrats. It was evident to all those involved in attempts to promote themselves or their families that the levels of status within the hierarchy of the *grands* were clearly linked to economic and political opportunities stemming from increasing proximity to the king and the chance of appropriate office and rewards—rewards which could easily involve powerful or lucrative marriages within the caste. Nor should it be forgotten that a principal aim of the *grands* in defining their status and their relationship with the crown remained the strengthening and consolidation of their regional or provincial power bases.

The advantages could equally well be non-material, yet still extremely valuable: one benefit of holding or acquiring the status of sovereign prince was that it brought with it a change in the relationship with the king of France. Ceasing to be an unconditional subject, the prince could introduce the notion of service to the monarch, potentially transferable to another power: actions which would be seen as treasonable in others could be defined more diplomatically in a sovereign prince's case. Frédéric-Maurice de La Tour d'Auvergne, duc de Bouillon, escaped punishment for his part in the Cinq-Mars conspiracy of 1642 by conceding the French occupation of Sedan, one of his sovereign territories on the eastern border of France. A decade later, in 1652, he was able to strike a further bargain with the crown, gaining formal recognition as *prince étranger* in return for

---

[10] BN MS Fr. 20564, fo. 118, 18 Oct. 1657. The efforts of the second duke to gain *prince étranger* status during the Fronde are described in Montglat's *Mémoires*, in C. Petitot and L. de Monmerqué (eds.), *Collection des mémoires relatifs à l'histoire de France . . .* (52 vols.; Paris 1819–26), l. 195–6.

[11] Labatut, *Ducs et pairs*, 366.

accepting the permanent cession of Sedan to France.[12] A further example of the privileges accepted at this level was the right to leave France without specific royal permission, and without any legal liability—an obvious advantage to members of the high French nobility with multifarious international connections. This was a privilege specifically accorded to the *princes étrangers*, and was not even shared by those at the top of the hierarchy of the *grands*, the *princes du sang*.

Status amongst the *grands* was critically important, and all of the families became involved, often by tradition, in rivalries and conflicts which had direct consequences for political influence and resources. Within the families themselves individuals could define and pursue very different policies or form alliances outside of their immediate group of relatives—either in their own interest or, more intriguingly, as an insurance policy for the wider family—'spreading bets', in effect.

Above all, in this context, the policies that were being pursued by the crown, or by Cardinal Richelieu, were not seen as some extraneous and distinctive force existing outside of all these rivalries. They fell within the mass of competing and conflicting aims of the *grands*, and to a great extent they were supported or opposed as a result of the existing conflicts and the aspirations of the participants.

The reasons which led a particular aristocrat or group of *grands* to oppose the policies of Richelieu would not necessarily entail the wider adherence of the *grands* to their cause. The whole question of status, aspirations, and traditional rivalries assumes vital importance in explaining why some families or individuals proved consistently hostile to the cardinal; why others gave him their explicit co-operation; and why a number occupied a central ground of careful and measured collaboration, from which they hoped to extricate themselves quickly if it served their interests.

The observation that the political motives of the *grands* should be understood in terms of individual, rather than corporate, self-interest has considerable significance for the control and management of the army during the ministry of Cardinal Richelieu. What gives it even greater relevance is Richelieu's own involvement as a major participant in the struggle for status and precedence amongst the *grands*.

For while we may assume that Richelieu somehow represented a higher level of political awareness and motive than the *grands* who

---

[12] E. Baluze, *Histoire généalogique de la Maison d'Auvergne* (2 vols.; Paris, 1708), ii. 813–17, 820; S. d'Huart, *Inventaire des Archives Rohan-Bouillon* (Paris, 1970), provides both a detailed introduction, and considerable evidence of the political power and family interests of the Bouillon: see pp. 111–40.

are taken to be his declared opponents, we are presented with the clearest evidence that Richelieu was himself seeking to establish his family within the topmost ranks of the aristocracy.[13] The conflict of motives that must have ensued is difficult to reconcile with what are usually thought to be Richelieu's achievements, except by assuming that his 'real' aims were enforcing unconditional service to the king and the development of authoritarian, absolutist policies; the apparently incompatible pursuit of aristocratic status for himself and his family has then to be regarded as a secondary motive, a mere foible of a great man.[14]

This attempt at reconciliation is unsatisfactory, as Joseph Bergin has convincingly demonstrated in his recent study of Richelieu's life before the achievement of ministerial status in 1624. In the introduction to this work he makes a number of remarks about what might be termed the myth of Richelieu, the notion that the cardinal, blessed from the outset of his career with 'un grand sens de l'État', somehow stood above the mundane world of his political contemporaries.[15] If we accept the propaganda of the *Mémoires*, Richelieu was the selfless servant of the king and of France, stoically prepared to accept whatever might be dealt him by fate: the possibility of the early death of Louis XIII, the succession of King Gaston, a royal regency controlled by Anne of Austria or a group of hostile *grands*— all scenarios that would probably lead to his political disgrace and the ruin of his family.[16]

In reality, of course, Richelieu sought to use all his power and influence to build up resources and position against such possibilities. Dr Bergin's first book provides the evidence of the systematic accumulation of the cardinal's fortune, and of his attempts to safeguard this fortune in his family's hands after his death.[17] An equally important aspect of Richelieu's ground-plan for political survival was dynastic. His pursuit of family links with the other *grands* was a consistent and extremely important motive underlying his choice and conduct of policy.

However, it would be quite misleading to suggest that this was a policy of conscious and cynical opportunism. Unlike the great majority of government ministers in seventeenth-century France,

---

[13] Bergin, *Cardinal Richelieu*, 119–31.

[14] Ranum, 'Richelieu and the Great Nobility', 200–2.

[15] J. Bergin, *The Rise of Richelieu* (New Haven, Conn., 1991), 1–11.

[16] See e.g. J. Caillet's, *L'Administration en France sous le ministère du Cardinal de Richelieu* (Paris, 1861), whose remarks on Richelieu are cited with due scepticism by R. J. Knecht, *Richelieu* (London, 1991), 217.

[17] Bergin, *Cardinal Richelieu*, 257–63.

who were drawn from backgrounds within the *noblesse de robe*,
Richelieu came from a traditional military family of long *épée* lineage. He could use this status to claim all the prerogatives of great
aristocratic rank: full membership of the order of the Saint Esprit,
rather than the secondary role of an office-holder within it; the
elevation of his territories to a *duché-pairie*; the nomination to army
command as the king's lieutenant-general. While the *robe* by definition held noble status, they were rigorously opposed in any attempt to
gain aristocratic rank or any of these trappings of 'true' aristocratic
status.[18] Chancellor Séguier was unique amongst the seventeenth-
century *robe* in using his loyalty during the Fronde to overcome this
opposition and to obtain the duchy of Villemor in 1650. It is significant, however, that Séguier had no male heirs, and that his
one daughter was married into a traditional *épée* family; the *pairie*
was registered a year later, in 1651, but explicitly in the name of
Séguier's grandson by this match, the marquis de Coislin.[19].

Established *épée* families, on the other hand, were always potentially able to assume the trappings of the great aristocracy, in that
they were considered to share a common identity with them, based
upon the values of a warrior class to which both groups traced their
origins. In a real sense the provincial *noblesse d'épée* was the lowest
tier of the hierarchy of the *grands*, excluded from most of the benefits
and power of the superior levels, but basic members of a structure in
which a few might succeed in achieving higher status. Richelieu was
an intrinsic member of this extended warrior caste, accepting its
claims to a monopoly of military command,[20] and was himself striving for advancement within its hierarchy, the fluidity of which
offered opportunities for one gifted member to raise the status of the
family as a whole. The behaviour and political assumptions of the
grands were shaped by membership of this dynamic and restless
hierarchy: nowhere is this clearer than in the organization and control of the army.

II

The French army of the early seventeenth century represented a
partnership involving the interests and activities of the crown and the

---

[18] Mousnier, *Les Institutions*, i. 126, 165–7.
[19] *Lettres et mémoires addressés au Chancélier Séguier*, ed. R. Mousnier (Paris, 1964), i. 34;
Labatut, *Ducs et pairs*, 96–7.
[20] *Test. pol.* 218–23.

grands. That part of the army that was genuinely 'royal' was extremely small: somewhere between 8,000 and 15,000 troops, depending on the strength at which the constituent units were maintained. It consisted of six regiments of infantry composed of the *gardes françaises*, the *gardes suisses*, and the four *vieux* regiments; and between twenty and thirty companies of cavalry, made up of a combination of armoured *gendarmes* and *cavalerie légère*. These were the *entretenue* units—those which the crown was prepared to pay on a permanent basis, even if their effective strength was severely reduced in time of peace.[21]

Even in these units, the crown's control was less than total. The *colonel général de l'infanterie française*, a post held by the duc d'Épernon since 1584, gave the right to present candidates for a number of officerships in five of these infantry regiments (the exception being the Swiss, responsible to its own *colonel général*), and to appoint directly the captain of one company in each regiment—usually composed of twenty companies.[22] Outside of this nucleus of troops at least nominally raised, staffed, and administered by the crown and its agents, was the great mass of the army which was raised, administered, and officered by the nobility. As war was a seasonal business, and as conflict was conceived in single, or small numbers of, campaigns, it seemed neither necessary nor financially practical to maintain a much larger, permanent army.

The crown frequently required large numbers of additional troops, but these needed to be raised at short notice and probably for a relatively brief period of service. The most practical means to achieve this was through reliance on the clienteles and influence of the nobility, especially the provincial aristocracy. They had access to a system of subcontracting through relatives and lesser noble supporters, who could themselves carry out the local recruitment of units of soldiers.

The crown had no alternative mechanism to achieve this rapid levy of an army. The military administrators consisted of a number of *commissaires* and *contrôleurs des guerres*, whose functions were primarily concerned with the supervision of payment and the discipline of both *entretenue* and recently raised units. In theory, *commissaires* could also be allocated the assignment of levying these new units in the name of the crown, given the funds to pay the enlistment

---

[21] V. Belhomme, *Histoire de l'infanterie en France* (5 vols.; Paris, 1893–1902), i. 333–96.

[22] G. Girard, *Histoire de la vie du duc d'Épernon* (Paris, 1655), 35, 270; L. Mouton, *Un demi-roi: Le Duc d'Épernon* (Paris, 1992), 142; N. Fessenden, 'Épernon and Guienne: Provincial Politics under Louis XIII' (Ph.D. thesis; Columbia Univ., 1972), 199–202.

premium, and dispatched to a designated area to carry out recruit-ment.[23] In practice, it would have meant giving money and responsi-bility to an *officier* who had no personal interest in carrying out the task honestly or efficiently, and who would be dispatched to an area in which he might well have limited or no local influence and no capacity to control the sources or the quality of recruits—even if he could find any.[24]

Practical considerations weighed heavily, so that the ministry con-tinued to rely overwhelmingly on traditional methods of recruitment. Provincial governors were appointed as the king's representative in the provinces with specific charge of military organization.[25] In the strategically critical frontier provinces, the appointment of a governor was a matter of vital importance. While, on the one hand, the crown wanted someone who would remain loyal to its service, it also needed a governor with sufficient local support and estab-lished military reputation to organize the war-effort and if necessary, defence, of the province.[26] Even when the provincial governor was not the key to local military organization, the crown looked to other powerful noble families in the province to raise troops for its armies.[27]

The crown also had a strong financial incentive for using local nobles to carry out recruitment rather than attempting to rely upon its own agents: even if it was able to obtain the funds to finance its projected campaign—and this itself became increasingly unlikely as the scale and expense of military operations increased—it was far less easy to ensure that those sums available could be collected and deployed at the times which corresponded to military requirements. The established provincial aristocrat would be in a better position than any crown representative to obtain the credit that would allow troops to be recruited and equipped against future revenues, or

[23] Richelieu, *Mémoires* MP ii. 170–1. Richelieu implies that a system of recruitment based upon *commissaires* was the usual practice; but the material in the Archives de la Guerre shows that this was not the case. In general, only additional troops raised during the campaign season for existing regiments were levied by *commissaires des guerres* or local *officiers*.

[24] The prescriptions in the 1629 Code Michaud, are far more pragmatic and give an indication of the real system: the captains were charged with the levy of their recruits, albeit supervised by a *commissaire* or local official, arts. 312, 315: Isambert, xvi. 223–342, 301–12. This was the system employed in practice, though it is difficult to establish how often the *commissaires* were actually present.

[25] R. Harding. *Anatomy of a Power Elite: The Provincial Governors of Early Modern France* (New Haven, Conn., 1978), 68–9.

[26] e.g. AG A¹24, fo. 167, 22 Mar. 1635: commissions to be sent to Schomberg, governor of Languedoc, for 4 regiments of infantry and 3 companies of cavalry.

[27] AG A¹24, fo. 59, Servien to Ventadour, a major provincial noble in the Limousin, 4 Feb. 1635; AG A¹29, fo. 1, de Noyers to Parabère, a great noble with substantial territorial holdings in Poitou, asking him to recruit troops in the province, 16 Aug. 1636.

indeed to provide credit for general military expenses which could be reimbursed at some point in the indeterminate future, or indeed reimbursed in some other, non-financial way. The example of the marquis de Villeroy, who in 1642 agreed to raise 500 additional troops for his regiment against later reimbursement, was typical of the shared assumptions about the financial obligations of the military nobility.[28] The other side of this coin are cases of royal 'gifts', such as that of 50,000 *livres* made to the maréchal de Châtillon in 1636, which were intended to recognize expenses previously incurred in the military service of the crown.[29] At a more generalized level, substantial crown pensions were regarded as a means to allow the *grands* in military service to maintain their commitments, as Richelieu made clear, with more than a hint of menace, in a letter to the prince de Condé.[30] Even when the officer was of a social level below the *grands*, financial 'service to the king' or indeed to Richelieu, was seen as a means to preferment and favour. In 1637 the intendant with the army of Italy singled out the governor of Bresme, Montgaillard, for praise and recognition in the light of his willingness to absorb the costs of fortification in his governorship while refusing to accept more than the 1,000 *livres* of his salary.[31] In this case, the intendant's good reports did not save the unfortunate governor from trial and summary execution a year later, when he was to be accused of showing insufficient resolution in the defence of his *place*.[32]

How did the *grands* benefit from this system? Why should they be willing to deploy their efforts and their social and financial credit in order to raise troops at the demand of the monarchy? The greatest advantage, as might be expected, was the opportunity to favour and advance their clienteles—above all, their adherents among the traditional lesser nobility.[33]

The status and prestige of a great aristocrat required constant affirmation within a society that placed great weight upon display and the visual trappings of power. The power and influence of a *grand* was measured by the number of clients, particularly of noble

[28] AAE France 843, fo. 167, Richelieu to de Noyers, 2 Aug. 1642.
[29] AG A^{1}31, fo. 193, Louis XIII to the Cour des Comptes, Paris, 30 Dec. 1636.
[30] Avenel, vi. 898–9, 20 Feb. 1642.
[31] AAE CP Savoie 25, fo. 237, Argenson to de Noyers, 14 July 1637.
[32] A. M. R. Vicomte de Noailles, *Le Cardinal de la Valette* (Paris, 1906), 380.
[33] J. Bérenger, *Turenne* (Paris, 1987), 102–3, 133–4; Harding, *Anatomy*, 203–4, presents the period after 1635 as one in which traditional military bonds between the great noble governors and the lesser *noblesse d'épée* were disintegrating; yet his evidence is ambiguous, concerned with the difficulties faced by the governors in raising support locally when, as one complained, 'the nobility of this *pays* is almost entirely in the armies of His Majesty'. However, the material in the Archives de la Guerre suggests that exactly these methods of selection and appointment through local patronage had been used to assemble the army in the first place.

rank, who were associated with him.[34] The extent to which the nobility in the seventeenth century still accepted and judged one another in terms of a traditional warrior culture should not be underestimated. The self-perception of the *grands* made it vital that each member should seek a major role in military activities, and use his influence as much as possible to favour his supporters in military appointments.[35]

One of the most prized aspects of holding a command in the field was the opportunity that it gave to present requests for promotions and new appointments. In the wake of any advantage achieved against the enemy, the crown and its ministers were deluged with requests by the commander for promotions to fill those places vacated by death or wounding or to reward meritorious service. In 1640, for example, the comte d'Harcourt, commander of the army of Italy, wrote to the court to announce the fall of Turin; in keeping with such an auspicious military event, he followed up his announcement with a long list of requests for promotions and favours for his officers.[36] Such requests could be rejected or held up by the ministers or those *grands* close to the king, but they were presented in the first place by the commanders; and this ability to act as highly influential 'brokers' in the distribution of patronage strengthened their practical power and prestige.

Richelieu, of course, was at the forefront of this concern to enhance his status as a *grand* and to enlarge his clientele through the sponsorship of military levies and commands in the field. He used his political bases in Brittany and Poitou for the creation of numerous infantry and cavalry units, both in his own name and those of his chief clients. One of these, the Régiment de la marine, he managed to promote, not only up to *entretenue* status, but into a fifth *vieux* regiment, with the accompanying precedence that this gave over most of the rest of the army.[37] His personal command of armies in the South-West, then in Italy, gave him the sought-after power to determine and control appointments and promotion, and to entrench his own supporters within the army.[38]

---

[34] K. Neuschel, *Word of Honor: Interpreting Noble Culture in Sixteenth-Century France* (Ithaca, NY, 1989), 93–5, 198.

[35] Ibid. 61–2. The assumption is present in numerous memoirs of the period, e.g. those written by Puységur, Bussy-Rabutin, Plessis-Praslin, Gramont. F. Billaçois, *Le Duel dans la société française des XVIe et XVIIe siècles* (Paris, 1986), 131–6, 146–61, considers duelling as an offshoot of this continuing conviction that military service defined and reinforced noble status.

[36] AAE CP Savoie 31, fo. 100, 23 Sept 1640.

[37] Belhomme, *Histoire de l'infanterie*, i. 364–5.

[38] Grillon, iv. 729–33, 24 Dec. 1629: commission for command of the army of Italy for Richelieu; the careers of de La Touche, lieutenant colonel of the Régiment de la marine, and

Overall military command in a particular campaign theatre was an extremely important aspiration for the *grands*. Representing an unambiguous sign of royal favour, it enhanced their perceived status within the caste.[39] The achievement of senior military command was the principal criterion for the promotion of an *épée* family to the rank of a *duché-pairie*.[40] Equally importantly, while it involved them in expense, it also provided opportunities for the distribution of patronage and favours. The broad expectation of the *grands* as a caste was that they had the right to commands in royal armies except when the king was personally present in the field. On what basis these commands should be allocated to the individual aristocrats was another matter, revealing clearly the complexities of, and internal rivalries within, the caste. In principle, generalships within the various army corps ought to have been allocated hierarchically, with the immediate royal family and the princes of the blood receiving commands in preference to any other *grand*, followed by the legitimized families, who were placed together with the sovereign princes of major foreign states, such as Lorraine and Savoy, and so on down through the ranks.

However, the situation was greatly complicated by the tradition that a provincial governor had the right to command an army operating in, or from, his territory, and would not expect to be subordinated to anyone of near-comparable status. Moreover, the status of maréchal clearly gave the holder a right, in general, to command the army corps with which he was serving. However, the granting of a baton of maréchal did not always imply that the holder was at the top of the aristocratic hierarchy, nor would it give him any clear-cut right to precedence. Both the maréchaux Toiras and Marillac were from provincial *épée* families of modest wealth.[41] In the court hierarchy a maréchal was judged to be equivalent to a duke in terms of rank and status.[42]

If some degree of preference was given to the maréchaux in the allocation of commands, possession of one of the major military *charges* could also enhance the prospect of appointment to control of an army corps: the *colonel général de l'infanterie*, of the *cavalerie légère*, and of the Swiss; the *grand maître de l'artillerie*. Richelieu's

Houdinières, captain of Richelieu's *gendarmes*, both indicate that they held military responsibility far greater than their nominal status: M. Deloche, *La Maison du cardinal de Richelieu* (Paris, 1912), 392–5.

[39] Neuschel, *Word of Honor*, 204–5.
[40] Labatut, *Ducs et pairs*, 125–9.
[41] M. Baudier, *Histoire du maréchal de Toiras* (Paris, 1644), 3–4; P. de Vaissière, *L'Affaire du maréchal de Marillac, 1630–32* (Paris, 1924), 13–18.
[42] *Dictionnaire du grand siècle*, ed. Bluche, 966–8.

newly created office of *surintendant et grand maître de la navigation* was also invoked to give him considerable, if ill-defined, status across the whole of the military. Once again, dispute and conflict was implicitly present in the coexistence of two separate sources of authority: the status conferred by senior military office, and the possibly divergent position that the holders of these officers held within the social hierarchy of the *grands*.

Richelieu certainly entered into these disputes in order to represent and to emphasize his own claims to military command. But for the cardinal the situation was complicated by larger issues at stake in control and command of the army. The achievement of Richelieu's personal and family aspirations rested heavily upon his ability to maintain himself as the king's *premier ministre*, and the opportunities that this provided to strengthen his power and status through patronage and the financial opportunities offered by senior government office and royal favour. The cardinal had managed to have himself appointed to the king's council in 1624 by presenting himself as the exponent of an assertive, anti-Habsburg foreign policy; identifying himself with this policy allowed him to overcome some of Louis XIII's previous dislike of him and to outmanœuvre potential rivals for his position. Yet despite launching an immediate propaganda offensive to try to justify his policies to those who were opposed to war against fellow Catholic powers, even when they were France's 'old enemies', it seems in retrospect inevitable that any attempt to achieve political reconciliation was doomed to failure.[43] Richelieu's personal hold on power came ultimately to rest upon explicit rejection of the political values and priorities of his opponents. In the struggle to defend his position against these rivals, Richelieu presented assertive policies and the prospect of territorial expansion to Louis XIII as a necessary means to achieve security and to satisfy the king's aspirations to dynastic *gloire*. Graphic evidence of this ambition can be seen in the wording of Richelieu's famous 'choice' to Louis XIII after the French capture of the Piedmontese fortress of Pinerolo in 1630, when the perennial obsession of French kings with their claims to parts of the Italian peninsula was pressed into service: 'si d'autre part, on veut la paix il faut quitter les pensées d'Italie pour l'avenir . . .'.[44] However, the consequence of this readi-

---

[43] W. F. Church, *Richelieu and Reason of State* (Princeton, NJ, 1972), 372–415. The practical consequences of this polarization are discussed in J. H. Elliott, *Richelieu and Olivares* (Cambridge, 1984), 146–8.

[44] Grillon, v. 208, (13 Apr. 1630). In view of the character of French foreign policy both before and after Richelieu's ministry, I find it profoundly unconvincing to regard these *pensées* as amounting to the disinterested defence of lesser Italian states against Spanish 'tyranny'. The conflict between the public rhetoric of Richelieu's ministry, and its practical—not to say pragmatic—aims has yet to be properly examined.

ness to slip into the traditions of an assertive, expansionist policy was that, faced with criticism which could quickly turn into outright opposition, Richelieu relied heavily on the prospect, and reality, of success to justify this foreign policy to the king. Success in the pursuit of France's diplomatic and military objectives would keep the opposition muted—at least in Louis XIII's presence—and ensure that Richelieu could maintain that combination of royal confidence and control of political resources that was critical to the survival of his regime.

The force lying behind diplomacy and war was the army, whether as a credible threat to other powers, or as an instrument of policy in its own right. While Richelieu's ambitions as one of the *grands* encouraged him to seek commands and to control patronage within the army, he had a wider priority, critical to his political survival: this was to ensure that the army was an effective support for the policies that he was presenting to the king. His hold upon political power depended upon the success of these policies; ultimately, this success would be determined by the decisions that he and others took with respect to the organization and command of France's military forces. The need for military effectiveness brought into focus two potentially contradictory requirements.

On the one hand, the ministry needed talented and capable military commanders. It was not necessary to find tactical geniuses or paragons of heroic leadership, but certainly Richelieu needed individuals who possessed a basic organizational ability, and a capacity to turn military instructions into practical operations. At the same time, Richelieu's control of government and promotion of his family aspirations depended upon the selection of commanders who were, as far as possible, personally loyal to the cardinal, although this loyalty had more to do with ambitions and alignments amongst the *grands* than with any shared sense of wider political objectives.

III

The rest of this discussion will be concerned with the policies and strategies that Richelieu pursued in making appointments to major military commands during his ministry, and which reflect the social and political structures, assumptions, and personal ambitions that have been examined in the preceding sections. Elsewhere I have suggested that it is easy to over-estimate the success of institutional and administrative expedients in turning the army into a more effective and better controlled instrument of royal or ministerial authority.[45] In contrast, a very great deal of the day-to-day management of the army continued to depend both upon the various means through which senior appointments might be controlled, and on the influence that could be exerted over the army commanders—whether or not they had been appointed through the patronage of Richelieu and his ministers.

Concentrating on the major military commands, it is possible to provide an overview of the factors that determined appointments. This will indicate, firstly, that Richelieu's control of such appointments was at best partial. Precisely because of this partial control, an examination of the individual appointments emphasizes the considerable skill with which Richelieu took advantage of political circumstances to rid himself of some of those *grands* who had customarily assumed military commands, but whose position posed a threat to Richelieu's political or family objectives.

The second point is that the criteria for appointment to commands almost never included explicit ideological identification with those aims and objectives that were the public justification for Richelieu's foreign policy. Those generals who were consistently loyal to the cardinal seem to have had no interest in presenting themselves as the agents of policies with which they explicitly identified, still less in emphasizing their commitment to the declared aims and public rhetoric of the ministry. Their loyalty was personal, and as such potentially—and in significant cases, actually—subject to revision or transfer. In consequence, Richelieu could not assume that his policies in themselves would be sufficient to command loyalty and commitment from those who were his allies amongst the senior officers. Instead, his decisions concerning nominations to the high command can very largely be explained in terms of his understanding of, and participation in, the tensions and rivalries that were inherent within the great aristocracy. Richelieu was working within a traditional system, and trying to bend it to serve his purposes: there is nothing in his policy which could contribute to the permanent creation of a controlled and subordinate military élite—as events after his death were to prove.

The military history of Richelieu's ministry can be divided for this purpose into two sections: the periods before and after the battle of Nördlingen in September 1634. For a number of reasons, Richelieu's ability to control and manipulate the whole structure of senior mili-

---

[45] D. Parrott, 'The Administration of the French Army during the Ministry of Cardinal Richelieu' (D.Phil. thesis; Oxford Univ., 1985); id., 'French Military Organization in the 1630s: The Failure of Richelieu's Ministry', *Seventeenth-Century French Studies*, 9 (1987), 151–67.

tary appointments and offices was substantially greater in the earlier period. Indeed, it was partly the success of the cardinal early in his ministry that contributed to the substantial problems that emerged later.

The period up to 1634 can be characterized as one of relatively small wars followed by the application of military pressure that fell short of any full-scale conflict. It was a period of conspicuous success for Richelieu and his foreign policy. The 1631 treaty of Cherasco was a clear vindication of the French war aims in North Italy, and one which wiped out the earlier humiliation of Richelieu's abortive involvement in the Valtelline. At home, the defeat of the English invasion, the siege of La Rochelle, the campaigns in the Midi, had all contributed to growing confidence in Richelieu's direction of policy, and the ability of the army to meet the military demands placed upon it.

The period after 1631 allowed Richelieu to cash in on this military and political credit. Avoiding any open commitment to her allies, France stood on the sidelines of the Thirty Years War, and used her military forces in successive campaigns to annex territory and strengthen her eastern frontier. Lorraine was invaded and occupied by the French, and the conditions for its return to independent sovereignty were deliberately left ambiguous.[46] Responding to the request of states on the Rhine and in Alsace for 'protection', France was able to establish a string of major fortified garrisons stretching from Coblenz down to Basle. French forces operated in Alsace and the Palatinate, clashing with Imperial and Spanish forces and preventing any secure consolidation of the 'Spanish Road'.[47] In Italy, France strengthened her garrisons and sought to sponsor an anti-Spanish League of Italian states.[48]

The Spanish and Austrian Habsburgs watched all of this anxiously, but were not prepared to act decisively against France unless their military situation elsewhere improved. They knew, as did Richelieu, that with the Swedish and German Protestant army the most effective force in Germany, and with the Dutch committed to an offensive

---

[46] R. Babel, *Zwischen Habsburg und Bourbon: Aussenpolitik und Europäische Stellung Herzog Karls IV. von Lothringen und Bar . . .* (Sigmaringen, 1989), 121–89.

[47] H. Weber, *Frankreich, Kurtrier, der Rhein und das Reich, 1623–35* (Bonn, 1969), 173–374; E. Straub, *Pax et Imperium: Spaniens Kampf um seine Friedensordnung in Europa zwischen 1617 und 1635* (Paderborn, 1980), 446–75; D. Parrott, 'The Causes of the Franco-Spanish War of 1635–59, in J. Black (ed.), *The Origins of War in Early Modern Europe* (Edinburgh, 1987), 94–105.

[48] G. Hanotaux and duc de La Force, *Histoire du cardinal de Richelieu*, (6 vols.; Paris, 1893–1947), ii. 420–1; Straub, *Pax et Imperium*, 449; Avenel, iv. 665–71, Ligue d'Italie (early Mar. 1635).

strategy since 1629, the Habsburg alliance was in no position to add France to the list of its open enemies, however provocative her policies.[49]

This successful foreign policy, achieved with a relatively low level of military commitment by contemporary European standards, shaped the politics of appointment to the command of army corps. Firstly, and importantly, there were not a great number of commands to allocate. Throughout this period, except during the campaigns against the Huguenots in late 1628 and 1629,[50] there were never more than three major army corps in operation, although overall authority might be shared by individuals within these. The more competition that existed, the easier it proved to block those who were obviously hostile to Richelieu. Moreover, both at the siege of La Rochelle, and during the 1629 and 1630 campaigns in North Italy, Richelieu assumed command of the main campaign army under the direct command of the king, who was present for at least part of these campaigns.

The king was prepared to support Richelieu and his clients, and to defer to Richelieu's advice in military appointments. Moreover, those who would have been able to lay claim to military commands by right of birth, and who were hostile to Richelieu, were, for one reason or another, out of the way. Gaston d'Orléans, above all, managed to rule himself out of claims to command for almost this entire period: the family crisis of the Chalais conspiracy was followed by a short *rapprochement* with Louis at the time of the brief Montpensier marriage. In late 1628, Gaston was being considered for command of the army that was to be sent down into Italy to assert the claims of the duc de Nevers to Mantua.[51] However Gaston's proposal to marry Marie de Gonzague, the daughter of the duc de Nevers, which would have tied Louis XIII more closely than he wished to the political fortunes of Mantua, and would have upset marriage plans that Louis found more congenial, ensured that

[49] J. H. Elliott, *The Count-Duke of Olivares: The Statesman in an Age of Decline* (New Haven, Conn., 1986), 472–3; R. A. Stradling, 'Olivares and the Origins of the Franco-Spanish War, 1627–35', *English Historical Review*, 101 (1986), 68–94, 79–83; Straub, *Pax et Imperium*, 468–9.

[50] In 1628 the army encamped around La Rochelle under Richelieu's direct command was supplemented by three small forces under Condé, Épernon, and Montmorency, ordered to *faire le dégât* in the countryside around the major Huguenot centres: Grillon, iii. 270, Richelieu to Condé, 9 May 1628. By mid-July an additional army of French troops acting in the name of Charles de Nevers-Gonzague had been placed under the command of d'Huxelles, and was preparing to enter Savoy in defence of Charles's claims to the Mantuan succession: Grillon, iii. 384, d'Huxelles to Richelieu, 16 July 1628.

[51] R. Quazza, *La guerra per la successione di Mantova e del Monferrato, 1628–31* (Mantua, 1926), i. 299; G. Dethan, *Gaston d'Orléans, conspirateur et prince charmant* (Paris, 1959), 81.

Gaston was kept away from a military role in which he would have considerable access to his prospective father-in-law.[52] Louis finally decided to command the army in person, with Richelieu as his *lieutenant général.* Until 1634, when he was finally persuaded to return to France, Gaston was either at the centre of conspiracies, under suspicion in their immediate aftermath, or in voluntary exile.[53] Richelieu therefore did not have to compete against the individual who had the strongest claim to military command under the king, and who would certainly have used this position in a manner harmful to the cardinal.

Instead, the path was eased to the establishment of the working relationship with Henri II, prince de Condé, who was to become a central figure amongst the commanders in the later 1630s. Next in line to the throne after Gaston, whose first marriage had produced only one daughter, Condé could see advantage in the progressive discrediting and weakening of Gaston's position in France.[54] At the same time, Condé himself felt threatened by the next princely line to the throne, represented by his cousin Soissons, who profited from rumours of Condé's illegitimacy to strengthen his own claim to a succession which, even after 1638, appeared anything but assured in the king's line.[55]

The result of this was that Condé proved an early and committed supporter of Richelieu, who proved willing to reciprocate the support.[56] Richelieu needed allies in the royal family, especially after the definitive break with the queen mother in 1630. Given the assumptions underlying senior military appointments, it was also important for Richelieu not to be seen as denying the claims of all the princes of the blood to military commands. The working relationship that was to culminate in the marriage of Condé's son to Richelieu's niece, Claire-Clémence de Maillé-Brézé, began with the appointment of Condé to the main army operating against Huguenot strongholds in the Midi during 1628.

The absence of Gaston spared Richelieu from one dangerous source of demands for high command in this period up to 1634; the

[52] M. C. Quazza, *Marie de Gonzague et Gaston d'Orléans: Un épisode de politique secrète au temps de Louis XIII* (Mantua, 1925), 6–10, 30–8. It is hard to avoid the conclusion that the most congenial of all solutions for both Louis XIII and Richelieu was to prevent Gaston remarrying at all.

[53] Dethan, *Gaston d'Orléans*, 83–129.

[54] Vittorio Siri, *Anecdotes du ministère du cardinal de Richelieu et du règne de Louis XIII* (Amsterdam, 1717), 111–12.

[55] I am grateful to James Inglis-Jones (Christ Church, Oxford) for bringing to my attention these rumours about Condé's illegitimacy, and their exploitation by Soissons.

[56] Henri d'Orléans, duc d'Aumale, *Histoire des princes de Condé pendant les XVIᵉ et XVIIᵉ siècles* (8 vols.; Paris, 1863–96), iii. 180–91; Jouanna, *Le Devoir de révolte*, 215–17.

alliance of the duke of Savoy with Spain during the second, 1630, campaign of the Mantuan war, and the French invasion of the territories of the duke of Lorraine, saved him from another hazard—the convention that the princes of foreign allies should receive the command of any forces operating within or close to their territory. However, Victor Amadeus I of Savoy was married to Louis XIII's sister, and when he was subsequently attracted into an alliance with France, Richelieu had no choice but to accept his appointment as *capitaine général* of the Franco-Savoyard army raised for the 1635 campaign in North Italy.[57] Yet from the outset suspicions were voiced about his commitment to the alliance and about his supposedly definitive break with Spain, and these suspicions proved justified by events. His reluctant subordinate, the maréchal de Créqui, accused him of sabotaging the siege of Valenza by permitting the entry of a Spanish relief force.[58]

How did Richelieu use the confidence of the king, and the relative scarcity of military commands, in the earlier period? In the first case he advanced a number of his family to high positions: Brézé, Richelieu's brother-in-law, was made a maréchal in 1632,[59] and given command of the forces operating in the Empire.[60] La Meilleraye, Richelieu's first cousin, was made *grand maître de l'artillerie* in 1634, an office which was subject to Richelieu, as *surintendant de la navigation*, in all important decisions about the artillery, but which none the less gave him a substantial claim to military commands.[61] D'Effiat, another of Richelieu's *fidèles* and linked by marriage with La Meilleraye, was made a maréchal in 1631,[62] after having held a joint command in Italy the year previously.[63] He died in 1632 in command of the forces trying to keep Habsburg troops from occupying the electorate of Trier.[64]

Such advancements, while not felt to be individually unacceptable—all three nobles were from traditional *épée* backgrounds—collectively aroused considerable antipathy amongst the great aristocratic families.

---

[57] AG A¹26, doc. 65, 15 July 1635.

[58] Hanotaux and La Force, *Richelieu*, v. 145.

[59] Anselme, *Histoire généalogique*, vii. 496.

[60] AG A¹21, fo. 74, *pouvoir* of *lieutenant général* for Brézé, 12 Nov 1632.

[61] AG A¹26, fo. 89, copy of the commission creating La Meilleraye *grand maître*, 21 Sept. 1635. The commission specifically states that La Meilleraye has been appointed as Richelieu's relative and as a person able to integrate the office with that of Richelieu's post of *surintendant de la navigation*.

[62] Anselme, *Histoire généalogique*, vii. 492.

[63] Grillon, v, 391, 13 July 1630; J. Jacquart, 'Le Marquis d'Effiat, lieutenant-général à l'armée d'Italie', *XVIIᵉ Siècle*, 45 (1959), 298–313.

[64] Avenel, iv. 337, Richelieu to Toiras, 7 Aug. 1632; R. J. Bonney, *The King's Debts: Finance and Politics in France* (Oxford, 1981), 159.

Had Richelieu tried to pursue such an appointment policy exclusively, he would have provoked intense opposition, and weakened his own wider bid to obtain the support and co-operation of the *grands*. In fact, by this stage he had effectively exhausted supplies of eligible males from his own extended family. A combination of marriages not notable for their fecundity and the pursuit of wide-ranging ecclesiastical ambitions had ensured that Richelieu never possessed a substantial number of male relatives to deploy in support of his political interests. His brother was dragged out of Carthusian seclusion, but in order to be made a cardinal and archbishop of Lyons, while his eldest sister's second husband, René de Vignerot, had died in 1625. The only son from this marriage, François de Pont Courlay, born in 1609, proved to be a less-than-adequate *général des galères*.[65] The marriage between Richelieu's youngest sister and the future maréchal de Brézé had also produced only one son, who served first as a second-rank commander, a *maréchal de camp*, but was then transferred to the navy, commanding the Atlantic fleet after the disgrace of Archbishop Sourdis.[66] The elder sister of the marquis de Brézé, Claire-Clémence, was married to the future Grand Condé. Of Richelieu's uncles on his maternal side, Amador de la Porte was made grand prior of the Order of Malta, thus remaining celibate, and also served as Richelieu's immediate subordinate in naval and maritime affairs, holding the office of *intendant général de la navigation*. The marriage of the other maternal uncle, Charles de la Porte, produced only one son, Charles, born in 1602, who was to become *grand maître de l'artillerie* and the future maréchal de la Meilleraye. Charles did not marry until 1630 and so Richelieu did not live to take advantage of any third generation of relatives able to fill military posts.[67]

Thus Richelieu could not draw upon a particularly extensive network of male blood-relatives to sustain his dynastic and political strategies. The limited pool of eligible males had to be spread thinly over the three areas of church, navy, and army. In consequence, his policy towards army command from the mid-1620s was largely based upon a shrewd and self-interested exploitation of aristocratic alignments. The hostility between Richelieu and the Guise/Lorraine family may have stretched back as far as Henri III's reign, when Richelieu's father had been subordinated to the duc de Guise at court.[68] Whatever the reason, from the outset of the ministry

---

[65] Anselme, *Histoire généalogique*, iv. 374–5.   [66] Ibid. iv. 368–9.   [67] Ibid. iv. 624–5.

[68] While François de Richelieu held the office of *grand prévôt* which subordinated him to the duc de Guise as *grand maître de France*, Dr Bergin warns against any facile assumption that this automatically created hostility between the two families: *Rise of Richelieu*, 20, 27–8. However

Richelieu's policy was to weaken and undermine the various branches of the Lorraine family, and to deprive them of any opportunities for military command. The hostility here was unambiguous, and can be seen as reaching its ultimate extent in the invasion and occupation of Lorraine, on whose sovereignty the status of the Guise and their cousins rested.

The creation of the charge of *grand maître et surintendant de la navigation*, to which Richelieu had himself appointed in 1626, allowed him to press for the elimination of the duc de Guise's *Amirauté du levant*, attempting to buy out the duke in 1629.[69] This attempt had become bogged down by Richelieu's refusal to pay the price demanded by Guise. However, when Guise supported Marie de' Medici in 1630, it provided an opportunity not merely to suppress the *Amirauté*, but to remove Guise from the governorship of Provence, breaking the power of the family in the south of France.[70] The duc de Guise died in exile in 1640; his brother, the duc de Chevreuse, never received a military command—despite distancing himself from the conspiratorial activities of his wife, Marie de Rohan.[71]

The Elbeuf branch of the Lorraine family was also excluded from commands: the duc d'Elbeuf, resentful of Richelieu's policies towards his family, was exiled when he gave support to Gaston's unapproved marriage in 1631 with Elbeuf's kinswoman, Marguerite of Lorraine.[72] Only one member of the Guise family was involved in the military activities of this period. In a strategy that is a recognizable and distinctive aspect of aristocratic family policy, the younger brother of Elbeuf, the comte d'Harcourt, served in the royal armies

as the hostility between Guise and Henri III became open and permanent in the later 1580s it is difficult to see how relations with the strongly royalist Richelieu could have been maintained. François de Richelieu was involved in action taken against the League after the murder of the Guise, and was one of the first courtiers to declare for Henri de Navarre after the assassination of Henri III: M. Deloche, *Les Richelieu: Le Père du cardinal* (Paris, 1923), 261–77.

[69] Grillon, i. 511–15, 'lettres d'erection en titre d'office de la charge de Grand Maître, Chef et Surintendant général de la Navigation . . .', Oct. 1626; for the removal of Guise, see Avenel, iii. 173–4 n. 4, (1628); Grillon, iv. 690, 1 Dec. 1629, makes reference to Guise's possible acquiescence in the loss of the *Amirauté du Levant*, but the negotiations continued into 1630.

[70] Bergin, *Cardinal Richelieu*, 112–13; J. M. Constant, *Les Conjurateurs: Le Premier Libéralisme politique sous Richelieu* (Paris, 1987), 79–80; *Dictionnaire du grand siècle*, ed. Bluche, 670.

[71] L. Battifol, *La Duchesse de Chevreuse* (Paris, 1924), 181–95; Constant, *Les Conjurateurs*, 95–96. The duchesse de Chevreuse was the widow of the duc de Luynes, and had produced a son by that first marriage who had inherited the title, which provided further grounds for Richelieu's suspicions and reluctance to place her second husband in any position of military importance.

[72] Avenel, iv. 109–10, Louis XIII to Mme d'Elbeuf (end Mar. 1631).

throughout the later 1620s and early 1630s, though he did not receive a senior command at this time.[73]

This offensive against the Guise had a number of advantages for Richelieu's relations with some of those families who had previously been known for hostility to the Guise/Lorraine nexus. In particular, it encouraged the *ralliement* of a group of traditional Huguenot aristocrats, above all, the duc de La Force, the maréchal de Châtillon, and the maréchal de Créqui. Richelieu's comments on La Force and Châtillon show that he had reservations about their military capacities, substantially borne out by their record in the field.[74] But both were prepared to support policies opposed to the interests of the Guise, and were heavily involved in the campaigns to overrun Lorraine.[75] When a commander was needed for the army sent against the comte de Soissons's invasion in 1641, it was Châtillon who was chosen, despite his mediocre military record. His forces remained loyal, but suffered heavy defeat at La Marfée, largely, Richelieu considered, through Châtillon's irresolution—a graphic demonstration of the dilemma faced by Richelieu in the appointment to commands.[76]

Most intriguing of all, Richelieu's obvious hostility to the Guise family permitted him to achieve a tenuous working relationship with the duc d'Épernon and his sons.[77] Both as a military power-broker in

[73] AAE France 815, fo. 101, Harcourt to Richelieu, Aug. 1635: affirms 'fidélité' to Richelieu and asks for Richelieu to intercede with the king to provide him with a *charge.*

[74] Hanotaux and La Force, *Richelieu,* iv. 438, 435–7. Comments extracted from a report dictated by Richelieu on the aptitude and character of all those who had served in senior commands since the siege of La Rochelle: BN MS Fr. 15644. Richelieu's opinions of the high command are characteristically partisan, but the low assessment of the capacities of these two generals is also reflected in the reports of the English ambassador in Paris, Viscount Scudamore, who, in 1635, wrote of de La Force's 'frigidy, whereunto his age disposes him', and that Châtillon was using the excuse of waiting for his baggage to return from Holland to avoid recommencing the campaign in Picardy: BL Add. MS 35097, fo. 7, early Oct. 1635; fo. 5, 18 Sept. 1635.

[75] La Force commanded the army of Lorraine from 1633: AAE France 808, fo. 119, Chavigny to Bouthillier, 27 Oct. 1633; Châtillon was nominated to command the army of Lorraine in 1635: AG A^{1}26, pièce 32, *projet de pouvoir,* Feb. 1635. This decision was changed and he was nominated with the maréchal de Brézé as joint commander of the Army of Flanders: Antoine Aubery, *Mémoires pour servir à l'histoire du cardinal de Richelieu* (2 vols.; Paris, 1660–1), i. 443, 30 Mar. 1635. Châtillon campaigned in Lorraine in 1639 and 1640, when he quarrelled vociferously and consistently with du Hallier: AAE CP Lorraine 31, fos. 419, 433; 7, 13 Sept. 1640.

[76] Hanotaux and La Force, *Richelieu,* iv. 437. A short account of La Marfée can be found in Aumale, *Histoire des princes de Condé,* iv. 469–70.

[77] With the exception of Noailles's study of the Cardinal de La Valette, (see n. 32 above), historians have tended to concentrate attention upon the first duke, rather than the wider family (see n. 22 above). M. Chaintron, *Le Duc d'Épernon* (Paris, 1988), 154–8, provides a brief overview of the family after 1642.

South-West France, one of the most important areas for recruit-ment,[78] and as holder of the office of *colonel général de l'infanterie*, Épernon was an important key to Richelieu's management of the army. While the power of the colonel generalcy never extended to an exclusive right to appoint to all infantry officerships, it remained a formidable factor in military patronage. Moreover, as early as 1612, the *survivance* of the colonel generalcy had passed to Épernon's second son, the duc de La Valette.[79] Unable to suppress the office, but anxious to control it, Richelieu took the obvious step of an alliance with the future holder: in 1634, the duc de La Valette was married to Richelieu's first cousin, Marie de Pontchâteau.[80]

Épernon's hostility to the Guise, more clearly than that of Richelieu's own family, can be traced back to the 1580s.[81] His possession of the governorship of Metz, both a strategic prize and potentially the basis of some future claim to sovereign status for the family, also led him to look more favourably upon the cardinal's military activities which were consolidating French control in this disputed area. In 1626 he told Richelieu of Gaston's request that Metz be used as a base for the Chalais conspiracy.[82] In 1632 he refused to move out from Guienne in order to give military support to the rebellion of his relative, the duc de Montmorency.[83] Épernon was given command of one of the armies engaged against the Huguenots in 1628/9.[84] The quarrel over precedence between the

[78] R. Chaboche, 'Les Soldats français de la guerre de trente ans: Une tentative d'approche', *Revue d'histoire moderne et contemporaine*, 20 (1973), 10–24, 15: only the provinces on the eastern frontier and Normandy provided a higher proportion of the troops in French service.

[79] Girard, *Épernon*, 261–2; Noailles, *Cardinal de la Valette*, 69.

[80] Girard, *Épernon*, 503–4.

[81] The Guise were the main protagonists in the conspiracy which disgraced Épernon in 1588: Girard, *Épernon*, 77–82; J. M. Constant, *Les Guise* (Paris, 1984), 204–5. The two families achieved a temporary *rapprochement* after 1612 when the duchesse de Montpensier, Épernon's niece, made a second marriage to the duc de Guise: Girard, *Épernon*, 265, who calls the marriage, somewhat enthusiastically 'une entière et parfaite réunion'. The subsequent alignments of the Épernon family, together with the wholesale destruction of the political position of the Guise/Lorraine by 1631, ensured that this period of improved relations with the Guise was of limited significance in shaping Épernon family strategy. Far more important was the period in which Richelieu and the duke found themselves working together to re-establish their political fortunes through the *rapprochement* of the queen mother with Louis XIII: see Bergin, *Rise of Richelieu*, 188–97. It is also significant that the powerful *créature* of Cardinal Richelieu, Chancellor Séguier, began his career as a client of Épernon, and used his influence with Richelieu to support the interests of his first patron: *Lettres au chancélier Séguier*, ed. Mousnier, i. 32.

[82] Fessenden, 'Épernon and Guienne', 55; Mouton, *Le Duc et le roi*, 177.

[83] Girard emphasizes that Épernon's possible sympathy for Montmorency's revolt caused great concern in Paris, and that the slowness with which he moved to secure Montauban raised suspicions. This account is confirmed in Siri's *Anecdotes*, 275. Girard stresses, however, that Épernon's loyalty to the crown in this matter was never in doubt: *Épernon*, 467–9.

[84] Grillon, iii. 270, Richelieu to Condé, 9 May 1628.

duke and Archbishop Sourdis in Bordeaux certainly weakened his own position with Richelieu after 1633.[85] But this was counter-balanced by the duc de La Valette's marriage, and the establish-ment of the Cardinal de La Valette, his younger brother, as one of Richelieu's most trusted military commanders.[86] Again, in the case of the Cardinal de La Valette, it is not clear where the personal ambition of a younger son stops, and a sophisticated family *politique* of sustaining as many political interests as possible, begins. His political and military career gives evidence of both tendencies; what is quite clear is that, after the duc de La Valette's flight to England in 1638 and Épernon's disgrace, Richelieu remained convinced of the cardinal's loyalty;[87] he received increasingly important military commands up to his premature death a year later, despite a perform-ance in the field which Richelieu described, with masterly under-statement, as 'unfortunate'.[88]

If the exclusion of the Guise brought Richelieu considerable advantages in terms of the support of other families, his attack upon the Vendôme proved equally fruitful. The opportunity to remove them permanently from the political and military stage came in 1626, when the two Vendôme sons of Henri IV by Gabrielle d'Estrées were disgraced in the aftermath of the Chalais conspiracy: the grand prior died in prison in Vincennes in 1629, his brother finally escaped to England where he remained until Louis XIII's death.[89] Their close links with the Lorraine—César had married Françoise de Lorraine-Mercoeur—had won them enemies amongst the other families. Moreover, their position as the most recently legitimized family of royal bastards ensured the lasting animosity of the two earlier legitimized lines, the Longueville and the Angoulême. Richelieu's exclusion of the Vendôme was the basis of a relationship with these two legitimized families. While Richelieu's opinion of the military capacities of the duc d'Angoulême was not high, he was none the less prepared to give him commands, at least at the beginning of the war.[90] The duc de Longueville was consistently favoured in the distribution of military commands until his appointment as one of the plenipotentiaries for the Westphalia negotiations in 1644. It could be added that a further reason for Longueville's frequent military commands reflected another aspect of the power of the

[85] Fessenden, 'Épernon and Guienne', 87–120.
[86] Noailles, *Cardinal de La Valette*, 94–115.
[87] Ibid. 456–62.
[88] Hanotaux and La Force, *Richelieu*, iv. 444.
[89] Constant, *Les Conjurateurs*, 84–5.
[90] Hanotaux and La Force, *Richelieu*, iv. 439.

grands; his possession of the governorship of Normandy enabled him to raise substantial numbers of troops on his own account. In late 1636, for example, he had raised some 8,000 infantry and 2,000 cavalry in his province to reinforce the French army in Burgundy.[91]

The concern of these two families to strengthen their own claims to status against *arrivistes* was further rewarded by Richelieu when Annibal d'Estrées, the maternal uncle of the Vendôme, was disgraced while commanding an army moving towards Trier in 1633. Richelieu suspected him of complicity in Châteauneuf's conspiracy, and, while the charges against him were dismissed, the cardinal took the opportunity to bring his military career to an end.[92]

By 1630, Richelieu had a team of *grands*, flanked by promoted members of his own family, which provided him with a reasonable pool of military commanders. Their loyalty and commitment were ensured less by any positive sense of identification with Richelieu's policies, than by a common dislike of those families which Richelieu himself had identified as his chief political and dynastic opponents.

The final factor in shaping and defining this group of commanders was the prolonged fall-out from the Day of Dupes, and the elimination of the queen mother's supporters from military commands during the early 1630s. It is possible to detect growing uneasiness between Richelieu and the military commanders whose posts were owed to the patronage of Marie de' Medici throughout 1630. Louis de Marillac's letters from his command in Champagne are a litany of complaints about the progress of the war, and his fears about the inadequacy of his forces in the face of a possible imperial invasion.[93] Bassompierre, who had enjoyed the command of a separate force at La Rochelle in 1628, had been appointed ambassador to the Swiss cantons in 1630—a step taken, he believed, to remove him from the Italian theatre.[94] He joined the campaign in Savoy, and contributed to a successful engagement there. However, Richelieu had already marked him down as talented, but unreliable. His close links with the Guise family, which had culminated in a secret marriage to Louise de Lorraine, princesse de Conti, undoubtedly increased

---

[91] AG A¹30, fo. 31, de Noyers to Longueville, 7 Oct. 1636.

[92] La Chesnaye-Desbois, *Dictionnaire de la noblesse*, vii. 597–8; Hanotaux and La Force, *Richelieu*, iv. 453.

[93] See Grillon, v. 748, under the index entry 'Champagne (Armée de)', for some 15 letters of Louis de Marillac written between Mar. and Sept., concerning the poor state of his army.

[94] Bassompierre, *Mémoires*, in Petitot and Monmerqué, *Collection*, xxi. 236–7. Bassompierre initially blamed Maréchal Schomberg for this, but claimed that Richelieu aligned himself with Schomberg and against Bassompierre's counsel by supporting the 1630 invasion of Savoy: xxi. 239–42.

Richelieu's suspicions and hostility.[95] The opportunity was provided to remove both Marillac and Bassompierre in November 1630.

Richelieu's most illustrious victim was, of course, the duc de Montmorency. Tension between Richelieu and Montmorency went back to Richelieu's creation of the *surintendance de la navigation*, and pressure placed upon Montmorency to sell the title to the *Amirauté du Ponant*.[96] This in itself represented a challenge to Montmorency's military status; even more provoking was the realization in 1627 that Richelieu had acted to suppress the office of the *connétable*, rather than allowing it to pass into Montmorency's hands, as he could reasonably have expected.[97] The expedient nature of this abolition of the office of *connétable* can be inferred from Richelieu's alleged preparedness to revive the office as part of the dowry attached to his niece, Marie de Combalet, when he was attempting to attract the comte de Soissons to the match.[98]

Montmorency received military command in the army of Italy in 1630, and indeed was made a maréchal by the king in this year. He was too important and influential for Richelieu to deprive him of high military status until he had actually taken the step into active revolt. It is significant that the Montmorency legacy, rather than falling to the king, as was customary in cases of treason, was parcelled out to Condé, on the basis of his marriage to Montmorency's sister.[99] Once again, Richelieu was working to bind himself to a particular group of the aristocracy through the ruin or exclusion of others.

A victim of Richelieu's suspicions who did not need to cross the line into open treason was the maréchal de Toiras, disgraced in 1633 despite an outstanding military career which had included the heroic

[95] Bassompierre, *Mémoires*, xxi. 288–90; *Dictionnaire du grand siècle*, ed. Bluche, 168. Bassompierre stresses his great affection for the princesse de Conti in his *Mémoires*, but omits all mention of the secret marriage. His 'liaisons trop étroites' with the Lorraine family are emphasized as the reason for his disgrace in Anselme, *Histoire généalogique*, vii. 464.

[96] Grillon, i. 513, Oct. 1626; Hanotaux and La Force, *Richelieu*, iv. 514–15. Montmorency's *Amirauté du Ponant* was the Atlantic equivalent of Guise's *Levant* (Mediterranean) post. Richelieu was anxious to absorb both *offices* into his own jurisdiction. It is worth stressing that the office of *amiral* was revived in 1646 for the queen mother, then conferred on the duc de Vendôme in 1649/50: BN MS Fr. 4223, fo. 3, 4 July 1646; fo. 8, 1649.

[97] Siri, *Anecdotes*, 274, sees this as the chief motive for Montmorency's revolt. Montmorency was the obvious successor to the office of *connétable* after Lesdiguières's death; despite his execution it was considered necessary to reaffirm the abolition of the office in 1643: BN Châtre de Cangé 25, fo. 239, Apr. 1643. This did not prevent speculation that the post of *connétable* would be revived in favour of Turenne after 1658: Bérenger, *Turenne*, 337–8; C. Picavet, *Les Dernières Années de Turenne* (Paris, 1914), 59–62.

[98] Siri, *Anecdotes*, 320. Although Siri is not an authoritative source, the comments in the preceding footnotes about the provisional nature of the abolition of such *offices*, and Richelieu's concern to pursue his family's interests, give the allegation some credibility.

[99] Aumale, *Histoire des princes de Condé*, iii. 250–2.

defence of fort Saint-Martin on the Île de Ré against the English in 1627, and the lengthy defence of Casale in 1629/30.[100] Richelieu stood high in the king's favour in 1633; he had crushed most of his main rivals, and Toiras, who was neither a *créature* nor clearly aligned with Richelieu's group of *grands*, could be removed without any questions being raised about the wisdom of destroying the career of an outstanding field commander.[101]

IV

Richelieu had taken advantage of a favourable military and political climate to reshape the high command of the army into a group which reflected his own dynastic ambitions and aristocratic alliances. This worked well, provided that the scale of French military effort remained limited and that his policies appeared successful. The problem from 1635 was that neither of these conditions was fulfilled.

The battle of Nördlingen and the unanticipated overturning of Protestant and Swedish military dominance in the Empire changed everything. The Habsburg powers had already resolved that any substantial improvement in their military situation would be the signal to engage France in what they hoped would be a large-scale, but short, conflict.[102] Richelieu was being forced towards a conflict whose nature and extent were not of his own choosing. France was unprepared for a struggle on six or seven different fronts and did all possible to avoid it; the French declaration of war on 19 May 1635, specifically against Spain rather than the emperor, should be seen as a last, futile, attempt to avoid a war fought simultaneously against both branches of the house of Habsburg. The anticipated scale of the French war-effort, which can be seen from late 1634 in the costing of 125,000 troops for the coming year, and the large number of campaign theatres opened up from 1635, did not reflect a deliberate French choice. It was determined by the preparations that the Habsburgs had been making since October 1634 for a series of simultaneous pre-emptive strikes against French territory.[103] Yet despite the risks and burdens of a war on this scale, it looked initially as though all might still go well for Richelieu, with a demonstration of French military and material superiority followed by a quick

[100] Baudier, *Toiras*, 234–47; Toiras was permitted to serve with the army of the duke of Savoy, in which he was killed in 1636.
[101] Hanotaux and La Force, *Richelieu*, iv. 455–6.
[102] Stradling, 'Olivares and the Origins', 68–94; Elliott, *Count-Duke of Olivares*, 472–5.
[103] AAE France 811, fo. 120, 7 Nov. 1634; Stradling, 'Olivares and the Origins', 88–91.

peace. But initial euphoria caused by the victory of Aveins, three days after the French declaration of war, was soon replaced by disillusionment as France moved into a sustained period of military stagnation and set-back. Outside the circle of ministerial propagandists and *fidèles*, there was a growing recognition that France had become involved in a war which would drag on, at heavy financial and human cost, for the foreseeable future.

As a result, Richelieu was confronted by a number of problems: the sudden change from a position of manifest French success to something altogether more ambiguous, had reduced the king's willingness to accept all of Richelieu's choices in the matter of military command. Moreover, increases in the scale of warfare required a larger pool of commanding officers, and therefore forced Richelieu to reverse much of the policy of restricting appointments that he had pursued before this time. Obviously the scale of the conflict from 1635—the result of the Habsburg decision to try to overwhelm France on as many fronts as possible—created huge problems of overall control and supervision. This was combined with doubts about the commitment of many of the commanders to a war which seemed far removed from previously successful policies. A combination of excessive demands and an increasingly vindictive response to military failure began to undermine the support of even the most loyal sections of the military leadership.

The burdens of supporting the war-effort after 1635 became very much greater for the commanders in the field: inadequate funding, constant shortages of food and equipment, units that were well under strength, all presented formidable problems for commanders who were being urged to pursue offensive strategies that would push the war on to foreign territory. Commanders such as La Force and Châtillon came under increasingly severe criticism from the centre for what was felt to be their lack of resolution in the pursuit of the war—though in the circumstances cautious policies were entirely justified. Chavigny, Richelieu's *créature* and secretary of state for foreign affairs, expressed the undoubted frustration of the ministry in writing of these two commanders in north-east France during the campaign of 1638: 'Le Roy et Mons. le Card[al] se sont avancez jusques en ce lieu d'Abbeville pour faire agir messrs de La Force et de Châtillon qui demeuroient les bras croisez a une lieu et demie des enemies sans rien faire avec vingt deux mil hommes de pied et sept mil chevaux effecti.'[104] Yet the commanders were very aware that a

---

[104] BN MS Fr. 6644, fo. 315, 29 July 1638: the numbers of troops attributed to this army are certainly exaggerated.

campaign army that outran its fragile supply lines would be faced with dissolution, and a punitive response from the ministry directed against those in command. Alternatively, keeping the army together required the employment of personal credit and resources on a huge, and probably unrecoverable, scale in a bid to hold the force together. The Cardinal de La Valette, the recipient of Chavigny's letter, knew this all too well, having been reduced to selling off his personal baggage to provide some basic supplies for his army on its retreat from Mainz during the campaign of 1635.[105]

Increasingly, and in a gesture of distrust that was noted and resented, the ministry took to pairing the established *grands* with a commander drawn from amongst the *créatures*. Châtillon, La Force, Angoulême, even Condé, found themselves sharing commands with Brézé, La Meilleraye, the Cardinal de La Valette; later in the ministry, they were paired with La Mothe-Houdancourt and Guébriant— commanders whose position and prospects were also owed directly to Richelieu. That the *créatures* were, as a rule, a generation younger than the traditional *grands* with whom they shared commands probably did not make co-operation any easier to achieve. The result seems to have been at best mixed; the long-term outcome was to undermine still further the commitment of the existing *grands* aligned with Richelieu, while not giving outright control to the *créatures* who might have directed the armies more effectively. Monitoring was combined with direct interference: extraordinarily frank letters went so far as to reproach even Condé for failing to use his funds to maintain his regiments at a high effective strength;[106] other grandee commanders, after military set-backs which owed far more to the overall inadequacy of the military administration than any particular blunder on their part, were subject to criticism and biting sarcasm.[107] When the success of the war-effort depended so much on the personal effort and resources of commanders, such reiterated complaints, which could extend to menace and threat, were undermining the fragile bonds of interest that held these commanders in their commands and led them to accept Richelieu's policies.

This kind of interference and these abrasive communications may seem short-sighted, but to Richelieu the consequences of the failure to pursue coherent and effective military operations were all too clear. In 1636, partly as a result of the decision to give priority to

[105] B. Kroener, *Les Routes et les étapes: Die Versorgung der französischen Armeen in Nordostfrankreich, 1635–61* (Munster, 1980), 87–8 and app. vi.
[106] Avenel, vi. 898, Richelieu to Condé, 20 Feb. 1642.
[107] e.g. Avenel, v. 845, Richelieu to D'Hémery, 27 Aug. 1637.

Condé's lengthy and unsuccessful siege of Dole in Franche-Comté, which had gravely weakened French military strength in the north-east,[108] a substantial Spanish army was able to push down into France from Flanders, capturing Corbie in August, and throwing Paris into turmoil. The organization of a relief army seems to have depended more upon the efforts of the king than on Richelieu.[109] In a gesture which indicates Louis's declining confidence in Richelieu's management, the army was placed under the command of Gaston and the comte de Soissons.[110] Châtillon and La Force were attached to the army, but took a largely passive role in all the decisions of the *conseil de guerre*, presumably because they were anxious to distance themselves from Richelieu's declining fortunes. Only La Meilleraye tried to sustain the ministerial interest, but with little success. Gaston deployed the entire army around Corbie and disregarded Richelieu's instructions to engage the retreating Spanish forces.[111] Only when the king arrived could the army be pushed, belatedly, into a wider offensive. Richelieu's presence in an atmosphere of frustration and uncertainty permitted the Amiens assassination plot to be hatched against him, with the support of both Gaston and Soissons.[112]

His need to counteract the political and personal dangers of this type of situation undoubtedly coloured Richelieu's attitude to his commanders, and explains his scarcely disguised anger at military failure which might have wider consequences for his control of the war-effort.[113]

The changing nature and scale of warfare adversely affected Richelieu's working relationship with many of his own team of commanders: even his *créatures* began to show frustration and anger at the pressures being placed upon them. Brézé simply announced in 1636 his intention of giving up the governorship of Calais—vital to the position of his forces in Picardy—on grounds that the personal financial burden had become impossible to sustain.[114]

The war also forced Richelieu to look further afield or simply

---

[108] AG A¹27, fo. 420, 19 May 1636; A¹28, fo. 124, 23 June 1636.

[109] Hanotaux and La Force, *Richelieu*, v. 162–8.

[110] AG A¹32, fo. 113, 7 July 1636 (Soissons); A¹32, fos. 165–6, 31 Aug. 1636 (Orléans).

[111] AAE France 1678, fos. 302–4 (misdated 1 Sept.) 1636.

[112] Claude de Bordeilles, comte de Montrésor, *Mémoires* in J. Michaud and J. Poujoulat (eds.), *Nouvelle collection des mémoires relatifs à l'histoire de France*, 3rd ser. (10 vols.; Paris, 1838), iv. 204–5; Constant, *Les Conjurateurs*, 122–5.

[113] Richelieu's celebrated comment that 'la douleur de Fontarabie me tue', Avenel, vi. 182, 17 Sept. 1638, was accompanied by his determination to prosecute the duc de La Valette for his supposed role in the defeat.

[114] AAE France 823, fos. 58, 61, 31 Aug. and 2 Sept. 1636.

to accept new commanders; by the end of his ministry this had amounted to the virtual abandonment of his earlier systematic policy. In the first case, the increase in the number of campaign theatres, bringing in Picardy, Provence, and, by 1636, Languedoc and Guienne, forced Richelieu to accept an *ad hoc* system of giving military commands to the provincial governors who were in place. French resources were committed to the main theatres of the Rhineland, Burgundy, Lorraine, Champagne, and Italy: faced with the need to counter small-scale, but disruptive, Habsburg incursions elsewhere, Richelieu relied upon provincial governors to raise troops at their own expense to supplement the small royal forces already present, and to lead these against the invaders. The results were unsatisfactory from all points of view.

A number of governors—Chaulnes in Picardy, Vitry in Provence, Schomberg and Épernon in Languedoc and Guienne—were confirmed in their opinion that they had the right to command all forces in their provinces, and to obstruct or resist anyone appointed over their heads. At the same time, with the notable exception of Schomberg who led a scratch force to defeat the Spanish invading army at Leucate in 1637, they were reluctant to commit their own financial resources or those of the provinces to any energetic pursuit of military objectives. Vitry was finally disgraced and imprisoned for what was felt to be his obstruction of the attempt to recover the Îles des Lérins.[115] Chaulnes was criticized for his failure to prevent Spanish incursions into Picardy in 1635,[116] just as Soissons, acting in his capacity of governor of Champagne, was to be in the following year.[117] In both cases, these commanders had far too few troops at their disposal: Soissons in 1636 was supposed to block the advance into Champagne of the Cardinal Infante's army of nearly 25,000 men with forces of less than 9,000.[118] Both Chaulnes and Soissons had seen large numbers of the better troops in their provinces reallocated elsewhere in France, and both felt with justification that they were being placed in overall command by a ministry whose main aim was to force them to raise new troops on their own credit in a dangerous and unstable military situation. One of the accusations levelled against Soissons in late 1636 was that he had written to Longueville

---

[115] Hanotaux and La Force, *Richelieu*, iv. 440; v. 264–5.

[116] Avenel, v. 242, 18 Sept. 1635.

[117] AAE France 821, fo. 106, Chavigny to Mazarin, 25 July 1636; France 1678, fos. 519–24 (Nov. 1636).

[118] AAE France 1678, fo. 193, 8 Aug. 1636; an earlier report had stressed that the retreating French had only 150 cavalry at their disposal—to face anything up to 13,000 horse in the Spanish army: AAE France 821, fo. 78, 7 July 1636.

expressing disgust with the 'grands employs' that he had received from the king, calling them 'commissions ruineuses' and complaining of the costs of maintaining his army.[119] Military command was not being used as a sign of confidence and the basis of a working relationship with aristocratic families, but as a desperate measure, thrust on to governors whose provinces were under threat and who suffered all of the financial and personal risks of command with none of the advantages.

This type of command could weaken and undermine those ties that had hitherto been cultivated by Richelieu. The demands placed upon Épernon and the duc de La Valette from 1636 became progressively heavier. Expected to raise the army to expel the Spanish from Saint-Jean de Luz entirely at their own expense, they were subsequently criticized by Richelieu for the failure to act sufficiently quickly or decisively against the invading forces.[120] As the war on the Spanish frontier grew more important, the clashes between Épernon and the central government grew more intense. Having been expected to organize the defence of the province in 1636, Épernon considered it an affront to his dignity that any other *grand* should be given overall command of a force within the province, and an indication that Richelieu was no longer abiding by the working relationship between the two families.

The arrival of Condé as commander-in-chief, with orders to organize an expedition into Atlantic Spain, brought these tensions to a head. They had been sharpened by the tactless way in which Condé's appointment had been presented, making it appear as a punishment for Épernon's dilatoriness during the 1637 campaign.[121] The subsequent defeat during 1638 at Fuentarrabia may to some extent have been brought about by Épernon's son, the duc de La Valette, who was accused of failing to co-operate with Condé's main besieging force; far more obvious was the general indecision and mismanagement that had dogged the French army since it had moved out of Guienne. But Richelieu wanted a scapegoat in the aftermath of the defeat and was unconcerned by the inadequacy of the evidence against La Valette. Moreover, the principal commander, Condé, was vital to Richelieu's political and dynastic strategies—above all, since

---

[119] AAE France 1678, fo. 519, (Nov. 1636). AAE France 822, fo. 189, Chavigny to Bullion, 10 Nov. 1636: details of the extent to which Chaulnes committed his own funds to the defence of Picardy in 1635/6.

[120] BN MS Fr. 6644, fo. 275, Girard to Cardinal de la Valette, 28 Oct. 1637; Avenel, v. 871, 10 Oct. 1637: letter from the king expressing great displeasure at Épernon's failure to engage the Spanish.

[121] Avenel, v. 871, 10 Oct. 1637.

the projected marriage of Condé's son to Richelieu's niece had yet to be finalized. So having previously tried to buy the support of the Épernon family, Richelieu now resolved to destroy the duc de La Valette and his father, and to abandon any attempt to work through the traditional source of power in Guienne.[122] The duc de La Valette fled to England to escape the inevitable consequences of the stage-managed trial that Richelieu had prepared for him; Épernon's governorship was exercised by Condé, and in 1641 he was exiled to his château at Loches where he died a year later.

The decisiveness of this break is underlined by the decision to appoint the comte d'Harcourt as governor of Guienne after the death of Épernon in 1642.[123] Richelieu's apparent volte-face, placing a member of the house of Lorraine in the governorship of one of their most inveterate opponents, can also be explained by the ever-increasing demands of the war-effort and the shortage of capable commanders. The comte d'Harcourt had served in a number of supporting roles throughout the 1620s and early 1630s. Despite quarrels with the maréchal de Vitry in Provence, when he was involved in the joint campaign to recapture the Lérins, it was Harcourt's action which finally regained the islands.[124] Harcourt's military ability and willingness to profess personal *fidélité* to Richelieu despite his family affiliations, attracted the cardinal's attention.[125] Faced with a choice between his established dynastic alignments amongst the *grands* and the need for competent military commanders, Richelieu showed the pragmatism that was characteristic of much of his political action. In 1639, Harcourt was married to Marguerite de Cambout, Richelieu's first cousin,[126] signalling that an

---

[122] Compare the account of the defeat at Fuentarrabia presented by Archbishop Sourdis—*Correspondance et dépêches*, ed. E. Sue (3 vols.; Paris, 1839), ii. 59–67, 9 Sept. 1638—with the *Factum du prince de Condé*, liberally rewritten by Richelieu: Avenel, vi. 195–209 (late Sept. 1638). The tribunal picked by Richelieu to ensure La Valette's prosecution proved equally unconvinced, and had to be bullied into bringing a verdict of guilty: Hanotaux and La Force, *Richelieu* v. 338 n. 4.

[123] *Dictionnaire du grand siècle*, ed. Bluche, 668. The governorship was restored to the duc de La Valette in 1643, immediately after the death of Louis XIII: Anselme, *Histoire généalogique*, viii. 220.

[124] Hanotaux and La Force, *Richelieu*, v. 261–7.

[125] See n. 73 above.

[126] Anselme, *Histoire généalogique*, iii. 499. Ironically, Marguerite du Cambout was the sister of Marie de Pontchâteau, who had been married by Richelieu to the duc de La Valette in 1634. Marguerite had first been married—at the same ceremony as her sister—to the duc de Puylaurens. However, Puylaurens's inability to honour his agreement with Richelieu that he should persuade his patron, Gaston d'Orléans, to renounce the marriage to Marguerite de Lorraine, was punished by confinement at Vincennes where he died a year later, freeing Marguerite de Cambout to play a second part in the cardinal's family strategy: B. Neveu, *Sebastien Joseph du Cambout de Pontchâteau (1634–90) et ses missions à Rome* (Paris, n.d.), 3–8.

arrangement had been reached to overlook traditional dynastic antagonisms. Tied into Richelieu's family network, Harcourt subsequently gained a series of prestigious commands and ever-growing military influence that continued under Mazarin and was to culminate in the viceroyalty of Catalonia in 1645.[127] Richelieu saw this as an important alliance: he needed the military skills of Harcourt to prop up the war-effort; Harcourt did more than anyone else to retrieve the French position in Italy that had deteriorated since the unexpected death of Victor Amadeus I of Savoy in 1637.[128] Yet it also implied the abandonment of a dynastic policy that had previously brought many families to support the cardinal. Harcourt's marriage allowed him to found a new cadet line of the Lorraine, distinct from the Guise and Elbeuf branches of the family, and to contribute greatly to the family's recovery in the later seventeenth century.[129] Moreover, dynastic affiliation to Richelieu's family did not ensure Harcourt's enduring loyalty to the cardinal's policies, as Mazarin was to discover in 1653 when Harcourt seized the fortress of Breisach in his own name, probably intending to set up an independent sovereignty close to the traditional territorial base of the Guise in Lorraine.[130]

Richelieu's venture into a marriage alliance with the house of Lorraine at least brought the military capacities of Harcourt into the high command. That which linked the comte de Guiche, the head of the house of Gramont and sovereign prince of Bidache, to Richelieu's family through his marriage to Françoise-Marguerite de Chivré, another of Richelieu's cousins on the Du Plessis side, was less fortunate.[131] Created a maréchal through Richelieu's intervention, Guiche was placed in command of the army in Flanders and led it to heavy defeat at Honnecourt in 1642.[132] Contemporaries drew the same conclusion that they had previously drawn about Brézé and La Meilleraye, that these military appointments reflected patronage

---

[127] *Dictionnaire du grand siècle*, ed. Bluche, 707–8.

[128] Most notably, of course, by the successful siege of Turin in 1640, which prevented the complete collapse of French influence in Piedmont: see N. L. Caron, *Le Tellier: Son administration comme intendant d'armée en Piémont, 1640–43* (Paris, 1880), *passim*.

[129] Anselme, *Histoire généalogique*, iii. 499–501.

[130] A. Chéruel, *Histoire de France sous le ministère de Mazarin, 1651–61* (3 vols.; Paris, 1881), ii. 45–7.

[131] Anselme, *Histoire généalogique*, iv. 616; Guiche—later maréchal de Gramont—gives details of the spectacular triple marriage of 1634, by which Richelieu simultaneously married three of his 'nièces' (actually cousins) to Guiche, the duc de La Valette and the duc de Puylaurens, in his *Mémoires* MP vii. 242.

[132] AG A¹71, doc. 45, *pouvoir* for Guiche, 26 Jan. 1642; Aumale, *Histoire des princes de Condé*, iv. 470–2, provides a brief account of Honnecourt.

based upon Richelieu's family interests and were not to do with military competence or general suitability.[133]

Appointment to other commands reflected the real practical difficulties faced by Richelieu in finding suitable *grands* who had not been previously disgraced or removed. The Protestant duc de Rohan, whose considerable military ability had been deployed against the crown in the 1620s, had been partially restored to royal favour in the early 1630s, and had served in a number of supporting roles.[134] Richelieu appointed him in 1635 to command the army operating in the Valtelline, one of the few areas of success during the first years of war.[135] Whether Richelieu continued to distrust Rohan, or whether it was assumed that he would seek to purge previous insubordination by committing unlimited private funds to the army of the Valtelline, is not clear; what is clear is that the army was starved of official financial support and collapsed in early 1637. Richelieu by this time felt his position even more threatened by military failure, and he made no attempt to hide his anger with Rohan, so that the duke ended his career as a gentleman volunteer in the army of the duke of Saxe-Weimar.[136]

The rise of Turenne towards senior military command was to have important consequences for the French war-effort after Richelieu's death. During the ministry, however, the willingness to promote the military careers of the La Tour d'Auvergne, Protestants who possessed the sovereign territories of Bouillon and Sedan, should be seen as a further sign of Richelieu's shortage of able generals, and of his acceptance of the conventional assumptions about the right of the highest aristocratic families to hold commands. The duc de Bouillon, head of the house, made little attempt to hide his hostility to Richelieu, and had been consistently implicated in conspiracies against the cardinal, organized from Bouillon's territories outside France. Yet in 1642, at the same time that he became involved in the Cinq-Mars conspiracy, he received command of the army of Italy.[137] Bouillon's opposition to Richelieu, together with the problems of controlling a

---

[133] For Brézé, see Bassompierre, *Mémoires*, xxi. 389–90; J. Chastenet de Puységur, *Les Guerres de Louis XIII et Louis XIV* (2 vols.; Paris, 1883), ii. 1–3, on La Meilleraye; Tallemant de Réaux, *Historiettes*, ed. A. Adam (2 vols., Paris, 1960), i. 326, on La Meilleraye; i. 529–30 for Guiche.

[134] A. Laugel, *Henry de Rohan, son rôle politique et militaire sous Louis XIII* (Paris, 1889), 273–318.

[135] Ibid. 319–33; Rohan, *Mémoire sur la guerre de la Valtelline*, in Petitot and Monmerqué, *Collection*, xix. 75–123.

[136] Avenel, v. 762, 28 Mar. 1637: blame was shared with the *surintendant des finances*, Bullion, but Rohan did not consider it safe to return to France to face Richelieu: Laugel, *Rohan*, 348–57.

[137] AG A^{1}71, fo. 44, 24 Jan. 1642; Hanotaux and La Force, *Richelieu*, iv. 486–7.

prince with a sovereignty outside the French borders, were both recognized. Nevertheless, after his previous reconciliation with the king in 1641, there was simply no reason, given the numbers of armies now in operation, to prevent him assuming a command for which his rank made him eligible. His younger brother Turenne, possibly playing a part in a wider family *politique*, had avoided complicity in conspiracies against the cardinal; however, he remained under suspicion as a consequence of his brother's activities throughout Richelieu's ministry.[138] Ironically, it was Turenne who had to wait until Mazarin's ministry to receive a full command and to be made a maréchal in 1643.[139]

The duc de Bouillon had benefited from the same conventions governing the military hierarchy within the *grands* as might other, yet more unreliable, sovereign princes. Richelieu was even prepared to envisage granting a military command to Duke Charles IV of Lorraine as one of the terms of the 1641 Peace of Saint-Germain, a prospect that was averted by the duke's decision to re-enter Spanish service, rather than by any reconsideration on Richelieu and Louis's part about the wisdom of such an appointment.[140]

The expansion of the army and the doubts about the reliability or competence of the *grands* available to command, eventually gave rise to a highly traditional expedient. In 1638, 1639, 1640, and 1642 the king and Richelieu took personal command of the main campaign army, both in the north-east and, in 1642, in Roussillon.[141] While the presence of the king and the concentration of resources led to the capture of a number of frontier cities, and went some way to silencing disputes between the other generals within the force directly under the crown, it reduced the overall control of the war-effort, and entailed even greater autonomy for the commanders of the other field armies. This autonomy was, however, hampered by the allocation of priority to the 'royal' army in the distribution of finance and supplies. The other commanders frequently found themselves deprived of promised support and, not surprisingly, developed a strong sense that they were being sacrificed to the requirement of ensuring success for the army that the king commanded in person.

---

[138] Bérenger, *Turenne*, 177–85; Avenel, vi. 946, Richelieu to de Noyers, 27 June 1642.

[139] Turenne received the baton of maréchal on 16 Nov. 1643, and was made *lieutenant général* of the army of Germany on 3 Dec.: Baluze, *Histoire de la maison d'Auvergne*, i. 459–60.

[140] Aubery, *Mémoires*, ii. 655–8, 29 Mar. 1641; Avenel, vi. 769, 771, Richelieu to Chavigny, 6 and 15 Apr. 1641.

[141] BN MS Fr. 6644, fo. 315, Chavigny to Cardinal de La Valette, 29 July 1638; Avenel, vi. 361, Richelieu to La Meilleraye, 22 May 1639; Aubery, *Mémoires*, ii. 541, Châtillon to Frederick Henry of Orange, 23 June 1640; Avenel, vi. 910, Richelieu to de Noyers, 3 May 1642.

Like the provincial governors, who had found themselves thrust into command in unfavourable circumstances, they too became increasingly defensive in tone and uncooperative, reluctant to make up shortfalls with their own funds, or to adopt ambitious strategies.

V

In this final section it has been stressed that, with the expansion of the ministry's war aims and the scale of military activities after 1634, Richelieu's difficulties in finding suitable commanders in terms of personal loyalty and military competence became more intense. His ability to regulate appointments in accordance with any clear political or dynastic plan became correspondingly reduced. Neither before nor after 1635 was there any ideological basis for the allocation of commands. Those of the *grands* who served as commanders did so because they considered this to be a right and duty within their caste; these *grands* were prepared to serve Richelieu's policies because their individual interests within the competitive world of the high aristocracy complemented, and coincided with, his. Even during Richelieu's ministry, this identification of interest was coming under severe strain as military expectations increased and the lines of Richelieu's aristocratic *politique* became blurred.

It was left to Mazarin to face up to the immense problems caused by the return and rehabilitation of Richelieu's aristocratic opponents, and to manage an aristocratic system in which he, although learning quickly, began as an outsider. But it was neither the Fronde, nor even Mazarin's longer-term miscalculations, that led Le Tellier, secretary of state for war, to refer in 1650 to the army as being like a republic, in which the individual corps commanders presided over constituent autonomous cantons.[142] It was a problem inherent in a system of military organization which accepted with few questions the rights of the aristocracy to be appointed to military command, which expected a heavy—and increasing—personal commitment from them, and yet which offered no means by which the interests and rivalries of a competitive and divided caste could be subsumed in wider notions of state or corporate service.

There were, of course, reasons other than the ambiguous relations with the high command for the relative lack of success of the French war-effort in the period after 1635: the chaotic state of the French

---

[142] R. J. Bonney, *Political Change in France under Richelieu and Mazarin* (Oxford, 1978), 262.

finances, which allocated an ever-increasing proportion of the crown's revenues to the servicing of loans contracted at high rates of interest; the universal problems of ensuring logistical support for armies and of poor communications; and inadequate provision for the real burden of a major campaign and no clear conception of what this would entail. Yet in the face of problems whose scale reflected the unprecedented level and duration of military commitments, it is notable that Richelieu remained firmly within a world of traditional assumptions and practices about the nature of military command and the character of army organization. Whether he had the power to achieve profound change in the organization of military authority or the *mentalité* of the senior commanders is certainly open to question, though his imposition of fiscal and administrative obligations upon the military commanders, and his punishment of failure with arbitrary severity, suggests that his ability to exploit his position as *premier ministre* of the king should not be underestimated. More critically, it must be asked whether, as a member himself of the traditional élite who staffed the upper reaches of the high command, he had any wish to make changes which might break the monopoly of the *grands* upon senior military posts, or threaten to disrupt the complex and multi-layered hierarchy within this caste. The appointment to military commands presents these questions in a particularly pointed manner. None the less, it is hard to resist the conclusion that this was merely a striking example of the ambiguities in Richelieu's relationship with the established élites throughout France, which combined an assertive and aggressive rhetoric of monarchical absolutism, and the demands of obedience to the monarch's servants, with a practical willingness to make concessions and to tolerate the reinforcement of privilege and the survival of independent authority. Some of this undoubtedly reflected the pragmatism of a politician who was far more constrained in his courses of action than generations of hagiography have been prepared to allow. Yet without a willingness to enter into the *mentalité* and the aspirations of Richelieu himself, and of the *grands* who have too frequently been depicted as an undifferentiated group of his opponents, much of the political action and motivation of this period will remain either contradictory or incomprehensible.

6

RICHELIEU AND HIS BISHOPS?
Ministerial Power and Episcopal Patronage under Louis XIII

JOSEPH BERGIN

I

It is striking that, despite the wide-ranging contributions of modern scholarship towards a better understanding of seventeenth-century France, religious and ecclesiastical issues should, to a considerable extent, still run somewhat parallel to the central concerns of political history, however broadly defined.[1] The subject of the present essay forms an interesting case in point. To the historian of French church, the period of Richelieu's ministry generally represents a strategically important phase in the development of the Counter-Reformation in France, which is usually seen as being borne along by the ever-widening influence of the *dévots*. To the political historian, it is a period when the monarchy tightened its grip on the levers of power throughout the kingdom, in the course of which Richelieu himself survived the most serious political challenge of all to his ministerial position from the same *dévots* whose influence he then proceeded to shatter.

The contribution of the episcopate to the French Counter-Reformation has been long, if inconclusively, discussed, but its contribution to the enhancement of royal power, hardly at all. Yet the possible relationships between the two developments scarcely need to be suggested. The most basic of these connections stems from the

This essay owes its origin to a research project still in progress on the French episcopate in the 17th cent., and is to be regarded as a provisional rather than definitive statement of that research. For that reason, no effort has been made to cite here all of the voluminous sources on which it is based. It is a pleasure to acknowledge the financial assistance I have received from the Univ. of Manchester, as well as the helpful advice I received from Mark Greengrass, who read an earlier draft of the essay.

[1] See the reflections of Wolfgang Reinhard, 'Möglichkeiten und Grenzen der Verbindung von Kirchengeschichte mit Sozial- und Wirtschaftsgeschichte', in *Wiener Beiträge zur Geschichte*, ed. G. Klingenstein and H. Lutz, viii (Munich, 1982), 243–78.

fact that since the Concordat of Bologna in 1516 the formal right to nominate bishops was the personal prerogative of the king of France. It was highly prized by successive monarchs, who resisted all attempts to alter or dilute it, and who repeatedly and successfully insisted on its extension to bishoprics acquired subsequent to the Concordat, or initially excluded from its terms. How that prerogative was exercised during successive reigns can reveal a great deal about the realities of power and the extent to which the French crown could treat its ecclesiastical patronage in a manner that differed from other forms of patronage at its disposal.[2] Because of the prestige, power, and wealth attached to episcopal rank, it was only natural that the crown would be subject to intense pressure from individuals, families, and lobbies anxious to benefit from royal largess. Inevitably, one effect of this is to focus the historian's attention on those figures—whether they be ministers, favourites, or courtiers—who served as mediators between the king and those in search of ecclesiastical preferment, figures whose power was both cause and consequence of their capacity to influence the distribution of episcopal office in the largest 'national' church in Christendom.

As a chapter in the wider history of royal patronage and policy towards the church, the long ministry of Richelieu would automatically deserve attention. Moreover, for perhaps the first time in the monarchy's history, ministerial and other papers are sufficiently numerous and interesting for a study of ecclesiastical patronage at the highest level to be possible and, it is to be hoped, illuminating. Of course, these papers are far from full or complete, and the historian is all too often reduced to guesswork concerning ministerial influence over numerous royal decisions—and indeed over the precise grounds of those decisions themselves.[3] But there are other reasons why the subject is worth pursuing. First of all, it enables us to approach from a somewhat unusual angle the perennial question of Richelieu's relations with Louis XIII, and specifically the extent of his ministerial powers to fashion decisions which the king could be expected to approve. Secondly, there is the often-ignored fact that Richelieu the cardinal-minister remained as committed as he had been throughout his own episcopal career to improving the condition of the French church. How far did he attempt to use, and succeed in

---

[2] See Pierre Blet, 'Le Concordat de Bologne et la réforme tridentine', *Gregorianum*, 45 (1964), 241–79.

[3] The exact role of the papacy and its nuncios in influencing the choice of French bishops would require extended study, and is not dealt with in the present essay. But it is worth noting that nuncios' correspondence in the Vatican archives and library is a relatively poor source of information on episcopal appointments generally.

using, his ministerial influence to pursue such objectives through episcopal patronage? How far was he—or indeed anyone in his position—free to ignore the pressures and interests of families and social groups clamouring for episcopal preferment? Clearly, not all of these questions can be treated adequately in a short essay: the pages that follow will focus primarily on the evolution of the episcopate during Richelieu's ministry and the successive phases of Richelieu's contribution to that change.

II

However much historians may remain sceptical about the value of the *Testament politique* as an expression of Richelieu's thinking, it is worth remembering that—as befitted a prince of the church— Richelieu's discussion in it of French society began with a chapter, by far the longest apart from that treating the power of the prince, on the church and the problem of its reform. Although less well-known than other parts of that controversial document, this chapter also attempted to influence, perhaps even to pre-empt, future discussion of the record of Louis XIII's reign. One of its best-known passages offered a combination of reminiscence and advice to the king on ecclesiastical appointments:

Quand je me souviens que j'ai vu, dans ma jeunesse, des gentilshommes et autres personnes laïques posséder, par confidence, non seulement la plus grande part des prieurés et abbayes, mais aussi des cures et des évêchés . . . J'avoue que je ne reçois pas peu de consolation de voir que ces désordres aient été si absolument bannis sous votre régne . . . Pour continuer et augmenter cette bénédiction, V[otre] M[ajesté] n'a autre chose à faire, à mon avis, que d'avoir un soin particulier de remplir les évêchés de personnages de mérite et de vie exemplaire.[4]

As has happened with other issues, the cardinal's comparison of the experiences of his youth and of subsequent improvements has been broadly accepted by his biographers and by historians of the church. Yet this consensus rests on remarkably slight foundations, as little serious research has been done on the French episcopate in general, let alone on Richelieu's and Louis XIII's contributions to its reform at the point where they could exercise greatest influence—namely, in the selection and nomination of bishops, since virtually all abbeys and priories referred to in the *Testament* were held *in commendam* and

---

[4] *Test. pol.* 151.

hence virtually secularized.[5] Thus, the claim made by Richelieu requires, apart from a general perspective on the episcopate, some attempt to describe and define the roles of both king and cardinal in achieving the results with which the author of the *Testament politique* clearly wished to associate himself. In order to do so, it may be useful to begin with a brief comparative sketch of their respective background and experiences where bishops and bishoprics were concerned.

III

In 1605, Henry IV made a claim essentially similar to that made a generation later by Richelieu for his son, Louis XIII: rejecting allegations of substandard appointments as the work of his predecessors, he characteristically asserted that he had substantially improved the quality of episcopal nominations. Leaving the question of reform to one side, it is clear on closer examination that Henry IV made numerous episcopal appointments of the kind that Richelieu would so strongly decry in the *Testament politique*.[6] During the decade following his death, many appointments of a similar kind were made, in particular of under-aged coadjutor-bishops who, once appointed, enjoyed automatic succession rights on the death or resignation of incumbent bishops. Old noble families benefited most from the instability and changing political balance of these years, of which they availed to acquire or strengthen their hold on the dioceses in question. Rome strongly objected from 1615–16 onwards to the intense pressure being put on existing bishops to accept 'coadjutors' who were frequently incapable of performing any useful coadjutorial functions at all. At the same time, reformist circles within the French church were beginning to raise the wider question of how to improve the exercise of episcopal patronage, with both the Estates General of 1614 and especially the 1617 Assembly of Notables at Rouen making concrete suggestions how to do this. Significantly, these considerations and pressures for action were surfacing just as Louis XIII was himself emerging from the shadows, after the destruction of Concini's regime in April 1617. The king's personal

---

[5] The only modern study of the ancien régime episcopate as a whole is that by Michel Péronnet, *Les Évêques de l'ancienne France* (2 vols.; Lille, 1978).

[6] See Frederic J. Baumgartner, *Change and Continuity in the French Episcopate: The Bishops and the Wars of Religion, 1547–1610* (Durham, NC, 1986), ch. 10, and Joseph Bergin, 'Henri IV and the Problem of the French Episcopate', in Keith Cameron (ed.), *From Valois to Bourbon: Dynasty, State and Society in Early Modern France* (Exeter, 1989), 127–43.

responses during the following years on questions of episcopal patronage, especially over debatable nominations, offered encouragement to church leaders and reformers, stimulating proposals to ensure that the king's conscience would be adequately enlightened where episcopal appointments were concerned. The role played by successive royal confessors like Jean Arnoux and Gaspar Seguéran, and especially by senior churchmen like Cardinal de La Rochefoucauld, grand almoner of France after 1618, in dealing with some unacceptable royal appointments is unthinkable apart from the king's anxiety to discharge his duties to the full, and his susceptibility to arguments centred on questions of conscience.[7] But in the uncertain political climate of the early 1620s, it still remained unclear how far the king was capable of marrying his perceived good intentions with traditional pressures from courtiers, patrons, families, and individual clerics, as well as with politico-ecclesiastical considerations generally. Perhaps Louis XIII himself did not quite know how far he would actively seek, let alone allow himself to be guided by, counsel concerning episcopal nominations from any one minister, even if that minister were at the same time a leading figure in the French church. It was, however, characteristic of this strong-willed but taciturn monarch that he never repeated, either before or during Richelieu's ministry, his father's boast of having transformed the French episcopate.

One claim that the naturally less modest Richelieu did *not* make in the *Testament politique* was that on taking office in 1624 he had recommended specific ecclesiastical objectives to Louis XIII. But if he did not have anything resembling a 'policy', he did, at least, have considerable personal experience of episcopal patronage. The record of his own promotion to Luçon in the early 1600s and the manner in which he had resigned it to a hand-picked successor as recently as 1623 are evidence enough, not merely of experience, but also of a strongly proprietary view of one particular diocese. In his early career, he had sought at least once to exchange Luçon for another, better diocese, but had been frustrated in his attempts—a not uncommon experience for French bishops.[8] Of even greater significance is the fact that Richelieu had also seen something of the wider problem of bishoprics in general, chiefly as a consequence of his position after 1619 as Marie de' Medici's principal adviser. Her jointure included presentation rights to the seven Breton and the two

---

[7] These remarks are drawn from J. Bergin, *Cardinal de La Rochefoucauld: Leadership and Reform in the French Church* (New Haven, Conn., 1987), 127 ff.

[8] J. Bergin, *The Rise of Richelieu* (New Haven, Conn, 1991), 58–63, 70–3, 75.

Auvergne bishoprics of Clermont and Saint-Flour. How, or indeed whether, she should be permitted to exercise these rights at all was a bone of contention during her years of exile and disgrace between 1617 and 1620.[9] Despite this opposition, she obtained formal royal confirmation of her presentation rights, and throughout the 1620s she effectively exercised them.[10] But this required vigilance, as the king and other parties were not averse to springing candidates of their own on her for approval.[11] In addition, Marie was governor of Anjou after 1619, and when Bishop Charles Miron of Angers became archbishop of Lyons in 1626, hers appears to have been the dominant voice in the choice of a successor to Miron at Angers.[12] For these reasons, Richelieu, even had he not become a royal minister, would have been far more closely associated with bishop-making politics on the queen mother's behalf throughout the 1620s than virtually any of his fellow ecclesiastics.

If this suggests that Richelieu's experience and concerns were focused purely on the political mechanics of episcopal nominations, his place in the queen mother's entourage should also remind us that he was part of the *dévot*-reformist movement, and moved in circles which were increasingly active in seeking to improve episcopal nominations, either by promoting candidates of whom they approved, or by ensuring that unsuitable nominations would not get past king and pope. They had already had, as we saw earlier, a limited measure of success on both counts, but as Cardinal de La Rochefoucauld admitted in 1622, major benefices like bishoprics involved so many powerful interests and pressures that intervention to influence nominations was extremely risky. Vincent de Paul, the *dévots'* champion under Anne of Austria and Mazarin, would find that things had not radically changed in the intervening years.[13]

[9] AAE France 771, fo. 157ᵛ, abbé Tantucci to Richelieu, 13 July 1617, relating the objections of members of the council to Marie retaining her ecclesiastical patronage.

[10] AAE France 772, fo. 132, *brevet* of 24 Sept. 1619 confirming her rights. See also BN MS Fr. 15699, fos, 413ᵛ–14ʳ, Marie de' Medici to Cardinal de La Rochefoucauld, 23 June 1619, insisting on presenting the bishop of Marseilles to the see of Rennes: 'c'est une affaire où il n'y a nulle difficulté'.

[11] AAE CP Rome 23, fos. 36–7, Sébastien Bouthillier to Claude Bouthillier, Rome, 1 June 1621, urging vigilance lest benefices be filled without the queen mother's knowledge.

[12] ASV, Nunziatura di Francia 66, fo. 163, Bernadino Spada, papal nuncio in France, to Cardinal Antonio Barberini the elder, 24 Oct. 1626; fos. 275–6, same to Cardinal Francesco Barberini, 4 Dec. 1626; fos. 279–83, same to same, 20 Dec. 1626.

[13] Pierre Blet, 'Vincent de Paul et l'épiscopat de France', in *Vincent de Paul: Actes du colloque international d'études vincentiennes* (Rome, 1983), 81–114, esp. 86 ff.

IV

The subject of Richelieu's role as a royal minister in episcopal patronage itself is best approached indirectly, and needs to be prefaced by a comment on sources, followed by a brief outline of the structure and evolution of the episcopate itself.

It is essential to realize from the outset that the sources available for the study of episcopal patronage in this period are far from adequate or comprehensive. The French monarchy kept nothing like systematic records, not least because it made no systematic attempt to organize and structure that patronage. Consequently, it is often extremely difficult to ascertain either the identity or the number of candidates for a given bishopric, or to identify those figures who patronized candidates' efforts to obtain a mitre; in certain cases, the actual dates on which royal nominations were made cannot be established with any accuracy. No formal record at all seems to have survived of discussions between Louis XIII, Richelieu, royal ministers, or other interested parties concerning the relative claims or merits of candidates, so that we can only guess as to which considerations or criteria eventually determined a royal decision. There is nothing remotely similar to the impressive dossiers and discussion papers compiled on the contemporary Castilian episcopate by the officials of the *Cámara de Castilla*.[14] Richelieu's own papers do, of course, refer to questions of episcopal patronage, if only because he received requests to support individual claims, and because he had names of his own to recommend to the king.[15] But even this documentation is distinctly haphazard and while it obviously helps to illuminate the cardinal's views, preferences, and behaviour, the lack of similar documentation for the other parties, Louis XIII included, means that a study based on Richelieu's papers alone risks being seriously one-sided. Because of the consequent difficulty of generalizing from such direct evidence as does exist, the analysis of Richelieu's role in church patronage must also be based in part on inferences from the factual, chronological record of episcopal appointments.

Even a brief look at that record can provide part of the framework essential for an understanding of Richelieu's activities as minister

---

[14] See Helen Rawlings, 'The Secularization of Castilian Episcopal Office under the Habsburgs *c.*1516–1700', *Journal of Ecclesiastical History*, 38 (1987), 53–79; Christian Hermann, *L'Église d'Espagne sous le patronage royal (1476–1834)* (Madrid, 1988).

[15] These requests, which more often concern pensions on bishoprics rather than the bishoprics themselves, appear far more frequently in the vols. of the Grillon edn. of Richelieu's internal state papers than in the Avenel edn.

and patron. Between May 1624 and December 1642, eighty-five episcopal nominations involving eighty individuals in all were made by the crown. This figure includes seven coadjutor-bishops who lived long enough to enjoy their guaranteed succession rights and become full bishops; in appointing coadjutors, the crown was in effect resolving individual succession cases in advance of a see falling vacant. In fact, more than eighty individuals received episcopal nominations during Richelieu's ministry, but an unknown number of them resigned or returned their nominations either voluntarily or as a result of difficulties they could not overcome before obtaining or, in some cases, even seeking, their papal provisions. The list of those who either refused or failed to secure preferment, incidentally, includes some distinguished names: Saint-Cyran, Charles de Condren, Bérulle's successor as superior general of the Oratory, Olier, the founder of Saint-Sulpice, Mathieu de Morgues, the doughty pamphleteer, Charles Talon, brother of Omer, and doubtless others. Unfortunately, the haphazard character of the information about such cases makes it virtually impossible to explore the reasons for success, failure, and even refusal where episcopal office was concerned.[16]

Fifty-four out of the eighty-five nominations made between 1624 and 1642 were occasioned by the death of reigning bishops creating a vacancy which in theory made the royal decision relatively straightforward. But nine resulted from resignations, which usually involved protracted or complex prior negotiations, while a further eleven nominations involved the transfer or promotion of existing bishops to other dioceses. Perhaps the most unusual and problematic of all were the three nominations which resulted from the deposition of bishops compromised by flight abroad with Marie de' Medici or by implication in the 1632 revolt in Languedoc, and the 'resignation' for similar reasons of the last Guise archbishop of Reims in 1640.[17] Arithmetically, these eight-five nominations would account for about three-quarters of the 114 dioceses in France at the time; but, in fact, only seventy bishoprics, or just over 60 per cent, were affected, as several dioceses experienced more than one change of bishop between 1624 and 1642, and others none at all. Nor were all the

---

[16] In the case of Talon, it was apparently the problems created by nomination to a see, Saint-Pol de Léon in Brittany, whose bishop had recently been deposed for going into exile with Marie de' Medici, which dissuaded him from seeking papal confirmation: Avenel, iv. 653 n. 3.

[17] The papal records use the term 'privatio' to describe the termination of Guise's tenure: *Hierarchia Catholica Medii et Recentioris Aevi*, ed. C Eubel *et al.* (5 vols.; Munich, 1898–1958), iv, art. 'Rhemensis'.

bishops involved new to the episcopate: six of those transferred or promoted under Richelieu were bishops first appointed during the 1610s or early 1620s. More specifically, episcopal nominations were not evenly spaced out across the years of Richelieu's ministry: instead, the bulk of them was concentrated in the years 1625, 1627–9, 1631, 1635–7, and 1640. Clearly, reshaping the French episcopate was not the work of a day, and the crown's ability to have an episcopal bench 'à son souhait', as Richelieu put it, was limited by episcopal independence and longevity as much as by anything else.

An equally cursory examination reveals certain general changes in the character of the episcopate which bear out some of the claims later made in Richelieu's *Testament politique*. For example, the number of under-aged appointees—a long-standing problem despite the fact that the required age in France was four years less than the canonical 30 in force elsewhere in Catholic Europe—declined steadily during the 1620s, disappearing almost completely during the 1630s. It is perhaps symbolic of the changing face of the episcopate during these years that the youngest appointment of the 1620s was Henri de Lorraine-Guise, aged 14 when nominated to Reims in 1628, while the youngest bishop seated in the 1630s was François Foucquet, son of one of Richelieu's closest councillors, who was only two months short of the required age of 26 when nominated to Bayonne in May 1637. At the same time, the mean age of all appointments climbed steadily rather than spectacularly towards 35 years and beyond, finally standing at nearly 38 years for the period of Richelieu's ministry as a whole. This trend towards a more mature episcopate was also reinforced by the sharp decline in the number of coadjutor-bishops appointed during the same period—fewer of whom were in any case the kind of under-aged, aristocratic *fils de famille* who had received most of the coadjutorships granted under Henri IV and during the 1610s. Likewise, more and more men with experience in pastoral and administrative activities, both ecclesiastical and secular, filled the ranks of the episcopate—a development which certainly corresponds with Richelieu's stated personal preference for men of action, energy, and authority over the men of mere book learning or mystics. Only eleven of the eighty nominees were members of religious orders, with the Oratorians and the Minims, both active orders, claiming three each. Only one, a Carthusian, could be classified as a contemplative, but he may properly be regarded as a special case, being Richelieu's own elder brother, Alphonse.

The phenomenon, also alluded to in *Testament politique*, of bishoprics being held by straw men, or *confidentiaires* as they were known, was also on the decline by the 1620s. The last known instances of this kind of arrangement, which for obvious reasons is extremely difficult to uncover, were the control of Agde and Lodève by the Montmorency-Ventadour family, and that of Toulouse, Mirepoix, and Aire by the duc d'Épernon, though there may have been others in Provence.[18] This form of domination disappeared in the 1620s, though not before Épernon secured the see of Mirepoix for an illegitimate son who in the event proved to be an active and conscientious bishop.[19] Instead, the control of bishoprics through *confidentiaires* gave way to a more 'rational', or at least legalized, practice of assigning often substantial, and sometimes multiple, pensions from episcopal revenues to a wide range of individuals, both ecclesiastical and secular. One important effect of this development was that, when it came to filling vacant bishoprics, candidates for pensions rather than for mitres would make themselves and their demands known, using family and patrons to press their case at court; Richelieu certainly received his share of such petitions. This obviously widened the circle of those interested in episcopal vacancies, so that delays and difficulties in reaching decisions over bishoprics might just as easily result from demands for pensions as from indecision over whom to nominate to the bishoprics themselves. It may well be that a certain number of those originally nominated to bishoprics returned their nominations because they were unable either to satisfy those seeking pensions or to prevent them from undermining their efforts to secure royal *expéditions* and papal provisions. However, direct evidence for this tenebrous sphere of episcopal patronage is less abundant for the ministry of Richelieu than for that of Mazarin.

V

The changes experienced by the French episcopate in the second quarter of the seventeenth century were, if far from radical or sudden, substantial and sustained. Because of the multiple influences and interests which lay behind this, the question of who may be regarded as instrumental in engineering such changes cannot be

---

[18] For the three successive Levy de Ventadour 'bishops' of Lodève between 1611 and 1625, see the careful work of Ernest Martin, *Histoire de la ville de Lodève*, ii (Montpellier, 1900), 373–4.

[19] For Épernon's control of Mirepoix, see Bishop Pierre de Donnaud's letter to him in BN MS Fr. 20477, fo. 287, 9 July 1623, protesting that he would not do anything to dispose of his see without Épernon's prior approval.

answered as rapidly or confidently as in the past. In particular, the power enjoyed by Richelieu as Louis XIII's leading minister cannot be taken as a sufficient, even if it was in the event a contributory, cause. His role must be approached, here as in other fields of activity, in as broad a context as possible.

There can be little doubt that, as he returned to office in 1624, Richelieu saw himself as playing a part in the crown's episcopal patronage—a part which his cardinal's rank seemed to make all the more natural. But how much influence he expected to wield is harder to determine. A cryptic note from late 1624 on the presentation of requests to Louis XIII gives only the most general indication of his early thinking:

le Cardinal gardera cet ordre en toutes les demandes qu'on voudra faire au Roy: (savoir) qu'il en advertira Sa Majeste, et se chargera en sa personne du reffus de celles que Sa Majeste ne pourra accorder. Et pour celles qu'elle [Louis XIII] voudra donner, il fera semblant de n'en vouloir parler; cependant il conseillera les parties de faire leurs demandes eux-mesmes au Roy, afin que la grace vienne purement de luy et qu'ils ayent obligation à luy seul.[20]

Such a self-imposed code of practice would only make sense if, as Cardinal Bérulle recognized a few years later, Richelieu already had a general permission to present all kinds of petitions directly to the king.[21] How far Richelieu gave his support to the idea of an ecclesiastical council to deal with episcopal and other matters in the proposed *Règlement général* of 1625 we can also only guess, but he made no attempt to resurrect it subsequently.[22] That he chose not to press for a formal *conseil de conscience* at any time during his ministry adds weight to the argument that he was not interested in institutions. By contrast, his reaction to the disgrace of Gaspar Seguéran, the king's confessor, in late 1625, is far more revealing. Seguéran was removed shortly after having been sharply attacked by Richelieu's old friend, Bishop Laubespine of Orléans, for his presumption concerning the distribution of major church benefices.[23] Seguéran's less combative successor, Jean Suffren, was long known to Richelieu as Marie de' Medici's confessor, and the cardinal's warning to him could hardly have been more explicit: 'N'ayez point l'ambition de

---

[20] Grillon, i. 105. This document is not dated, but is related to proceedings against La Vieuville in late 1624.

[21] Ibid. iii. 241, Bérulle to Richelieu (28 Apr. 1628).

[22] Ibid. i. 248–69, *Règlement pour toutes les affaires du royaume* (1625), at p. 249. See the discussion of this document and its authorship by Robin Briggs in Ch. 3 above.

[23] E. Griselle, *Louis XIII et Richelieu* (Paris, 1911), 21–2, quoting the diary of Robert Arnauld d'Andilly.

disposer des éveschez et des abbayes, estant chose qui doit dépendre immediatement du roy, ainsy que toutes autres graces'—though Richelieu did concede that Suffren could warn the king directly if a matter of conscience arose concerning such appointments.[24] Suffren claimed in 1628 that he had been only too happy to behave in accordance with Richelieu's guidance.[25]

If it is characteristic of Richelieu's political style to seize such an opportunity to neutralize a royal confessor, it would be hasty to see it as heralding an immediate move on his part to monopolize advice to the king on episcopal patronage. Indeed, there is ample evidence that Richelieu was extremely cautious over bishoprics during his early years as a minister. Successive royal favourites such as Baradat and Toiras secured bishoprics for sons, brothers, or uncles between 1625 and 1627, and there are no signs that Richelieu tried to come between the king and his favourites.[26] Much the same could be said of several promotions between 1625 and 1629, mostly of young and inexperienced scions, or clerical dependents, of powerful noble houses like the Guise, Épernon, Souvré, Matignon, or Montmorency; the aristocratic newcomers were as personally inexperienced and undistinguished as their family names were prestigious.

However, Richelieu's caution during these early years should not be interpreted as a lack of interest or activity. He was also constrained by forces other than the great nobility. A number of sources show that he experienced difficulty, even failure, in getting bishoprics for a small group of individuals, at least one of whom was a close personal associate; just as significantly, some of the opposition came from fellow churchmen rather than from courtiers. In 1626, Mathieu de Morgues was prevented from becoming bishop of Toulon by Cardinal de La Rochefoucauld who regarded him as being too outspokenly Gallican, with the result that de Morgues abandoned his efforts, blaming Richelieu for his discomfiture.[27] La Rochefoucauld also held up for a time the appointment of Henri de Sponde to Pamiers, as well as successfully frustrating the young Henri de Béthune's designs on Lyons. Both of these men were known to be supported by Richelieu.[28]

---

[24] Grillon, i. 239, undated letter but probably late 1625.

[25] Ibid. iii. 374–5, letter of 10 July 1628.

[26] See ibid. iii. 52–3, 'mémoire concernant M de Toiras', 6 Feb. 1628, in which Richelieu criticizes Toiras, noting that his brother and uncle both received bishoprics during his term of favour.

[27] BN MS Fr. 23200, fos. 3ᵛ–4ʳ, Morgues to Richelieu, 16 June 1626, thanking him for nomination to Toulon.

[28] Bergin, *La Rochefoucauld*, 133–4.

This evidence of limited success in influencing episcopal nominations—both in preventing certain nominations and in promoting others—also fits with the overall record of appointments during Richelieu's early years in office. That record strongly suggests that Richelieu experienced much less difficulty when he was promoting the claims of candidates who were *dévots* or members of the queen mother's wider circle rather than purely personal clients; and that a policy of collaboration with the queen mother and her entourage in turn facilitated the advancement of those candidates who did enjoy close personal association with Richelieu. It would be misguided to assume that Richelieu, even after his ministerial elevation, effortlessly dominated the queen mother's entourage, or that he was able to use its power at will in order to secure vacant bishoprics for his own personal protégés. For example, less than half a dozen opportunities arose between 1620 and 1631 to fill dioceses directly subject to Marie's right of presentation. In 1621, Richelieu's former university mentor, Philippe Cospeau, was given the important see of Nantes; ten years later, Achille de Harlay obtained that of Saint-Malo, but the original nominee had been Michel de Marillac's son, who died before receiving his provisions.[29] None of the other nominees was especially favoured by Richelieu, and it is clear that Marillac, Bérulle, and others felt free to compete with him in pressing the claims of their own candidates, protégés, or family members. Bérulle actively sought the see of Dol in Brittany for the abbé de Saint-Cyran in 1629; on that occasion, it was not Richelieu, but the queen mother's chief physician, Vautier, who appears to have frustrated him by engineering an appointment of his own.[30]

Nevertheless, Richelieu did register several striking personal successes as a patron of episcopal hopefuls during these early years, and not just in Brittany. In addition to known *dévots* like Miron of Lyons, Montchal of Toulouse, Jaubert de Barrault of Arles, Bonzi of Béziers, Dony d'Attichy of Riez, Grillet of Bazas—all strongly supported by the queen mother and others of her circle, Richelieu himself included—we can list Richelieu's own brother, Alphonse, successively archbishop of Aix and Lyons; Victor Bouthillier, successively bishop of Boulogne and coadjutor-archbishop of Tours; Henri de Sourdis, elevated, despite some strong *dévot* criticism, from

[29] Harlay, who would play a leading role in writing Richelieu's so-called *Mémoires*, was a contemporary of the cardinal's at the Univ., and had been nominated by Henri IV to the diocese of Lavaur in his youth.

[30] Jean Orcibal, *Jean Duvergier de Hauranne, abbé de Saint-Cyran et son temps* (Louvain, 1947), 284.

Maillezais to the archbishopric of Bordeaux; Harlay de Sancy, bishop of Saint-Malo; and Sylvestre de Marcillac, bishop of Mende.[31]

These developments, and the influence which accounted for them, did not go unnoticed. If Richelieu's surviving correspondence can be taken as a reliable indicator, it was in 1628 that he began to receive letters and petitions explicitly requesting his favour or intervention over appointments to vacant dioceses. Marie de' Medici, Gaston d'Orléans, Marillac, Bérulle, and others were among those regularly soliciting his intercession with the king; but while Marie and Gaston would also approach Louis XIII directly, and would say so in their letters to Richelieu, others such as Marillac or Bérulle would generally not enjoy such direct access to the king.[32] This resort to Richelieu as intermediary could perhaps be seen as a consequence of his accompanying Louis XIII on the military campaigns of the late 1620s and of the petitioners' temporary absence from the royal entourage, but it amounted to rather more than that by 1628. Interestingly, Richelieu's own first direct, written request to Louis XIII to appoint a particular individual (Raymond de Montaigne) to a given diocese (Condom) also dates from February 1628.[33] Unfortunately, the text of the king's reply, if indeed there was one at all since the 'vacancy' proved to be a false alarm, has not survived, but a few months later, it was Louis XIII's own turn to write to Richelieu on hearing that the archbishop of Paris was dead. If Paris was now vacant, the king wrote tantalizingly, 'vous sçavez bien pour qui c'est'.[34] But Paris was not vacant either and, unfortunately for historians, neither Louis XIII nor Richelieu was to have the opportunity of revealing the name of their choice as the next archbishop of Paris. Yet what emerges clearly from these two instances is that by 1628 consultations and exchanges between king and minister over episcopal patronage were taking place, and that in at least some cases, provisional decisions were being made in advance of actual vacancies.

---

[31] Richelieu's association with Sourdis was greatly strengthened during the siege of La Rochelle, when Sourdis proved his organizational abilities. Marcillac was a *maître de chambre* in Richelieu's own household. See M. Deloche, *La Maison du cardinal de Richelieu* (Paris, 1912), 75–7.

[32] For examples of this, see Grillon, iii. 419–20, Marie de' Medici to Richelieu, 8 Aug. 1628; ibid. iii. 538, Gaston to Richelieu, 21 Oct. 1628.

[33] Ibid. iii. 66, *précis* of letter of 13 Feb. He had been informed, wrongly as it transpired, that the bishop of Condom was dead. Montaigne had formerly been president of the *présidial* court at Saintes.

[34] Ibid. iii, no. 550, letter of 27 Sept. 1628.

VI

The gradual expansion of Richelieu's episcopal patronage, and of the king's readiness to seek his advice, continued up to, and especially after, the political crisis of 1630, and can be explored from a number of convergent angles.

Continuity and expansion are clearly visible in the fate of the queen mother's ecclesiastical patronage. After her flight abroad in July 1631, her presentation rights in Brittany and the Auvergne lapsed. Neither Clermont nor Saint-Flour fell vacant before 1642, but Brittany was a different matter, with all but one diocese being vacated through death between 1629 and 1642. Richelieu, who became governor of the province in 1631, clearly inherited Marie's influence in filling its bishoprics. Direct evidence of how he exercised it is scant, but the record speaks for itself. It begins in 1631 with Victor Bouthillier's strategically important move from the bishopric of Boulogne to the coadjutorship of Tours, a highly unusual move for a reigning bishop. But Tours was the metropolitan see for all the Breton dioceses, and persuading both Louis XIII and Bertrand d'Eschaux, the reigning archbishop and an old mentor of Richelieu, to agree to this particular succession arrangement was a considerable success for the cardinal.[35] During the next decade, the key Breton bishoprics—Saint-Malo, Nantes, Rennes, and Saint-Brieuc—all went to men who were unmistakably clients of Richelieu. Lesser, more remote dioceses like Tréguier or Quimper went to men known to him at least by repute, and who obtained his approval and support.

However, neither before nor after 1630 were Richelieu or the *dévots* confined to Brittany or the Auvergne when it came to bishoprics. There is no obvious geographical logic or limitation to episcopal appointments of Richelieu clients during the 1630s which embraced dioceses as wide apart as Arles, Marseilles, and Grasse in Provence, Bazas, Dax, and Bayonne in Guyenne and Gascony, and Auxerre, Chartres, and Lisieux closer to Paris.

One instance of episcopal musical-chairs involving well-scattered dioceses—Boulogne, Bayonne, and neighbouring Aire-sur-l'Adour—provides a particularly telling illustration of this. Sébastien Bouthillier, the first of all Richelieu's friends to become a bishop, got the see of Aire in 1621 when Philippe Cospeau vacated it to move to Nantes,

---

[35] See Michel de Marillac's view of Tours, expressed when the archbishop was rumoured to be dying in 1628: 'C'est une pièce digne d'un grand et sage prélat, ayant ces trois grandes provinces et toutte la Bretagne': Grillon, iii. 483, letter to Richelieu (*c*.12 Sept. 1628).

but Bouthillier died suddenly in January 1625. Soon afterwards his
brother, Victor, was nominated to succeed him at Aire, but he
evidently did not relish moving to such a remote diocese, so he
resigned his title to Gilles Boutault, whose exact connection to
the Richelieu–Bouthillier circle at that point remains obscure. A
year later, however, in 1626, Victor Bouthillier became bishop of
Boulogne, which he in turn resigned in 1632 to Jean Dolce after
becoming coadjutor-archbishop of Tours. Meanwhile, Richelieu had
secured for Raymond de Montaigne the vacant see of Bayonne,
whose incumbent, supported by the queen mother, had moved to
Angers in 1626. When Montaigne died in 1637, Bayonne went to
eldest son of François Foucquet. And when Foucquet later moved
from Bayonne to Agde, very soon after Richelieu's death, it was the
bishop of Boulogne, a nephew of Bertrand d'Eschaux, himself a
former bishop of Bayonne, who moved all the way from Boulogne to
Bayonne. These exchanges were facilitated by the survival of the
older practice, much disliked by certain reformers, of resigning
benefices in favour of named individuals, though in the case of
bishoprics resignations were naturally subject to royal approval. How
much pressure was put on reigning bishops to resign or accept
coadjutors is extremely difficult to determine, but it seems as if the
bishop of Boulogne at least was happy to move to Bayonne, his
native region.

In this example, the evidence of a clientele's growing confidence in
its power as well as of certain bishoprics becoming the virtual *chasses
gardées* of a limited number of ministerial rather than noble families,
is unmistakable. Such an impression is in turn borne out by the
record of episcopal nominations between 1631 and 1642. Of the
forty-three nominations made, at least half were of men who were
close enough to Richelieu, either through personal service or other
associations, to be regarded as owing their preferment to his personal
influence. Only a handful of them were members of his personal
ecclesiastical household, which was relatively small. Among them, it
is perhaps significant that it was his successive *maîtres de chambre*,
dignitaries with important administrative functions, who fared best,
and that the last Richelieu household member to get a bishopric, in
late 1641, was the cardinal's confessor, Jacques Lescot. The remaining episcopal clients were drawn from the cardinal's wider circle.
The most prominent among these were members or relatives of ministerial families, actual or future, who owed their political fortunes
to Richelieu—for example, the Bouthilliers, the Séguiers, the
Foucquets. After them came the sons or relatives of important
royal officials such as Malier du Houssay, an *intendant des finances*,

Pavillon, a prominent tax-farmer, or Danès de Marly, a former *maître des requetes* and intendant in Languedoc. Beyond this particular circle we find the many religious figures whom Richelieu knew personally or who were strongly recommended to him by others: Godeau the poet, the Gault brothers (members of the Oratory and very active in Sourdis's diocese of Bordeaux), Jean de Lingendes (a highly appreciated preacher whose papal provisions Richelieu insisted on paying for himself), the Vialarts, uncle and nephew, and so on.

Further, more pointed evidence of the cardinal's influence is provided by the fact that, of the six bishops transferred or promoted during the last decade of his ministry, five were known clients of his. This hardly needs further comment in the case of bishops with names like Bouthillier, Séguier, Étampes, and Cospeau, but reliable bishops were also required in troubled Languedoc sees like Uzès and Albi in the aftermath of the Montmorency revolt; this was duly achieved by transferring existing bishops from other sees.[36] Moreover, only four coadjutor-bishops were appointed during the 1630s, all in 1633–4, but by then royal policy on coadjutorships had changed considerably. The new coadjutors were experienced men intended to offer positive assistance to ageing bishops, rather than relatives of incumbent bishops anxious to maintain or assert a quasi-patrimonial claim to a bishopric. In one significant and extensively documented case, that of Montauban, the coadjutor, Pierre de Bertier, son of the first president of the Toulouse *parlement*, was only appointed after five years of intense pressure on a reluctant reigning bishop from leading figures in the Toulouse *parlement* and from Richelieu himself.[37]

Moreover, it is worth noting that, as Richelieu's entourage became the beneficiary of his episcopal patronage, it tended to be approached by those seeking bishoprics and other benefices to intercede with Richelieu himself—in other words, to become a secondary source of

---

[36] Bishop Daillon du Lude, transferred from Agen to Albi, was a nephew of Schomberg, the new governor of Languedoc and a political ally of Richelieu. Barrault, promoted from Bazas to Arles, was one of the 4 bishops specially commissioned to judge their colleagues implicated in the 1632 revolt.

[37] The campaign against Murviel was launched by Gilles Le Masuyer, *premier président* of the Toulouse parlement in 1629, and continued after his death by his successor, Bertier: See the letters in Grillon, iv. 682, Le Masuyer to Richelieu 23 Nov. 1629; ibid. v. 623–4, same to same, 28 Oct. 1630; ibid. v. 729–30, Richelieu to Murviel (1630?); vi. 48–9, Murviel to Richelieu, 20 Jan. 1631; Avenel, iv. 540–1, Richelieu to Murviel (Feb.) 1634. Murviel probably lacked the stomach for a Catholic reconquest of Montauban similar to that being attempted in the other former Protestant stronghold of Nîmes: see Robert Sauzet, *Contre-Réforme et réforme catholique en Bas-Languedoc: Le Diocèse de Nîmes au XVIIe siècle* (Louvain, 1979).

patronage and support. Begging letters and letters of thanks to secretaries and close associates of Richelieu all testify to this.[38] Quite how active or successful his entourage was remains difficult to assess, not least because such activity was something which Richelieu, never keen on having subordinates make up his mind for him, was determined to keep under strict control. In 1629, for example, Claude Bouthillier reported to Richelieu on a wide-ranging discussion between himself, Bérulle, Marillac, and the cardinal's own niece as to which of several candidates was best suited to fill one of the Breton dioceses then thought to be vacant. Bouthillier evidently received an instant rebuke from Richelieu for his pains, for he assured him virtually by return of post that he had not opened his mouth, nor would he, on the subject, and declared that he had no wishes other than those of Richelieu himself on such matters.[39] In 1639, Sublet des Noyers was reported as making moves to obtain a bishopric for the abbé de Champigny, but, despite his high favour with the cardinal, he had no success whatsoever.[40]

Richelieu's influence can also be gauged from an examination of the speed or slowness with which episcopal vacancies were filled. In an age when rumour was rife, news of episcopal vacancies might take some time to confirm, depending on where the diocese was, or whether the court was itself on the move. Allowing for this, it is remarkable how quickly decisions to appoint known Richelieu clients were made, though there are some interesting exceptions. Alphonse de Richelieu's nominations to Aix and to Lyons came within three days and five days respectively after the previous archbishops' deaths.[41] Henri de Sourdis was appointed to Bordeaux on the very day his brother died. Most of the other nominations came between a week and a month of a predecessor's death, but with most of them clustering at the shorter end of that spectrum. Admittedly, Abra de Raconis got Lavaur three months after it fell vacant, but this delay seems due to his reluctance to accept it because of its remoteness. Grasse in Provence was vacant for six weeks before Antoine Godeau was nominated, but this was largely because Richelieu had attempted to find a Provençal for that see. Where the transfer of Richelieu

[38] BN MS Fr. 23200, fos, 1–2, Charles Talon to Michel Le Masle, Richelieu's Secretary, 2 Sept. 1635. Similar letters to another secretary, Charpentier, who corresponded with a wide range of bishops and other figures, are to be found in BN MS Baluze 333.

[39] Grillon, iv. 556, Bouthillier to Richelieu, 19 Aug. 1629; ibid. 570–1, same to same, 31 Aug. 1629.

[40] BN MS Fr. 15610, p. 168, Henri Arnauld to Président Barillon, 4 Sept. 1639.

[41] Grillon, iii. 427, Louis XIII to Richelieu, 11 Aug. 1628: 'l'on me vient de dire que l'archevesque de Lion est mort. Je vous ay voulu escrire ce mot pour vous dire que, en ce cas, je le désire donner à Mr l'archevesque d'Aix, vostre frère.'

clients from one diocese to another was concerned, the speed of the decision is no less striking. The frequently prolonged vacancies of French bishoprics during the 1630s and early 1640s were not due to royal negligence, but were the direct consequence of increasingly tense relations with the papacy which, for reasons that had nothing to do with candidates' suitability, took several years to ratify numerous royal nominations.[42]

VII

With so many converging, if often indirect, indices of Richelieu's success in peopling the episcopal bench, we return to the question of his relations with Louis XIII over the exercise of that very personal royal prerogative of nominating bishops. Understandably, the cardinal's success in obtaining benefices for protégés and clerical acquaintances encouraged, both at the time and since, the tendency to think that Louis XIII simply ratified the cardinal's choices. But it would be a mistake to perpetuate a view which is partly based on throwaway comments of members of Richelieu's entourage itself. We need not take at its face value the statement of d'Effiat, the *surintendant des finances* who, in passing on information to the cardinal in early 1629 about the reputedly vacant bishopric of Lodève, wrote that he did so 'affin que vous en disposiès comme il vous plaira'.[43] Instead, the practice of consultation and even prior agreement between king and minister already noted in 1628 was extended and became routine in subsequent years; there is little to suggest that Louis XIII found this particular aspect of their relationship irksome. Indeed, it is precisely because he found it so normal to seek the cardinal's opinions over major church appointments that there is much less direct evidence of exchanges of opinion between them during the 1630s. For much the same reason, Richelieu was under less pressure than ever to consider a formal *conseil de conscience*, and the appointment of his brother as grand almoner of France in 1632 ensured that he would not need to fear competiton from another leading ecclesiastic. Clearly Louis XIII, who had from time to time consulted the previous grand almoner, Cardinal de La Rochefoucauld, down to 1630, was now willing to allow Richelieu to add to his

---

[42] See P. Blet, *Le Clergé de France et la monarchie: Étude sur les assemblées générales de 1615 à 1666* (2 vols.; Rome, 1959), i, *livre* ii, chs. 5–7, for the best study.
[43] Grillon, iv. 106–7, letter of 15 Feb. 1629.

existing role the one previously filled by La Rochefoucauld of ensuring that episcopal appointments were of an acceptable standard.[44]

But while enjoying considerable liberty to advise and guide the king, Richelieu was careful not to overreach himself, and he appreciated the political dangers that doing so entailed. For example, in August 1630, he replied to Louis XIII that he had no one to recommend for the see of Orléans, but advised him in a general way to take his time before deciding whom to nominate.[45] In the event, Louis did precisely the opposite, and filled the position as fast as possible in order to prevent his brother, Gaston, from staking a claim to it for one of his clients. Gaston did indeed protest during the following months at the lack of respect shown for his interests on this occasion. In August 1630, as the major crisis of his ministry was brewing, Richelieu could certainly not afford to antagonize Gaston, whose interest in the see of Orléans he presumably realized; in the circumstances, leaving the decision to Louis XIII made eminent political sense, while also making it more difficult for Gaston to blame the cardinal for the outcome.[46]

Problems of this kind seem to have been less frequent in the 1630s, with fewer sons of well-placed nobles or clients of the *grands* finding a place among the episcopate. Yet there was no observable change in Richelieu's behaviour towards Louis XIII. Hearing the diocese of Tréguier was vacant in 1635, he wrote to Bouthillier: 'Sy le roy considère le père Deslandes, qu'il avoit destiné pour Périgueux, qui n'est pas vacant, pour Tréguier, je croy qu'il s'en acquittera bien. Sy cependant Sa Majesté a quelque autre pensée je m'y sousmets, sçachant bien que la prudence de S.M. est telle qu'Elle ne sçauroit faire un mauvais choix'.[47] In recommending candidates for benefices to the king, Richelieu frequently covered himself by letting them understand that he could not vouch for the king, who might already have given his word to someone else. That may appear, and indeed may occasionally have actually been, a convenient pretext, but we would be well advised to view it in the context of a sharp reminder which Richelieu issued to Bouthillier's son, Chavigny, in 1638: 'quand je propose une chose au roy, ce n'est

[44] Bergin, *La Rochefoucauld*, 135.

[45] Grillon, v. 490–1, Richelieu to Bouthillier, 8 Aug. 1630.

[46] Ibid. v. 578–9, Claude de Bullion to Richelieu, 30 Sept. 1630; ibid. 622–3, Louis XIII to Richelieu, 28 Oct. 1630; ibid. 628–9, Suffren to Richelieu, 1 Nov. 1630. Gaston did not enjoy presentation rights to dioceses within his apanage of Orléans, Chartres, and Blois, but felt strongly that he had a rightful interest in the choice of bishops there. In 1641, when Lescot, Richelieu's confessor was appointed to Chartres, Gaston again tried to prevent him from accepting it: see Blet, 'Vincent de Paul et l'épiscopat de France', 88–9.

[47] Avenel, v. 246, letter of 20 Sept. 1635.

pas une demande, mais une simple proposition'.[48] This suggests either that Chavigny had been too forward with Louis, or perhaps that the king had been irritated by a suggestion from Richelieu himself. At any rate, four days later, Richelieu wrote to the king, possibly on this same issue but almost certainly in response to a direct request from Louis: 'Sa Majesté ne scauroit mieux faire, à mon avis, que de gratiffier M de Lavaur de l'évesché d'Evreux, s'il vient à vacquer'.[49] Two days after that, he was able to write thanking Louis XIII for agreeing to transfer the bishop of Lavaur to Evreux. But there had been another candidate for Evreux, the abbot of Saint-Denis of Reims, and Louis evidently sought the cardinal's comments on him, too. Richelieu's answer is again instructive on several counts: 'Quant à la prétention du sr de Saint Denis, je n'ay rien autre chose à dire sinon que je croy que le roy doit persister à la resolution qu'il a prise de ne se haster pas de donner les éveschez, afin d'avoir le temps de faire une bonne perquisition de vita et moribus. Je ne sçay rien à dire contre M de Saint Denis'.[50]

This standing responsibility to inform the king and protect his conscience, which Louis XIII expected Richelieu to exercise, is also implicit in a number of the cardinal's other remarks. When the princess of Condé asked Richelieu, in 1631, to intervene with Louis XIII in order to get the see of Auxerre for her 2-year-old son, the prince of Conti, the answer was reasoned and polite but firm, the idea of such a promotion being 'une proposition que, vous scavez bien, le roi ne peut effectuer'.[51] Likewise a candidate for suffragan-bishop of Metz in 1634 was peremptorily turned down with the words, 'je ne voudrois pour rien du monde proposer de le faire evesque, estant tel qu'il est'.[52]

This entente cordiale between king and minister over appointments, and Richelieu's lack of interest in a formal mechanism or *conseil de conscience*, did not entirely preclude the development of certain working arrangements concerning the distribution of episcopal patronage. Richelieu was certainly aware of the need to avoid snap nominations and the dangers they entailed, an awareness expressed most clearly in 1630 when he wrote that bishops 'doivent

---

[48] Ibid. vi. 113, letter of 25 Aug. 1638.

[49] Ibid. vi. 118, letter to Louis XIII, 29 Aug. 1638.

[50] Ibid. vi. 132–3, letter to Chavigny, 31 Aug. 1638. In the event no nomination to Evreux was made at this time, since news of the incumbent bishop's death was false.

[51] Grillon, vi. 594–5, letter of 21 Sept. 1631. Within days, Dominique Séguier, brother of Pierre, keeper of the seals, was appointed to Auxerre.

[52] Avenel, iv. 711, letter to Cardinal de La Valette, 20 Apr. 1635. As the bishop of Metz was the unconsecrated Henri de Bourbon-Verneuil, Louis XIII's illegitimate brother, the diocese was effectively administered by his suffragan.

estre pris non par hasard, mais par grande eslection, ayant dès cette heure en l'esprit ceux qu'ils voudroient y pourvoir dans un ou deux ans'.[53] Eight years later, as we saw, he wrote to the king recommending that he persevere in his resolution not to nominate bishops hastily, so as to have sufficient time to conduct a proper inquiry into candidates' life and morals.[54] Unfortunately, nothing further is known about the nature or date or the king's resolution, or the arrangements made for its implementation. Though the evidence is slight, Richelieu also seems to have developed an awareness that not all French bishoprics, especially those in distant provinces, were equally attractive to potential, even worthy, candidates, an awareness which probably derived from a combination of personal experience and from his extensive voyages around France in the late 1620s and 1630s. Writing to the incoming bishop of Saint-Papoul in March 1636, Richelieu promised: 'la façon dont il s'acquittera de sa charge donnera lieu à Sa Majeste de rechercher dans le fonds des provinces d'autres personnes de bonne reputation'.[55] A month later, when the bishop of Grasse in Provence died, Richelieu could think of no one to recommend to the king, but wrote to Louis that Sublet des Noyers, the secretary of state, would attempt to find out who the worthy clerics in Provence were, as a small diocese like Grasse was unlikely to attract outsiders.[56] Sublet evidently proved unsuccessful, and Richelieu's own scepticism was confounded when Antoine Godeau, a northerner and a distinguished founding member of the Académie Française, accepted the royal nomination.

Despite—or perhaps even because of—these difficulties, it may be argued that something like a pool of potential candidates did emerge over the years, at least to the extent that their names were mentioned more than once when vacancies arose. Here also, the evidence is anything but comprehensive, yet it does have the advantage of affording an additional glimpse at the nature of the exchanges between the king and his minister. Ironically, as we have already seen in a few cases, much of the evidence exists only because of the repeated reports reaching the king and ministers, as well as candidates, their patrons, and families, of bishops who had died, were in imminent danger of death, or were held to be beyond all hope of recovery. As in the case of Paris in early 1628, king and minister would exchange views and names, and patrons would begin pressing

---

[53] Grillon, v. 490–1, letter to Bouthillier, 8 Aug. 1630.
[54] Avenel vi. 132–3, Richelieu to Chavigny, 31 Aug. 1638.
[55] Ibid. v. 992, letter to Bernard Despruetz (late Mar./early Apr. 1636, and not Oct. as Avenel suggested, Despruetz having been nominated by Louis XIII on 30 Mar.).
[56] Ibid. v. 468, Richelieu to king, 19 May 1636.

candidates of their own. In at least some instances, an actual decision to nominate was made, clearly with some speed, and even a *brevet de nomination* given to the successful candidate. When the news proved to be false, the process obviously had to stop, but not before it had produced some acknowledgement that a particular individual had been deemed worthy to join the episcopal bench. This did not necessarily imply any express right to succeed if or when the diocese in question became vacant, or even to become a bishop, but such a candidate's claims would be even harder to resist in future. We noted above how Richelieu reminded Louis XIII in 1635 that the Dominican Noël Deslandes had previously been recommended for Périgueux when it was thought to be vacant, and suggested that he could now offer him Tréguier instead. Tréguier *was* indeed vacant, and Deslandes was duly appointed two days later.[57]

There is considerably more evidence of this both before and after 1635. Raymond de Montaigne did not get Condom, as Richelieu had hoped he would in 1628 when it was mistakenly thought to be vacant, but he did obtain Bayonne the following year. When Henri de Sourdis was moved to Bordeaux in 1628, the queen mother promptly asked that his former see of Maillezais go to her almoner, Nicolas Grillet, who, as she reminded Richelieu, had earlier been promised Vence when it, too, was rumoured to be vacant.[58] The following year she renewed her appeal for Grillet when it seemed the see of Maillezais would be moved to La Rochelle and, later in 1629, Grillet's name was also suggested for the see of Dol in Brittany.[59] Finally, he got Bazas in 1630, only to be moved to the troubled diocese of Uzès a few years later. Achille Harlay de Sancy was first recommended for the southern diocese of Vabres, when it was rumoured vacant in April 1631, and duly got Saint-Malo a few months later when Marillac's son died before receiving his papal provisions.[60] A similar impression of certain individuals being designated for preferment emerges no less clearly from Louis XIII's admittedly isolated request to the pope in early 1631 to confer a titular bishopric on Dominique Séguier, brother of the future chancellor, 'en attendant qu'il soit nommé à quelque évêché en nostre Royaume'.[61] It is hardly surprising that by September 1631 it

[57] Ibid. v. 245–6, letter of 20 Sept. 1635.
[58] Grillon, iii. 397–8, letter to Richelieu, 25 July 1628.
[59] Ibid. iv. 61–2, Marie de' Medici to Richelieu, 29 Jan. 1629; ibid. 556, Bouthillier to Richelieu, 19 Aug. 1629.
[60] Ibid. vi. 225, Châteauneuf to Richelieu, 11 Apr. 1631.
[61] Biblioteca Apostolica Vaticana, MS Barberini Latini 7942, fo. 22, letter to Urban VIII, 14 Feb. 1631. By Sept., Séguier had in fact been nominated to the see of Auxerre.

was Séguier, and not the infant prince de Conti, who should be nominated to the see of Auxerre. Towards the end of the decade, in November 1639, Henri Arnauld reported the common view that Bishop Étampes of Chartres was already selected to become archbishop of Reims once Henri de Guise-Lorraine had finally been ejected or obliged to resign.[62] Étampes duly got Reims, but it took a full year to force Guise out. Henri Maupas du Tour, abbot of Saint-Denis of Reims, was a contender not merely for Evreux in 1638, as we saw, but also for Avranches in 1640 before he finally got Le Puy in 1641.[63]

It would, however, be hasty to conclude from this evidence that a full-blown 'system' of episcopal appointments, with a clearly defined waiting list of acceptable candidates, took shape during Richelieu's ministry. It was not until much later in the century, under Louis XIV, that a move was made in that direction with the institution of the *feuille des benefices*. Yet even then episcopal appointments remained 'political' in the broadest sense, with far too many religious, personal, and political considerations arising in each case for them ever to become a matter of bureaucratic routine.

VIII

Yet to a cardinal who until the end of his life saw himself as a champion of church reform, episcopal patronage could not be reduced to an elaborate exercise in political fixing. Richelieu's capacity to shape the character of the episcopate was naturally greater during the 1630s, when his political position was stronger and the king's willingness to take his advice over bishoprics more certain. But the evolution of the episcopate during those years has been obscured by the historians' acceptance of the view, also enshrined in the *Testament politique*, that Richelieu had a clear preference for sons of the old nobility as being better fitted by birth and their inherited qualities for the challenges of episcopal authority. Not only is the language of the *Testament* more elusive and nuanced than that, but it provides no guide at all to what actually occurred.[64] First of all, the episcopate was increasingly a highly educated body, one which in effect came into line for the first time with the terms of the Concordat of Bologna, which required that bishops hold a degree 'from a

---

[62] BN MS Fr. 15610, p. 305, letter to Barillon, 27 Nov. 1639.
[63] Avenel, vi. 132–3, Richelieu to Chavigny, 31 Aug. 1638; BN MS Fr. 15610, p. 412, Arnauld to Barillon, 15 Jan. 1640; MS Fr. 15611, fo. 250ᵛ, same to same, 7 Sept. 1641.
[64] See *Test. pol.*, esp. 152–5.

famous university', and with the promptings of both the Council of Trent and subsequent royal legislation. Bishops without university degrees disappeared altogether by 1635 at the latest, having been in a distinct minority since the later 1620s. Moreover, an increasing proportion of the episcopate held either doctorates or licences in theology or law, not mere baccalaureates (like Richelieu himself); both the doctorate and the licence, especially in theology, required serious, sustained study. No less interestingly, the balance between bishops holding law and theology degrees, which had strongly favoured law in the 1620s and early 1630s, tilted increasingly towards theology during the later years of Richelieu's ministry. Though the antithesis between law and theology, and their respective capacity to shape episcopal styles, has been exaggerated, the trend towards theology is nevertheless significant: even some of those bishops taking law degrees are known to have devoted several years to studying theology.[65] In the emergence of an episcopate that was increasingly literate theologically, we may see a concrete result of Richelieu's own attempts to reform the theology faculty of the University of Paris, and make it an unofficial seminary for future higher clergy.[66]

This shift is closely connected to another equally significant development, the declining presence of the aristocracy and *noblesse d'épée* among the episcopate. Scarcely one-third of all bishops nominated between 1631 and 1642 can be regarded as stemming from the older nobility, and not one of them, with the exception of a Daillon du Lude or a Maupas du Tour, was the bearer of a distinguished name; all of the others were of middling families of provincial nobility. However, if Bishop Étampes de Valençay was elevated to the archbishopric of Reims in 1640, it was not because of his genealogy but because he was a well-known Richelieu factotum: neither his record nor his new rank would save him from being disgraced by his master in 1642. A further illustration of this change is provided by the fate of a typically small diocese of the Midi, that of Conserans, south of Toulouse. Since the 1580s, its three successive bishops had owed their elevation to the patronage of Roger de Bellegarde, *grand écuyer de France* and companion of successive monarchs, but also a loser

---

[65] This discussion of the educational background of the French episcopate is based upon information gleaned from their papal provisions, and esp. from the depositions made before the papal nuncio concerning recently nominated bishops, and which are to be found in the Vatican Archives, *Processus Consistoriales* for the period *c.*1612–61. Some of the depositions were made by univ. professors in respect of former students recently nominated bishops by the king.

[66] See Ch. 8 below, by Laurence Brockliss. I would like to thank him for additional information and advice on educational questions.

in the political crises of 1630 and 1632. In 1639, he approached Richelieu reminding him of his past influence and asking him to nominate one of his nephews as coadjutor with succession rights to the ageing bishop, Bruno Ruade; and, as if to precipitate a decision, he added that Ruade was himself negotiating to resign the see in favour of the son of a Toulouse lawyer, Bernard Marmiesse.[67] But, by 1639, Bellegarde's influence had evaporated at court, where the kind of aristocratic succession-arrangement he sought was out of season. Ruade's own independent efforts were no more successful, and only weeks after Richelieu's death a coadjutor was nominated of whose learning and experience, if not his outspoken Gallicanism, the cardinal would have approved: the celebrated Pierre de Marca.[68] Of course, a relative lack of success did not render the aristocracy indifferent to the fate of bishoprics. When Orléans was rumoured vacant in April 1641, Condé's son, the comte de Béthune-Charost, and the Ventadour family all interceded with Richelieu for their own candidate.[69] No decision needed to be made, as Orléans proved not to be vacant, but the aristocracy, and the Ventadours in particular, were to begin their episcopal come-back under Mazarin.

If Richelieu was able to carry the king along with him in his preference for bishops drawn largely from office-holding families, and who were well-educated and experienced either administratively or pastorally, it was due in part because the principal losers in the power-struggles around 1630 were not so much the *dévots* as the aristocracy. Thereafter, Richelieu's increasingly secure position meant that he could rely on second-generation *dévots* whose non-political, reformist activities he was perfectly ready to support; many of them were drawn from the second-order clergy and some, as we saw, refused to accept bishoprics for themselves while being anything but indifferent about the condition of the episcopate. Indeed, it can be argued that their influence on the evolution of the episcopate was more pervasive than was that of their better-known predecessors in the 1610s and 1620s. Biographers of leading figures like Père Joseph, Vincent de Paul, or Charles de Condren have always claimed that they had sufficient influence with, or were well-enough regarded by, Richelieu to present the names of deserving candidates to him. To date, independent evidence of this has not been found, but the appointment of members of the Oratory, like the Gault brothers to

---

[67] AAE France 834, fo. 59, Bellegarde to Chavigny, 11 Sept. 1639.

[68] BN MS Fr. 15611, fo. 598, Henri Arnauld to Barillon, 31 Dec. 1642. Arnauld heard that Marca had not been Richelieu's candidate, but this was little more than third-hand gossip.

[69] BN MS Fr. 15611, fos. 90, 96, 103, letters from Henri Arnauld to Barillon, 24 Apr., 5 and 12 May 1641; AAE France 840, fo. 55, Béthune to Richelieu, 26 May 1641.

Marseilles, as well as of ecclesiastics who, like Pavillon of Alet and Vialart of Châlons-sur-Marne, had been involved in missions and other projects sponsored by Vincent de Paul, points to Richelieu's receptivity to such influence and advice.[70] The surprise which Henri Arnauld, future bishop of Angers and attentive observer of court politics between 1639 and 1642, frequently evinced over these unexpected episcopal appointments leads to the same conclusion: that those who, by virtue of a combination of blood, connections, court almonerships, and so on, expected preferment were being passed over in favour of men with *dévot* and pastoral credentials. Indeed, the message was understood by more conventionally ambitious clerics, such as the future Cardinal de Retz, who made a point of attending, and made a favourable impression at, Vincent de Paul's early conferences of future clergy.

If this constitutes evidence of continuing *dévot* influence in Richelieu's entourage, it should not be inferred that he was somehow being propelled in a direction in which he was reluctant to go. That he took an increasing interest in, and responsibility for, the behaviour of France's bishops is also evident from a number of steps he took during the 1630s. Two cases have emerged from the late 1630s of new bishops writing detailed reports on the state of their dioceses to Richelieu at his explicit request, but it is not known if they were isolated episodes or part of a more systematic interest on his part.[71] Furthermore, it would be difficult to think of any other period in the sixteenth or seventeenth centuries when recalcitrant, non-resident, or negligent bishops were subject to so much admonition from a royal minister. During the four years that it took the elderly bishop of Montauban to accept that he needed a younger man as his coadjutor, he received some stinging criticism from Richelieu about his obligations towards his Huguenot-dominated diocese.[72] The bishops of Nîmes, Reims, and Rouen, and elsewhere, were also lectured over their behaviour or their opinions.[73] The archbishop of Paris was rebuked to his face for his negligence, with Richelieu's confessor in attendance as a witness.[74] Richelieu's concern was such that in 1638 he even requested Urban VIII to authorize a commission of French bishops directed against 'evesques mal vivans par

---

[70] See Blet, 'Vincent de Paul', 85–6.

[71] AAE France 836, fos. 12–13, Hugues Labatut on diocese of Comminges, 6 Aug. 1640; ibid. 838, fos. 138–9, Godeau on Grasse, 12 Apr. 1641.

[72] See esp. the letter from Richelieu in Avenel, iv. 540–1, Feb. 1634.

[73] Ibid. iv. 510–11, late 1633 (Harlay of Rouen); ibid. v. 960, 1636 (Saint-Bonnet of Nîmes); ibid. vi. 378–9, 8 June 1639 (Guise of Reims).

[74] BN MS Fr. 15610, pp. 389–90, Arnauld to Barillon, 8 Jan. 1640.

l'appréhension de la recherche de leur vie'.[75] Nothing ever came, or was indeed ever likely to come, of this proposal—yet another instance, one may feel, of Richelieu's liking for special commissions—but, as other essays in this volume make clear, a similar fate befell many of his schemes.

Richelieu could not, by the nature of things, literally claim—as Henry IV did, and Louis XIII might have done had he so wished—the bishops to be his men, but the evidence presented here should, for all its lacunae, leave no doubt as to the extent to which he contributed to shaping the episcopate, especially in the second half of his ministry. If he did so, it was firstly because, being both cardinal and leading minister, he was uniquely placed to play such a role. Even more crucial was the willingness, even alacrity, of Louis XIII, a king with his share of scruples, to accept Richelieu as both purveyor of advice, patron of would-be bishops, and guardian of his conscience. There is no sign that Louis ever chafed at this particular element of his relationship with Richelieu, however different other features of their association might be. All of this took place in the context of institutional inertia. Yet behind this inertia lay the gradual emergence of an unmistakable readiness to treat royal episcopal patronage as something which required information, reflection, and even a measure of foresight and anticipation. As such, there is some justification in claiming that the result was a significant shift in what Denis Richet once called *l'esprit des institutions*.[76]

---

[75] Avenel, vi. 228–9, memorandum for Chavigny, 1 Nov. 1638.
[76] Denis Richet, *La France moderne: L'Esprit des institutions* (Paris, 1973).

7

RICHELIEU AND THE ARTS

EDRIC CALDICOTT

The assessment of Richelieu's career as a collector and a patron of the arts is beset with contradictions. He has been both condemned and praised for his involvement in the artistic life of France: condemned for self-aggrandizement, but praised for enhancing the authority of the king; accused of introducing forms of censorship, but lauded for bringing order into the intellectual and artistic periphery of the monarchy. In addition, the sheer scale of this activity, his building programmes, the size of his collections, the extent of his influence in literary reform, the weight of his authority in the creation of new publishing procedures, as well as in the administration of the arts, is such that it escapes quantification. Not only that but, as Deloche points out, the cardinal often disguised his hand by delegating responsibility for acquisitions to a limited number of tried and trusted *créatures*: 'chez le Cardinal, le paiement de ces pensions même [to literary figures of the day] n'était pas fait dans la forme comptable usuelle rigoureusement suivie pour l'administration de la maison, puisque c'était Desbournais, le valet de chambre de Richelieu, qui l'effectuait lui-même directement'.[1] This, too, is entirely typical of him; driven constantly forward, developing a tentacular network of controls, he mobilized all the instruments at his command, the *conseil du roi*, the parlements, the Académie française, the provincial intendants, ambassadorial delegations, his ministers, and other more lowly *créatures* such as Lopez, Boisrobert, or Desbournais, to reach his determined goals, whether in the realm of the arts or of domestic and foreign policy. The question is further complicated by the fact that, following his apprenticeship as *surintendant* in the household of Marie de' Medici, in his capacity as principal minister and through the agency of Sublet des Noyers (*surintendant des bâtiments du roi*), Richelieu also assumed responsibility for construction, decoration and restoration in the household of

---

[1] M. Deloche, *La Maison du cardinal de Richelieu* (Paris, 1912), 'Aumônes, dons et pensions', 177.

the king. The overriding effect is thus one of comprehensiveness masked by dissimulation.

What sense of priorities, then, can one derive from this restless activity? A new look at original sources, allied to a synthesis of the material which has been produced since the quatercentenary of Richelieu's birth,[2] will help us to understand the growth of his ambition, from the construction of his principal residences and collections to his initiatives in the realm of cultural diplomacy, via his relations with the great writers of the day. It will then become clear how, following the example and influence of contemporary political figures, Richelieu's patronage of the arts was used to serve his own strong sense of image; it will also be seen that this in turn was heavily dedicated to a 'certaine idée de la France'. In a complex, mutually supportive interplay, the ambitious images of Richelieu and French pre-eminence fed upon each other, leaving an enduring example of vigorous state 'dirigisme' in French cultural affairs. The growth from assertion of his personal position to a sense of royal and national mission can be traced through a lavish early building programme and subsequent administration of the arts; from bricks and mortar to a politico-cultural policy.

In an even wider perspective, it is significant that the course of his career as a patron of the arts not only confirms Krzysztof Pomian's observation of the general movement of the mid-seventeenth century away from the unsystematic *esprit de la curiosité*,[3] but also shows that Richelieu was ahead of his time in this tendency in France. Put more bluntly, he spurned the process of gratuitous collection in the single-

---

[2] A. Tuilier (ed.), *Richelieu et le monde de l'esprit* (Paris, 1985); R. Mousnier (ed.), *Richelieu et la culture* (Paris, 1987); H. Levi, 'L'Inventaire après décès du Cardinal de Richelieu', *Archives de l'art français*, NS 37 (1985), 9–83; H. Levi and D. Helot-Lécroart, 'Le Château et les jardins de Rueil du temps de Jean de Moisset et du Cardinal de Richelieu 1606–42', *Fédération des Sociétés historiques et archéologiques de Paris et de l'Île de France*, 36 (1985), 19–95; *L'Album Canini du Louvre et la collection d'antiques de Richelieu* ed. J. Schloder and M. Montembault (Notes et documents des Musées de France, 21; Paris, 1988); H. Gaston Hall, *Richelieu's Desmarets and the Century of Louis XIV* (Oxford, 1990); J. H. Elliott, *Richelieu and Olivares* (Cambridge, 1984); J. Bergin, *Cardinal Richelieu: Power and the Pursuit of Wealth* (New Haven, Conn., 1985); R. J. Knecht, *Richelieu* (London, 1991). In addition to the numerous specialized contributions contained within Tuilier, *Richelieu et le monde de l'esprit* and Mousnier, *Richelieu et la culture*, there are also many important studies of patronage and patrons at the time of Richelieu in R. Mousnier and J. Mesnard (eds.), *L'Age d'or du mécénat 1598–1661* (Paris, 1985). Levi, 'Inventaire Richelieu', deals more particularly with the objects held in the Palais-Cardinal and inventoried, with the notaries, by Simon Vouet, Laurent de la Hire, Jacques Sarrazin, and Simon Guillain; it needs to be complemented by A. Boislisle, 'Les Collections de sculptures du Cardinal de Richelieu', *Mémoires de la Société Nationale des Antiquaires de France*, 32 (1882), 71–128, and E. Bonnaffé, *Recherches sur les collections de Richelieu* (Paris, 1883).

[3] K. Pomian, *Collectionneurs, amateurs et curieux* (Paris, 1987).

minded pursuit of his personal political interests. National histories have tended to concentrate on the later phases of his patronage, on his literary interests and his administration of the arts, in order to highlight his contribution to the cultural heritage of France, but no examination of Richelieu's strategy for the arts could be considered complete without some illustration of the way in which, in an earlier phase of his career, he deployed his considerable talent as an image-maker and publicist for more personal ends. Such was the success of the public persona which the cardinal created for himself that, in playful provocation, Christian Jouhaud has recently asked if the real man ever existed at all.[4] It is precisely because the early phase of his career offers such a tangible expression of his priorities, creating an essential platform for later patronage, and because it has remained little-known, that it will be given greater emphasis in this study. The final phase of the cardinal's patronage, literary and administrative, is already well known to the general reader and is thus given correspondingly less coverage.

Richelieu confessed to an instinctive taste for display in an early letter to Madame de Bourges, dating from 6 June 1610 when he was still only 25 and penniless. He wrote revealingly of himself that, 'tenant de vostre humeur, c'est-à-dire étant un peu glorieux, je voudrais bien, estant plus à mon aise, paroistre davantage'.[5] It should be recalled that, as the 'marquis' de Chillou until the age of 17, he had already been formed as a *noble d'épée* at the time that the family succession to the see of Luçon passed to him. As the physical shelters for the bulk of Richelieu's collections, the most tangible declaration of his desire to 'paroistre', the palace built by Jacques Le Mercier at Richelieu (Poitou), where the statuary described by Canini was originally installed, the Palais-Cardinal in Paris, and the rural retreat at Rueil (near Saint-Germain-en-Laye), were his most visible and most costly investments. It is therefore proposed to study the first two of these sumptuous residences, for which the sources are most abundant, with particular attention to the decorative work lavished upon them. It will then be possible to add their permanent fittings—which included paintings by Claude Deruet (1588–1660), Claude Lorrain (1600–82), Philippe de Champaigne (1602–74), Charles Le Brun (1619–90), Nicolas Poussin (1594–1665), and Simon Vouet (1590–1649)—to an inventory of Richelieu's moveable masterpieces, those *tableaux à chevalet* which were executed for the most part by the Italian masters appearing in the final version of

---

[4] C. Jouhaud, *La Main de Richelieu, ou le pouvoir cardinal* (Paris, 1991).
[5] Avenel, i. 55–6.

Vasari's *Lives of the Painters*, several copies of which existed in Richelieu's library.[6]

Richelieu's building projects developed in the wake of his brother's death in 1619 and, as Joseph Bergin has shown,[7] were initially an extension of the deceased Henri's policy to recover and restore the family's dispersed estates. It was coincidentally at this time that Richelieu also acceded to the post of *surintendant* in the household of the queen mother, Marie de' Medici, and then purchased in 1621 the ancestral family seat and lands of Richelieu. It would be difficult to say at what stage the policy of recovery of family property was adjusted to one of aggrandizement. The munificence, and example, of his patron the queen mother were undoubtedly critical factors in the process of change: she assisted him with the purchase of Limours (near Fontainebleau) in 1623 and made him a gift of the Petit-Luxembourg in 1627, followed by a further gift of 180,000 *livres* for the purchase of Bois-le-Vicomte in 1628. The elevation of the estate of Richelieu to a *duché-pairie* in 1631, enhanced by the exchange of Bois-le-Vicomte for the Montpensier property of Champigny (contiguous to Richelieu, and owned by his inveterate enemy Gaston d'Orléans) in 1635, indicates a combination of emulation, opportunism, and consistent consolidation in the expansion of his estates.

In addition to her material support, Marie de' Medici offered her *surintendant* a vigorous example of patronage in the cultivation of magnificence. As Voltaire was to say of them in his *Le Siécle de Louis XIV* (chapter 33), 'Il s'en fallut beaucoup que le Cardinal de Richelieu, avec autant de grandeur dans l'esprit, eût autant de goût qu'elle'. The formative role of Marie de' Medici in the image-making cultural policy of the Bourbon dynasty has been traditionally neglected, but the careful work of Deborah Marrow, and Sara Mamone's exciting re-examination of this aspect of her career, based on Medici state papers in Florence, have brought precious new insight to the question.[8] It was Richelieu's great good fortune to serve his apprenticeship in patronage to the superb 'Augusta Regina', the only queen of France to have herself so styled.[9]

---

[6] Bibliothèque Mazarine, MS 4270–1, 2 folio vols.; see MS 4271, nos. 4297–4300, fos. 651ᵛ–652; G. Vasari, *Le Vite de piu eccellenti architetti, pittori e scultori italiani* (Florence, 1568). See also P. Gasnault, 'Note sur les livres de Richelieu', *Mélanges de la Bibliothèque de la Sorbonne*, 8 (Paris, 1988), 185–9.

[7] See Bergin, *Cardinal Richelieu*; also J.-P. Babelon, 'Le Château de Rueil et les autres demeures du cardinal', in Tuilier (ed.), *Le Monde de l'esprit*, 75–81.

[8] D. Marrow, *The Art Patronage of Maria de' Medici* (Studies in Baroque Art, 4; Ann Arbor, Mich., 1982); S. Mamone, *Paris et Florence, deux capitales du spectacle pour une reine, Marie de Médicis* (Paris, 1990).

[9] M. Jones, *A Catalogue of the French Medals in the British Museum*, ii. *1600–72* (London, 1988), nos. 88–90, pp. 132–3. Compiled by the assistant keeper of coins and medals at the

Mamone's work has shown how the dramatic circumstances of the death of Henri IV accelerated the process of heroization of the first Bourbon monarch, both during and after his funeral arrangements; it was in Florence (birthplace of the widowed queen), at the cathedral of San Lorenzo, that the process of heroization was most clearly marked, with the creation of twenty-six tableaux representing the dead king's exploits presented by Giuliano Giraldi in his *Les Obsèques d'Henri IV* (Florence, 1610). This glorification in death of the founder of the dynasty appears to have served as a critical stimulus to Bourbon propaganda, exploited to the full by his widow in her ostentatious two-year period of mourning; whether represented as a bare-breasted Juno by Barthélémy Prieur, as the mother of Europe in the marriage alliances and the famous (first) *Carrousel* of 1612,[10] or as the heroine of the twenty-four tableaux painted by Rubens for the gallery of her Luxembourg palace, she maintained the heroic, starring role for herself by manipulation of the arts. Mamone has also illustrated an extraordinary process of politico-artistic translation by showing that the Rubens project executed for Marie was directly inspired by the work of Giraldi for the mausoleum of Henri IV at San Lorenzo in Florence.[11] It was this example of self-promotion within, and for, a higher cause which Richelieu himself was to follow. Perhaps the most valuable lesson he was to learn in the household of Marie de' Medici, it was further refined under his guidance to make an indelible mark on the image and propaganda of the Bourbon dynasty.

The ultimate artistic achievement of Marie de' Medici in France was the construction of her new Luxembourg palace; the architect Clément Métezeau (1581–1652) was sent to Florence in 1611 to copy the plans of the Pitti palace for her, and the first stone was laid in 1615; temporarily delayed by Marie's period of detention in Blois, the work resumed in 1620 under the direction of Salomon de Brosse (1571–1626), with the greatest artists and craftsmen of France, Flanders, and Italy recruited to work on the building, and Richelieu employed as her *surintendant*. Most, if not all, of the craftsmen employed in the Luxembourg were subsequently recruited by Richelieu

British Museum, this catalogue offers important insights into the iconography of the queen mother, as perpetuated in the medals of Guillaume Dupré and Pierre Régnier. Needless to say, Richelieu was subsequently also immortalized in metal, by Jean Warin: ibid., nos. 182–96, pp. 191–6. Under Louis XIV, the *histoire métallique du règne* became the responsibility of the Académie des inscriptions.

[10] Mamone, *Paris and Florence*, 180 (Prieur's statue of Juno); 243 (Ziarnko's engraving of the *Carrousel*).

[11] Ibid. 214–24.

for his own projects. Nicolas Duchesne (died *c.*1630) painted the ceilings, and his future son-in-law Philippe de Champaigne executed his earliest commissions in France for her (winning the supreme recompense of the gift of a painting by Marie de' Medici herself in 1629). Orazio Gentileschi (1565–1647) completed an allegory of *La Félicité publique* (1623–5) for her chamber, and she also had paintings by Guido Reni (1575–1642) sent to her from Italy. At the same time (*c.*1623), the young Nicolas Poussin began a brief spell of work at the Luxembourg, as did Simon Vouet. In addition, the suite of paintings of the Muses by Giovanni Baglione (*c.*1573–*c.*1645) from Mantua was hung in the palace, launching a French taste for Muse paintings flattering their patrons;[12] Peter Paul Rubens (1577–1640) painted the immense series of twenty-four allegorical works for the justly famous gallery; Guillaume Berthelot (died *c.*1648) executed the statuary for the exterior, including a series of eight bronze *Femmes illustres* designed in collaboration with Rubens;[13] and the architect Marin de la Vallée completed work on the building after the retirement of Salomon de Brosse (1624). During this time, Marie was also resident periodically at the Louvre where she had the chapel and her suite on the south side ground floor altered by Jacques Le Mercier (*c.*1585–1654) in the years 1627–9, with adjudication of the contract dating from 1624.[14] Directly involved in the queen mother's plans and negotiations for the Luxembourg, Richelieu was able to use most of these artists, architects, and craftsmen in his own service. Duchesne worked on the ceilings at Limours, and was later invited to work on the early phases of the Palais-Cardinal; Salomon de Brosse, too, made his contribution to Limours, as did Berthelot before he went to Richelieu to design the much-admired ceremonial entrances;[15] it was Jacques Le Mercier, assisted by Marin de la Vallée, who drew up plans for the grandiose projects of the Palais-Cardinal and the Sorbonne (also commissioned by Richelieu in his capacity as its *proviseur*) prior to his preparation of drawings for the palaces of Richelieu and Rueil (and before his construction of the *Cour de l'Horloge* at the Louvre). Needless to say, Poussin, Vouet, and Philippe de Champaigne were to provide invaluable, well-documented services for the cardinal in subsequent years.

If, in the sphere of the arts, Richelieu was later to implement

[12] Marrow, *Art Patronage*, 29.
[13] Ibid. 28.
[14] A. Erlande-Brandeburg, 'Les Appartements de la Reine Mère Marie de Médicis au Louvre', *Bulletin de la Société de l'histoire de l'art français* (1965), 106.
[15] Grillon, i. 459, letter of 8 Sept. 1626.

much of what he learnt from the royal example of Marie de' Medici, it should also be added that he appears to have developed his own less munificent ways of exploiting this association with her and her artists during his period in her household. Nicolas Peiresc (1580–1637) relates in a letter of 4 May 1623 to his friend Peter Paul Rubens (then seeking payment for his work on the Luxembourg gallery) a conversation with Claude Maugis (abbé de Saint-Ambroise), intendant of the queen mother's household: the advice given to Peiresc on behalf of his friend was that Richelieu should be offered a sweetener in the form of a small painting in order to elicit payment. Writing in Italian, Peiresc communicated the following:

I had forgotten to inform you that after your last letter, and in conversation one day with M. l'Abbé about the difficulties that Cardinal Richelieu had created for M. de Brosse [the architect] and which ceased as soon as the cardinal completed the purchase of Limours, when M. de Brosse made several journeys in order to provide plans for reconstruction to be done on the building, M. l'Abbé added that if you were to offer some small painting of yours which might be appropriate for a 'cabinet', everything would 'andarebbono molto piu facile tutte le cose sue.'[16]

Even though the cardinal's method seems to have entailed the careful maintenance of relations with artists already known to him, or whom he had seen at work, he never again worked with Rubens. This is probably due as much to political reasons as to artistic taste: as we shall see, a number of works by Rubens were retained in his collections, but he presumably preferred to avoid the embarrassment of working with a diplomatic emissary of Philip IV. It goes without saying that Rubens would also have had his own views on the matter of future collaboration with Richelieu.

As a consequence of the collapse of the queen mother's patronage after the Day of Dupes in November 1630, Richelieu was able to play a more dominant role as a patron of the arts. Not only did he adopt many of the queen mother's craftsmen, but he also reproduced her ideas. The gardens of the Luxembourg, of which the fountains were a distinctive feature, were emulated at the Palais-Cardinal, the

---

[16] *Correspondance de Rubens, et documents épistolaires concernant sa vie et ses œuvres*, ed. C. Reulens and M. Rooses (6 vols; Antwerp, 1889–1907), v. 160–1. 'Io mi scordava di mandarte che doppo l'ultima mia lettera sendomi trovato un giorno a raggionare col Sr Abbato delle difficolta che il Sr Card. de Richelieu haveva fatta al Sr Brosse, le quali si sonno hora supprate subito che il Sr Cardinale ha havuto finito il trattato della compera del contado di Limours dove detto Brosse ha fatto diversi viaggi per dissegnare certa fabrica nuova nel castello chi egli ha da condurre. Egli m'aggionse che se v. s. portava qualche quadretto di sua mano al detto Sr Card^{le} da potersi mettere in qualche studiolo . . .' (author's trans.).

palace of Richelieu, and at Rueil.[17] The most striking feature of the
Luxembourg was the queen's gallery, surviving now in the twenty-
four great canvases of Rubens in the Louvre;[18] although not calling
again on the services of Rubens, Richelieu repeated this most famous
feature of the Luxembourg in all his principal palaces. His use of the
gallery, a centre-piece of all his residences, is so striking that it
deserves particular attention. Although he brought many innovations
to the concept of the gallery, Richelieu's projects were necessarily
marked by the cultural legacy of an earlier age and by the mental
attitudes described by Michel Foucault in *Les Mots et les choses*. The
gallery was a stage for the representation of magnificence and great
achievements; answering a need for the promotion and interpretation
of those achievements, it had the qualities of a theatre, a monument,
and a shrine. It appears to have been a semiotic space as well as a
representational one, manipulating the naïvety of the seventeenth-
century viewer, and paradoxically naïve itself in the talismanic
force that its recurring emblems, devices, and historical allegories
appeared to convey. Clio, the muse of history was dominant in
Richelieu's galleries, and her role was both predictive and recapitula-
tory. With the parallels artfully created by great artists between
achievements of the present and the universal classical past, with the
artists' works themselves exemplifying qualities of timelessness, the
career of the glorious patron was presented as a pre-ordained ascent
towards immortality. In a similar fashion, the taste for punning or
polyvalent devices indicates a self-fulfilling role: like the images
for which they served as commentary, partaking of the reality
they represented, words could be perceived as both causative and
descriptive.

The gallery was not an invention of Marie de' Medici; a frequent
feature of palaces in Italy, the gallery had been used for politico-
artistic purposes by a number of French monarchs, and most notably
by Francis I at Fontainebleau—with his own *galerie François I* and
the *galerie d'Ulysse*. Having had work done at Fontainebleau through
the agency of Sublet de Noyers, Richelieu knew these galleries very
well; when designing his own galleries he undoubtedly combined his
knowledge of Fontainebleau with his immediate experience of the
work on the Luxembourg, thus creating a sense of continuity from

---

[17] See Levi and Helot-Lécroart, 'Rueil'; the fountains and 'cascades' were a well-known
feature of the gardens of Rueil, at the *château du Val* as it was sometimes called. Inventories of
internal decoration indicate far more modest surroundings than in the cardinal's other palaces.
[18] The gallery was destroyed in 1800 in Chalgrin's renovations for the Senate; the paintings
are now displayed at the end of the Grande Galerie of the Louvre. It is planned to display them
permanently in the Richelieu wing of the Grand Louvre, when it is completed.

Valois style to Bourbon political propaganda. As Jacques Thuillier has pointed out,[19] the very concept of the gallery had become a subject for political speculation and innovation in the reign of Henry IV. The proposal put to Sully by Antoine de Laval, *géographe du roi*, dated 1600 and published in 1605 under the title *Des peintures convenables aus Basiliques et Palais du Roy, memes à sa Gallerie du Louvre à Paris*, offered a blueprint for the design of a contemporary gallery which broke with the traditions of the past and appears to have been followed very closely by French statesmen and architects subsequently, even to the *Galerie des Batailles* of Louis-Philippe at Versailles; it was the contention of Laval that, to judge from the Italian inspiration of the galleries at Fontainebleau (by Primaticcio, Rosso, and dell'Abbate), their concept and design were of too much political importance to be left in the hands of the artist or architect alone:

Je veus me persuader que la grande opinion que l'on avoit de ces peintres italiens (qui taillent tous des Princes) fut cause que l'on les mit sur leur foy, & qu'on leur bailla la carte blanche pour inventer & peindre ensemble: comme j'ai ouy dire que Du Breul [Toussaint Du Breuil, 1561–1602, one of the foremost painters of the court of Henri IV, delegated to decorate the new gallery of the Louvre] espère que le Roy fera pour sa galerie [au Louvre]: qui serait du tout difformer l'oeuvre, étant jeux bien différents celuy de l'esprit & celuy de la main, l'un requiert une grande connaissance d'Histoires, de Poésie, de sciences diverses, de considérations des choses de nature, des célestes, bref d'une infinité de secrets cachés dans les fonds inépuisables des bonnes lettres, auquel ces grands peintres n'ont pas bien le temps, ni le loisir, de fouiller plus avant qu'en la surface: & ne savent guère bien rapporter & assortir les choses l'une à l'autre.[20]

Even if the notion of political manipulation was not explicitly articulated, it is everywhere apparent in Laval's text; his concept of the gallery is clearly reaching for an easily assimilable, manipulative presentation of royal authority. 'L'histoire des rois de France', he argues, 'la plus belle de la terre', should be presented with a succession of portraits in chronological order, enhanced and explained 'avec les ornements d'architecture, emblèmes, devises, figures, titres, vers, éloges, et inscriptions dont je les veux accompagnés'.[21] It was to this style that Rubens's allegorical presentation of the life of Marie de' Medici was adapted for the Luxembourg, and it was precisely

[19] J. Thuillier, 'Peinture et politique: Une théorie de la galerie royale sous Henri IV', *Etudes d'art français offertes à Charles Sterling* (Paris, 1975), 175–205.
[20] Ibid. 196–7; the treatise of Laval is reproduced in its entirety as an appendix to Thuillier's article, pp. 195–205.
[21] Ibid. 199.

according to Laval's prescriptions that the *Galerie des Hommes Illustres* of the Palais-Cardinal was designed, as Vulson de la Colombière's commentary, *Les Portraits des hommes illustres français qui sont peints dans la gallerie du Palais Cardinal de Richelieu*, illustrated by Heince and Bignon (Paris, 1650), so clearly demonstrates. This tendency towards discipline and relevance in the graphic arts matches the literary influence, identified by Marc Fumaroli, of Jacques Davy du Perron (1556–1618), archbishop of Sens, on Richelieu.[22]

The work on the Palais-Cardinal had begun as early as 1624 with the purchase by Richelieu of the Hôtel d'Angennes, but the construction of the gallery, with the distinctive motif of anchors and ships' prows adorning the supporting colonnade, only began after confirmation by the parlement of Rouen in April 1627 of Richelieu's appointment as *grand maître et surintendant général de la navigation et commerce de France*.[23] Marin de la Vallée was responsible for the early work on the Hôtel d'Angennes, but it was Jacques Le Mercier, fresh from his start on the Sorbonne, who designed the new gallery wing of the expanding palace. The gallery wing was to the west of the second (northern) courtyard; running north–south, along the line of the present rue Montpensier, it was almost 50 metres long and 6 metres wide and, with the lighting problems of the Luxembourg gallery fresh in mind, it was illuminated by eight windows along the eastern inner wall and by a further two in the northern wall abutting the gardens. This was but the start of a new phase of building; in 1633, Guy Patin wrote in his journal that the cardinal had begun to 'construire puissamment',[24] indicating expansion to the west of the gallery; this was followed in 1637 by the construction of the huge new *salle de comédie*, and by the reconstruction in 1638 of the first courtyard, with a new *petite galerie* incorporating ceilings by Philippe de Champaigne which Sauval declared to be the most perfect artistic representation of the cardinal's career.[25] In 1642, plans were launched for the construction of a library to be called the Palais Brion, on the western perimeter of the palace. The library, too, was adorned with a sufficient number of portraits to be considered a gallery of sorts;[26]

[22] M. Fumaroli, 'L'Empire de l'Hercule Gaulois', in J. Mesnard (ed.), *Le Précis de la littérature française du XVIIe siècle* (Paris, 1990), 81–2.
[23] Grillon, i. 511.
[24] Quoted by Françoise Bercé, 'Le Palais-Cardinal', in Tuilier (ed.), *Le Monde de l'esprit*, 64.
[25] H. Sauval, *Histoire et recherches des antiquités de la ville de Paris* (3 vols.; Paris, 1724), bk. vii. 164.
[26] There were 58 portraits in the cardinal's library: C. Chardigny, 'Les Portraits de la bibliothèque de Richelieu au Palais-Cardinal', in Tuilier (ed.), *Le Monde de l'esprit*, 149–54.

with the gallery which was later incorporated into the renovations at Rueil, this brings to five the total number of galleries constructed for Richelieu. Of these, the most significant were at the Palais-Cardinal and the palace of Richelieu.

The reconstitution of Richelieu's galleries is not easy since they have all disappeared, as have their putative models in Fontainebleau and the Louvre; as will be seen, however, there is more than enough evidence to indicate that, mediated by the childhood memories of Louis XIV (resident with his mother in the Palais-Cardinal, then the Palais-Royal, in the period preceding the Fronde) and by the less youthful memories of Le Brun (apprenticed to Simon Vouet who was commissioned by Richelieu to work on the Palais-Cardinal), the concept of these galleries was imitated at Versailles on the ceilings of the *Galerie des Glaces*, the *Salon de la Guerre*, and the *Salon de la Paix*. With the creation of the two famous galleries, at the Palais-Cardinal and the palace of Richelieu, the cardinal asserted his own personal presence in the political and social hierarchy of France. Subsequent initiatives suggest a merging of his own interests with those of a policy of national prestige, but we should first of all examine the evidence of the two galleries, not forgetting the *petite galerie* of 1638 so admired by Sauval.

Bernard Dorival's study of the political symbolism of the *Galerie des Hommes Illustres* is a fundamental reference point on the subject.[27] He extrapolates five main lines of interpretation for the twenty-five portraits executed by Champaigne and Vouet, with their accompanying devices and emblems. These are: (1) loyalty to the monarch; (2) fidelity to the Church; (3) a placatory homage to the great noble families of France who formed the military caste (amongst whom Richelieu is included by association); (4) defence against foreign incursions (including the English in the past, as well as the Habsburgs in the present); (5) a readiness to give one's life in the service of France. There is little doubt that Richelieu maintained direct control of the plans and portraits for the gallery, in conformity with the recommendations of Laval's treatise. All the twenty-five figures (abbé Suger, Simon de Montfort, the constables of France— Bertrand du Guesclin, Gaucher de Chastillon, Anne de Montmorency, and Lesdiguières—Olivier de Clisson, Marshal Boucicaut, Dunois, Jeanne d'Arc, Cardinal d'Amboise, Louis de la Trémouille, Gaston de Foix, Bayard, Charles de Cossé-Brissac, François de Guise, the Cardinal de Lorraine, Blaise de Montluc, Armand de Gontaut-Biron,

---

[27] B. Dorival, 'Art et politique en France au XVIIᵉ siècle: La Galerie des Hommes Illustres du Palais-Cardinal', *Bulletin de la Société de l'histoire de l'art français* (1973, publ. 1974), 43–60.'

Henri IV, Marie de' Medici, Louis XIII, Anne d'Autriche, Gaston d'Orléans, and Richelieu himself) express one or several of his political priorities; with the exception of the representatives of the Bourbon dynasty, all the heroes and statesmen presented were precursors, in a sense, of the cardinal. Strikingly modern, with not one deity of antiquity among them, the figures converge towards, and climax at, the most recent contemporary event of moment: the siege and capture of La Rochelle, a mere incident in British history, but presented by Richelieu as much more momentous for the French. The event was prominently depicted in the gallery, and Richelieu naturally cast himself in a heroic role in it as a *miles christianus*. All the portraits are presented in identical fashion, surrounded by four medallions showing emblems, and seven square tablets showing representative exploits; at the top of the portrait were framed Latin hexameters, and a framed distych beneath. The portraits were by Champaigne and Vouet, the hexameters by Roland Desmarets (1584–1653), and the emblems and devices by Guisse, *interprète royal* according to Sauval.[28]

The portrait of the cardinal produced here (Plate 1) is typical of the uniform design of the collection. Above the Richelieu portrait is the following inscription (not in hexameters, and imperfectly reproduced on the print): 'Tot ex[t]ant Latis quos Universus orbis | Audiit Laboribus hoc Unum praestitisse | Sibi Visus est, quod Summa rerum | a Domino suo sibi concredita, Tanti | Regis mentem Ingenio Assuquutus, | Secundante Caelo sorti animo | Faeliciter Executus est'. (There exist so many of whom the world has heard, he seemed to himself to have provided by his labours this single benefit: the fact that when supreme power was entrusted to him by his master, he divined by his ability the intention of that great king, and successfully accomplished it, supported by Heaven's will.) Beneath the portrait is the distych: 'Grandia qui tot facta vides tollatur imago. Dices hac non sunt Unius acta Viri'. (Let his portrait be raised when you see so many great deeds accomplished by him; it may be said that no one man could accomplish them all.) Moving clockwise from the top right-hand tablet, the figures are as follows: Tablet 1. *La prise de Nancy 1633 (plan of the town)*; Medallion 1. Eagle carrying thunderbolt (*Expertus fidelem Jupiter*/the faithful executor of Jupiter); Tablet 2. *La prise de Pignerol* (with landscape and horsemen); Medallion 2. Sundial exposed to the sun (*Nec monumentum sine linea*/No achievement is possible without clear direction); Tablet 3. *Secours de Casal* (with map and horsemen); Tablet 4 (lower central).

---

[28] Sauval, *Antiquités de Paris*, 166.

PLATE 1. Engraving by Heince and Bignon of Champaigne's portrait of Cardinal Richelieu in the *Galerie des Hommes Illustres* of the Palais-Cardinal; *c.*1635, in the series 'à col noué par des lacets courts', and one of the first of Richelieu's famous official portraits by Champaigne; emblems and battle-scenes by Charles Poërson and Juste d'Egmont. From Marc Vulson de la Colombière, *Les Hommes illustres et grands capitaines français qui sont peints dans la Galerie du Palais Royal [. . .] Avec leurs portraits, armes et devises, dessignez et gravez par les Sieurs Heince et Bignon* (Paris, 1650), 1690 edn., fo. 91. See also Bernard Dorival, *Catalogue raisonné*, nos. 206 and 389.

[*La*] *prise de La Rochelle* (with horsemen, including the cardinal, and chart), flanked on right and left by sprays of laurel leaves; Tablet 5. *Le secours de* [*l'Île de*] *Ré 1627* (horsemen, including the cardinal, and map); Medallion 3. Purple carnation flecked with white (*Candorem purpura servat*/he serves the purple and the white together); Tablet 6. *La prise de Moyenvic 1631 et de Marsal 1632* (horsemen, including cardinal, and map); Medallion 4. Three lilies (*Sola mihi redolent*/ Their fragrance alone delights me); Tablet 7. *La prise de la ville de Trèves* (with map).[29]

If the figures represented in the portraits were all of the modern period, the accompanying devices and emblems, although typical of the time in their allusive, elliptic qualities, indicate a different way of preceiving the world and reality. In the *impresa*, or the emblem, which was so popular in the Renaissance, the essence of the figure's being and achievement were captured and encapsulated in a teleological order in which *les mots* and *les choses* were one; in the new gallery, the emblems preserve the same qualities, but they are made subservient to the cardinal's specific vision of the past as a cipher for present policies. The devices and instruments of an early humanist tradition were thus exploited in a remarkably modern, manipulative way; it was propaganda, in which the artists Vouet and Champaigne were conscripted as publicists in the cardinal's design.

Both of the artists worked on a contractual basis, although Félibien asserted in his *Entretiens* (1666–85)[30] that Richelieu had tried unsuccessfully to persuade Champaigne, the younger man, to become a member of his household. Vouet brought with him a number of protégés and former pupils, including Charles Poersen (1609–67) and Justus van Egmont (1601–74), who worked on the peripheral decorations and the emblems of the gallery. Champaigne executed seventeen portraits, but Vouet, whom Richelieu is said to have disliked, only eight; although all the portraits have been preserved as prints by Heince and Bignon, only six of the originals now survive.[31] Champaigne's portrait of Richelieu marks a turning-point in the public image of the cardinal. As perhaps the first of a series of full-length portraits of Richelieu executed by Champaigne, identified as the sequence 'à col noué par des lacets courts' and

[29] It will be appreciated that for the 25 portraits the 11 accompanying panels constitute a major exercise of exegesis. In the *salle longue* of the palace of Richelieu there were 43 such devices.

[30] Reprinted by Gregg, foreword by Sir Anthony Blunt (Farnborough, 1967).

[31] By Vouet: Suger (Musée des Beaux-Arts, Nantes), Simon de Montfort (Château de la Treyne, Lot), and Gaucher de Chastillon (Louvre). By Champaigne: Gaston de Foix (Musée de Versailles), Louis XIII (Louvre), and Blaise de Montluc (Château de Marsan).

painted between 1634 and 1636, it was one of an estimated fourteen to be completed by Champaigne, at the rate of one a year until the cardinal's death, in all of which a new regal presence is projected.[32] This series of portraits also marked the end of the association with Michel Lasne, a painter of most court figures, who had been the first recognized artist to execute Richelieu's portrait in 1626. As Dorival has shown in his famous study of Champaigne's work, the portraits of the cardinal *en pied* also broke new ground by representing for the first time an ecclesiastical figure standing like a monarch in full length.[33] Significant, too, is the fact that Vouet sought the likenesses of his portraits in the work of Bunel in the *petite galerie* (now the *galerie d'Apollon*) of the Louvre, while Champaigne executed his work from portraits by Pourbus and prints from André Thevet's *Les Vrais Pourtraits et vies des hommes illustres* (1584).[34] Since the *petite galerie* was later destroyed by fire in 1661, and final projects had not yet even been approved for the long *galerie au bord de l'eau* (also known as the *Grande Galerie*) running from the old Louvre to the Tuileries, the surviving portraits from Richelieu's gallery represent a rare line of continuity with the very earliest Bourbon portraiture. Indeed, everything in the cardinal's patterns of patronage indicates that it was his intention to ensure a line of continuity with royal policy.

If the portraits were necessarily modern, the statuary surrounding them was resolutely classical; as inventoried in its later arrangement in the gallery, it appears to have come from the crates of statues shipped out of Rome in 1633 and 1637 under the supervision of Mazarin, and destined, for the most part, for the palace at Richelieu.[35] The juxtaposition of modern and classical art forms was, of course, an affirmation of the patron's immortal qualities, but the precise relationship between the two in the *Galerie des Hommes Illustres* appears to have been still evolving during Richelieu's lifetime. A similar affirmation was made in a more explicit, tightly woven fashion at the palace of Richelieu; the gallery there was also an exercise in image-making, but even more complex and ambitious than the work being completed at the Palais-Cardinal. Unlike the Paris gallery, the one at Richelieu was a *galerie des batailles*; it

[32] B. Dorival, 'Richelieu, inspirateur de Philippe de Champaigne', in Mousnier (ed.), *Richelieu et la culture*, 153–61.

[33] Ibid., and also Dorival, *Philippe de Champaigne, 1602–74: La Vie, l'œuvre et le catalogue raisonné* (2 vols.; Paris, 1976), ii. 113, no. 204.

[34] Sauval, *Antiquités de Paris*, 166.

[35] *Album Canini*, ed. Schloder and Montembault, intro., 33–42. See also G. Dethan, *Mazarin* (Paris, 1981). The *Album Canini* contains drawings and an inventory of statutes drafted by a contemporary Italian (Canini) for the cardinal.

presented not portraits of illustrious predecessors and contemporaries, but battle-scenes from Richelieu's career as a military commander. Of the surviving descriptions of the gallery at Richelieu, the most detailed is Vignier's *Le Chasteau de Richelieu ou l'histoire des dieux et des héros de l'antiquité avec des réflexions morales* (Saumur, 1676).[36] The eight *Promenades* in verse of Desmarets de Saint-Sorlin, published in 1653, offer a hauntingly beautiful and more contemporaneous description, but they probably tell us more about Desmarets than about Richelieu. In addition to the verbal descriptions, the drawings of the palace building by Jean Marot, executed in 1649, are a precious visual source of information; they constitute the largest dossier ever to cover a princely house in France.[37] Vignier's description reveals a scale and complexity which were literally monumental; transcending the Paris galleries of both the Luxembourg and the recently completed Palais-Cardinal, the gallery at Richelieu was 70 metres (35 *toises*) long, 10 metres (5 *toises*) wide, with a ceiling 8 metres high. The Luxembourg gallery was only 32 *toises* long, but the largest gallery in France remained the *Galerie d'Ulysse* at Fontainebleau, over 100 metres long.[38] Within the Richelieu gallery, the lower level of each lateral wall carried a series of ten paintings, each showing contemporary French military triumphs and flanked by a classical bust. Above these paintings was an ornamental plaster-work frieze showing the now-familiar ships' prows; above that, along the upper level of each wall, was a series of ten triumphs of classical antiquity, each chosen to match the modern French triumphs below. Thus the capture of La Rochelle was echoed by Alexander's capture of Tyr, or the reduction of Privas (1629) by Scipio's destruction of Carthage; all the French battle-scenes shared the common property of the cardinal's presence and responsibility for victory. Each of the upper sections of the lateral walls was illuminated by a window adorned with the shell motif of St James, which itself contained Richelieu's coat-of-arms of the chevrons, surmounted by cardinal's hat and ducal coronet. Each window had a gilded latch repeating the same motif. Above each window was another aperture, an *œil-de-bœuf* (which Vignier calls an 'O'), which illuminated a third series of

[36] The contents of the palace, as described by Vignier, may have been modified by the cardinal's heir, the duc de Richelieu, who particularly admired the work of Rubens; the gallery would almost certainly have been left intact.

[37] BS Fonds Richelieu, nos. 55–85; the most accessible reproductions of these drawings are to be found in Tuilier, the illustrated catalogue of the exhibition held in the Sorbonne in Nov. 1985.

[38] The principal source of information on the now-vanished *galerie d'Ulysse* is the superb study by S. Béguin, J. Guillaume, and A. Roy, *La Galerie d'Ulysse à Fontainebleau* (Paris, 1985).

paintings on the ceiling. The ceiling bore eleven ovals depicting scenes from the life of Ulysses, each designed to match an incident in the cardinal's life. In summary, the walls of the gallery were adorned with representations of twenty military exploits attributable to Richelieu; these were given spatial extension by the classical busts which flanked them, and temporal allegorical extension by the twenty classical triumphs and eleven scenes from the life of Ulysses which matched them: a total of fifty-one paintings celebrating the achievements of the cardinal. In addition, at each extremity of the gallery, facing each other over the entrance and the fireplace respectively, were equestrian portraits of Richelieu himself and Louis XIII. The military scenes of past and present therefore created a stage on which the king and his minister met each other in an expression of triumphal partnership: icons of the enduring power of France. Above their combined triumphs, the exploits of the stoic and sagacious Ulysses stretched in an allegorical representation of the powers of diplomacy, high enough to be admired from one end of the gallery to the other. Although not compatible with the essentially Roman inspiration of the emergent official art of France and the Bourbons (he is an arch-villain for the Trojan founders of Rome in the *Aeneid*), the figure of Ulysses was clearly inspired by the great gallery of Fontainebleau, and probably stimulated by Van Thulden's *Les Travaux d'Ulysse* of 1633, with maxims by Melchior Tavernier.[39]

Even though Laval had denounced the freedom with which the Italian painters had developed their own themes at Fontainebleau, the *galerie d'Ulysse* (demolished by Louis XV) stood as the visible high-water mark of Valois patronage, and therefore to be emulated by their successors. It was emulated not only in its substance but in its mode of presentation, because Richelieu, for the first time, resorted to decoration of the ceiling. Decoration of the ceiling was an Italian convention introduced by Francis I for the *galerie d'Ulysse*, but subsequently abandoned for the timbered ceilings of the *galerie François I*. Marie de' Medici had also fluctuated between the two conventions: after having the *galerie de la reine* in the Louvre decorated by Ambroise Dubois (*c.*1542–1614), with ceilings depicting allegorical victories of Henri IV, she reverted to the French tradition of the plain ceiling for the the Luxembourg palace. It was therefore Richelieu who restored the decoration of the ceiling, so conspicuously maintained at Versailles, to French palace art, even if it was initially for his own glorification.

[39] Publ. in Paris by Melchior Tavernier; for a commentary on this work and its 58 maxims, see Béguin, Guillaume, and Roy, *Galerie*, 106–15; for the imagery of Ulysses in France, see also N. Hepp, *Homère en France au XVIIᵉ siècle* (Paris, 1968).

As explicit as it appears to be in its fusion of ideology and art, the gallery at Richelieu preserves an enigmatic quality. The arrangement of the pictures, with the portraits of Louis XIII and Richelieu facing each other across a very crowded room, suggests a moment of perfect reconciliation, with nothing more to be accomplished: any further additions would destroy the artistic symmetry of the whole. The associations between the three levels of painting and the décor were too closely woven to accommodate an updating process. But a *mise-en-scène* of this kind, complete in every detail, implies an audience. Who, exactly? In 1640, the approximate date of completion of the gallery, Louis XIII was only 39 and could have been reasonably expected to add to his exploits. But that was probably not the point: it was Richelieu, after all, who was the prime focus of the gallery, with the imagery of Ulysses illustrating not the king's career but his own, even if it had been previously used to glorify the career of the most dazzling of the Valois, Francis I. With the completeness and symmetry of a final statement, the gallery implies that the cardinal saw his great work behind him; the gallery elevated that career to the perfection of a work of art. Perhaps too self-centred to be safely exposed in Paris, the gallery was in an appropriate setting in the ancestral residence of Richelieu (where some historians claim that the cardinal was born). Although remote enough not to be provocative, the gallery did have a public planned for it, because the palace was the centre-piece of the whole new town of Richelieu which had been planned for construction; within the privacy of the family seat, the gallery did therefore aim to address a certain posterity.[40] Its message obviously served family pride, but it was also set in the context of service to France and the king. It carries a final irony in that its undisputed architect and *maître d'œuvre*, Richelieu himself, probably never saw it.[41]

The process of allegorical representation observed in Richelieu's galleries corresponds to the literary device of *antonomasia* (Condé as Achilles, or the king as Apollo); it presupposes the enlistment not only of the artist and the architect as artisans of glory, but of the historian, too. The images adorning the gallery (as distinct from the chapel or suites of *appartements*) all served an interpretation, if not manipulation, of history: in this regard they can be seen to derive

[40] I am grateful to Robert Knecht, emeritus professor of history at the Univ. of Birmingham, for his reflections on the kind of public envisaged for the Richelieu gallery. Probably an important constituency would have been formed initially by the young nobles of the short-lived Richelieu academy: see Ch. 8 by Brockliss.

[41] In his eighth *Promenade*, Desmarets wrote: 'Richelieu fit bâtir la merveille et ne la vit jamais'.

from well-established programmes of learning, going back via Bodin's *Methodus ad facilem cognitionem historiarum*, and Budé's *Institution du prince* (1547), to the portraits and parallels of Plutarch (several copies of which are listed in the catalogue of Richelieu's library).[42] As Orest Ranum points out in his study of history as propaganda, Bodin's interest in history lay 'in the capacity to motivate the minds of men'.[43] As the Emperor Suleiman was spurred to the conquest of Asia Minor by reading a translation of Caesar, so Caesar admired Alexander, who in turn discovered an admiration for Achilles in the work of Homer. Through his astute observation of what Traian Stoianovich calls 'exemplar history',[44] with human behaviour as a universal constant, Richelieu plainly used history as an instrument in the struggle for the minds of men. To suggest, however, that he was capable not only of manipulating this kind of humanist optimism to such advantage, but also of believing in it himself would be to strain credibility. The cardinal's sensitivity to the uses of history is revealed as rather more complex through his relationship with François de la Mothe le Vayer (1588–1672), the sceptic Oratius Tubéro. Occasionally commissioned by Richelieu to conduct historical studies for him, he was also entrusted with the education of the Dauphin; his *Instruction de Monseigneur le Dauphin* appeared in 1640, but previous to that he had written a *Discours sur la bataille de Lützen* (1633), and a *Discours de l'histoire* (1638).[45] The latter work was dedicated to Richelieu, and it sets out to expatiate on the aberrations of the Spanish history of the reign of Charles V by Sandoval; if the exposure of history as fable is a sceptical device employed as a means of discrediting official Spanish history, it has to be said that Richelieu's own use of history as self-promotion appears just as sceptical, even cynical.

The research of John Schloder has brought much new light to bear on the craftsmen and artists who worked at Richelieu.[46] He has located the surviving paintings of the gallery, and indicated that, as *premier peintre du roi*, Simon Vouet acted as overseer for the bulk of the decorative work in the palace, even if executing relatively little himself. With Vouet came a host of contractual workers: their names

---

[42] Bibliothèque Mazarine MS 4271, fo. 472ᵛ.

[43] O. A. Ranum, *Artisans of Glory: Writers and Historical Thought in Seventeenth-Century France* (Chapel Hill, NC, 1980), 89.

[44] T. Stoianovich, *French Historical Method: The Annales Paradigm* (Ithaca, NY, 1976), 28–9.

[45] For an absorbing study of La Mothe le Vayer as historian, see P.-J. Salazar, 'La Mothe le Vayer ou l'impossible métier de l'historien', *Seventeenth-Century French Studies*, 13 (1991), 55–7.

[46] *Album Canini*, ed. Schloder and Montembault.

cross the archival records and reappear in the pages of Félibien, with
little being known about them: the Crosnier brothers, Edmé Jacob,
or François Bougnet. Schloder suggests that two of the most important of these background figures were François Perrier and Nicolas
Prévost. With an estimated 2,000 craftsmen working on the site at
one stage, it was clearly on a scale comparable to Vaux-le-Vicomte or
Versailles. Claude Deruet and his pupil Claude Lorrain completed a
series of landscapes for the palace's *Cabinet de la Reine*; the landscapes commissioned by Marie de' Medici for the Luxembourg were
perhaps echoed here, as were Berthelot's *Femmes illustres* in a series
of murals, probably also by Deruet and Lorrain. The link between
the Luxembourg and this last series is quite explicit because we
know that the Richelieu sequence included Artemisia, Dido, and
Semiramis, three figures originally suggested by Rubens for the
Luxembourg but not accepted.[47] Jacques Stella (1596–1657) worked
at Richelieu, as did Louis Fréminet (1617–51) whose father Martin
decorated the chapel at Fontainebleau. Poussin executed his two
Bacchanales for the palace in 1636;[48] with his *Triomphe d'Amphitrite*,
these were perhaps the most prized of the contemporary French
works of the palace collection. There were also many foreign and
past masters at Richelieu; the work of Rubens, Van Dyck, and Reni
was represented, as well as that of Dürer, Titian, Caravaggio,
Carracci, Mantegna, Perugino, and Lorenzo Costa (the last three
coming in loot from the sack of Mantua in 1630). The meticulous
maître d'œuvre of this great project was Richelieu himself, who
adhered firmly to his injunction that 'les peintures que je voy en tous
les lieux où je vas, me font désirer que les miennes soient fort
bien'.[49] The instruction to others to secure the best available work is
characteristic of the exercise, and also of Richelieu's criteria as a
collector. It appears to have been the 'biddability' of an artist within
a master scheme, or the perceived reputation of an artist among
his peers, which determined his judgement. His association with
Philippe de Champaigne was a long and fruitful one, but there was
never any question of the artist's right to self-expression. Indeed,
there is evidence of considerable tension when he encountered the
claims of great artists to personal creative freedom, whether they
were called Rubens, Poussin, Bernini, or Pierre Corneille; the kind
of latitude sought by artists such as these was probably found more

---

[47] Marrow, *Art Patronage*, 22.
[48] R. Pintard, 'Rencontres avec Poussin', in A. Chastel (ed.), *Nicolas Poussin* (Paris, 1960),
33.
[49] Avenel, iv. 304.

frequently in Italy than in France, evidence of the growth of Laval's ideas on the ideological enlistment of the artist.

These criteria of artistic selection were particularly valid in Richelieu's acquisition of the extraordinary collection of antique statuary at Richelieu. The Canini album inventoried no less than 250 statues at Richelieu;[50] these included a *Vénus et Cupidon* (*Canini* 60a), a *Bacchus* (*Canini* 77a), and an *Alexander* (*Canini* 158) which were hailed at the time as priceless masterpieces. The *Alexander* was even attributed to Praxiteles. Present-day assessments of the artistic worth of the collection are certainly not as flattering, and it is evident that, in reality, the collection of classical statues was worth far less than the collection of approximately 200 paintings. The purchase of the statuary was entrusted by Richelieu to agents such as Benedetti and Frangipani, with the occasional intervention of a French ambassador such as the duc de Créquy, who acted for him in Italy; his instructions were simply to find and procure the most highly prized works. It was in this way that he created a situation which was vulnerable to artistic and commercial fraud. The most significant message of such an imposing collection was that it cost a fortune, and was only accessible to a figure of great eminence; a massive testimony to what Francis Haskell would call 'the lure of the antique'. In a relative assessment of value and quality, the collection of statues at the Palais-Cardinal was calculated by Bonnaffé and Boislisle as standing at 150, while the paintings numbered 300 (with a significantly higher concentration of old masters than at Richelieu).[51] Compared to the Vasari shopping-list of works in the Palais-Cardinal, the collections of the palace at Richelieu were more modern and more tightly integrated into an overall design. It would be impossible to put a price on these collections; the *inventaires après décès*, dramatically rediscovered in the recent past,[52] do indeed list the estimated value of items, but they cover only movable objects. All the interior decorative work of the palaces, including the galleries, was part of the fabric and fittings of the buildings themselves.

The external design of the palaces played a part in the development of royal palace architecture in France. The architect in both cases was Le Mercier; at Richelieu he proceeded by quadrupling the size of the original *cour d'honneur* of the family seat, doubling the length of the original *corps de logis* in such a way that the original corner *pavillon* became an enhanced central *pavillon*. As Claude

---

[50] *Album Canini*, ed. Schloder and Montembault.
[51] See n. 2 above.
[52] See Levi, 'Inventaire Richelieu', and Levi and Hulot-Lécroart, 'Rueil'.

Mignot has pointed out,[53] this was precisely the plan proposed for the extension of the Louvre by Métezeau in 1624. As it happens, it was Le Mercier who finally undertook the extension of the Louvre in 1639; having initially completed the same experiment at Richelieu, he confidently proceeded to double the length of Pierre Lescot's *corps de logis* at the Louvre, transforming the original corner *pavillon* into the main central structure now known as the *pavillon de l'Horloge*, and quadrupling the size of the *Cour carrée*. It was thus the renovation of the ancestral seat of Richelieu which led to the extension of the Louvre, and the cardinal's commission which entrusted it to Le Mercier, first Marie de' Medici's architect and then his own.

The final mark of Richelieu on royal palace architecture in France was, of course, in the design of the galleries and ceilings. This is well illustrated by the work done on the new gallery of the Palais-Cardinal by Champaigne, and by the work that Poussin finally did not do in the Louvre. The ceilings executed by Champaigne in the new *galerie de l'avant-cour* have been inventoried by Dorival as follows. (1) *La Félicité publique*, (2) *La Gloire immortelle de Richelieu*, (3) *Apollon avec les Muses*, (4) *Junon ou la Paix*, (5) *Génie, Prudence et Générosité de Richelieu*.[54] These heroic themes will be immediately recognized as having their origin in the work executed for Marie de' Medici in the Luxembourg almost twenty years previously by Rubens, Gentileschi, and Baglione. Champaigne's work was described by Sauval thus:

des blanc et noirs, des tableaux, des rostres [ships' prows], imités de l'antique, et des chiffres du Cardinal de Richelieu, environnés de lauriers, étaient répandues dans cette voûte sur un grand fond d'or peint en mosaïque avec autant d'ordre que d'esprit et composaient ensemble comme une sorte de panégyrique à l'honneur du Maître de la Maison [. . .] on tient qu'il prenait plaisir quelque fois de faire réciter à Champaigne l'histoire de sa vie que ce peintre avait représenté dans la voûte d'un bout à l'autre.[55]

It is to be hoped that the theme of Richelieu's munificence to the Muses stemmed as much from the artist's inspiration as from the cardinal's formal instructions. Bearing in mind that the *galerie de l'avant-cour* adjoined the *appartements de la Reine* in the former Palais-Cardinal where, apart from some unplanned excursions to Saint-Germain, the young Louis XIV lived from the age of 5 to 12 with his widowed mother, it can easily be imagined how the

---

[53] C. Mignot, 'Le Château et la ville de Richelieu en Poitou', in Tuilier (ed.), *Le Monde de l'esprit*, 67–74.
[54] Dorival, *Champaigne: Catalogue raisonné*, ii., nos. 420*b*–420*f*.
[55] Sauval, *Antiquités de Paris*, 164.

child's simple curiosity about his father's absence from such heroic allegories would grow into a determination to insert a monarchical presence into them. A further presence of significance was to be found in the *appartements de la Reine* where, as Vouet's assistant, Le Brun had executed an early canvas for Richelieu, *Hercule et les chevaux de Diomède*. According to Sauval, it was a work which assured the reputation of Le Brun, 'Poussin lui-même dit au Cardinal de Richelieu que Le Brun était un homme de grande espérance, et tel que si jamais il passoit les monts quelques jours, ce serait un excellent peintre.'[56] It would take the creative intuition of an Orson Welles to determine to what extent the young child's experience led, like Citizen Kane's, to the later affirmation of his own power. It was, in any event, Charles Le Brun who gave it expression at Versailles.

The final piece of evidence in the reconstruction of the line of continuity maintained in Bourbon official art by Richelieu, between Marie de' Medici and Louis XIV, is to be found in the Poussin incident of 1640. Félibien informs us in his eighth *Entretien* (iv. 38) that, continuing his work of restoration at the Louvre, Le Mercier had drawn up plans for the *Grande Galerie* and, in a description which calls to mind the *Galerie des Glaces*, 'dans la voûte [il] avait déjà disposé des compartiments pour y mettre des tableaux avec des bordures et des ornemens à sa manière, c'est-à-dire, soupesants et massifs'. Brought back to Paris at the express wish of Richelieu to decorate this same ceiling, Poussin protested at the concept which was inflicted upon him, and had it changed. It was then Le Mercier's turn to complain and to mobilize resistance. There is little doubt that his own approach was informed by his long association with Richelieu, and designed to serve the allegorical representation of power; the symbolism of the monarchy was particularly important in the *Grande Galerie* where the miracle of kingship, the healing of scrofula, was staged five times a year.[57] In a trenchant letter to Sublet des Noyers, quoted in its entirely by Félibien (iv. 47), Poussin complained that 'on ne lui a jamais proposé de faire le plus superbe ouvrage qu'il pût imaginer: et que si on eût voulu l'y engager, il aurait librement dit son avis'; disgusted with the aesthetics of grandeur, Poussin gave three principal objections to the project asked of him. His arguments were bruising for Richelieu; they were 'premièrement à cause du peu d'ouvriers à Paris capables d'y travailler; secondement à cause du longtemps qu'il eût fallu y employer; et en troisième lieu à cause de l'excessive dépense qui ne lui semble pas bien employée'. In September 1642, having reduced

[56] Ibid. 168–9.
[57] G. Bresc, *Mémoires du Louvre* (Paris, 1989), 42–3.

Richelieu's design to the level of a Jay Gatsby extravagance, Poussin packed his bags and left for Rome. It had been an error of judgement to seek the assistance of Poussin in a project which had relatively little to offer to the artist's freedom of inspiration; the result, *faute de mieux*, was to confirm the grandiose manner of early Bourbon absolutism. At the same time, the Bernini bust of Richelieu, considered too frivolous, was refused in favour of the statesmanlike 'Champaignesque' *gravitas* of Jean Warin's work (Plate 2); similarly, Louis XIV was later to prefer Warin and Coypel to Bernini.[58]

This is not to say that Richelieu systematically turned his back on Italy in favour of a French artistic school; nothing could be further from the truth. He was steeped in Italian culture, and profoundly marked by Italian art and ideas; his reliance on Mazarin's taste, (offering in 1635 to make him *surintendant de ses collections*),[59] the preponderance of Italian books in his library (including editions of Bacon's *Essays* and Molina's theatre in Italian translation),[60] and above all, the distinctive design of the Sorbonne chapel, 'le premier dôme vraiment romain de Paris',[61] with its slavish imitation by Champaigne of the Raphaëlesque decoration of the dome of St Peter's, executed by the Cavalier d'Arpino almost forty years before,[62] all provide eloquent testimony to this.

The colossal building programme summarized here, which does not even touch the plans of his rural retreat at Rueil (perhaps a haven from the all-pervading grandeur), covers a sixteen-year period from 1624–40; at one period in the 1630s there was work proceeding apace at Richelieu, the Palais-Cardinal, Rueil, and the Sorbonne. The building corresponded to the advances in his own career; the Palais-Cardinal was, of course, begun in the wake of his elevation to the college of cardinals (and he incurred some derision in erudite circles for having inscribed in gold letters, above the main entrance, the apparent solecism of the two juxtaposed nouns, 'Palais-Cardinal').[63] The correspondence between his appointment as *surintendant de la navigation* and the construction of the *galerie des proues* below the *Galerie des Hommes Illustres* has been noted, and in 1631, the elevation of the estate of Richelieu to a *duché-pairie* prompted the development of the ancestral domain. Not only that,

[58] Jones, *French Medals*, ii. 181–2, 'Jean Warin'; H. Himmelfarb, 'Du Louvre au Louvre, le Louis XIV équestre du Bernin (1665–1989)', *XVIIe Siècle*, 165 (1989), 437–48.

[59] M. Laurain-Portemer, 'Mazarin militant de l'art baroque au temps de Richelieu', *Études mazarines* (Paris, 1981), i. 177 n. 3.

[60] Bibliothèque Mazarine MS 4271, fos. 631^v and 857^v.

[61] Mignot, 'La Chapelle et maison de Sorbonne', in Tuilier (ed.), *Le Monde de l'esprit*, 93.

[62] Dorival, 'Richelieu, inspirateur de Champaigne', 156–7.

[63] Sauval, *Antiquités de Paris*, 158.

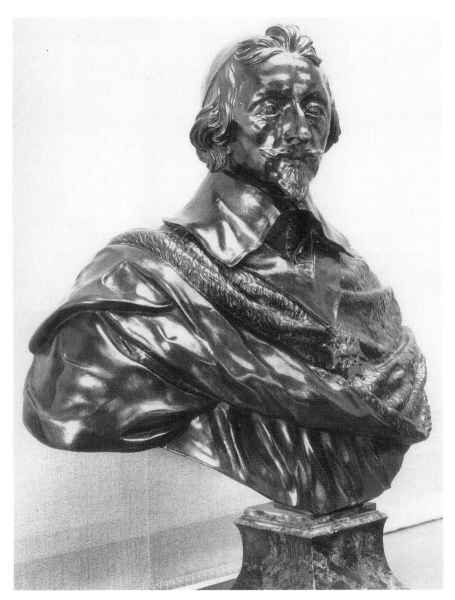

PLATE 2. Bust of Cardinal Richelieu, after Jean Warin; the Barber Institute of Fine Arts, the University of Birmingham. Possibly one of the four casts after Warin's plaster model (1641, now lost) for which the sculptor Hubert Le Sueur was paid in 1643. Other casts are in the Bibliothèque Mazarine and the Musée Jacquemart-André, Paris, in the Albertinum at Dresden, and in Windsor Castle. He is wearing the collar of the Order of the Holy Spirit.

but having become principal minister in 1629, and been released
from the joint incubus of Marie de' Medici and Gaston d'Orléans in
1631, he was free to propagate an image of himself as the king's right
hand. This is presumably the message implicit in the development of
the estate and new town of Richelieu (which was never finished). It
was an attempt to emulate, and perhaps outshine, Sully, the great
minister of Henri IV, who had also had plans for a palace and a new
town. Begun in 1608, the construction of Henrichemont (Berry)
under the direction of Salomon de Brosse lost its purpose and its
funding after the assassination of the king in 1610. The campaign of
total architecture, in which even the window latches reproduced the
main design, appears to have served for Richelieu as an expression
for the maturing concept of total politics. By 1634–5, the main lines
of direction of his building programme were well established, with
all that that implied and defined for patronage of the arts. It is
against that background, and arising out of it, that Richelieu's subsequent creation of the Académie française and his administration of
the arts are best understood.

The recruitment of the artist in the service of first the cardinal and
then the state did not occur without some external stimuli. First
and foremost was the need to consolidate his own position as a
pre-eminent minister, and then there was the inadequacy of the
household of the king, upon whom his position depended. There is a
hard-hitting passage in Richelieu's *Testament politique* which deals
specifically with the 'état présent de la Maison du Roi';[64] explaining
that 'un testament met au jour beaucoup d'intentions que le testateur
n'avait osé divulguer pendant sa vie, Celui-ci conviera Sa Majesté à la
réformation de sa Maison.'[65] The king's household should normally
be magnificent, but Louis XIII's was deplorable, and his miserliness
legendary, even if he did have talent as a painter and a musician. The
assertion of French authority in Europe required a court of appropriate splendour, like those of Granada or the Escorial, with portraits
of royal magnificence comparable to those created by Titian or
Velázquez. Charles I of England had also required a reputation for
magnificence and munificence as a patron of the arts; he had commissioned Rubens to decorate a gallery at Whitehall which was
longer than the one at the Luxembourg, and he had swept away the
prized Gonzaga collections from under the noses of the French at the
Mantua sale of 1629; as Roy Strong has amply illustrated, art was for
princes a manifestation of power.[66] The palaces of the Farnese

---

[64] *Test. pol.* 279–86.   [65] Ibid. 280.
[66] R. Strong, *Art and Power: Renaissance Festivals* (Woodbridge, 1989).

and the Barberini in Rome excited the admiration of all, and the Rome of 1630 was a centre of artistic attainment such that Yves Bonnefoy chose that year as his privileged point of vision.[67] And yet, Castiglione's mocking dismissal in the *Cortegiano* of the French nobility as uncultured men of war, with only Francis I showing promise, stood unanswered a century later. Small wonder that Richelieu worked so single-mindedly to enhance the image of the dynasty (and by extension, the nation) created by Marie de' Medici.

It thus appears that Richelieu's early involvement in the arts served first the promotion of his own image, and then that of the monarch; perhaps his most 'innocent' collection was the set of rock crystal vases inventoried in the Palais-Cardinal, and valued modestly in the *inventaire après décès* at 5,543 *livres tournois* (the movable paintings were valued at 80,000 *livres*, and the jewellery and silver kept in the palace at 372,000 *livres*).[68] The foundation of the Académie française was certainly not perceived by his contemporaries as innocent; suspicious of the cardinal's encroaching, omnivorous authority, the parlement of Paris refused for over two years to register the letters-patent of the new institution. There is little to add here to the circumstances of the Academy's foundation and its early skirmishes, which have all been well documented,[69] but it is important to note that it was called not the Académie Cardinale, not the Académie Royale, nor the Académie des polis (as was originally intended), but the Académie française, a strikingly bold, modern, and efficient expression of its priorities. It was an invention of Richelieu's to link in this way the genteel concept of the academy, traditionally a refuge in polite society for the pleasures of a cultured *otium*, with the more overtly political notion of national prestige. The cardinal was named the protector of the academy, and its seal bears his effigy.[70] If one recalls his involvement in the famous *querelle du Cid*, it is evident that he acted in a far more decisive, interventionist way than would normally be expected of a disinterested *mécène*. The Maecenas of Guez de Balzac (1597–1654) for example, one of the arbiters of taste of the time, was a figure who 'dora un siècle de fer, qui rendit

---

[67] Y. Bonnefoy, *Rome 1630: L'Horizon du premier baroque* (Paris, 1970).

[68] These figures have been reached on my own calculations, on the basis of the *inventaire après décès* in Levi, 'Inventaire Richelieu'; they are most certainly conservative because they do not include items which were not sold or which are in the Boislisle inventory (see n. 2, above).

[69] See P. Pellisson, *Relation concernant l'histoire de l'Académie Française* ed. C.-L. Livet (Paris, 1858; 1st. edn. Paris, 1653); A. Gasté, *La Querelle du Cid: Pièces et pamphlets d'après les originaux* (Paris, 1898). There are also many more recent studies by scholars in the field, with Antoine Adam and H. Carrington Lancaster offering a basic starting-point.

[70] A photograph of the seal can be seen in T. Murray, 'The Académie Française', in D. Hollier (ed.), *A New History of French Literature* (Cambridge, Mass., 1989), 269.

supportable la monarchie à des âmes passionnées pour la liberté' (*Entretien*, 21). In fact, Balzac's ideal of the patron of the arts was designed, as Jean Jehasse has pointed out, as an anti-Richelieu. The sequence of four *Discours* ('Le Romain', 'La Conversation des Romains', 'Mécénas', 'La Gloire') addressed to the marquise de Rambouillet, the incomparable 'Arthénice' of Paris salon life, all imply an *allure d'opposition*,[71] and in consequence they also imply the alienation of the cardinal from the fashion-setting literary salons; this provided further good reason for founding an academy under his aegis. It might also serve to explain the adoption of Desmarets de Saint-Sorlin (*c.*1600–76) as his house-dramatist and propagandist; Gaston Hall's comprehensive recent study of Desmarets's career reveals that he was a well-received habitué of the Rambouillet salon before becoming a *créature* of the cardinal.[72]

Following his early associations with François le Metel de Boisrobert and the Compagnie des Cinq Auteurs—Boisrobert (1592–1662), Corneille (1606–84), Rotrou (1609–50), Colletet (1598–1659), and Lestoille (1597–1652)—in the period 1635–7, the partnership with Desmarets proved to be the most enduring in Richelieu's career; it was with Desmarets, and his ambitious stage productions of *Aspasie*, (1636), *Les Visionnaires* (1637), *Scipion* (1638–9), *Roxane* (1639–40), *Mirame* (1641), *Erigone* (1641–2), and *Europe* (1642), presented at the rate of one a year for the last six years of the cardinal's life, that Richelieu brought a new sense of spectacle, as well as political commitment, to the French stage. Inaugurating his superb new theatre, subsequently to become the home of Molière's troupe, at the Palais-Cardinal with *Mirame* on the 14 January 1641 (with the décor designed by Bernini), hosting state occasions in his theatre, he undoubtedly prompted the royal decree of 24 April 1641 which gave civic status to actors in France, and he contributed more than anyone else to the magnificent flowering of French theatre later in the century.[73] Whether or not this was accomplished in a spirit of continuing *realpolitik*, it remains a considerable achievement; it is a received view in France that Richelieu played a part in the formation of French literary classicism.[74] But there was a price to pay. In commenting on the career of Boisrobert, a writer of light and entertaining verse and comedy until his absorption into the entourage of

[71] J. Jehasse, *Guez de Balzac et le génie romain 1597–1654* (Saint-Étienne, 1977), 354.

[72] See n. 2 above.

[73] G. Couton, 'Richelieu et le théâtre', in Mousnier (ed.), *Richelieu et la culture*, 79–101.

[74] See amongst others, R. Bray, *La Formation de la doctrine classique* (Paris, 1927), 358–60; Antoine Adam, *L'Âge classique, 1624–60*, i, in C. Pichois, *Littérature française* (Paris, 1968); R. Zuber, 'Le Temps des choix', in Mesnard, *Précis de la littérature française*, 153–69.

Richelieu led him to the compilation of elogious *œuvres de circonstance*, such as *Le Sacrifice des muses au grand cardinal de Richelieu* (1635), Antoine Adam wrote one of the most damning of modern appraisals of the cardinal's literary influence, 'sous les apparences de l'ordre et d'une fausse grandeur, le régime de Richelieu aboutissait à domestiquer les talents et à rendre stériles les écrivains les plus heureusement doués'.[75] Wolfgang Leiner provides quantified evidence for the growing weight of the cardinal's presence in literary circles during those years following the concentrated period of building and image-making.[76] Ministerial patronage supplanted princely patronage throughout the 1630s and into the 1640s, with Richelieu outstripping all others with an average of three books a year dedicated to him in the years 1631 to 1640. It must also be said that this is as much due to the writer's own perception of personal advantage as to ministerial encouragement, and not all the writers concerned were of the top rank.[77]

Amid the conflicting appraisals of Richelieu's career as a patron of the arts, the question of his 'innocence' provides a useful point of focus on which to conclude. The period 1624–35 was certainly marked by systematic building and consolidation of his place in public life, by what one French historian has called, in another context, 'l'art et la manière d'accommoder les héros de l'histoire de France'.[78] The subsequent years brought greater involvement in literary and theatrical life, but it is not possible to determine with any certainty whether that later activity reveals an intimacy of personal interests, a face behind the heroic mask, or not. If the cardinal did have genuinely 'innocent' pastimes and interests, they probably lay in the area of theatre, music, and dance. The phenomenon of high-level ministerial involvement in the composition of plays by the Cinq Auteurs (a group formed by the cardinal) demonstrates how the signals can be confused. Was it as a theatre-lover at play, or indeed as a royal minister, that Richelieu turned to this activity? The three plays composed by this assembly of writers were *La Comédie des*

---

[75] A. Adam, *Histoire de la littérature française au XVIIᵉ siècle*, i (Paris, 1962), 349.

[76] W. Leiner, *Der Widmungsbrief in der französischen Literatur (1580–1715)* (Heidelberg, 1965).

[77] One of the most complete lists of recipients of pensions from Richelieu is to be found in Antoine Aubery, *Mémoires pour l'histoire du cardinal duc de Richelieu* (Cologne, 1666), 433: he gives a 'liste assez exacte' which mentions 'Silhon, Chapelain, Faret, Scudéry, Colletet, Baro, Rotrou, L'Estoille, Tristan, P. Corneille, Magdelenet, Benserade, La Mothe le Vayer, Duchesne, Mézeray, Baudouin, Duret, Baudier, Hennequin, Halier, Gaudin, Véron, de la Place, Valens, Geoffroy, de Rians.'

[78] C. Amalvi, *De l'art et la manière d'accommoder les héros de l'histoire de France: Essais de mythologie nationale* (Paris, 1988); see also T. Gaehtgens, *Versailles: De la résidence royale au musée historique* (Paris, 1984).

Tuileries (1635), *La Grande Pastorale* (1637), and *L'Aveugle de Smyrne* (1637); it is assumed that Richelieu's role in the composition of these plays was to provide an outline plot for exploration and elaboration, but in his *Relation contenant l'histoire de l'Académie française* (1653), Pellisson suggested that Richelieu wrote five hundred lines of *La Grande Pastorale*, a play never published and now lost.[79] Even if Richelieu's involvement in these plays was, for reasons now impossible to fathom, ministerial and political, it has to be said that not only did they have positively no impact on the cultural life of France, but they also had a damaging effect on the cardinal's own image. Both this episode and the evidence provided by the catalogue of Richelieu's library suggest a genuine love of theatre. Drafted after the cardinal's death as an inventory of the superb library of the Palais-Cardinal which Richelieu bequeathed to the nation, the catalogue lists all the dramatic authors of Greek and Roman antiquity, as well as Lope de Vega, Molina, and a number of lesser known Italian and Spanish dramatists; the library also held pastoral novels, a collection of *rimes burlesques*, and the works of Ariosto and Tasso. The amount of work in English is minimal, with no theatrical work represented. The absence of French dram- atists, and more particularly of Desmarets de Saint-Sorlin, from this catalogue is striking; it includes a supplement for the library at Rueil, where the cardinal may have pursued more leisurely activities, but it cannot be determined whether the catalogue and its supple- ment, which betray all the signs of a hasty and uninformed compila- tion, were complete or not. The library was dominated by Italian treatises on political theory, historical commentaries, canon and Roman law, and theology, and the overall proportion of theatrical works is small, but one tantalizing, unverifiable entry is an *Argumenta des tragédies latines et françaises écrites in Aula Cardinalis de Richelieu*.[80] The creation of Latin and French tragedies at the Palais-Cardinal, completely undocumented to date, suggests even more involvement in theatre than hitherto suspected.

Disinterested as Richelieu's interest in the theatre may originally have been, there is also evidence that his encyclopaedic, calculating mind began to contemplate ways of turning it to advantage. The style of the productions organized by Desmarets indicates attention to political opportunity;[81] even if his original interest was purely for 'la beauté de la chose', Richelieu always seemed drawn to the

---

[79] Couton, 'Richelieu et le théâtre'.

[80] Bibliothèque Mazarine MS 4271, fo. 1932, no. 5754.

[81] See Couton, 'Richelieu et le théâtre'; also Hall, *Richelieu's Desmarets*.

opportunity to make one set of solutions operate for a number of other, different issues. He appears ultimately never to have acted gratuitously. If he enjoyed the excitement and colour of the theatrical spectacle, the opportunity of a more active participation than for the plastic arts, and also perhaps the vanity of self-dramatization (as, for example, in the role of Scipio),[82] he would also have been very sensitive to the political advantage derived by the Medici family from the full panoply of their spectacular pageants (including Marie's own wedding to Henri IV). Arthur Blumenthal's *Theater Art of the Medici*,[83] and the work of Sara Mamone provide ample evidence of the ways in which such spectacles were used to express political goals, or to sway influential opinion; as control of the 'air waves' is considered essential to the success of a new political regime, so the opportunities of court spectacle would have been put in the same context as the creation of the *Gazette* in 1631, the Académie française in 1634, and the Imprimerie royale in 1640.

It is Margaret McGowan's assessment that from 1635 most court ballets were performed at Richelieu's instigation.[84] These include *Le Ballet des Quatre Monarchies Chrétiennes* (1635), which stated the political aspirations of the time; *Le Ballet de la Marine* (1635), for which the *surintendant de la navigation* had a particular interest; the *Ballet de la Félicité* (1639), which celebrated the birth of Louis XIV; the *Ballet de la Prospérité des armes de la France* (1641), celebrating the union of his family (through his niece Clémence de Maillé-Brézé) to the blood royal (through the duc d'Enghien, future Grand Condé); and by no means least, the final superb statement of national political strategy with *Europe* (1642). The spectacular social and theatrical occasion created by the production of *Europe*, allied to the ideological gallocentricity of its subject, indicates not only a line of direct descent from Marie de' Medici's theatrical *Carrousel* of 1612 in the Place Royale, but a determination on Richelieu's part to bring to an influential public the ideas of one of his favourite books, the neo-Latin *Argenis* (1621) of John Barclay (1581–1621).[85] It can thus be

---

[82] Desmarets's play of that title is dedicated to Richelieu; there were busts of Scipio in the collection at Richelieu (*Album Canini*, ed. Schloder and Montembault, 108); there were parallels presented in the Richelieu gallery between Scipio's victories and those of the cardinal, and Puget de la Serre wrote *Le Portrait de Scipion l'Africain ou l'image de la vertu représentée au naturel dans celle de Mgr le Cardinal de Richelieu* (Bordeaux, 1641): this work was dedicated to the cardinal and he possessed a copy of it in his library, Bibliothèque Mazarine MS 4271, fo. 2035, no. 142.

[83] Dartmouth, Va., 1980.

[84] M. McGowan, *L'Art du ballet de cour en France* (Paris, 1963), 184.

[85] For *Europe*, see H. Gaston Hall, '*Europe*, allégorie théâtrale de propagande politique', in Mousnier and Mesnard, *L'Age d'or*, 319–29; for Barclay, see Fumaroli, 'L'Empire', 83–5.

argued that, under the impulsion of Richelieu, the *ballet de cour* went beyond eye-pleasing entertainment to reach a new level of meaningful political persuasion; even at play, he appears to have concentrated on predetermined goals.

In commenting upon Richelieu's impact on court spectacle, McGowan has suggested that the work of the Dominican visionary Tomasso Campanella (1568–1639), *De Monarchia Christianorum* (1593), was a source for the ballet which translated that title. This association with Campanella, to whom Richelieu offered political refuge in Paris, is a reminder that it was Richelieu's librarian of the time, Jacques Gaffarel (1601–81), who first made contact with Campanella; author of *Les Curiosités inouyes* (1629) and *Des Talismans ou figures faites sous certaines constellations* (1636), Gaffarel was interested in alchemy and the arts of the occult. Could Richelieu himself also have been interested in what we now call the occult? This may well have been possible and is certainly an area for further study; in an age when most princely households had a spagyric physician the definitions of science and medicine were very different from today, but it is certainly no basis for overheated speculation of the kind provided by Eliphas Levi (l'abbé Constant).[86] It is interesting to note that the intellectual climate of the court of the Habsburgs in Prague and Vienna was far more steeped in superstition and the occult than would have been possible in Paris.[87]

Here lies the first point to be made in an assessment of Richelieu's career as a patron of the arts; his activity was committed to clearly defined, practical goals, with little time for the gratuitous speculation of a *curieux*. Related to this is the second general point, that his personal survival and the success of his political objectives were inextricably related; he could not attain his goals if he fell, and if he did not attain his goals he would certainly fall. As a consequence of this, his interest in the arts was used for the promotion of personal, dynastic, and national interests; in this regard he followed the example of Marie de' Medici and opened the way for Colbert and Louis XIV (it was Colbert who bought the collections of the duke of Richelieu in 1665 for the *Cabinet du roi*).[88] The subjugation of all else to central political concerns in which his own interests were

---

[86] E. Lévi, *Dogme et rituel de la haute magie* (Paris, 1972), 243; also L. Thorndike, *A History of Magic and Experimental Science*, vii and viii. *The Seventeenth Century* (New York, 1958), vii. 300, 304.

[87] R. J. W. Evans, *The Making of the Habsburg Monarchy 1550–1700* (Oxford, 1979), esp. the ch. 'The Compromise with Educated Magic'.

[88] Jean-Claude Boyer, 'Les Collections royales', in *Colbert 1619–83* (Paris, 1983), catalogue of tercentenary exhibition, 373.

enmeshed introduced a new order, as unwelcome, alien, and as virulent for his contemporaries, as any ideological heresy of today might appear. If he was cordially detested in his own time and later (derided by Fénelon in his *Dialogue des morts*, reviled by Montesquieu in *L'Esprit des lois*),[89] it was undoubtedly due to the suspicion that the ends and the means had become confused, and that he was the beneficiary in a certain loss of idealism. On the other hand, the form of official art that he created was part of a new, assertive French presence in the world. He accomplished this by working tirelessly and systematically, with vision and ambition, from consolidation of his own position to the expansion of new horizons in the mid-1630s, maintaining a legitimizing continuity from Valois to Medici and Bourbon styles,[90] and finally reaching aspirations to administer the intellectual life of the nation as a whole. His ultimate success is best measured by the fact that the arts policy of contemporary French governments (both left and right) is still marked by the belief that 'la France ne peut être la France sans la grandeur'.[91]

[89] 'Quand cet homme n'aurait pas eu le despotisme dans le coeur, il l'aurait eu dans la tête', Montesquieu, *L'Esprit des lois*, ed. Roger Caillois (Paris, 1951), 388.

[90] It should be pointed out that what has become known as the *style Louis XIII* actually predates the accelerating growth of official art introduced by Richelieu.

[91] C. De Gaulle, *Mémoire de Guerre: L'Appel, 1940–42* (Paris, 1945), 1.

8

RICHELIEU, EDUCATION, AND THE STATE

LAURENCE BROCKLISS

I

On his death Richelieu bequeathed an unspecified, but modest portion of his fortune to endow a new *collège de plein exercice* at the University of Paris.[1] On first sight the cardinal's limited generosity seems scarcely worthy of comment, all the more since the mooted college was never established.[2] After all, it had long been common for princes and prelates to curry favour with posterity and appease the wrath of their God by leaving money for educational purposes. Arguably, Richelieu was merely acting within a hallowed tradition. Indeed, the cardinal had little choice in the matter for the bequest was not so much a gift as a debt repaid. In the late 1620s another Parisian *collège de plein exercice*, the Collège de Calvi, had been pulled down in order to enlarge the Sorbonne and construct the magnificent college chapel in which the cardinal intended to deposit his bones.

Yet it would be a mistake to dismiss the cardinal's donation as a simple act of piety or a publicity stunt. Rather, it was a reflection of his long-standing interest in the extent and nature of the educational provision for the social and professional élite. Throughout his public career Richelieu was an educational reformer. For various reasons he was dissatisfied with the state of élite education and in a number of memoranda and preambles to personal educational initiatives he set out an alternative vision. Admittedly, like many of his reforms, his educational policy was consistently espoused rather than vigorously

I would like to thank Dr Ann Blair of Harvard University for verifying certain refs. below to MSS in Parisian libraries.

[1] The bequest was part of a larger, unfinished building programme entrusted to his niece; the college was to be called the Collège de Richelieu: see BN MS Fr. 20653, fo. 206ᵛ.

[2] Eventually Richelieu's executors gave 100,000 *livres* from the estate to repair another Parisian *collège de plein exercice*, the Collège du Plessis, which had fallen on hard times: see AN M 182, esp. nos. 22 and 42; AUP 115, fos. 1–5 (minute-book concerning the affairs of the college 1643–8). As the abbot of Marmoutiers, Richelieu had been the college's visitor.

pursued. Education, even more than finance and trade, played second fiddle to foreign affairs. Nevertheless, it is strange that the cardinal's educational interests are scarcely mentioned by his biographers and that in recent years (with so much interest in the educational history of early modern France) there has been only one, very inadequate, account of his aims.[3]

The system of élite education with which Richelieu found fault was built around two institutions: the college and the university. The college, a new institution of the sixteenth century, primarily provided a generalist education in the civilization of classical antiquity, which the Renaissance humanists believed should be the common cultural cement of the social and professional élite.[4] Smaller colleges offered courses only in the Latin and Greek humanities, but the *collèges de plein exercice* (some hundred in number by the mid-seventeenth century) also gave instruction in Aristotelian philosophy, traditionally a university subject. At first, the colleges had been run by seculars but by the 1620s many were in the hands of the regular orders, especially the Jesuits. The university, in contrast, trained entrants to the liberal professions. This was done in the three 'higher' faculties of theology, law, and medicine, while the faculty of arts, no longer a teaching faculty, assayed the linguistic and philosophical competence of graduates from the *collèges de plein exercice* who needed an MA to take a degree in theology or medicine. There were sixteen universities in France during Richelieu's ministry, but of the three professional sciences only law was taught everywhere.[5]

Richelieu objected to this system in the first place on the grounds that it condemned large numbers of the *noblesse d'épée* to the educational wilderness. Despite the humanist rhetoric, the cardinal believed that the colleges of the early seventeenth century were largely filled with would-be entrants to the liberal professions. Few nobles bound for a career of arms or a life of leisure graced their portals, while those that did so left before the philosophy class. Whether the

---

[3] R. Mousnier, 'Richelieu et l'enseignement: Le Cardinal, précurseur de la Convention', in Mousnier (ed.), *Richelieu et la culture* (Paris, 1987), 17–28.

[4] On the humanist campaign in favour of a classical education, see J. Hexter, 'The Education of the Aristocracy in the Renaissance', in id., *Reappraisals in History* (London, 1961), ch. 4. Typical of the genre was Erasmus, *Declamatio de pueris statim ac liberaliter instituendis* (1529), ed. and trans. J. C. Margolin (Travaux d'humanisme et Renaissance 77; Geneva, 1966), 406–58.

[5] L. W. B. Brockliss, *French Higher Education in the Seventeenth and Eighteenth Centuries: A Cultural History* (Oxford, 1987), esp. 13–27, 478; G. Huppert, *Public Schools in Renaissance France* (Chicago, 1984); R. Chartier, M.-M. Compère, and D. Julia, *L'Éducation en France du XVIe au XVIIIe siècle* (Paris, 1976), chs. 5–6.

cardinal was correct in this contention is difficult to say. Contemporaries frequently bemoaned the ignorance of the *épée* but no detailed study has yet been effected of the noble component of college attendance to test the assertion.[6] Whatever the truth of the matter, Richelieu's actions as minister make it clear that he found the *épée*'s ignorance (real or imaginary) disquieting and that he was anxious to end its cultural isolation.

Secondly, the cardinal felt that the colleges processed too many students, especially from the lower orders. While their doors were closed to most members of the *épée*, they were opened wide to the sons of artisans and *laboureurs*. Here Richelieu was on firmer ground. Modern research has demonstrated that in the 1620s the sixty-three Jesuit colleges contained some 40,000 students. At the same date the colleges of Oxford and Cambridge which offered a similar education contained only 2,000–3,000. Admittedly the comparison is flawed in that the English colleges did not teach classics from scratch but received students who had already studied the elements of Latin and Greek in the grammar schools. Nevertheless the comparison is not without point. Moreover, many students at the Jesuit colleges were from humble backgrounds: some 20,000–25,000 were the sons of artisans, merchants, or *laboureurs*.[7]

Thirdly, Richelieu was concerned about the faculty of theology at Paris. The cardinal seems to have felt that the other higher faculties at Paris and elsewhere functioned satisfactorily for they were never the subject of public comment. Presumably he shared in the dismay evinced in the Code Michaud at the general level of corruption surrounding appointments and the awarding of degrees, but there is no evidence that he made this the subject of a personal crusade.[8] The Paris faculty of theology, however, was different. In Richelieu's eyes a university was not a forum for the discussion and development of

[6] As an undifferentiated group nobles formed about 10% of college intake in the 17th cent. but it is impossible to know what proportion was comprised of younger sons or *robins* bound for the church or bar. See F. de Dainville, 'Collèges et fréquentation scolaire au dix-septième siècle', *Population*, 12 (1957), 470; and id., 'Effectifs des collèges et scolarité aux dix-septième et dix-huitième siècles dans le nord-est de la France', *Population*, 10 (1955), 476–9. For examples of nobles who did attend college, see M. Motley, *Becoming a French Aristocrat: The Education of the Court Nobility 1580–1715* (Princeton, NJ, 1990), 97–122.

[7] Dainville, 'Collèges et fréquentation scolaire', 467–73.

[8] Isambert, xvi. 253–8 (arts. 43–51). One reform that Richelieu does seem to have been interested in was the introduction of civil-law teaching into the Univ. of Paris on the grounds that its knowledge was essential for the study of canon law. Civil law had not been taught at Paris since the 12th cent. See BN MS Fr. 18938, fos. 265–6, anon. memo. in favour of the reform which cites Richelieu as its moving spirit. The cardinal also fostered botanical studies by supporting the establishment of the Jardin du roi in Paris, in 1635: see Rio C. Howard, 'Gui de la Brosse: The Founder of the Jardin des Plantes' (Ph.D. thesis; Cornell Univ., 1974), ch. 2.

controversial ideas, but an institution for the dissemination of professional knowledge. As a result, the Paris faculty in which he had been educated was judged inadequate. Unlike the faculties of law and medicine it was not a dedicated agent of professionalization: the education it provided was too unstructured and academic; theological study was not a necessary passport to a successful career in the church; and the faculty was the scene of unseemly and politically unhelpful doctrinal disputes.

II

Richelieu's concern that the *noblesse d'épée* receive an education in the classical humanities and philosophy sprang from his understandable paranoia about political stability. In his opinion, a humanist education was a potent instrument of acculturation. As he declared in the preamble to an educational project of 1636 'l'entretennement et bonne nourriture de la jeunesse' was one of the most important concerns of the ruler. The young were likened to a nursery, 'd'où le corps politique prend incessament sa subsistance et son entretien successif'. Depending upon their instruction they would bear good or bad fruit. A properly inculcated knowledge of letters would produce the ideal, virtuous subject, one who would display until the end of his days 'la crainte de Dieu, l'obéyssance aux princes, la submission aux lois, le respect envers les magistrats, l'amour de la patrie, et la practique des actions vertueuses'. It was thus essential that the *noblesse d'épée*, not just the *robe* and noble churchmen, received a classical education. Indeed, a knowledge of letters was of greater importance for those bound for a career of arms than for any other sections of society: '. . . la corruption des choses excellentes est la pire, et cause de la débauche et dépravation des gentilshommes, faute de nourriture et bonne discipline'. The *épée*'s failure to attend college, the text of the preamble implies, was the root cause of its *frondeur* mentality.[9]

The solution that Richelieu eventually championed to the problem of the purportedly ill-educated *noblesse d'épée* was not based on his own educational odyssey. Although intended originally for a military career, the cardinal himself had been sent at a young age to study the Latin and Greek humanities at the Paris Collège de Navarre. This was the reason why he had been able to make such a rapid career shift when his elder brother had taken the cowl. Richelieu, however,

---

[9] Isambert, xvi. 466–70, 'Règlement du cardinal de Richelieu pour la fondation d'une école militaire à l'usage de la jeune noblesse'.

whatever his views might have been earlier in life, ended his days uninterested in increasing *épée* attendance at the existing *collèges de plein exercice*. We can only speculate that he came to see this as an unrealistic policy, believing (rightly or wrongly) that nothing would induce large numbers of provincial noblemen to immerse their sons for seven or eight years in the study of classical antiquity if there was no immediate and obvious professional and social benefit. Possibly, too, always conscious of the dignity of his caste, he felt uncomfortable with the intermingling of the orders such a policy would have encouraged.[10]

Instead Richelieu promoted the development of an alternative institution: the academy. Specialist academies for training the courtier-soldier were already in existence in the France of Louis XIII. In the course of the second half of the sixteenth century a new concept of the gentleman, based on the *Courtier* of Castiglione, had gradually filtered into France. According to the new ethic, nobles were not supposed to be learned but accomplished in the polite as well as the military arts. To create this paragon of gentility the Italians invented a new institution and in 1594 the first of its kind was founded in Paris by Pluvinel, director of the royal stables (d. 1620). In this academy, for an exorbitant fee, the scions of the great nobility could learn under one roof to dance, sing, play a musical instrument, fence, wield a pike, and above all handle a horse in a decorous fashion. As the stable was inevitably a major outlay of such institutions, they were usually called *académies d'équitation*.[11]

Richelieu himself was no stranger to the new noble ethic and was an accomplished dancer and courtier. It was from Pluvinel's academy that he had been plucked in 1603 for a life in the church. But Richelieu saw in the academy an institutional base for the extension of a humanist education to the *noblesse d'épée*. The academies offered boarding facilities; their clientele was limited to wealthy aristocrats and their provincial clients; and in training young noblemen in a complex of courtly and military arts they were ineluctably teaching a sense of discipline. As such, the academies were obviously an ideal forum for promoting caste consciousness and inculcating civil obedience. All that was required was to transform their curriculum and extend the student's length of stay, at this date often no more than a matter of months.

---

[10] At one stage in his career Richelieu even dreamt of educating noblemen entering the church in a separate institution: see the plan for endowing a college for 400 noble clerics in Avenel, v. 721–3.

[11] The development of this new institution in France is most fully discussed in Motley, *Becoming an Aristocrat*, ch. 3.

The direction in which the cardinal's mind ultimately travelled can be seen in his *projet* of 1636. The purpose of the project was to establish twenty *bourses* (worth in total 22,000 *livres* per annum) in the new Académie royale, an *académie d'équitation* established by the king on Richelieu's encouragement in the 'old' rue du Temple.[12] Richelieu's endowment was intended primarily to allow the sons of poor Catholic nobles a chance to learn how to be gentlemen. Its beneficiaries were to be drawn from the youth 'de maisons nobles, lesquelles incommodées, et par nombre d'enfans, ou [sic] par les despenses excessives, à quoy ils sont obligez par leur qualité, ou par autres accidens de fortune, se trouvent en impuissance de la faire eslever dans les vertueux exercices convenables à leur extraction'. But the *boursiers* were expected to study more than the courtly and martial arts. Besides learning alongside the other *pensionnaires* how to 'monter à cheval, voltiger, faire des armes, les mathématiques, fortification et autres [choses]', the *boursiers* were to be taught a variety of extra-curricular subjects aimed at character-building. The first of these was philosophy. The *boursiers* were to spend two years at the academy, the same length of time as a college course in philosophy, during which they would study the four philosophical sciences: logic, physics, metaphysics, and especially ethics (the science of rational behaviour). The language of instruction would be French, thereby resolving the problem that *boursiers* would not have studied Latin and Greek (at least not extensively). The second extra-curricular subject consisted of two disciplines, history and geography, both taught to a certain extent in the colleges as part of the rhetoric course but never to the depth envisaged by Richelieu. By the end of their stay the *boursiers* were to have studied:

la carte géographique, des notions générales de l'histoire universelle; de l'establissement, déclinaison et changement des empires du monde, transmigrations des peuples, fondemens et ruines des villes, noms, actions et siècles des grands personnages, comme aussi de l'estat des principautez modernes, singulièrement de l'Europe, dont les intérests nous touchent de plus près que leur voisinage; surtout au long ils apprendront l'histoire romaine et françoise.[13]

Richelieu, then, was not advocating that his *boursiers* replicate in the academy the humanities and philosophy course of the college: he was, however, insisting that they took a course in the liberal arts

---

[12] Very little is known about this academy.

[13] Unfortunately, the document gives no indication of the texts that were to be used as the basis of this course. For college history and geography teaching, see Brockliss, *Higher Education*, 151–63.

which would suit their linguistic skills and mental development. It would presumably hold their attention while it worked its stoical message.

The cardinal's conception of a humanist education appropriate to the needs of the *noblesse d'épée* found its complete expression in the foundation of a college and academy at Richelieu in 1640. The preamble of the royal declaration establishing the joint institution began by emphasizing again the importance of instructing the young.[14] It then proceeded to bemoan the fact that so many gentlemen quit their studies 'avant de pouveoir parvenir à la cognoissance des sciences' because of their reluctance to spend many years learning dead languages. This was a grave mistake. Not only was a knowledge of letters one of the ornaments of nobility, but it was also the source 'dont ils pourroient puiser les meilleurs preceptes de l'art militaire et les plus utiles instructions pour composer leurs mœurs'. If only French gentlemen, brave by nature, could cultivate prudence as well as military skill, they would be far better placed to 'servir le public et d'achever les entreprises glorieuses, ausquelles ils sont destinez par leur naissance'.

The way to remedy this problem, went on the *Déclaration*, was to establish an academy where the sciences were taught in French. In contrast to Richelieu's instructions in 1636, however, the study of the sciences was now integrated into a carefully articulated programme of teaching. According to the statutes of 11 September 1640 the academy would consist of six classes, just like a *collège de plein exercice*. Lessons would be held every morning. In the sixth (and lowest) class the curriculum would consist of French grammar, poetry, and rhetoric, and in the fifth map-identification, chronology, genealogy, and history. The student would then commence the study of the sciences: logic and physics in the fourth; the elements and application of geometry, arithmetic, and music in the third; mechanics, optics, astronomy, geography, and gnomonics in the second; and ethics, economics, politics, and metaphysics in the first.[15] Interestingly, the afternoons would be given over to the study of classical languages. Evidently, Richelieu had not abandoned the hope that the nobility could become part of a larger élite founded on a common cultural inheritance. Again the course was divided into six classes. In the first four the students would learn Latin and

---

[14] BN MS Fr. 18828, fos. 439–46, *Déclaration du roy portant establissement d'une académie et collège royal en la ville de Richelieu* (1641).

[15] In contrast to the *collège de plein exercice* philosophy began in the 4th class, not the 2nd. This was because 2 of the final 4 classes were mathematics classes and mathematics was poorly taught in most colleges: see Brockliss, *Higher Education*, 381–90.

Greek grammar and rhetoric, an ambitious programme given the lamentable state of Greek studies in the *collèges de plein exercice*.[16] In the last two the course would consist of comparative linguistics. In the second the student would learn the advantages of the Greek language over all others; in the first the origins of the Greek, Latin, Italian, Spanish, and French languages, and their differences and similarities. The emphasis on Greek presumably reflected the belief of a number of sixteenth-century linguisticians in its close affinity with French. The ancient Greeks were thought to have been a Celtic people.[17]

The foundation at Richelieu was clearly a novelty. Not only was its curriculum different from that of any contemporary college but so too was its ethos. Other colleges were strictly denominational, but the new foundation had an eirenicist tone. The college possessed an almoner and a chapel where mass would be said daily, but the professors, although they had to be Catholics, were forbidden to discuss religion in their courses, especially in philosophy. The institution aimed to rear pupils 'en la crainte de Dieu, en la fidélité, et en l'obéissance qu'ils doivent au Roy'. It was an institution which was intended to integrate as well as educate the noble élite. At the same time, despite the emphasis given to classical studies, the academy was intended to foster a pride in French culture. The absence of any detailed provision for studying other modern languages besides French is particularly notable, given the fact that a knowledge of Italian and Spanish was commonly seen as a genteel accomplishment.[18] Richelieu wanted the *épée* to value their own language above all other vernaculars. It is also instructive that the new institution was to enjoy the same privileges as those accorded the recently founded Académie française 'établie pour la réformation de la langue'.

Like many of Richelieu's reform initiatives, the creation of the academy at Richelieu was the work of a number of people.[19] The possibility of a new type of academy may first have been placed in Richelieu's mind by a proposal that the duc de La Force presented to

---

[16] It proved very difficult to get college students to apply themselves to Greek, given its limited utility in professional life. See Brockliss, *Higher Education*, 113–16.

[17] e.g. J. Picard, *De prisca Celtopaedia* (Paris, 1556).

[18] On the other hand, there is little evidence that modern-language teaching was an automatic part of the curriculum of the *académie d'équitation* at this date. This was a later development. Compare, for instance, the subjects taught at the academy at Aix in 1627 with those offered by a Paris academy in 1678: see AN O^1 915, nos. 34 and 18.

[19] For a history of the institution, see M. Bataillon, 'L'Académie de Richelieu, Indre et Loire', in *Pédagogues et juristes* (Congrès du Centre d'Études Supérieures de la Renaissance de Tours 1960; Paris, 1963), 255–70.

the Assembly of Notables in 1626–7.[20] The actual patent of foundation, on the other hand, was the result of a petition to the king
by the academy's first director, Le Gras, intendant of the queen's
household. The ideological underpinning of the institution was provided by yet another figure, François de Grenaille, who in 1642
published a work which expatiated at length on the virtues of an
educated *épée* and extolled Richelieu's contribution to its realization.[21]
The success of the venture, however, depended on Richelieu's survival. Although some 400 noblemen were reported to be studying at
the academy immediately after it opened, the institution quickly
collapsed on his death.

III

While Richelieu was anxious that the *noblesse d'épée* received a suitable education in the humanities and philosophy, he was reluctant
that the same opportunity be afforded the lower orders. Just as a
poorly educated nobility threatened the stability of the state, so
an overeducated people threatened its prosperity. This conviction,
expressed briefly in the 1625 *Règlement pour toutes les affaires du
royaume*, was clarified in the *Testament politique*. Richelieu recognized
that a knowledge of letters was essential for the republic, but insisted
that a state where everyone was educated would be monstrous (his
word). Once educated, the sons of the poor would desert the productive occupations of their parents for the comfort of office. An
overeducated public would be disobedient, drive out commerce, and
ruin agriculture. France, as a result, would have no soldiers and be
filled with *chicaneurs* who would be the ruin of honest families. For
this reason Richelieu was alarmed by the apparent social 'openness'
of the *collèges de plein exercice*. In his opinion, they were filled with
members of the lower orders attempting to escape their destiny, and
in consequence they were sapping the life-blood of the state.[22]

Richelieu throughout his ministry entertained a simple solution to

---

[20] He called for an academy teaching history and moral philosophy: see Motley, *Becoming an
Aristocrat*, 138.

[21] François de Grenaille, *L'Honneste Garçon, ou l'art de bien élever la noblesse . . .* (Paris,
1642), esp. bk. ii.

[22] Grillon, i. 267; *Test. pol.* 204. Given Richelieu's belief in the moral value of letters it
seems paradoxical that he should equate an overeducated public with disobedience. It seems
likely that he did not mean that members of the lower orders who were educated in the colleges
would become subversives, but rather that they would refuse to pursue the occupation to
which they were born.

the problem of a socially heterogeneous college population: the number of colleges should be drastically reduced. Implicit in this solution
was the belief that the pattern of attendance reflected ease of access.
If the majority of students could not live at home and had to board in
a strange town, the attractions of study for the lower orders would
quickly diminish. In addition, the surviving colleges should be
divided equally between the regular orders and secular masters,
thereby introducing an element of competition which would improve
the quality of teaching.[23] In the 1625 memorandum Richelieu proposed a swingeing educational cut. Henceforth there should be colleges only in twelve designated towns.[24] Each town would have two
colleges, except Paris, which because of its size would have four. The
number of *collèges de plein exercice* would thus be reduced to a
quarter of the existing total. Redundant colleges were to be put to
more profitable use. In the *Testament politique*, on the other hand,
Richelieu was far less draconian. Rather than calling for the abolition
of a large number of colleges (obviously difficult to achieve because
of their corporate status) he contented himself with controlling the
scope of their activities. Only metropolitan towns were to be allowed
to possess *collèges de plein exercice*; colleges in other towns were to be
restricted to three or four classes and to teaching the humanities.
The smaller colleges would have a twofold purpose. On the one
hand, they would provide a humanist education for a broad section
of society: future soldiers and merchants as well as lawyers, doctors,
and clerics. On the other, they would allow parents to learn which
of their children was really suited to a career based on detailed
academic study.

Both observations are intriguing. In the *Testament*, probably composed in the late 1630s, Richelieu seems to hold fast to the sixteenth-
century humanist belief that, initially at any rate, there should be a
common educational experience for all members of the élite, indeed
for the well-to-do generally. This belief, however, would seem to
contradict the apparent thinking behind his promotion of a specific
noble-orientated humanist programme, which came to fruition in the
1640 foundation. One answer to the conundrum would be that
throughout his life Richelieu retained a sentimental attachment to
the traditional humanist viewpoint about the education of the *épée*,
while for all practical purposes his mind had moved by the mid-

[23] In the 1625 *Règlement* Richelieu maintained that many of the professors in the existing
colleges were inadequate.

[24] The towns were Paris, Rouen, Amiens, Troyes, Dijon, Lyons, Toulouse, Bordeaux,
Poitiers, Rennes, La Flèche (privileged as the college there had been founded by Henri IV),
and Pau. A number of university towns were not included in the list.

1630s in a different direction. Another, perhaps more plausible explanation, would be that the sentiment reflected the private opinion of one of his entourage who helped compose the *Testament*. This explanation might also account for the equally puzzling emphasis on the need to test an individual's suitability for a career in the liberal professions, which was scarcely a commonplace educational viewpoint. This was an era where the parental right to decide a child's career was given ideological support by the convenient Plutarchian doctrine that children were empty vessels which could be filled in many ways. Within the constraints of birth it was education, not native talent, which ensured functional capacity. It seems, moreover, an unlikely viewpoint for Richelieu in particular to champion, given his personal history: after all, he was living proof of the adaptability of youth.[25]

None of Richelieu's plans for altering the structure of collegiate education was put into effect. Not only did the number and scope of the colleges remain the same, but their take-over by the regular orders continued apace. Between 1620 and 1640 the number of Jesuit colleges rose from sixty-three to ninety-three and the number held by the Oratory from three to eighteen. By the cardinal's death few secular colleges outside Paris remained and there was little genuine educational competition. In part Richelieu was hamstrung by lack of power. He was not the only figure whose advice the king listened to on educational issues and the Jesuits were well-placed to press their case as one of their order was always the king's confessor.

That Richelieu would have done more had he had the opportunity is evident from the history of his relations with the University of Paris. In the second quarter of the seventeenth century, there were some twelve *collèges de plein exercice* in the capital, one run by the Jesuits and the rest under the protection of the university. The university, as much as Richelieu, disliked the expansion of collegiate provision, for the expansion had had a dramatic effect on the number of students pursuing a course in arts in its colleges. Consequently, as we shall see, the rector had been campaigning since the Estates General of 1614–15 for only colleges attached to a university to be allowed to provide instruction in philosophy.[26] The plight of the Paris colleges was worsened by their financial state. Most were too poor to stipend their professors who relied instead on gratuities from

[25] Of course, it might be argued that Richelieu thereby unconsciously expressed his own unhappiness at being forced to enter the church. Richelieu did express similar sentiments on another occasion. In the plan for a college of noble clerics (see n. 10 above) he specified that students who proved unsuitable should be directed to a life of arms.

[26] See sect. v below.

a dwindling student body, one that declined all the faster since the rival Jesuit college in the capital provided free education. Not surprisingly, friends and critics of the university felt that its education in arts was of an inferior quality.[27]

Ostensibly, there was every reason for Richelieu and the University of Paris to be allies and for the university to have knocked on the cardinal's door whenever its colleges felt threatened by fresh moves of the Jesuits to increase their educational sway. In fact no alliance was forged. Although the university evinced continual concern about the growing Jesuit stranglehold throughout the 1620s and early 1630s, Richelieu was never officially approached for assistance. Instead the university relied on the good offices of the Paris parlement.[28] Indeed, there was no official discussion with the cardinal about the university's plight until 1633 and even then the subject was only broached in the course of negotiations over an entirely separate threat to the university's privileges. As a result, the cardinal was ever only asked to stymie one Jesuit foundation in the provinces: the attempt to establish a college at Senlis in 1638.[29] On this occasion Richelieu eventually promised support but emphasized that success 'would be difficult since [the Jesuits] had already got at the mind of the king'.[30]

The university's failure to involve the cardinal in its fight against the Jesuits and other regular orders can hardly have been due to its ignorance of his views.[31] Rather it reflected the fact that the harmony of interests between the two was apparent rather than real. The

---

[27] e.g. Anon., *Réponse d'un étudiant en l'université de Paris à un sien ami* (1616), pamphlet in BN MS Fr. 15782. For an account of the rewards of teaching in the Paris colleges throughout the ancien régime, see M. Targe, *Professeurs et régents de collège dans l'ancienne université de Paris aux XVIIᵉ et XVIIIᵉ siècles* (Paris, 1902), ch. vii.

[28] A conclusion based primarily on the study of the univ. minute-book (1621–58) and the minute-book of the German Nation (1613–60): see AUP reg. 25–7. The German Nation was one of the four associations of MAs resident in the univ.; membership was determined by geographical origin; members of the German Nation came from the Holy Roman Empire, Switzerland, the British Isles, Scandinavia, and Eastern Europe.

[29] The rectoral assembly decided to approach Richelieu on 4 May: see AUP reg. 26, fo. 254. As we shall see later in this sect., the univ. had already agreed on the same day to accept the cardinal's plans for 3 of its residential colleges; presumably, the assembly hoped for his support as a *quid pro quo*. The assembly found the Jesuits' attempt to establish a college at Senlis particularly galling because of its closeness to the capital. The univ. colleges drew most of their arts students from north of the Loire: see L. W. B. Brockliss, 'Patterns of Attendance at the University of Paris, 1400–1800', *Historical Journal*, 21 (1978), 524–8.

[30] AUP reg. 26, fo. 262, *sub* 2 Oct. 1638. It was reported that the cardinal said '. . . hoc admodum difficile, cum iam invaserint Ingenium Regis; se tamen curaturum, ut hoc fiat secundum Academiam'.

[31] The educational provisions in the 1625 *Règlement* seem to have been immediately known beyond the cardinal's entourage. The Jesuits were certainly informed of Richelieu's ideas: see sect. v below.

university's desire to monopolize philosophy teaching conflicted with Richelieu's belief in educational competition. More importantly, the cardinal wanted to reduce the number of teaching colleges attached to the University of Paris and not just the number of colleges *tout court*. Eleven in his eyes was far too many. In consequence, any move by the university to elicit his help in its quarrel with the Jesuits would have been greeted by the demand that the university put its own house in order.

This was exactly Richelieu's response when the university finally did approach him in 1633 over an attack on the livelihood of its diocesan messengers. The venal office of university messenger was much sought after because it brought the holder the fiscal privileges of a student (including exemption from the *taille*), and the outlay could be recouped by carrying private letters. In late 1632 the rewards of the office were suddenly threatened when Bullion arranged a contract with the financier Le Barbier to sell royal messengerships. These offices had existed sporadically since 1576 but on their individual creation the crown had always been careful to respect the university's rights. Le Barbier, however, was anxious to recoup his investment of one million *livres* and insisted that the university's couriers must compound with him if they wished to continue to carry non-university mail.[32] The university understandably objected to this attack on its privileges and Richelieu was asked to assist. In May 1633 Richelieu agreed to help and in early August the university's rector, Grangier, and censor, Aubert, had an audience with the chief minister who was accompanied by Séguier and Bullion.[33] In May Richelieu had expressed support for the university's suggestion that in future the money obtained from the sale of its messengerships should be used to endow college professors, rather than being distributed among the resident MAs, as was customary.[34] But at the August meeting the cardinal produced a counter-proposal. The rights of the university's messengers would be protected but in return the number of its teaching colleges should be reduced to four. To sweeten the pill the crown would provide the professors with a

[32] I have not seen the contract; the sum is deduced from statements made in various entries in the minute-book of the univ. and the German Nation 1633–6. Louis Le Barbier died in 1641, his business in ruins: see R. J. Bonney, *The King's Debts: Finance and Politics in France 1589–1661* (Oxford, 1981), 141. An account of the trials and tribulations encountered by the univ. messengers in the 17th cent. from the greed of Le Barbier and other financiers is given in BN MS Fr. 21734, fos. 308–12, 'Notes sur les messagers', and BS U9 in-4°, no. 2, list of court rulings on the office (printed).

[33] AUP reg. 25, fo. 250; reg. 26, fos. 191–2.

[34] The messengers were appointed by the nations. This idea was first floated by Aubert in a meeting of the univ. of 30 Oct. 1632: see AUP reg. 26, fo. 181.

permanent stipend, Bullion agreeing that 30,000 *livres* per annum could be put aside from the recently introduced tax on paper. The university's deputies replied by arguing that there was no need to cut the number of university colleges if the provincial colleges were forbidden to teach rhetoric and philosophy. The cardinal, however, continued to insist that its colleges must be reduced to six. When the results of the meeting were debated in the rectoral assembly the discussion was lengthy but without result. The university was impaled on the horns of a dilemma. It neither wanted to annoy the cardinal, nor to close down half of its teaching colleges. Eventually, after several years of inconclusive negotiations, the offer was rejected.[35] All the same Richelieu never abandoned the hope of rationalizing the number of teaching colleges. In April 1641 the faculty of theology contacted the cardinal over a different university matter. In the course of the conversation, its delegates were informed that the government would still provide 12,000 *livres* to fund the professorships if the number of colleges was reduced to six.[36]

Richelieu was just as keen to reduce the number of purely residential colleges attached to the University of Paris. There were some thirty of these which, together with the *collèges de plein exercice*, theoretically provided free board and lodging for some 600 indigent students.[37] Given the cardinal's views about the evils of educating the poor, he can scarcely have viewed such foundations sympathetically. Rather, he seems to have believed that the smaller colleges should either be amalgamated with the *collèges de plein exercice* or given to the new charitable orders of the Counter-Reformation in need of a base.

Thus, in 1638 he engineered the amalgamation of the Collège de Boissy and the Collège de Tournai with his Alma Mater the Collège de Navarre, and located the Missionary priests of Vincent de Paul (one of his clients) in the Collège de Bourgogne. The university was not amused. In mid-March it organized a deputation to Richelieu and the king to thank them for their desire to embellish the Collège de Navarre but to remind them of the value of the residential colleges. These had been founded 'so that diverse nations and provinces would have a secure place to live for their alumni, both students and professors of the noble arts, whence well-trained and furnished with a master's degree they would return to their homeland to be of future use to the church and the state'. The foundations

---

[35] See AUP reg. 26, fos. 204, 263 and 265, *sub* 7 Jan. 1634, 5 Dec. 1635, and 17 July 1636.

[36] AUP reg. 26, fo. 295, *sub* 13 April. The univ. continued to fight for the rights of its messengers and these were finally confirmed by the council in late 1641.

[37] The reality was rather different: see Brockliss, 'Patterns of Attendance', 533–7.

of the three colleges therefore, indeed the foundation of any Parisian college, should not be altered.[38] In this instance, however, the university had to admit defeat. On 4 May 1638 it agreed to sanction the amalgamation of Tournai and Boissy, provided the scholarship endowments were maintained, and accepted the introduction of the Missionary priests to Bourgogne as long as they obeyed the statutes of the university. In the second case, Richelieu had appealed to the university's patriotism. The Collège de Bourgogne was an alien foundation filled with the enemies of France (presumably Franc-Comtois). A change of ownership was a matter of *raison d'état*.[39]

The Collège de Bourgogne, however, was not the only residential college that Richelieu presented to a regular order. Far worse, in the university's eyes, was his gift to the Jesuits of the Collège de Marmoutiers in 1641.[40] The university at once suspected a plot to hand over large parts of its property to its arch-enemy. Well aware that many smaller colleges were ill-governed and the statutes neglected, it quickly moved to prevent the cardinal using this as an excuse to expropriate other foundations. On 27 September 1642 the rector was empowered to carry out a thorough inspection of all the colleges so as to forestall the criticism of 'those who seek to harm the university and who strive with all their might to restrict the number of colleges to four or six'.[41]

Richelieu and the university, therefore, had different conceptions of the way collegiate education should be reformed. On the other hand, the relationship between the two was not always strained. Richelieu could not afford to antagonize the university completely for he often needed its support in minor acts of patronage. On a number of occasions, for instance, he asked the rectoral assembly on behalf of clients if it would waive the conditions usually required to

---

[38] AUP reg. 26, fo. 256, *sub* 16 kal. April: '. . . ut diversa nationes et provincias certa suis alumnis et bonarum artium studiosis atque professoribus haberent domicilia, unde honestis disciplinis imbuti et magisterii gradus adepti ad sua redierent ecclesiae et reipublicae utiles futuri'.

[39] AUP reg. 26, fo. 258. *sub* 27 March; fo. 259, *sub* 4 May.

[40] Marmoutiers was eventually restored to the univ. after Richelieu's death when the parlement of Paris, always its supporter, once more came into its own: see AUP regs. 25 and 26, *sub annis* 1641–4, *passim*. As the abbot of Marmoutiers, Richelieu was the college visitor (see above, n. 1). The Jesuits claimed to need more space and continually attempted to take over a univ. residential college. Their move against the Collège du Mans in the early 1630s may have been frustrated with the cardinal's support: see BS U 87 in-12°, *Cenomanica*, anon. oration given on the first day of term, Oct. 1632.

[41] AUP reg. 26, fo. 302. 'Censuerunt proceres Academiae lustranda esse propediem accurate collegia ex academiae statutis et curiae decretis [reference esp. to 1601 *arrêt* of the Paris parlement]; ne sit, quod conquerantur, qui eidem Academiae perniciem moliuntur. Cum pro virili conantur omnia et singula collegia ad 4 aut 6 restringere.'

supplicate for an MA.[42] The cardinal also knew how to flatter the university when one of its number attempted to curry favour by dedicating their theses to the chief minister. When the rector did this in 1639, Richelieu's response, recorded in the university minutes was short but sweet: 'I am not the man whom you and other well-wishers pretend, nor the man my enemies claim. But whatever I may be, I am always a patron of letters. Rest assured that I will be pleased to be at your disputation in spirit if not in body, weighed down as I am by the cares of state.'[43]

IV

Richelieu's interest in the education of the *noblesse d'épée* and the size and social character of the college population sprang from his larger concern for the good of the kingdom (as he understood it). For the state to flourish, it was necessary that the social élite as a whole should receive an education in the humanities and philosophy appropriate to its needs, while the access of the lower orders to such an education had to be strictly curtailed. In contrast, Richelieu's concern about the role of the Paris faculty of theology primarily, although not exclusively, reflected his commitment to the Counter-Reformation. This was a commitment in evidence even before he entered his diocese. The fact that he decided to prepare himself for his trust by studying theology at Paris and taking a degree (albeit only a bachelor's degree) marked out the young Armand-Jean du Plessis as peculiar.[44] Only a small minority of bishops in post in the first decade of the seventeenth century had had a rigorous theological training; most, if they had trained at all, had studied canon law.[45] Richelieu, however, represented the new world of the Council of Trent in which theology was the queen of the sciences in fact as well as theory and where a theologically literate hierarchy was seen as the key to the reduction of Protestantism. For Richelieu the cardinal, the

---

[42] For the first time on 17 Dec. 1629; earlier, on 27 Oct. 1629, the university had waived its regulations on behalf of a client of Gabriel Florand, Richelieu's *prévôt*. see AUP reg. 26, *sub datis*.

[43] AUP reg. 26, fos. 278–9, *sub* 12 Dec., letter transcribed in the univ. minute-book. 'Non is sum, quem tu et benevoli me praedicant, aut quem invidi dicunt, sed qualiscunque sim, semper ero fautor literarum; vestris disputationibus si non corpore propter negotia quibus obruor, saltem animo lubens adero.'

[44] Richelieu became a bachelor of theology on 30 Oct. 1607: for a correct account of Richelieu's studies, see J. Bergin, *The Rise of Richelieu* (New Haven, Conn., 1991), ch. 2.

[45] Of the 108 bishops in office in 1614, only 11% had a theology degree; 27% had a law degree: see J. M. Hayden, 'The Social Origins of the French Episcopacy at the Beginning of the Seventeenth Century', *French Historical Studies*, 10 (1977), 33.

chief theological faculty of France, indeed of Catholic Europe, was a key institution in the campaign to revitalize the church.

Admittedly, Richelieu has left no policy statements about his anxieties concerning the Paris faculty of theology. Nevertheless, as his relationship with the faculty was far closer than that with any other educational institution, his policy in this regard is easy to reconstruct. This closeness sprang not only from the fact that Richelieu was a churchman concerned with the state of theological studies, but also from the fact that this was the one important educational institution over which he could exercise a degree of direct control. He had no automatic right of access to faculty meetings as he was not a doctor of theology. He was, however, from September 1622 the *proviseur*, or visitor, of the Sorbonne, the élite university theological college, whose fellows were all theology graduates and within whose walls many faculty lectures and *actes* took place.[46]

As a Counter-Reformation bishop Richelieu found the faculty wanting in several respects. In the first place, the teaching was scarcely organized in a professional manner. Traditionally, teaching in the faculty had been left to annually elected professors and bachelors who lectured as part of the requirement for becoming licentiates. The situation had begun to change in the reign of Henri IV with the appointment of permanent royal professors in scholastic theology attached to the Sorbonne and the Collège de Navarre.[47] On the king's death, however, there was still only a handful of stipendiary posts and Richelieu himself must have been chiefly taught by part-time professors. At the same time, the faculty's clientele hardly suggested that the school was functioning as the educational vanguard of the Counter-Reformation. There were about 500 students attending lectures at the Sorbonne in the first decades of the seventeenth century.[48] Very few, however, would have shared Richelieu's pedigree. There was little sign that France was about to be blessed with a new generation of theologically literate bishops and canons.[49] Most Paris theology students were members of the third

---

[46] For the Sorbonne's official invitation, see AN M 74, no. 25, letter 4 Sept.; the election took place on 29 Aug. Richelieu's letter of thanks is publ. in Avenel, vi. 519–20, 14 Sept. 1622. Richelieu had become a fellow of the Sorbonne in 1607: see AN MM 269, fo. 11, college minute-book.

[47] e.g. AN M 74, no. 59, 1597 letters-patent, Sorbonne foundation.

[48] A figure quoted on several occasions in the MS history of the Paris doctor of theology, Edmond Richer: e.g. BN MS Lat. 9947, fo. 177, Richer's speech to the faculty, Sept. 1610.

[49] The higher clergy was under no obligation to study theology. According to Henri IV's comprehensive church edict of 1606, bishops and canons were expected to hold a degree in either theology or canon law: see Isambert, xv. 312 (art. 312).

estate whose sights were set no higher than on gaining a parish cure in a walled town.[50] Admittedly, we know nothing precise about their backgrounds but even a cursory survey of the lists of those who became licentiates or doctors suggests that the large majority were *roturiers*. Not suprisingly, only two or three faculty doctors in the early seventeenth century ever became bishops, most notably Harlay of Champvallon, abbot of Saint-Victor and archbishop of Rouen.[51] Most resident faculty doctors were monks or Paris *curés*.[52]

Above all, the faculty presented an unseemly profile. The premier intellectual jewel in the crown of the French church, it was riven by theological disputes which could only give succour to the church's enemies. In the cardinal's lifetime the field of conflict was ecclesiology. The majority of the doctors were Gallicans who insisted on the primacy of councils above popes, the right of bishops to control the pastoral activities of monks, and the strict separation of church and state. A strong minority, however, especially the doctors who were members of regular orders, espoused an Ultramontane line, if their commitment to the power of the papacy in temporal affairs was understandably never openly expressed.[53] The division, moreover, was one that was hard to keep out of the public domain. From time to time the faculty's bachelors expressed their preference in an intemperate fashion in the printed abstracts of their graduate dissertations. On occasion, too, faculty doctors were known to air their positions in print. But in general most faculty members showed restraint in their personal statements. Graduands in particular had difficulty being provocative because their theses could not be printed until the content had been verified and signed by the syndic.[54] The division chiefly became a matter of public knowledge because the faculty claimed the right to investigate and censure any theological publication by Roman Catholics which one of its number denounced as unorthodox. As a result, each faction continually tried to embar-

---

[50] According to the Concordat of 1516 such cures had to go to graduates in theology or canon law.

[51] Licensed 1608. Unless otherwise stated, biographical details of faculty doctors mentioned in the text can be found in P.-Y. Féret, *La Faculté de théologie de Paris et ses docteurs les plus célèbres: Époque moderne* (7 vols.; Paris, 1900–12), iii.

[52] Some doctors came from quite humble backgrounds. Richer was the son of a *laboureur*. He had hopes of becoming a prebend of Notre-Dame but his patron, Louis Séguier, dean of the chapter, died unexpectedly in 1610. See BN MS Lat. 9948, fos. 129–33.

[53] The Gallicans also tended to be suspicious of new devotions associated with Counter-Reformation spirituality.

[54] For nearly 20 years from 1614 the syndic was the moderate Gallican, Filesac. The syndic's watchdog role was introduced in 1608 as a means of checking the Ultramontane party: see *Histoire du syndicat d'Edmond Richer* (Paris, 1753), 6–8.

rass the other by demanding the condemnation of any work which pushed the Gallican or Ultramontane line beyond acceptable limits.[55]

This unseemly division not only hindered the struggle against Protestantism but also affected the conduct of international relations. Given the faculty's status in the Catholic world its censures automatically carried great moral authority, although in France as elsewhere they had no legal weight. When the faculty moved to condemn a theological work, it was immediately a matter of interest outside the assembly. The papal nuncio in particular intervened from the wings to promote or frustrate the endeavour, and as the nuncio's sympathies could make or mar relations between the crown and Rome, the factional division in the faculty could ultimately jeopardize French foreign policy. In this way Richelieu's concern about the faculty's profile also became a matter of state. Indeed, when analysing Richelieu's response to specific instances of the faculty's ecclesiological wrangling, it is difficult to know which was uppermost in his mind: the good of the church or the good of the kingdom.[56]

Richelieu's desire to make the faculty's teaching more professional is evidenced by his interest in increasing the number of permanent faculty professors. He showed his commitment in this direction as early as 1616 when he encouraged Marie de' Medici to found a new royal chair in the Sorbonne. Significantly, this was a chair in theological polemic to which, to quote the royal letters patent, 'nos sujets puissent avoir recours pour s'instruire particulierement des matières controversées par ceux de la religion P[rétendue] R[éformée] et autres semblables lesquels se sont desnoués deladite Eglise'.[57] Apparently the foundation was entirely on Richelieu's initiative. One of the points that commended the cardinal's election to the Sorbonne in 1622 was that he had acted unsolicited in 1616 'et mesme a nostre desceu'.[58] As cardinal-minister Richelieu did not neglect this early concern. Always anxious to promote educational competition, he founded another chair of theological controversy in 1638, this time attached to the Collège de Navarre, his own Alma Mater and the other theological power-house in the university.[59]

[55] Information relating to most of the works subject to the faculty's censure in the Richelieu era are to be found in BSG MSS 960–1; also AN MM 71.

[56] The best account of the nuncio's activities in favour of the papal dignity is found in P. Blet, *Le Clergé de France et la monarchie 1615–1666* (2 vols.; Rome, 1959).

[57] AN M 74, no. 68, Oct. 1616: the chair was given to Nicolas Ysambert.

[58] AN M 74, no. 25. This letter is the sole source of our knowledge that Richelieu was behind the 1616 *fondation*.

[59] BN MS Lat. 9962, fo. 86. The chair was given to Jacques Perreyet and endowed with 1,000 *livres* p.a. Unlike the Sorbonne, the Collège de Navarre also taught the humanities and

Richelieu also took an interest in the appointment of faculty professors when chairs fell vacant. It was the custom for initial appointments to be made by the founder. After that the chair was in the gift of the college to which it was attached. As *proviseur* of the Sorbonne Richelieu had the right to vote in professorial elections and he used it. When Philippe de Gamaches, one of the two royal professors of theology at the Sorbonne appointed by the king in 1597, died in 1625, Richelieu insisted that the election of a successor be delayed until he could be present. Writing from Courances on 26 July 1625 he joined the Sorbonne in mourning the death of such a great man. At the same time he urged the fellowship to look to the future and search for a worthy replacement among the candidates emerging from the theological schools. 'This is a weighty affair, one not to be handled lightly, and the importance of the matter, the dignity of the society, and the consideration due my office persuade me that I should be present.' Richelieu presumably played an important part in the subsequent election for the choice fell on Jacques Lescot, later his confessor and bishop of Chartres.[60]

Richelieu's concern that the upper clergy become theologically literate can be deduced from the amount of money he invested in renovating the Sorbonne. The cardinal seems to have planned to rebuild the college from the moment he became *proviseur*. He and Le Mercier worked on the plans in secret and their scheme was apparently placed before the society in June 1626 without warning. The building programme was begun immediately and was still incomplete on his death. By then the cardinal had spent about one million *livres* on the project and another half a million was needed to finish the job. Several historians have discussed the undertaking, so no further details need be given here.[61] What does require analysis is the intention that lay behind such munificence. On one level, Richelieu was image-building. As with all the other monuments he patronized, he was writing his epitaph in stone. Richelieu was ensur-

---

philosophy. Before 1638 there was no 'community' of theologians at Navarre and it was in the hope of creating such a fellowship that Richelieu sponsored the union with Boncourt and Tournai. See J. Launoy, *Academia Parisiensis illustrata, quatuor partibus divisa. Iᵃ contient quae ab annis 1304 ad anuum 1640 in Regio Navarrae Gymnasio gesta sunt* ... (2 vols.; Paris, 1682), ii. 1067–9. There is also an undated *règlement* for such a society in Avenel, iv. 76–8.

[60] Grillon, i. 194–5. 'Res gravis nec leviter pertractanda, cui, ut intersim ego, et rei pondus, et societatis dignitas, et officii mei ratio suadent.' Lescot became a fellow of the Sorbonne in 1620.

[61] See Claude Mignot, 'La Chapelle et la maison de la Sorbonne', in A. Tuilier (ed.), *Richelieu et le monde de l'esprit* (Paris, 1985), 87–93; R. Pillorget, 'Richelieu, rénovateur de la Sorbonne', in Mousnier (ed.), *Richelieu et la culture*, 43–54; L. Batiffol, *Autour de Richelieu* (Paris, 1937), 95–141.

ing that, ever after, his own name and the name of his family would be associated with the patronage of letters and support of the Catholic Church. However, the project had arguably a deeper significance. The renovation of the Sorbonne was the most important of the cardinal's building schemes in his own eyes. Significantly, he seems to have conceived the project *before* he returned to the government and thus at a time when he could not possibly have anticipated the immense resources which would soon be at his disposal. More importantly, the Sorbonne was entrusted with his bones. Great men in the seventeenth century did not distribute their mortal remains haphazardly. When Henri IV gave his heart to the Jesuits of La Flèche he was making a statement; so too was Richelieu when he arranged for his body to be interred in the college chapel.

Richelieu, it may be supposed, intended through the renovation of the Sorbonne to raise the social status of theological studies. While the Sorbonne remained decrepit and Spartan, it was scarcely surprising that the faculty lecture halls were attended only by the aspiring sons of the middling sort. Richelieu aimed to turn the Sorbonne into an educational show-place, an ecclesiastical palace fit to receive the sons of the nobility.[62] At the same time, through bequeathing the society his ashes, he bestowed on its walls in perpetuity the aura of his ecclesiastical and secular dignity. Richelieu's actions are those of a man who realized that royal edicts change nothing on their own. Theological studies had to be made socially acceptable and this could be done only by the faculty shedding its hair-shirt image.[63]

Admittedly, this reading of the cardinal's actions may be disputed. When we turn to look at Richelieu's involvement in the faculty's internal disputes, on the other hand, the facts speak for themselves. His continual interventions to quieten discord can only be the actions of a man who found its divisions unseemly and troublesome. Richelieu himself was a moderate Gallican. While abhorring papal claims to intervene in secular affairs in France and steadfastly upholding the dignity of the episcopate, he nevertheless recognized the peculiar position of the papacy as head of the Church. He was also

---

[62] Richelieu certainly made the Sorbonne visible. On 30 June 1628 the fellows wrote to the cardinal saying that the recently completed Great Hall (the first part of the building programme) had made the college a tourist attraction. See Grillon, iii. 363–4.

[63] Richelieu was not just interested in the education of the higher clergy but wanted parish priests to receive an appropriate training too. At a time when, despite the wishes of the Council of Trent, seminaries were still few and far between in France, he called for their establishment in every diocese. See the 1625 *Règlement*: Grillon, i. 254. He also supported the endeavours of others to establish seminaries by giving money to this end to Vincent de Paul, Bourdoise, Jean Eudes and Olier: see Batiffol, *Autour de Richelieu*, 113.

aware that a general council had never ruled on the question of
the papal power in the temporal realm, so that supporters of Ultra-
montanism could not justly be accused of heresy. The cardinal, then,
would not have appreciated the hard-line conciliarism of Bossuet's
Exposition de la foi.[64] Ideally, Richelieu would have liked the faculty
to have rallied behind his own position, but he evidently realized,
both as a theologian and a politician, that unanimity was unattain-
able. For the very reason that, within limits, ecclesiology was a
recognized area for theological debate, it was difficult to command
obedience. As a result, Richelieu's interventions in faculty affairs
were aimed at damage limitation rather than the imposition of a
particular party line. He was concerned chiefly to lower the level
of animosity within the faculty and ensure that no one promoted
doctrines that were definitely contrary to the teaching of the Church.
The cardinal had no time for the radical ecclesiology of the Gallican
Edmond Richer whose *De Ecclesiastica et Politica Potestate* (1611)
had posited that, just as the pope was subject to the episcopate, so
bishops should be subject to their clergy. Richer was called on to
recant and in 1629, shortly before his death, he signed a deposition
before Richelieu, tempering his views.[65]

Richelieu's most forceful move to contain faculty strife was to
establish an alternative system of censorship whereby the judgements
of the faculty were potentially devalued in the outside world. From
1628 there existed a committee of royal censors of theological books
whose imprimatur had first to be sought before a work could be
published in France. The committee proved short-lived but in the
1630s Séguier used the powers granted the chancellor under the
Code Michaud to appoint *ad hoc* censors who served the same
purpose.[66] The faculty's traditional right to censure books, however,
was never questioned. Richelieu must have sensed that such a move

[64] Richelieu may well have agreed with Cardinal Du Perron that aristocracy in the church
led to aristocracy in the state. The best source for Richelieu's ecclesiology is his *Mémoires*
where he sets out his position clearly in discussing the various moments of tension between
church and state in the 1610s and 1620s. For Bossuet's views, see A. Martimort, *Le
Gallicanisme de Bossuet* (Paris, 1953).

[65] For Richer's recantation, see BN MS Fr. 15734, fo. 27, 7 Dec. 1629. Richelieu was
particularly pleased by Richer's recantation, for he seems to have believed that the French
Church was threatened with schism: see *Mémoires* SHF x. 420–7. Richer, *Histoire du syndicat*,
89–104, says Richelieu attended the special council called by Du Perron in Mar. 1612 to
censure his book.

[66] H.-J. Martin, *Livres, pouvoirs et société à Paris au XVIIᵉ siècle: 1598–1701* (2 vols.; Paris,
1969), ii, ch. 6. An attempt seems to have been made to establish the committee first of all in
late 1626: see BN MS Fr. 18827, fo. 300, from a memorandum entitled 'Esclaircissement des
differends meus en la Faculté de Théologie de l'université de Paris touchant le nombre de
Bacheliers que les quatre ordres de Mendiants peuvent mettre en chaque licence . . .'.

would have produced unnecessary conflict. The faculty was angered enough by the way some of their number were being used as official government censors. Moreover, Richelieu appreciated the value of the faculty's condemnation in the wider world. He was quite willing to encourage the faculty to censure works that he himself found distasteful, and, for instance, was behind the faculty's attack on the Oratorian Séguenot's, *De la sainte virginité* in 1638. This was a work that emphasized that penitents must be contrite not attrite if priestly absolution was to have any effect, a doctrine which Richelieu loathed.[67]

Richelieu's usual method of proceeding was to send word to the faculty of his displeasure in the hope that a provocative censure or thesis would be withdrawn. In the first years of his ministry, however, he lacked the moral authority that he later gained and he was not always obeyed. On one occasion, in 1626–7, the faction-fighting got out of hand and Richelieu had to resort to the *conseil d'état* to bring the unruly flock to heal. The dispute arose over the censure of Santarelli,[68] an Italian Jesuit who had published a book extolling the papal power over temporals in terms redolent of Boniface VIII, and who regarded kings as papal vassals.[69] The Gallican faction in the faculty was appalled when the book came to its attention and immediately pushed for its censure. On 1 April 1626 the work was duly condemned but only by a majority of thirty-seven to twelve. A minority headed by the professors Ysambert and Duval (always on the side of the Ultramontanes) agreed that the doctrine was abhorrent but declared that the faculty should withhold its censure until the government had been consulted. Three days later the censure was put to the faculty again and this time a hard core of

---

[67] For the text of the censure, see BSG MS 960, fos. 151–8. Séguenot maintained that sinners should only be absolved if the confessor was convinced that they abhorred their sin out of a perfect love of God's goodness, rather than from a simple fear of His justice. In the first case they were contrite; in the second only attrite. Opponents of the doctrine of contrition claimed that priestly absolution and penance were thereby made pointless, for the sacrament was intended to be the occasion when God took pity on the fearful sinner and gave him the divine grace that he needed to hate his sin out of pure love for his maker. Richelieu's penitential views are outlined in his *Instruction de la chrestien* (1619). It was for supporting Séguenot that Saint-Cyran was placed in the Bastille.

[68] The best secondary account of the Santarelli affair is V. Martin, *Le Gallicanisme politique et le clergé de France* (Paris, 1929), 163–244; documents in Charles Du Plessis d'Argentré, *Collectio judiciarum de novis erroribus* . . . (3 vols.; Paris, 1728–36), ii. 205–56; AN M 71, nos. 57–75; for the Jesuit viewpoint, see *Mémoires du père Garasse* . . . , ed. C. Nisard (Paris, 1860), 180 ff.

[69] Antonio Santarelli, *Tractatus de haeresi* . . . (Rome, 1625). Santarelli (1569–1649) espoused an extremely uncommon position in the early 17th cent.: the usual Ultramontane view was Bellarmine's that the pope had the power to intervene occasionally in the secular realm but that normally kings were independent princes.

opponents voted against. Duval accepted that Santarelli's views on papal power were impolitic but denied that they were contrary to the Word of God as the censure proposed. The opposition, however, could now only muster fifteen votes, for many regular clergy were absent from Paris preaching Lenten sermons. The censure was therefore accepted and recorded.

Richelieu and the government did not take kindly to the Gallicans' behaviour in defence of the king's inviolability. The cardinal had already forced the Paris Jesuits to sign a disavowal of Santarelli in mid-March after the book had been burnt by the parlement and he did not want the society to be humiliated further when the government was at a delicate stage in its Valtelline policy. Moreover, he feared political unrest if the persecution continued and the papacy reacted.[70] As a result, on 3 May and 18 July the crown ordered that all discussion over the censure should cease and that the offending passages of the book (chapters 30–1) should be referred to the *conseil d'état* for examination. However, the majority in the faculty ignored the request, secure in the knowledge of the parlement's support, and by the end of the year the Gallicans had involved the university in the quarrel. In October the university demanded that the censure should be read publicly every year.[71] The Ultramontanes, not surprisingly, did not take their defeat lightly. In late November a Dominican called Testefort tried to sustain a thesis arguing that the papal *Decretals*, including the *Liber sextus* of Boniface VIII, were the Word of God. As this implied that papal pronouncements could not be revised by a general council and as the *Liber sextus* had never been accepted as law in France, the Gallicans in the university and the Paris parlement were incensed. Testefort was expelled from the university and the rectoral assembly ordered that the denuciation of his views should also be read publicly each year.[72]

At this point Richelieu lost patience. Political worries aside, the cardinal disliked the unequivocal line of the original censure which labelled Santarelli a heretic. On 13 or 14 December the university was ordered by an *arrêt* of the *conseil* not to meddle in ecclesiastical affairs, and on 2 January Richelieu organized a *coup* in the faculty. The bishop of Nantes (Cospeau, the cardinal's former theology tutor) stood up at the faculty meeting saying that he had orders from the

---

[70] Grillon, i. 314–15: letters to Bouthillier (Apr. 1626) and Marillac (undated). See also Richelieu's account of his policy in his *Mémoires* SHF v. 242–7.

[71] AUP reg. 26, *sub dato*.

[72] AUP reg. 26, *sub* 3 non. Dec.; AN MM 71, theses of Testefort, plus marginal comment (no number).

king to move that the censure of Santarelli be rescinded. The faculty
was duly cowed and the motion carried: the Ultramontane vote rose
from fifteen to fifty-seven.[73] On 13 January the king (presumably
on Richelieu's prompting) wrote the faculty a propitiatory letter,
explaining his actions. He thanked the bishop of Nantes for obeying
the royal will and expressed his gratification at the faculty's loyalty.
All further discussion of Santarelli was forbidden until further
notice.[74] In early February Richelieu appeared before the parlement
of Paris and urged the *conseillers* to trust the king's judgement in
what, he declared, was a matter of *raison d'état*.[75]

After 1630 the cardinal usually got his way by less drastic means.
On occasion, however, he still had to threaten and cajole and the
faculty continued to cause him anxiety until he died. Even in the last
years of his life he had to diffuse ecclesiological bickering which
threatened to spill over into the public domain. A case in point is the
well-documented Constantin affair. On 16 June 1640 Robert Constantin sustained a Gallican doctoral thesis which maintained *inter
alia* that the donation of Constantine *might* be a forgery. Ultramontane
attempts to have the theses condemned were met by a strategic
appeal to Chancellor Séguier, who gave his support to Constantin.
The quarrel within the faculty was on the point of flaring up into
a major clash between church and state when Richelieu (initially
absent from Paris) intervened to pour oil on troubled waters. He
ordered Constantin, who described himself as the cardinal's client, to
produce a written explanation of certain 'ambiguous' passages in his
theses that might seem derogatory to papal authority. This done to
his satisfaction, he ordered the Ultramontanes on 12 July to cease
harassing the new doctor. Thereby, although obedience was not
instantaneous (Lescot had to be used to enforce Richelieu's wishes),
the ground was laid for a satisfactory solution to the crisis which left
honours even.[76]

---

[73] Richelieu's account of the faculty meeting of 2 Jan. can be found in *Mémoires* SHF vii.
10–15. He claims that the decision was taken on a free vote.

[74] AN MM 71, no. 65 (ii): letter 13 Jan. 1627. The censure was struck out but the decision
was not confirmed at the next faculty meeting as constitutionally should have happened. The
Gallicans later in 1627 tried to get Testefort declared insane (see MM 71, no. 73).

[75] Du Plessis d'Argentré, *Collectio judicarum*, ii, *sub mense*. On this occasion, Richelieu
purportedly said: 'Je dirai encore, et il est vrai, que le mécontentement que Sa Sainteté a eû sur
ce sujet [Santarelli] depuis un an, ont fait que l'exécution de la Paix de la Valtelline, qui coûte
tous les mois six ou sept cent mille francs, ne s'est point faite jusqu'à présent.'

[76] BSG MS 960, fos. 172–82; for the printed thesis abstract, see fo. 172; for Richelieu's
letter to the faculty (signed and appended by the cardinal), see fos. 180–1. Nothing is known
about Constantin except he came from Angers and was a high-flyer. He had come 5th in the
license of 1640, and higher places than this were always given to the socially prestigious.

V

In the previous sections it has been demonstrated that Richelieu believed that the existing state of élite education was in crucial respects unsatisfactory. By going beyond the 1625 *Règlement* and the *Testament politique* and examining the cardinal's relationship with the University of Paris and its faculty of theology in particular, it has been possible for the first time to construct a detailed account of Richelieu's educational policies. As was shown above, these policies were not always governed by secular concerns, if *raison d'état* had a habit of continually intruding on his interest in church reform. In this concluding section, however, the emphasis will be placed entirely on Richelieu the secular statesman. Its purpose is to see to what extent Richelieu's analysis of the inadequacies of the system, and the strategies that he adopted to overcome them, fits into the long-term history of the crown's educational policy in the early modern period. In this wider context, should Richelieu be viewed as a conservative or a radical?[77]

Richelieu's aim as chief minister to stop the Paris faculty of theology undermining the crown's authority at home and abroad was certainly not novel. Throughout the sixteenth and early seventeenth centuries the French monarchy had understood the importance of gaining at least the faculty's tacit support for its largely self-centred religious and foreign policy. The faculty's influence in the outside world was too great for the crown to relish the prospect of conflict. Richelieu was merely more successful than earlier ministers in keeping the faculty under relative control. From the conclusion of the Concordat in 1516 the Paris theologians had been a continual thorn in the crown's flesh. The relationship between the two reached its nadir in 1589 when the doctors completely independent of the papacy declared Henry III an ungodly tyrant and henceforth deposed.[78] Although relations improved considerably with the defeat of the League, it was only after 1630 that the faculty was finally tamed. Admittedly, Richelieu's task was eased by the death of the most vocal and prickly faculty members—notably Richer in 1631 and Duval in 1638.[79] Nevertheless, the fact that the cardinal eventu-

---

[77] The educational policy of the early modern French state has never been properly studied. For a short overview, see H. A. Lloyd, *The State and Education: University Reform in Early-Modern France* (Inaugural lecture; Hull, 1987).

[78] Brockliss, *Higher Education*, 299; the fullest account of the faculty in the 16th cent. is Féret, *La Faculté de théologie*, i.

[79] Richer had an extremely elevated, 'Protestant' vision of the faculty's international role. He wanted the universities to replace the general council as the arbiter of Catholic doctrine: see his MS history, BN MS Lat. 9948, fos. 25–36.

ally managed to bring the lid firmly down on the hitherto public quarrels which had threatened to discomfort his diplomacy in the early years of his ministry is a tribute to his masterly managerial skills. Moreover, his achievement was permanent. The Jansenist movement which developed in the years after Richelieu's death was to prove a lasting headache for the ministers of Louis XIV. The Paris faculty, however, gave little cause for concern, for the hard-line Jansenists in its midst, led by Antoine Arnauld, were expelled in 1656.[80] The faculty became a nuisance to the crown again after Louis's death, over the Bull *Unigenitus*, but only temporarily. Brought to heel by another cardinal, Fleury, the faculty throughout the eighteenth century was a pillar of the establishment.[81]

Similarly, Richelieu's belief in the important contribution that institutionalized education could make to political and social stability was already current in governmental circles long before he arrived at the helm. Henri IV in particular had been an enthusiastic believer in the regenerative powers of instruction. One of his first acts as king, after the submission of the capital in 1594, was to establish a commission headed by Chancellor Hurault to look into the state of the University of Paris. According to the preamble of the letters-patent, the commission's justification lay in the value of education to the state.

Entre les premieres et principales actions qui font fleurir et prosperer les royaumes et les republiques est la bonne et fidele instruction de la jeunesse tant en la crainte et cognoissance de Dieu qu'en bonnes mœurs et instruction aux bonnes lois ou gist le seminaire des hommes virtueux, qui par ceste premiere institution se rendent dignes et loyaux administrateurs des Republiques et Royaulmes: comme au contraire cessant ceste bonne institution ne peut un état se maintenir en son entier et splendeur, mais par la barberie et ignorance tourne en ruyne et dissipation.[82]

The continuation of the war with Spain prevented the commission from beginning its task, but with peace in 1598 the investigation was resumed by the Paris parlement. The result was the promulgation of a new set of statutes for the four faculties of the university in 1601.[83] This was a significant moment in the history of French education for it was the first time that a thorough reform of the statutes of a

---

[80] The best account of French Jansenism in this period is Antoine Adam, *Du mysticisme à la révolte: Les Jansénistes du XVIIe siècle* (Paris, 1968).

[81] Féret, *La Faculté de théologie*, iv–v; Brockliss, *Higher Education*, 272–6.

[82] BN MS Fr. 15518, fos. 240–1, 'au camp devant Paris 26 July 1594'.

[83] *Liber supplex* of the univ. to the parlement 1600, to be found in a collection of printed speeches in BS U 20 in-4°. For the statutes, see *Réformation de l'université de Paris* (Paris, 1601), esp. De Thou's preamble, 6–12.

French university had been undertaken by a secular authority.[84] However, the reform was only one of many royal initiatives during the reign aimed at improving the provision of élite education.[85] The most spectacular was the decision to recall the Jesuits, exiled from most of France in 1594 for their association with regicide. Henri IV was under great pressure from the papacy to recall the society but he also grasped the Jesuits' popularity and value as educators. In December 1603 the Jesuits were readmitted to the kingdom and immediately given the right to reopen most of their former colleges. When the parlement of Paris objected to the Jesuits' return the king emphasized their utility: 'Ils attirent, dites-nous, les Enfans qui ont d'esprit bons et croissent les meilleurs, c'est de quoi je les estime'.[86]

The underlying assumption behind Richelieu's interest in the provision of institutionalized arts education could therefore be called traditional. He was the heir to a deep-rooted humanist belief in the social and political value of literary and philosophical studies. On the other hand, in important aspects his policy broke new ground. In the first place, the cardinal's originality was displayed in his conviction that members of the *épée* were reluctant to attend the *collèges de plein exercice* and that their hostility to 'letters' was best met by the development of an alternative educational institution. As has been pointed out, the actual depth of the *épée*'s antipathy to college education is impossible to measure. What is certain is that from the 1580s a number of *épée* apologists rejected the traditional post-Reformation belief that immersion in the classical humanities and scholastic philosophy was a fit education for a gentleman. Their mentor was the *robin*, Montaigne, who maintained in his *Essais* that a gentleman ought to be primarily skilled in prudence, an art best acquired from practical experience and the study of history.[87] For these educational pundits, the lengthy study of Latin and Greek was a waste of time. The classical tongues were for scholars and pedants.

---

[84] Prior to this, state intervention in the life of the universities had been limited to the promulgation of specific *arrêts* and the general administrative provisions laid down in the Ordonnance of Blois (1579).

[85] Henri IV was particularly interested in establishing stipendiary lecturers throughout the univ. system. Besides the theological lectureships at Paris already mentioned, the king founded permanent posts in all 4 faculties at Aix: see F. Belin, *Histoire de l'ancienne université de Provence . . . Première période 1409–1679* (Paris, 1896).

[86] BN MS Dupuy 74, fo. 78, from 'Escrit dressé par les Jésuites'. This is a Jesuit account of the society's fortunes on its immediate return and should be treated with caution. For the history of the order in France, see H. Fouqueray, *Histoire des Jésuites en France* (5 vols.; Paris, 1910–23), and P. Delattre, *Les Établissements des Jésuites en France depuis quatre siècles* (5 vols.; Enghien, 1940–55).

[87] Michel de Montaigne, *Essais*, ed. A. Micha (3 vols.; Paris, 1969), i. 193–225 ch. xxvi, 'De l'institution des enfans'.

A courtier and a man of action needed rather to be able to converse and write in French and other modern languages. Institutionalized education for the young nobleman could be safely restricted to a brief sojourn in his mid to late teens at an *académie d'équitation* to learn the art of arms and politeness.[88]

For nearly half a century the crown and its ministers seem to have been unaffected by this propaganda which clearly aimed at keeping the military and court nobility a separate caste. All the evidence suggests that, in government circles before Richelieu's ministry, it was assumed that the *épée* should be initially trained in the same way as those destined for the church or bar. Henri IV certainly had no qualms about placing the *épée* in college, demonstrating his commitment to a formal classical education by founding thirty scholarships for the sons of poor gentleman at his Alma Mater, the Paris Collège de Navarre, and a further hundred at the new Jesuit college at La Flèche.[89] And this was only a beginning. Towards the end of his reign, Henri was supporting a grandiose plan associated with Du Perron and De Thou to amalgamate the Paris Collège de Boncourt with Navarre and create a boarding-school for 1,200 indigent gentlemen.[90] The cardinal, in contrast, at least towards the end of his life, responded positively to the *épée* critique. At the same time, however, he did not succumb to the propaganda completely. Rather, in developing a new kind of academy which taught classical languages and philosophy as well as the military and polite arts, he combined two hitherto antithetical conceptions of *épée* education.

In the second place, Richelieu was the first royal minister to voice concern about the proliferation of the college system. Here again the cardinal's policy was inspired by a propaganda campaign of some antiquity, one primarily associated with the University of Paris. As we have seen, the university was extremely worried by the growth in the number of municipal colleges which it believed, quite rightly, was behind the collapse in the number of its arts students in the second half of the sixteenth century.[91] This fear was first raised by

---

[88] e.g. François de la Noue, 'De la bonne nourriture et institution qu'il est nécessaire de donner aux jeunes gentilshommes françois', in his *Discours politiques et militaires* (Geneva, 1586); *Mémoires de . . . Gaspard de Saulx, seigneur de Tavanes*, in J. Michaud and J. J. F. Poujoulat (eds.), *Nouvelle collection des mémoires . . .*, 1st ser. (12 vols.; Paris, 1836), viii. 55–62; Nicolas Faret, *L'Honnête Homme ou l'art de plaire à cour* (Paris, 1630), dedicated to Gaston d'Orléans.

[89] BSG MS 277, fo. 54, from an account of the state of the Univ. of Paris, *c.*1660; also BN MS 10841, fo. 75, 14 Mar. 1595, royal order of payment; BN MS Fr. 15781, fos. 284–312, collection of royal letters-patent concerning the Jesuits, *sub* 2 July 1605.

[90] BN MS Lat. 9947, fos. 76–8, plans for restoration of the univ. recorded by Richer under late 1609.

[91] See Brockliss, 'Patterns of Attendance', 511–20, table and analysis.

the university's supporters in the years 1594 to 1602, being deployed as one of several excuses to have the Jesuits exiled and then to prevent their return.[92] By 1614, however, the university had recognized that the problem lay with the plethora of colleges generally, not just the Jesuits; hence the demand in the *cahier des doléances* presented by the rector to the Estates General that university colleges at Paris and elsewhere should henceforth have a monopoly in philosophy teaching and that all other foundations should be restricted to teaching Latin grammar.[93] The justification in the *cahier* remained one of self-interest but by this date supporters of the university (and its sisters throughout the kingdom) had developed a more cunning strategy. Early defences of the university's position had warned of the evil political and social consequences of not allowing students to attend the capital and benefit from mixing in polite society and seeing the king and his court. A pamphlet published by the Toulouse law professor, Maran, in 1615, now raised the spectre of a surfeit of semi-educated wastrels who were a threat to the health of agriculture and commerce.[94]

By the 1620s this was a common university trope. In 1624 the universities of France banded together to resist the Jesuits' attempt to found a university at Tournon, and warned, in terms redolent of Richelieu's strictures the following year, that unless philosophy teaching was not immediately restricted to university towns, the result would be 'l'anéantissement de la milice, de la marchandise, de l'agriculture, sans laquelle nul Estat ne peut estre conservé ni maintenu'.[95] However, by the time Richelieu took up his seat on the council, other voices besides those of the universities were demanding a rationalization of the college system. Apologists for the *épée* had

---

[92] e.g. Jacques-Marie d'Amboise (univ. rector), 'Oratio' (1594), BS U 20 in-4°; Étienne Pasquier, *Le Catechisme des Jésuites ou l'examen de leur doctrine* (Villefranche, 1602), fos. 134–7; Antoine Arnauld, *Le Franc et Veritable Discours au roy sur le restablissement qui luy est demandé pour les Iesuites* (n.pl., 1602), 5–6.

[93] BUP U 87 in-4°, no. 1, 8–13: accepted by the univ., 13 Dec. 1614.

[94] *Remonstrance de la necessité de restablir les universités pour le reestablissement de l'estat et les moyens de se faire* (1615). Pamphlet in Richer's MS history, BN MS Lat. 9948, fos. 189–249 (esp. fo. 207). Richer records himself commenting on the adverse economic effects of the proliferation of colleges in the course of a conversation with the president of the parlement, Nicolas de Verdun, in 1611 (see MS Lat. 9947, fo. 257), but it is impossible to know when this passage of the history was written.

[95] Cited in *Mercure curieuse ou recueil de pièces contre les Jésuites 1620–6* (n.pl., n.d.), 291. Not all *universitaires* deployed this argument, doubtless because many professors were from quite humble backgrounds and did not want to exclude the poor from élite education altogether. Some apologists tended to emphasize that the proliferation of educational opportunity encouraged those with little intellectual potential to study and created a society of lazy semi-literates: e.g. Gabriel Dabes, *Avis pour le bien et la conservation de l'Université de Paris* (n.d. [1630s]). Pamphlet in BS U 44 in-4°, esp. p. 7.

begun to suggest that college endowments could be used to establish military academies.[96] More interestingly, there were signs that rationalization was being discussed in the queen mother's coterie. In 1617 Richelieu's later *bête noire*, Matthieu de Morgues, published a pamphlet which accused the Jesuits of ruining the commonweal.[97] Moreover, the critique was not limited to France: in February 1623 Olivares showed the same concern in his *Articles of Reformation*.[98]

Nevertheless, until the presentation of the cardinal's memorandum in 1625 this propaganda campaign equally received scant attention in government circles. Except for a cautious interlude during the regency, both Henri IV and the young Louis XIII championed the extension of the college system and its growing domination by the regular orders without hesitation. The Jesuits were particularly patronized. In 1604 the king supposedly declared that a Jesuit college should be founded in every province. 'Aussi que par ce moyen toute France si pourra peupler de gens doctes, d'autant que plus facilement pauvres et riches pourrient estudier, que s'il falloit comme auparavant envoyer a grand pas les enfans a Paris.'[99] By his death the king had become even more devoted to the society's expansion. Henri's erstwhile confessor, Père Coton, writing to Louis XIII in July 1625, maintained that the dead king had intended that the Jesuits establish a college in each of the 114 dioceses.[100] The only place where Henri did not allow the society to reopen its former college was in the capital, but permission would almost certainly have been granted had he lived. As it was, the Paris college was finally resurrected in 1618, one of the first independent educational acts of a pious Louis XIII. The preamble of the letters-patent must have made bitter reading for the University of Paris. Discounting totally the university's claim that the reopening of the Jesuit college would spell its own demise, the king turned the argument on its head. Repeating the jibe that his father had supposedly made in 1604, Louis claimed that the university was deserted anyway. Parisians were sending 'la plus grande partie' of the town's youth to Jesuit colleges in the provinces in order to receive a decent education.[101]

For the next six years the Jesuits could do no wrong in royal eyes.

---

[96] Motley, *Becoming an Aristocrat*, 126.

[97] M. de Morgues, *Contrepoids aux Jésuites et aux ministres de la Religion* (n.pl., 1617), 14.

[98] J. H. Elliott, *Richelieu and Olivares* (Cambridge, 1984), 68.

[99] 'Escrit dressé par les Jésuites', BN MS Dupuy 74, fo. 81: purportedly the king's own words.

[100] Letter to the king, Rennes, 13 July 1625: Chantilly, Jesuit seminary, Fouqueray papers, unclassified document. Of course, Coton's assertion must be treated with caution.

[101] AN MM 71, no. 52, letters-patent, 5 Feb. For Henri IV's jibe, see 'Escrit dressé par les Jésuites', BN MS Dupuy 74, fo. 78.

The order was given permission to take over colleges at Orléans, Aix, Angoulême, Pontoise, and Sens, and was even empowered to establish two Jesuit universities at Angoulême and Tournon. The old universities fought tooth and nail in the courts to scotch these projects. That in several cases their resistance was successful can almost certainly be attributed to Richelieu's rise to power. The elderly Coton had no illusions that the cardinal's presence in the council threatened the society's expansion. The letter to the king already cited primarily concerned a plan to take over the secular college at Tours. Coton realized that the wind had changed and the response was unlikely to be favourable. Invoking the name of the dead king, he immediately took issue with the claim that the expansion in collegiate provision was socially and economically harmful:

Que ce qui empesche le labourage ou le marchandise n'est pas l'estude de bonnes lettres divines et humaines, mais le nombre effrené des sergentz, notaires, clercz, solliciteurs d'affaires et procez et d'un monde de gratepapiers, et quant aux sergentz il y en a de compte faict plus de 6000 à pied, à cheval, ou à baguette qui relevent du Châtellet de Paris pour ne rien dire des autres. Et ce grand Prince [Henri IV] estimoit que c'est là où il faudroit du retranchement, et non aux colleges esquels soit nostres ou autres, il n y a pas assez d'escoliers pour fournir ce qu'il faudroit au seul ordre ecclesiastique.

In the margin another (presumably Jesuit) hand has added the revealing comment that Coton's words were intended 'pour respondre en general aux estranges impressions que le grand favori a mis depuis peu en l'esprit du roy'.[102]

Richelieu's arrival in power, then, heralded an important change of direction in royal educational policy. Moreover, the change was permanent. This is not the place to discuss at length the history of the education policy of the French government in the period 1650 to 1789. Suffice it to say that no subsequent regime embraced the cause of collegiate expansion or supported the imposition of a traditional humanist education on the *épée*.[103]

[102] See above, n. 100. Assuming the marginal annotation was a reference to the 1625 *Règlement*, it becomes possible to date this document more precisely; until now only the year of its composition was known.

[103] Like Richelieu, Mazarin left money to found a *collège de plein exercice* at the Univ. of Paris. The college was also to be the home of 60 gentleman and bourgeois scholars from recently annexed parts of the kingdom who were to be taught *inter alia* 'combien il est advantageux d'être soumis à un si grand Roy'. As the college was also to be provided with an *académie d'équitation* presumably Mazarin expected the scholars to pursue a career in the army. However, in seeing a traditional humanist education as a suitable education for a military man, Mazarin was definitely out of step with government opinion. The project was entrusted to a committee which included Colbert and Le Tellier and at its very first meeting a decision was

Richelieu's fears about the social and economic consequences of the easy access to élite education became a commonplace of government thinking. Few new colleges were permitted to open after 1650 and on several occasions the government of Louix XIV threatened the smaller institutions with closure. In 1667 and 1685 the government even moved to prepare the ground by asking the intendants to report in detail on the state of élite education in the localities.[104] As in Richelieu's case such initiatives came to nothing. Even when the Jesuits were expelled again from France in 1762 their 100 colleges were simply transferred to lay hands.[105] The sole significant development that resulted from their departure was the much mooted rationalization of the college-system of the University of Paris.[106] In general, local vested interests—represented by the bishop and the municipality—which had demanded the foundation of the colleges in the first place were always too strong to be overridden. France's 400 colleges (large and small) were seriously threatened only right at the end of the ancien régime when municipal élites began to doubt their educational value for the first time. The *philosophes* had questioned the utility of a traditional classical and philosophical education for all social groups, not just the *épée*, and by 1789 this was a view espoused by many members of the liberal professions.[107]

By and large, however, Louis XIV and his ministers inherited Richelieu's educational prejudices but not his vision. After the

taken to separate the college and the academy. The Collège de Mazarin opened in 1688; the plans for an academy were jettisoned. See BN MS 18828, fo. 447, patent of foundation 6 Mar. 1661; AN MM 462, fos. 21–3, college minute-book, 20 Mar. 1661.

[104] Several examples of the instruction sent to the intendants in 1667 survive: e.g. BN MS Fr. 10226, fos. 29–32. So, too, do the replies: for the generality of Toulouse, see C. de Vic and J. J. Vaisette (completed by E. Rosschah), *Histoire générale de Languedoc avec des notes et les pièces justicatives* (16 vols.; Toulouse, 1872–1905), xiv. 1030–60. The government moves are discussed in Dainville, 'Collèges et fréquentation scolaire', 479–89.

[105] The fullest account of the fate of the Jesuit colleges is C. Bailey, 'French Secondary Education 1763–90: The Secularization of Ex-Jesuit Colleges', *Transactions of the American Philosphical Society*, 68/6 (1978).

[106] Charles Brechillet Jourdain, *Histoire de l'université de Paris aux XVIIe et XVIIIe siècles* (2 pts. in 1 vol.; Paris, 1862–6), 399–420. The Univ. lost one *collège de plein exercice* but was given the Jesuits' Paris college in compensation. At the same time all the non-teaching colleges were closed and their scholarship foundations (those that survived) attached to the former Jesuit college. Calls for a far more dramatic reorganization were frequent in the late 17th and 18th cents.: e.g. BN MS Fr. 18828, fos. 489–92, anon., 'Le Moyen infallible de rétablir dans l'université de Paris l'étude des lettres' (*c.*1700).

[107] A classic statement of Enlightenment thinking about élite education is the article 'collège' in D. Diderot, *Encyclopédie ou dictionnaire raisonné des sciences, des arts et des métiers* (17 vols.; Paris, 1751–65), ii. 526–8. Agitation for reform of the college curriculum eventually came from the parlements: see D. Julia, 'Une réforme impossible: Le Changement du cursus dans le France du 18e siècle', *Actes de la Recherche en Sciences Sociales*, 47–8 (1983), 53–76. A list of colleges extant in 1789 is given in D. Julia and P. Presley, 'La Population scolaire en 1789', *Annales: Économies, sociétés, civilisations*, 30 (1975), 1516–61.

failure of the cardinal's academy, there was no further attempt in the seventeenth century to establish an alternative educational network for the *noblesse d'épée*. Academies continued to be founded with royal approval but these only provided a professional education in the military and courtly arts.[108] None offered the wider training in the humanities and philosophy which Richelieu deemed so necessary if the *épée* were to become fit members of the community. Nor did Louis XIV show any interest in subsidizing the attendance of indigent nobleman at the military academies. This had been a constant demand of noble apologists in the first part of the century and it was another plank of their programme to which the cardinal had responded, if only slightly.[109] In the reign of Louis XIV the educational needs of the military nobility were never part of the political agenda. The *épée* had to fend for itself. Wealthy nobles had a choice: they could either accept the traditional humanist ethic, however inappropriate, and give their sons an exacting classical education in a college *pensionnat*, or they could employ a private tutor to provide a more worldly education. Poorer gentleman had no choice at all: most entrusted their sons to the local *curé* until such time (usually their early teens) as they left home to join a regiment.

Fresh initiatives in providing an alternative institutionalized education for the *épée* eventually came from outside government circles. From the turn of the eighteenth century a new type of college began to be founded, particularly by the Benedictines, which bore strong resemblances to the ill-fated academy at Richelieu. The new colleges were boarding-schools which offered a hybrid education in the classical humanities, modern languages, mathematics, and philosophy, and placed a great emphasis on physical activity. Their clientele was not exclusively noble but their social profile was very different from that of the traditional college.[110] At the same time the more prestigious traditional colleges, such as the Jesuits' Paris Collège de Louis-le-Grand (until 1680 the Collège de Clermont)

---

[108] Many of the letters-patent granting these academies a privileged status can be found in AN o¹ 915–17.

[109] Saulx-Tavanes had demanded that the state support the military education of 2,000 young gentlemen. Besides the foundation of 20 scholarships in the Académie royale Richelieu also considered establishing an academy where 600 nobles would receive subsidized tuition in the military arts; this was to be located in the college for noble clerics: see above, n. 10.

[110] The most famous of these new colleges was at Sorèze: see J. Fabre de Massaguel, *L'École de Sorèze de 1758 au 19ᵉ Fructidor an IV* (Toulouse, 1958). On the Benedictines, see D. Julia, 'Les Bénédictins et l'enseignement au XVIIᵉ et XVIIIᵉ siècles', in *Sous la règle de Saint Benoît: Structures monastiques et sociétés en France du moyen âge à l'époque moderne* (École Pratique des Hautes Etudes, IVᵉ Section: ser. v, no. 47; Paris, 1982), 345–400.

responded to the new competition by beginning to organize extra-curricular tuition in the military and the polite arts.[111]

As a result, by 1750 the *épée* no longer had reason to believe that the educational system largely ignored their cultural needs. The poor nobility, however, were still left out in the cold. The situation was remedied to a degree only when Louis XV, after twenty-five years of government debate, established the Paris École militaire in 1751. This was a state-funded boarding-school which offered an education in Latin, modern languages, mathematics, and military science to 500 sons of poor gentlemen.[112] The school functioned in this guise for only a couple of decades. In 1776 the government established eleven provincial *écoles militaires* and divided up the scholars between them. These were not new institutions as such but the most success-ful of the new colleges, thereby emphasizing the latter's formative influence on the original foundation. The Paris school became a specialist military academy for training officers after they had received a generalist education. It took its place alongside a num-ber of other *grandes écoles* on the eve of the Revolution preparing students for state service whose establishment had been necessitated by the growing sophistication of military and naval science.[113] Richelieu would have approved of the provincial *écoles militaires* and the new type of college that inspired them, although he would have wished them even more socially exclusive.[114]

Given that Richelieu's educational ideas were embraced by his ministerial successors and to some extent eventually put into prac-tice, his reform programme in this instance can scarcely be dismissed as a failure. Indeed, it is unlikely that the cardinal would have

---

[111] Brockliss, *Higher Education*, 91, 120. From the beginning of the 17th cent. a number of Jesuit colleges had offered specialist courses in mathematics (including the science of fortification) which were not part of the traditional curriculum: see F. de Dainville, 'L'Enseignement des mathématiques dans les collèges jésuites de France du seizième au dix-huitième siècle', *Revue d'Histoire des Sciences et de leurs Applications*, 7 (1954), 6–21 and 109–23.

[112] Robert Laulan, 'La Fondation de l'école militaire et Mme de Pompadour', *Revue d'histoire moderne et contemporaine*, 21 (1984), 284–99.

[113] The most famous was the engineering school at Mézières: see the essays by Serbos, Birembaut, and Taton in R. Taton (ed.), *L'Enseignement et diffusion des sciences au dix-huitième siècle* (Paris, 1963), 345–64, 365–418, 559–66.

[114] By 1789 the *écoles militaires* represented merely the privileged tip of an alternative educational iceberg. The new colleges founded by the Benedictines and other orders had a public, corporate personality granted by royal letters-patent, like the traditional *collèges de plein exercice*. As a knowledge of drawing, mathematics, and modern languages became more and more valued in both bourgeois and noble circles for a variety of careers a plethora of private schools were established in Paris and other large towns pandering to the demand. These have been dubbed *maisons particulières*: see esp. P. Marchand, 'Un modèle éducatif original à la veille de la Révolution', *Revue d'histoire moderne et contemporaine*, 22 (1975), 549–67.

judged his educational policy so harshly, despite its manifest lack of achievement within his lifetime. The kind of educational changes that Richelieu espoused could only have been carried through by an omnipotent state which commanded large resources of men and money. Louis XIII and his successors never enjoyed such authority. General statements of reform could be transformed into political action only after lengthy negotiation with a wide variety of interested parties—largely privileged corporate bodies. It was the Revolution of 1789 that first created the kind of state in which reform proposals could be swiftly and often ruthlessly put into effect.[115] Richelieu understood the restrictions under which he worked and accepted them as part of the nature of things. There is no evidence that he had a conception of a different kind of French state where royal authority was truly absolute. Reform programmes, therefore, were utopian statements, largely outside the political realm. In a fallen world they marked out an ideal which could at best be realized piecemeal. They had achieved much of their purpose if they frightened opponents, like Coton, into moderating their demands. In such a world the politics of reform was an endless game of petty diplomacy as ministerial gifts were traded for corporate concessions. As long as neither side resorted to arms, there could be no absolute winners or losers. Richelieu in the course of his ministry would never have expected to change dramatically the educational map. It would have been sufficient that he passed on his vision to his successors.

[115] In the field of education the French revolutionaries aspired to create a truly national system of instruction embracing the primary, secondary, and tertiary sectors. Ideological divisions, political rivalries, and war prevented wholesale reform before the advent of Napoleon. The best recent surveys are R. R. Palmer, *The Improvement of Humanity: Education and the French Revolution* (Princeton, NJ, 1985); H. C. Harten, *Elementarschule und Pädagogik in der Französischen Revolution* (Munich, 1990).

Bibliography

The bibliography contains a list of recent or important secondary works on Richelieu and seventeenth-century France. Not all the secondary literature cited in the notes to the chapters above is included in it.

ADAM, ANTOINE, *Grandeur and Illusion* (London, 1971).
—— et al., *Richelieu* (Collection Génies et Réalités; Paris, 1972).
BAXTER, DOUGLAS CLARK, *Servants of the Sword: French Intendants of the Army 1630–1670* (Urbana, Ill., 1976).
BAYARD, FRANÇOISE, *Le Monde des financiers au XVIIe siècle* (Paris, 1988).
BEIK, WILLIAM, *Absolutism and Society in Seventeenth-Century France: State Power and Provincial Aristocracy in Languedoc* (Cambridge, 1985).
BÉNICHOU, PAUL, *Morales du grand siècle* (Paris, 1948).
BERCÉ, YVES-MARIE, *History of Peasant Revolts* (Cambridge, 1990).
BERGIN, JOSEPH, 'A Prelate's Progress', *History Today* (Feb. 1991).
—— *Cardinal de La Rochefoucauld: Leadership and Reform in the French Church* (New Haven, Conn., 1987).
—— *Cardinal Richelieu: Power and the Pursuit of Wealth* (New Haven, Conn., 1985).
—— *The Rise of Richelieu* (New Haven, Conn., 1991).
BILLACOIS, FRANÇOIS, *The Duel: Its Rise and Fall in Early Modern France* (New Haven, Conn., 1990).
BLET, PIERRE, *Le Clergé de France et la monarchie 1615–1666: Étude sur les assemblées générales de 1615 à 1666* (2 vols.; Rome, 1959).
BLUNT, ANTHONY, *Art and Architecture in France 1500–1700* (2nd edn.; Harmondsworth, 1970).
BOITEUX, LUCAS A., *Richelieu 'grand maître de la navigation et du commerce de France'* (Paris, 1955).
BONNEY, RICHARD, 'Jean-Roland Malet: Historian of the Finances of the French Monarchy', *French History*, 5 (1991), 180–233.
—— *L'Absolutisme* (Paris, 1989).
—— *Political Change in France under Richelieu and Mazarin 1624–1661* (Oxford, 1978).
—— *Society and Government in France under Richelieu and Mazarin 1624–1661* (London, 1988).
—— *The King's Debts: Finance and Politics in France 1589–1661* (Oxford, 1981).
BRIGGS, ROBIN, *Communities of Belief: Cultural and Social Tensions in Early Modern France* (Oxford, 1989).
—— *Early Modern France 1560–1715* (Oxford, 1977).
—— 'Noble Conspiracy and Revolt in France 1610–60', *Seventeenth-Century French Studies*, 12 (1990), 158–76.
BROCKLISS, L. W. B., *French Higher Education in the Seventeenth and*

Eighteenth Centuries: A Cultural History (Oxford, 1987).

BURCKHARDT, CARL J., *Richelieu and his Age*, Engl. trans. (3 vols.; London, 1967–70).

CAMERON, KEITH C. (ed.), *From Valois to Bourbon: Dynasty, State and Society in Early Modern France* (Exeter Studies in History, 24; Exeter, 1989).

CARMONA, MICHEL, *La France de Richelieu* (Paris, 1984).

—— *Marie de Médicis* (Paris, 1981).

—— *Richelieu: L'Ambition et le pouvoir* (Paris, 1983).

CARRIER, HUBERT, *La Presse de la Fronde (1648–1653): Les Mazarinades*, i (Geneva, 1989).

CASTAGNOS, PIERRE, *Richelieu face à la mer* (Rennes, 1989).

CHARTIER, R., COMPÈRE, M.-M., and JULIA, D., *L'Éducation en France du XVIᵉ au XVIIIᵉ siècle* (Paris, 1976).

CHÂTELLIER, LOUIS, *The Europe of the Devout: The Catholic Reformation and the Formation of a New Society* (Cambridge, 1989).

CHEVALLIER, PIERRE, *Louis XIII, roi cornélien* (Paris, 1979).

CHURCH, WILLIAM F., *Richelieu and Reason of State* (Princeton, NJ, 1972).

—— (ed.), *The Impact of Absolutism in France* (New York, 1969).

CLARKE, J. A., *Huguenot Warrior: The Life and Times of Henri de Rohan 1579–1638* (The Hague, 1966).

COLLINS, JAMES B., *Fiscal Limits of Absolutism: Direct Taxation in Early Seventeenth-Century France* (Berkeley, Calif., 1988).

CONSTANT, JEAN-MARIE, *Les Conjurateurs: Le Premier Libéralisme politique sous Richelieu* (Paris, 1987).

COOPE, ROSALYS, *Salomon de Brosse and the Development of the Classical Style in French Architecture from 1565 to 1630* (London, 1972).

COVENEY, P. J. (ed.), *France in Crisis 1625–1675* (London, 1977).

DAGENS, JEAN, *Bérulle et les origines de la restauration catholique (1575–1611)* (Paris, 1952).

DELOCHE, MAXIMIN, *Autour de la plume de Richelieu* (Paris, 1920).

—— *La Maison du cardinal de Richelieu* (Paris, 1912).

DELUMEAU, JEAN, *Catholicism between Luther and Voltaire*, Engl. trans. (London, 1977).

DENT, JULIAN, *Crisis in Finance: Crown, Financiers and Society in Seventeenth-Century France* (Newton Abbot, 1973).

DESSERT, DANIEL, *Fouquet* (Paris, 1987).

DETHAN, GEORGES, *Mazarin: Un homme de paix à l'âge baroque 1602–1661* (Paris, 1981).

—— *The Young Mazarin*, Engl. trans. (London, 1977).

DEWALD, JONATHAN, *Aristocratic Experience and the Origins of Modern Culture: France, 1570–1715* (Los Angeles, Calif., 1992).

DUCCINI, HÉLÈNE, *Concini: Grandeur et misère du favori de Marie de Médicis* (Paris, 1991).

DULONG, CLAUDE, *Anne d'Autriche* (Paris, 1980).

—— *La Fortune de Mazarin* (Paris, 1990).

ELLIOTT, J. H., *Richelieu and Olivares* (Cambridge, 1984).

—— 'Richelieu, l'homme', in R. Mousnier (ed.), *Richelieu et la culture* (Paris, 1987), 187–98.

—— *The Count-Duke of Olivares: The Statesman in an Age of Decline* (New Haven, Conn., 1986).

FUMAROLI, MARC, *L'Age de l'éloquence* (Geneva, 1980).

GOLDEN, RICHARD M. (ed.), *The Huguenot Connection: The Edict of Nantes, its Revocation and Early French Migration to South Carolina* (Dordrecht, 1988).

GOUBERT, PIERRE, *Mazarin* (Paris, 1990).

—— *The French Peasantry in the Seventeenth Century* (Cambridge, 1986).

GREENGRASS, MARK, *France in the Age of Henry IV: The Struggle for Stability* (London, 1984).

HALL, H. GASTON, *Richelieu's Desmarets and the Century of Louis XIV* (Oxford, 1990).

HANOTAUX, GABRIEL, and LA FORCE, duc de, *Histoire du cardinal de Richelieu* (6 vols.; Paris, 1893–1947).

HARDING, ROBERT R., *Anatomy of a Power Élite: The Provincial Governors of Early-Modern France* (New Haven, Conn., 1978).

HARTH, ERICA, *Ideology and Culture in Seventeenth-Century France* (Ithaca, NY, 1983).

HAUSER, HENRI, *La Pensée et l'action économiques du cardinal de Richelieu* (Paris, 1944).

HAYDEN, J. MICHAEL, *France and the Estates General of 1614* (Cambridge, 1974).

HICKEY, DANIEL, *The Coming of French Absolutism: The Struggle for Tax Reform in the Province of Dauphiné* (Toronto, 1986).

HILDESHEIMER, FRANÇOISE, *Richelieu: Une certaine idée de l'état* (Paris, 1985).

HILL, H. B. (ed. and trans.), *The Political Testament of Cardinal Richelieu* (Madison, Wis., 1965).

HOLT, MACK P. (ed.), *Society and Institutions in Early Modern France* (Athens, Ga., 1991).

HUPPERT, GEORGE, *Public Schools in Renaissance France* (Chicago, 1984).

ISHERWOOD, ROBERT M., *Music in the Service of the King: France in the Seventeenth Century* (Ithaca, NY, 1973).

JOUANNA, ARLETTE, *Le Devoir de révolte: La Noblesse française et la gestation de l'état moderne 1559–1661* (Paris, 1989).

JOUHAUD, CHRISTIAN, *La Main de Richelieu, ou le pouvoir cardinal* (Paris, 1991).

KETTERING, SHARON, *Patrons, Brokers and Clients in Seventeenth-Century France* (New York, 1986).

KIERSTEAD, RAYMOND F. (ed.), *State and Society in Seventeenth-Century France* (New York, 1975).

KLEINMAN, RUTH, *Anne of Austria, Queen of France* (Columbus, Oh., 1985).

KNECHT, ROBERT J., *Richelieu* (Profiles in Power; London, 1991).

LADURIE, EMMANUEL LE ROY, *The French Peasantry 1450–1660* (Aldershot, 1987).

LAURAIN-PORTEMER, MADELEINE, *Études Mazarines*, i (Paris, 1981).

LOCKYER, ROGER, *Buckingham* (London, 1981).

LUBLINSKAYA, A. D., *French Absolutism: The Crucial Phase 1620–1629* (Cambridge, 1968).

—— *La France au temps de Richelieu: L'Absolutisme français* (Moscow, 1982).

MCGOWAN, MARGARET, *L'Art du ballet de cour en France 1581–1643* (Paris, 1978).

MAJOR, J. RUSSELL, *Representative Government in Early Modern France* (New Haven, Conn., 1980).

—— 'The Revolt of 1620: A Study of the Ties of Fidelity', *French Historical Studies*, 14 (1986), 391–408.

MARVICK, ELIZABETH WIRTH, *Louis XIII: The Making of a King* (New Haven, Conn., 1986).

—— *The Young Richelieu: A Psychoanalytical Study in Leadership* (Chicago, 1983).

MÉTHIVIER, HUBERT, *La Fronde* (Paris, 1984).

—— *L'Ancien régime en France* (Paris, 1981).

METTAM, ROGER, *Power and Faction in Louis XIV's France* (Oxford, 1988).

MEYER, JEAN, *La Noblesse française à l'époque moderne* (Paris, 1991).

—— *1638: La Naissance de Louis XIV* (Brussels, 1989).

MILLER, JOHN (ed.), *Absolutism in Seventeenth-Century Europe* (London, 1990).

—— *Bourbon and Stuart: Kings and Kingship in France and England in the Seventeenth Century* (London, 1987).

MOOTE, A. LLOYD, *Louis XIII, the Just* (Berkeley, Calif., 1989).

—— *The Revolt of the Judges: The Parlement of Paris and the Fronde, 1643–1652* (Princeton, NJ, 1971).

MORIARTY, MICHAEL, *Taste and Ideology in Seventeenth-Century France* (Cambridge, 1988).

MOTLEY, MARK, *Becoming a French Aristocrat: The Education of the Court Nobility, 1580–1715* (Princeton, NJ, 1990).

MOUSNIER, ROLAND, *La Vénalité des offices sous Henri IV et Louis XIII* (2nd edn.; Paris, 1971).

—— *Les Institutions de la France sous la monarchie absolue* (2 vols.; Paris, 1974–80). Eng. trans.: *The Institutions of France under the Absolute Monarchy* (2 vols.; Chicago, 1979–84).

—— (ed.), *Richelieu et la culture* (Actes du Colloque international en Sorbonne; Paris, 1987).

—— *The Assassination of Henry IV*, Eng. trans. (London, 1973).

PAGÈS, GEORGES, 'Autour du "grand orage": Richelieu et Marillac, deux politiques', *Revue historique*, 179 (1937), 63–97.

—— *The Thirty Years' War*, Engl. trans. (London, 1970).

PARKER, DAVID, *La Rochelle and the French Monarchy* (London, 1980).

—— *The Making of French Absolutism* (London, 1983).

PARKER, GEOFFREY, *The Thirty Years' War* (London, 1984).

PARROTT, DAVID, 'French Military Organization in the 1630s: The Failure of the Richelieu Ministry', *Seventeenth-Century French Studies*, 9 (1987), 151–67.

—— 'The Administration of the French Army during the Ministry of Cardinal Richelieu' (D.Phil. thesis; Oxford Univ., 1985).

—— 'The Causes of the Franco-Spanish War of 1635–59', in Jeremy Black (ed.), *The Origins of War in Early Modern Europe* (Edinburgh, 1987).

PETIT, JEANNE, *L'Assemblée des notables de 1626–27* (Paris, 1936).

PITHON, RÉMY, 'Les Débuts difficiles du ministère de Richelieu et la crise du Valtelline, 1621–1626', *Revue d'histoire diplomatique*, 74 (1960), 298–322.

RANUM, OREST A., *Artisans of Glory: Writers and Historical Thought in Seventeenth-Century France* (Chapel Hill, NC, 1980).

—— *Paris in the Age of Absolutism* (New York, 1968).

—— *Richelieu and the Councillors of Louis XIII* (Oxford, 1963).

—— 'Richelieu and the Great Nobility: Some Aspects of Early Modern Political Motives', *French Historical Studies*, 3 (1963), 184–204.

RAVITCH, NORMAN, *Sword and Mitre: Government and Episcopate in France and England in the Age of Aristocracy* (The Hague, 1966).

REPGEN, KONRAD (ed.), *Krieg und Politik 1618–1648: Europäische Probleme und Perspektiven* (Schriften des Historischen Kollegs: Kolloquien 8; Munich, 1988).

RICHELIEU, ARMAND-JEAN DU PLESSIS, cardinal de, *Lettres, instructions diplomatiques et papiers d'état*, ed. D. L. M. Avenel (8 vols.; Paris 1853–77).

—— *Mémoires*, ed. J. F. Michaud and J. J. F. Poujoulat (Nouvelle collection des mémoires pour servir à l'histoire de France, 2nd ser., vols. 7–9; Paris, 1850).

—— *Mémoires*, ed. Société de l'Histoire de France (10 vols.; Paris, 1908–31).

—— *Les Papiers de Richelieu: Politique intérieure, correspondance et papiers d'état*, ed. P. Grillon (6 vols. to date; Paris, 1975–85).

—— *Testament politique*, ed. Louis André (Paris, 1947).

RICHET, DENIS, and CHARTIER, ROGER, *Représentation et vouloir politiques: Autour des états généraux de 1614* (Paris, 1982).

ROWEN, HEBERT H., *The King's State* (New Brunswick, NJ, 1980).

SALMON, J. H. M., *Renaissance and Revolt* (Cambridge, 1987).

SAWYER, JEFFREY, *Printed Poison: Pamphlet Propaganda, Faction Politics and the Public Sphere in Early Seventeenth-Century France* (Los Angeles, Calif., 1991).

SOLOMON, HOWARD M., *Public Welfare, Science and Propaganda in Seventeenth-Century France: The Innovations of Théophraste Renaudot* (Princeton, NJ, 1972).

STURDY, DAVID, *The D'Aligres de la Rivière: Servants of the Bourbon State in the Seventeenth Century* (Woodbridge, 1986).

SUTCLIFFE, F. E., *Guez de Balzac et son temps: Littérature et politique* (Paris, 1959).

TALLON, ALAIN, *La Compagnie du Saint-Sacrement (1629–1667): Spiritualité et société* (Paris, 1990).

TAPIÉ, VICTOR-LUCIEN, *France in the Age of Louis XIII and Richelieu*, Eng. trans. (Cambridge, 1974).

—— *La Guerre de trente ans* (Paris, 1990).

—— *La Politique étrangère de la France et le début de la guerre de trente ans (1616–1621)* (Paris, 1934).

TAVENEAUX, RENÉ, *Le Catholicisme dans la France classique 1610–1715* (2 vols.; Paris, 1980).

THUAU, ÉTIENNE, *Raison d'état et pensée politique à l'époque de Richelieu* (Paris, 1966).

TREASURE, G. R. R., *Richelieu and the Development of Absolutism* (London, 1972).

TUILIER, ANDRÉ (ed.), *Richelieu et le monde de l'esprit* (Paris, 1985).

WEBER, HERMANN, 'Chrétienté et équilibre européen dans la politique du cardinal de Richelieu', *XVII Siècle*, 42 (1990), 7–16.

—— 'Dieu, le roi et la chrétienté: Aspects de la politique du cardinal de Richelieu', *Francia*, 13 (1985), 233–45.

—— 'Richelieu et le Rhin', *Revue historique*, 239 (1968), 265–80.

—— 'Richelieu théoricien politique', in R. Mousnier (ed.), *Richelieu et la culture* (Paris, 1987), 55–66.

ZELLER, BERTHOLD, *Louis XIII, Marie de Médicis chef du conseil 1614–1616* (Paris, 1898).

—— *Louis XIII, Marie de Médicis, Richelieu ministre* (Paris, 1899).

—— *Richelieu et les ministres de Louis XIII de 1621 à 1624* (Paris, 1880).

Index

Note: A number of the main themes of this volume have been highlighted in the index by the use of bold typeface